T MECCA MYSTERY

Probing the Black Hole
at the Heart of Muslim History

PETER TOWNSEND

Contents

Introduction

There is total silence in the mosque as the Imam begins his Friday sermon. Over the next few minutes he holds the congregation in breathless sway as he recounts the glorious occasion of the Prophet Muhammad entering Mecca, after years of struggle, at the head of a victorious army. You can almost feel the elation as the assembled believers hang on to every word of the preacher as he transports them to a time and place that are in some ways more real to them than their present surroundings. As they delight in their beloved prophet's victory in the name of Allah, at a location which some of them have visited in person, not a few of those present reflect on how very grateful they are that their faith is based on such a rock-solid historical foundation.

History. It underpins every aspect of the Muslim faith. From the descriptions of how a man named Muhammad was called from his humdrum existence to a life of prophethood, to blow-by-blow accounts of the major battles of the post-Muhammad conquests. Historical accounts are pervasive when it comes to Muslim self-understanding and these accounts act as the foundation for Islamic faith and practice at every turn. How could it be otherwise? Islam is based upon the fundamental idea that God intervened at a specific time, in a specific place and through a specific person to bring his message to an unbelieving world. It is, therefore, of the utmost importance that the historical record upon which Islamic teaching is based should be accurate and verifiable.

Most practicing Muslims would instinctively and passionately argue that this is indeed the case. As far as they are concerned, there exists an unbroken and impeccable historical record that links modern Muslims with the distant Islamic past; a past during which events played out exactly as

1

described in the countless biographies of the prophet and descriptions of the early Arab conquests that line the shelves of Islamic bookshops all around the world. A lot will depend on whether this is, in fact, the case.

In light of the above, it is of the utmost importance that historians honestly and seriously strive to get to the bottom of the questions relating to the origins of early Islam. A basic question to start with is: *"How reliable are the historical accounts upon which the faith of more than a billion Muslims rest?"* I fully realize that many people will see this question as verging on the nonsensical. It is, after all, common knowledge that Islam, as Ernest Renan memorably put it, emerged in the 'full light of history'.[1]

The problem is that the 'common knowledge' about Islam's origins rests, as is so often the case with common knowledge, on some potentially profound untested assumptions. Chief among these assumptions is the conviction that certain key historical documents, written hundreds of years after the time of Muhammad, are the most reliable window into the early origins of Islam that we have.

The issue of the reliability of the Islamic historical record is too important to allow the mostly uncritical acceptance of certain entrenched positions to remain untested. The purpose of this book is, therefore, to pursue the following related lines of enquiry:

- Whether the classical sources underpinning Muslim history stack up as reliable records of the period and the events they seek to describe?

- Whether there are other reliable sources, perhaps largely ignored by those responsible for the traditional accounts, that provide alternative yet credible perspectives into the periods and events under discussion?

These are the type of questions that historians should ask as a matter of course when the history of any period is discussed, but the traditional version of Islamic history has largely received a 'free pass' when it comes to serious critical scrutiny.

The result is that documents claiming to shed light on the earliest years of Islam are often accepted as intrinsically trustworthy without even the most basic questions about historical accuracy or reliable transmission being asked. This happens despite the fact that the key texts of other major world religions have now been subjected to more than a century of the most searching investigations.[2]

There are several reasons behind the fact that Islamic sources have so far escaped thorough historical re-examination. Perhaps most significant is the simple fact that this is an exercise fraught with danger. Scholars in the Muslim world face the prospect of being branded as apostates if they are perceived to be deviating too far from accepted versions of Islamic theology and history. This can have very serious consequences. Throughout history, those who challenged Islamic orthodoxy from within the bosom of Islam quickly discovered that this is not something to undertake lightly. The fact that this is not an observation that only applies to the distant past (e.g. the slaughtering of Mutazalite[3] scholars in 10th century Baghdad[4]) can be seen in the case of Muhammad Taha, who was executed by the Sudanese government in 1985 for proposing a re-evaluation of the way in which the Qur'an is interpreted.[5]

The fear-factor and the sheer ubiquity of the traditional sources means that very little is happening inside the Muslim world itself as far as a critical re-evaluation of the history of the earliest years of Islam are concerned. The handful of scholars who are working in this field are mostly doing so at Western universities and publishing their findings in obscure academic journals or very expensive scholarly texts.[6] All of this means that there is very little public consciousness, either in the Muslim or Western world, of the myriad of serious questions that are being asked about the early origins of Islam.

This book is a modest attempt to address this situation by providing an accessible overview of the state of research in this crucial area. In the process, I will be interacting with the work of a wide range of scholars. Such a discussion could potentially become very technical very quickly and this is precisely what I would like to avoid in this volume. Readers should, therefore, view this as a two-level work. In the main text, I will endeavor to keep things as readable, accessible and non-technical as possible. This does not mean, however, that I will simply make a series of untested claims. Those who would like to dig deeper, or who would like to verify the accuracy of my interaction with the sources that I refer to, are encouraged to consult the detailed notes and bibliography that are provided at the end of this work in order to identify resources for further reading and in-depth research.

Although I will be making extensive use of the work of other scholars, it should be noted that all views expressed are my own, except of course where the views of others are directly quoted or referenced.

With a project like this, there is a huge temptation to move too quickly from *'There are questions to be asked about a specific historical period'* to *'This is what actually happened'*. I am going to do my best to avoid that temptation (although it is obviously a great way to gain an audience, just ask Dan Brown[7]) by probing deeply into the problems with the traditional account of Muslim history and entering only lightly into possible alternative histories.

The reason for this is simple. Any alternative reading of history will, barring stunning archaeological or documentary discoveries to confirm it, necessarily operate in the realm of speculation and conjecture. This means that works asking significant questions about the history of Islam have in the past been all too easily dismissed by those who were able to poke holes in the alternative histories that were proposed. Critics then felt able to ignore the basic fact that there are significant problems with the traditional account itself. Let's be clear, the fact that alternative interpretations can be challenged does not automatically validate the traditional account as a kind of 'last man standing'. The questions remain.

I do realize that I will not be able to completely avoid the need to present some views on why the Islamic tradition developed as it did. I will, therefore, present some statements in Chapter 8 that will outline some of my views as far as an alternative understanding of Islamic origins is concerned. Please understand, however, that these are offered as rather tentative conclusions and that my views in this area should not be seen as the most important part of this book. The focus should remain on the questions that should be answered before we can declare that Islam was indeed 'born in the full light of history'.

The questions to be discussed in this book must necessarily be approached from a variety of angles. The following topics will be covered:

- Some basic principles of historiography (e.g. the scientific methods underpinning historical research and writing), especially as they apply to the topic under consideration

- The sources behind the traditional Islamic historical account and an evaluation of their reliability

- Pre-Islamic Arabia (i.e. the period before Muhammad) and how Muslim historians view this era

- The historicity of Mecca and its position in Muslim history

- The data surrounding the life and public ministry of Muhammad

- The history and composition of the Qur'an

- The early Islamic conquests

- The early development of Muslim faith and practice, including a discussion of non-Muslim primary sources

As mentioned before, I will contribute my own views as far as an alternative understanding of early Islamic history is concerned towards the end of the book. It should, once again, be emphasized that these views are tentative and should not be seen as the major focus of this work.

It is probably inevitable that the material presented in this work will be labeled as 'revisionist'. Revisionism can be defined as the critical re-examination of accepted historical accounts and the sources upon which such accounts are based. Revisionist projects are sometimes all too easily dismissed as foolhardy and quixotic. However, to reject revisionist questioning out of hand is to state that we should simply uncritically accept generally established historical convictions. Without the willingness, and in fact the duty, to question received wisdom, the task of the historian is reduced to simply finding ever more entertaining ways to tell the 'same old story'. Few, if any, historians would find this an appealing prospect. We should instead, in line with one of the most cherished convictions of the Western intellectual tradition, be willing to follow the evidence wherever it may lead. Even if it means tipping over a few sacred cows in the process.

Thank you very much for taking the time to investigate the crucially important questions of the historical reliability of the generally accepted accounts of Islamic origins.

Please note that this book will be quite narrowly focused on the issue at hand (i.e. Islamic history). For a more general critique of the truth claims of Islam, please see my book *Questioning Islam – Tough Questions and Honest Answers about the Muslim Religion* available at www.qi-book. com. For a discussion of the links between Islamic teaching and violence, please see 'Nothing to do with Islam? – Investigating the West's most Dangerous Blind Spot' available at www.ntdwi.com.

Peter Townsend
Sydney, May 2018

Navigating this Book

The topic that we will be discussing may well be quite unfamiliar to many readers and there is a danger that some people may feel a bit overwhelmed by the material that will be presented.

To help readers keep track of our progress as we move through different topics, a short paragraph will act as our guide. This paragraph is a summary of traditional Muslim historical orthodoxy that will be thoroughly 'interrogated' as we go along. Here it is:

> The classic Islamic sources tell us that the ancient city of Mecca was a site of immense spiritual and economic importance. However, by the time Muhammad was born (570 CE), it was adrift in a sea of paganism and barbarity that enveloped the entire Arabian Peninsula. Muhammad was a member of one of the most important tribes in Mecca, the Quraysh, and received a call from God to act as his prophet in a cave just outside the city. Acting upon this call, Muhammad received a series of revelations over a period of about twenty years, right up to his death in 632 CE. These revelations form what we now know as the Qur'an. After Muhammad's death, his followers burst out of the Arabian Peninsula in the name of Islam and conquered the Persian and much of the Eastern Roman Empire. The coming of Islam established the Muslim religion, with the message of Muhammad and the city of Mecca at its center, as the pre-eminent belief system from Egypt to Persia within 100 years of the death of the prophet.

This summary paragraph will appear above every chapter with the part that is being investigated in that chapter in **bold type.** Hopefully this will help orient readers in terms of exactly where we are in our investigation of Islamic history.

Every chapter will also end with a summary of the main points that were discussed.

Full references are provided at the end of the book. In cases where the Qur'an and traditions (*hadiths*) are quoted, these references will refer to versions that are available online so that readers can confirm that they have been accurately quoted.

A Brief Geographical Orientation

Throughout the course of this book I will be referring to a range of locations in what we now know as the Middle East. This is a region that many people do not know very well, beyond perhaps a few major cities, in terms of its contemporary geography. To complicate matters further, we will mostly not be looking at contemporary geography, but rather at on-the-ground realities during the period of Late Antiquity[8] (roughly the 4th to the 7th centuries CE). It would, therefore, be good to take a bit of a tour through the area while referencing some geographical features as they existed back then. A major focus of this tour will be an attempt to relate some of the names and features that existed during this period to modern realities.

It may be best to begin with the Roman presence in the Middle East. The Roman Empire, although it still gloried in its Roman heritage, was by the 3rd century not headquartered in the Eternal City (Rome) anymore. During the reign of the Emperor Constantine (272-334 CE), the capital was moved to a city which he, never one for modesty it seems, named after himself (i.e. Constantinople, the modern Istanbul).[9] Historians often refer to this phase of Roman history as the coming of the Byzantine Empire[10] (after the name of the town that originally stood on the site where Constantinople was built), although this term was not in general use in the period we will be studying. Most people still simply referred to the empire governed by the successors of Constantine as 'Roman'. The move towards the east, and away from Rome in the West, was in many ways a strategic one as it brought the heart of Roman Imperial power closer to the center of the empire. All the better to keep a wary eye on the Persian threat to the east.

As far as the Middle East is concerned, it can be stated that in general the Roman Empire controlled (in the immediate pre-Islamic period) the areas now taken up by Syria, Lebanon, Israel, Palestine and Jordan. This vast area was not administered as a single province while under Roman rule. Roman governmental demarcations and arrangements changed over time, but the most enduring of these arrangements was the division of what we now generally refer to as the Middle East into three Roman provinces. They were:

Syria: Roman Syria[11] was one of the most important, richest and influential of all the provinces of Rome. Its capital Antioch (now the Turkish city of Antakya) was the third largest city (after Constantinople and Alexandria) in the Eastern Roman Empire. Antioch was furthermore also a very important city in Christian history and over the centuries played host to intense debates between different Christian traditions. Another Syrian city which will loom large in our narrative is, of course, Damascus. This city, holding the distinction of being one of the oldest continuously inhabited settlements on earth, also came in time to be one of the jewels in the crown of early Arab rule. The importance of Syria was not only to be found in its wealth, but also in its strategic position very near to the frontline of the enduring Roman-Persian conflict (more about this below). When thinking about the ancient province of Syria, we should try to banish the boundaries of the modern state of Syria from our minds. The Roman province was much bigger than this, stretching into areas now occupied by Turkey, Jordan, Lebanon and Iraq. It should also be noted that the cultural influence emanating from Roman Syria spread way beyond the province itself. Religious, cultural and linguistic (through the Syriac language) ideas from Syria put down deep roots in neighboring Roman provinces as well.

Palestina (Judea): The Roman Province of Palestina[12] covered much of the territory now held by the modern state of Israel. This province went through a series of political up and downs. The Romans initially named the province Judea and tried to rule through local proxy-rulers, but eventually they decided to exert direct political control in response to two major Jewish rebellions (i.e. the Jewish Revolt 66-73 CE[13] and the Bar Khokba War 132-135 CE).[14] The Roman response to Jewish resistance was so heavy handed that they even tried to erase the memory of Jerusalem from the map (they renamed the city Aelia Capitolina[15] and the province Syria-Palestina). This policy endured until the Christianization of the Roman Empire suddenly and unexpectedly thrust the Holy Land back into the spotlight. The establishment of Jerusalem as a major center of pilgrimage from the reign of Constantine onwards massively raised its prestige and importance as a Roman city. This led to the name Aelia Capitolina being quietly forgotten and even the term Judea making a comeback. Safeguarding Jerusalem and emphasizing its place in Christian history was viewed as a priority, especially given the fact that Roman imperial authorities increasingly saw themselves as the guardians of Christian theological orthodoxy. One implication of this was that they had to ensure that the expressions of Christianity in Jerusalem, a major site of pilgrimage after all[16], aligned with their understanding of the faith. This approach necessitated much tighter control of the area and, over time, led to an influx of Christians from all over the Roman Empire.

Roman Arabia[17] (Arabia Petraea): The Romans also controlled parts of what is now Jordan, Egypt (the Negev Desert) and northern Saudi Arabia. This was known as Roman Arabia or Arabia Petraea. Roman dominance of this area came about after the Roman army conquered the Nabataean Empire in 106 CE. This empire, centered on Petra, was one of the major sources of the Arabic language as well as cultural and religious ideas. By the 6th century effective Roman control of much of Roman Arabia was significantly diminished, with the task of securing this part of the empire mainly outsourced to Arab tribes. These tribes were mostly settled in garrison cities on the edge of the provinces of Arabia and Syria.

The Syro-Arabian Borderlands: This is a term that will be employed throughout this book. It refers to territories on either side of the borders of the Roman Provinces of Syria, Palestina and Arabia. If this sounds a bit ambiguous, it is meant to be. The borders of these provinces were obviously not fixed lines, fences or walls, but most depended on a general understanding of how far Roman military power projected into the Arabian Desert. This means that there were many people on either side of the border who either accepted or rejected Roman rule and ideas. In the Syro-Arabian borderlands (between Syria and Northern Arabia), many people identified with the developing Arab language and culture. Some of them could be described as nomadic Arab tribes (to whom the term 'Bedouin' is often applied). Others settled in towns and small cities associated with trans-Arabian trade or in Roman and Persian supported garrison cities. These were settlements set up to house Arab tribespeople in the employ of the two great empires of the day. The most important of these garrison cities were Jabiya, under the control of a group of Christian Roman aligned tribes known as the Ghassanids.[18] Much further east, inside the Sassanian (Persian) empire, there was Hira, controlled by a pagan Arab dynasty known as the Lakhmids.[19] It will become obvious as we go along that the Syro-Arabian borderlands played a very significant role in the development of Islam so we will have occasion to return to this region at several points throughout this book.

Central Arabia and the Hejaz: Central Arabia, which is mostly covered by the modern state of Saudi Arabia today, was mostly arid and devoid of large-scale settlements. The exceptions were oases (e.g. the ones at Yahtrib, later known as Medina, and Ta'if). These settlements were often closely associated with trans-Arabian trade as way-stations on the route. A very important part of this region for our purposes is the Hejaz[20], the region where the modern city of Mecca is located. According to traditional Muslim historiography, this area was right at the heart of trans-Arabian trade networks and also had immense religious importance. We shall see later in this book that these convictions are not necessarily supported by historical and geographical evidence.

Southern Arabia: This area is mostly covered by the modern state of Yemen and parts of Southern Saudi Arabia. It was known by the Romans as 'Arabia Felix'[21] (or 'Happy Arabia'). The reason for this was that it was exceptionally fertile, unlike most of the rest of the territories where Arabs lived. It was also the source of the many of the spices and especially the incense that powered the trans-Arabian trade. For much of the pre-Islamic ara this area was dominated by the Kingdom of Himyar.[22] The Himyarites had strong links with tribes and groups further north, especially through trade. These links were reflected in the fact that several of the kings of Himyar belonged to the Jewish religion. In the immediate pre-Islamic era, Himyarite domination of Southern Arabia came to an end when Ethiopian armies, with Roman support, defeated the last Himyarite king in 527 CE.

The Arabian Peninsula: This is a catch-all term that I will use at several points throughout this book as shorthand for the territories with a significant Arab presence. It encompasses Southern Arabia, Central Arabia and into Northern Arabia (i.e. the Syro-Arabian borderlands).

Beyond the Arabian Peninsula to the West: In this part of the world, we need to briefly mention two geographical realities. The first is the Red Sea, which runs between the Arabian Peninsula and Africa. These days, since the opening of the Suez Canal, it is well-known as one the busiest shipping lanes on the planet, but this is not necessarily something new. It has always been much cheaper to transport goods by water than by land. This means that the Red Sea played a hugely important role in trade from southern to northern Arabia. A fact that we will revisit later. We also need to take note of the Christian Aksumite Empire of Ethiopia as one of the most significant pre-Islamic African entities, especially because of the links between this part of Africa and southern Arabia. Influence went both ways and had implications for political and religious life on both sides of the Red Sea.

The Sassanian (Persian) Empire: The Sassanian Empire[23] covered much of what we now know as Iraq and Iran and into parts of Afghanistan, Pakistan and the Central Asian republics. The heart of the empire could be found in the area known as Mesopotamia or the 'Land Between the Rivers'. The rivers in question were the Tigris and the Euphrates, and it was indeed between these rivers where some of the oldest traces of human civilization have been found. The capital of the empire in the immediate pre-Islamic period was Ctesiphon on the banks of the Tigris (about 22 miles southeast of present-day Baghdad), but there were also many smaller centers. Some of these cities could be described as garrison cities, while others were focused on scholarship. Zoroastrianism was the major religion of the Empire and the Sassanian Emperors were given special religious status within this religion. The Empire was also home to large communities of Jews and Christians. Many of the Christians in the Empire would have been regarded as unorthodox by the authorities in the Roman Empire since they belonged to what became known as 'The Church of the East', which followed a doctrine known as Nestorianism. The Jewish presence in Mesopotamia went back to the time when both the northern (722 BCE) and southern (586 BCE) Jewish tribes were brought to this region as exiles. It was especially in the erstwhile Babylonian lands where Jewish culture and learning flourished. One expression of this was the Babylonian Talmudic Academies that were strung between the towns of Pumbedita (modern Fallujah) and Sura, farther south down the Euphrates. It would be hard to overstate the importance of these academies on the development of Judaism. This importance is reflected in the name of the Babylonian Talmud, a collection of writings that continue to guide and inform Jewish life to this day.

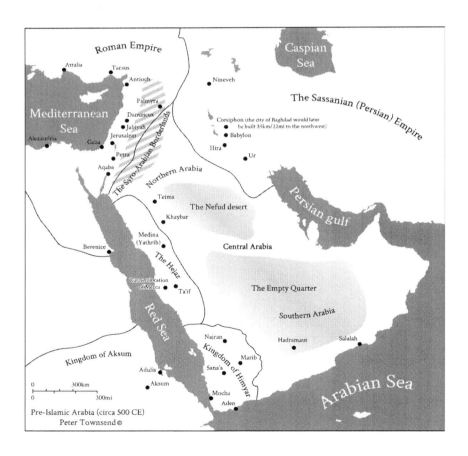

Pre-Islamic Arabia (circa 500 CE)
Peter Townsend ©

14

1.

What is the Basis for Traditional Beliefs About the Early Years of Islam?

*T*he classic Islamic sources tell us *that the ancient city of Mecca was a site of immense spiritual and economic importance. However, by the time Muhammad was born (570 CE), it was adrift in a sea of paganism and barbarity that enveloped the entire Arabian Peninsula. Muhammad was a member of one of the most important tribes of Mecca, the Quraysh, and received a call from God to act as his prophet in a cave just outside the city. Acting upon this call, Muhammad received a series of revelations over a period of about twenty years, right up to his death in 632 CE. These revelations form what we now know as the Qur'an. After Muhammad's death, his followers burst out of the Arabian Peninsula in the name of Islam and conquered the Persian and much of the Eastern Roman Empire. The coming of Islam established the Muslim religion, with the message of Muhammad and the city of Mecca at its center, as the pre-eminent belief system from Egypt to Persia within 100 years of the death of the prophet.*

1.1. The Past as a Battlefield

A particular interpretation of history can sometimes be so overwhelmingly presented as the accepted or canonical version that it is tempting to forego critical historical enquiry into whether the 'facts' that are presented are, in fact, anything of the sort. One of the central claims of this book is that the uncritical acceptance of supposed 'certainties' is a temptation that those writing about the early years of Islam all too often succumb to. The accepted narrative describing the early years of Islam have been retold in so many forms and formats over the centuries that there seems to be a kind of historical inevitability to them. Things had to have happened in this way, or so the argument goes, because so many people believe that it did. Needless to say, this is not a sufficiently solid foundation upon which to construct an entire historical edifice.

One of the most important insights that should underpin all historical research is the simple acknowledgement that the past can very often be contested territory. The identity of many groups around the world is quite explicitly based on certain interpretations of history, so much so in fact that it has often been stated that he who controls the past controls the present.[24] The usefulness of history as a tool with which to exert religious and political control is perhaps nowhere better illustrated than the use to which a particular version of early Islamic history has been put by Muslim religious leaders throughout the centuries since Islam was founded.

How is this control exerted? A major factor is that many Islamic teachings are supposedly based quite explicitly on the example of Muhammad and the first Muslims. In fact, the Qur'an calls Muhammad an 'excellent example' for those who hope to enter paradise (Qur'an 33:21).[25] In other words, if you can show that the prophet did or said something in the distant past, this is enough to, theoretically at least, settle the matter as to how modern Muslims should speak and act.

It should be blindingly obvious, in light of the above, that the temptation for early Muslim leaders to 'edit' Islamic history would have been almost overwhelming. Claiming to invoke the example of the prophet could potentially spur their followers into action in a way that hours of attempts at persuasion or even threats of violence could not hope to do.

The fact that many early Muslim leaders consciously chose to back-project certain events and sayings onto Muhammad's life is amply demonstrated by the multitudes of *hadiths* (traditions) that have Muhammad saying precisely contradictory things at certain specific points during his career.

There are, for example, traditions in which Muhammad appoints his nephew Ali[26] as his successor and others where he bestows leadership of the community on his friend Abu Bakr.[27] It does not take a genius to work out what happened here. The leaders of different traditions (Shi'a in the former, Sunni in the latter) simply invented traditions supporting their view of the succession. As such, the prophet was being enlisted on both sides of the most bitterly contested political debate within worldwide Islam, as questions related to political succession during the post-Muhammad period form the basis for the Sunni/Shi'a split.[28]

These contradictory traditions are, of course, endlessly argued over (in terms of which ones are accurate), but their mere existence should be enough to cause all sorts of red flags to go up for the historian. What we have here are two mutually exclusive readings of history, both supposedly supported by an impeccable line of narrators[29] (i.e. those who supposedly retold the traditions until they were finally written down). The purpose of citing this example is obviously not to attempt to resolve this contradiction, but to forcefully point out that anyone who begins to read Islamic history is entering a minefield.

Given the deeply contested nature of Islamic historical accounts, it is all the more important to be very suspicious of the mere repetition of supposedly accepted accounts or 'everybody knows that it happened this way' statements. If Muslim scholars cannot even remotely begin to agree among themselves on the history of their faith, why should outsiders meekly accept the confidently asserted certainties of one or the other of the Islamic schools of thought?

What is sorely needed is a thoroughgoing investigation of early Islamic history without being shackled by pre-conceived notions of what we're supposed to find during this investigation. In other words, when it comes to the early history of Islam, we need to be able to ask the very same questions that are asked about other historical periods and about the reliability (or otherwise) of the sources used to reconstruct those periods. This is exactly what motivated the writing of this book.

In asking these questions, we must spend a bit of time thinking about the way historical research is conducted and how historical accounts are written (a field of study known as historiography[30]). For many, if not most, readers this may sound like an impossibly dull pursuit, but a discussion of some of the basic principles of historiography is necessary. It will, however, be kept as non-technical and relevant to the topic at hand as possible.

1.2. Dealing with Sources: Some Basic Historiographical Principles

It has already been stated that an investigation of the sources used to write Islamic history will be at the heart of this book. In general, historians ask three basic source-related questions at the beginning of any historical research project. They are:

- What sources are mostly used to serve as the basis for reconstructing the history of the person, period or place in question?

- How reliable are these sources? Simply put, can they be trusted?

- Are there other sources, perhaps hitherto ignored, that can contribute to (or even radically alter) our understanding of the period, person or place in question?[31]

One of the purposes of this chapter is to work through these questions as far as the early history of Islam is concerned. However, before we go into specifics, a few general remarks about historical sources would be in order.

Historical sources come in all shapes and sizes. They can be:

- *Documentary:* This refers to books, letters, diary entries and a host of other forms of writing. Part of the task of the historian will be to gain access to reliable written sources.[32] Sometimes this can be as (relatively) easy as visiting an archive where specialists store carefully catalogued sources in conditions optimized for their long-term survival (many such archives are being digitized, which will make the task of consulting them even more straightforward in future). In other cases, finding written sources can be very difficult. This is a problem that becomes more acute the further back in time the research subject is. It will, for example, be much easier to conduct documentary research into Hitler's Third Reich (where the volume of available documents is likely to be overwhelming) than it would be for the empire of Alexander the Great where the sources at our disposal will be relatively few and quite likely secondary in nature (see below for the difference between primary and secondary sources). There are relatively many documentary sources available for the period that we are interested in, although nothing approaching an abundance. However, significant questions can be asked about the reliability of many of these sources (this issue will be discussed in much more detail below).

- *Oral Sources:* Sometimes historical evidence can be provided in the form of oral recollections by people who lived through the period in question. We obviously do not have any audio recordings dealing with firsthand memories of early Islamic history however. What we do have is entire collections of traditions that *claim to be* the result of the committing to paper of vast amounts of oral traditions. These volumes, therefore, exist in a kind of strange no-man's land between written and oral sources, and we will return to them with a view to assessing their reliability as historical sources.

- *Artifacts:* Anyone who has ever been to museum will have had the opportunity to observe plenty of historical artifacts.[33] Artifacts can be described as physical objects associated with the subject, period or person in question. In the case of ancient history, artifacts are often obtained through archaeology. There will sometimes be significant questions associated with the authenticity of artifacts supposedly originating from the distant past. We are, for example, entitled to raise an eyebrow at the many claims from the trustees of several sacred sites around the Middle East that each of them have been entrusted with the safekeeping of the actual head of John the Baptist. This kind of healthy skepticism should probably also be employed when it comes to certain objects supposedly directly associated with the person of Muhammad, like his cloak (supposedly in the possession of the Taliban in Afghanistan)[34] and hair from his beard (proudly displayed by the Topkapi Museum in Istanbul).[35]

- *Archaeological Evidence:* Archaeology can be particularly helpful as an aid to help reconstruct historical events or periods for which there is a lack of documentary and oral sources. In fact, there have been several instances in which archaeology significantly modified, or even completely altered, our understanding of specific periods of history. We will, therefore, need to look at what, if anything, archaeological sources can tell us about the period we are studying.

It is very important to remember that not all historical sources have been created equal, not by a long shot. Various considerations allow historians to attach different values to sources as far as their usefulness in drawing up a reliable historical account is concerned. These factors include the following yardsticks that will be particularly relevant for our purposes:

- *The reliability of an author (or narrator):* For example, historians would normally attach more authority to the testimony of a respected medieval chronicler than that of a storyteller known for spinning tall tales.

- *The distance in time and place from the event:* Documents or other pieces of evidence that can be accurately traced to the period and region in question generally carry more weight. In other words, historians interested in medieval life in Southern France will generally pay much closer attention to a document from Provence, dated to

20

1350, than to a document from Picardie (on the other side of the country) dated to 1650, even though they may claim to describe the same events.

- *Wide Distribution:* Although this is not a hard-and-fast rule, historians will generally assume that texts that were widely distributed (especially if distributed through official channels, e.g. royal chronicles) during the period in question are more reliable, as their wide distribution invites more opportunity for comment and possible correction.

- *Documentary evidence generally trumps oral/legendary material:* There are obviously many narratives out there that claim to be based on actual historical events, but that may be nothing of the sort. Most historians will, therefore, perhaps be willing to concede that legendary material (often based on oral retellings) may contain kernels of historical truth, but will not take every single claim that is made on face value. They will, instead, do their best to find reliable written sources and/or archaeological evidence to ascertain the reliability of such material.

1.3. Primary and Secondary Historical Sources

One of the most important historiographical distinctions between different types of sources is related to the distance from the time and place of the events being described. These differences are expressed in terms of primary and secondary sources.

At the most basic level this distinction has to do with presence. A primary source[36] is a source which can be shown to have been present (i.e. existed) during the period under discussion. If, for example, I am doing research into Napoleon's Russian Campaign, his diaries, letters and daily dispatches will be some of the most important primary sources that I can consult. Secondary sources are typically sources that were 'not present' (i.e. they were written or created after-the-fact). Let's stick with our example of Napoleon's Russian campaign. In this case, the most widely available secondary sources will be books, articles and reports written by others after the campaign. These can range from sources written shortly after the events and right up to the present.

It should immediately be obvious that primary sources are crucial for accurate history writing since they take us right to the heart of what is being discussed. Secondary sources are, of course, not unimportant, but here historians have their work cut out for them to sort the wheat from the chaff in terms of accuracy and reliability. An important part of the historian's craft is, therefore, to 'weigh' and evaluate sources in terms of their reliability and usefulness in reconstructing the past. It is, for example, logical, that a history of the Napoleonic wars written while many of the participants were still alive will be regarded as a much more important source than a summary article that appeared in a 21st century encyclopedia. Most historians will, in fact, regard contemporary summaries of historical events (like encyclopedia entries) not so much as historical sources in the strict sense, but rather as useful (depending on the quality of course) introductions to historical subjects for non-specialists.

In case this is not abundantly clear already, an important principle should be stated outright: primary source research represents the gold standard when it comes to the writing of history. In other words, when it comes to the early history of Islam, we need to be able refer to (and give preference to) documents, artifacts and archaeological evidence that can be reliably dated to the period under discussion (roughly 570 CE to 732 CE, i.e. from the birth of Muhammad to about a hundred years after his death).

Much of the discussion over the coming chapters will focus on the quality (or perhaps lack thereof) of the primary sources upon which the traditional accounts are based. We will also be looking at the question of whether there are not perhaps alternative primary sources that are routinely being excluded from the discussion because they do not fit in with a particular ideological agenda.

1.4. The Place of Oral Tradition in Historiography

Readers may wonder why a section on oral traditions as historical sources was included in a book about the early history of Islam? Simply because this is more-or-less what the accepted Islamic historical tradition has to offer by way of primary source support. The bulk of Muslim historical accounts as taught in mosques and *madrassas* (Islamic schools) around the world rest upon a vast bulwark of oral retellings supposedly stretching all the way back to the time of the prophet.

In most cases, these traditions were only finally committed to paper about 200-300 years after the date (632 CE) generally associated with the death of Muhammad. This is essentially what you will find in the stacks of books on Muslim history lining the bookshelves of Muslims scholars: written-down versions of supposedly reliable oral traditions. It is important to repeat, however, that there was a period *of at least two centuries* when the oral versions were supposedly all that there was.

We need to begin our investigations by asking if oral sources are, in fact, admissible as primary source evidence. In the writing of modern history, the answer would, in most cases, be a resounding 'yes'.[37] A historian writing the history of the Watergate Scandal would, for example, be able to refer to recordings of the testimony of the major protagonists. He may even, if this could be negotiated, get to interview some of them. This is, however, not the kind of oral sources that we are faced with in the writing of ancient history where ways of accurately transmitting and preserving oral records were still many centuries in the future.

The problem with validating oral sources that originated before the advent of recording technology should be immediately obvious. These sources can really only be taken seriously if we can trust the accuracy of transmission up to the point where the oral accounts were finally written down. Transmission in this context refers to the process of 'retelling' a story or tradition from its point of origin to the point when it is finally committed to paper. The biggest challenge in this context is that corruption may have occurred at some stage during the transmission process.

Corruption in the historiographical sense obviously has nothing to do with bribe-taking, but rather refers to the way in which a historical tradition can be altered, sometimes radically so, in the process of being passed from one person to another. In other words, the original meaning or message gets corrupted. Anyone who has ever played a game of Chinese Whispers will immediately be aware of how significant this problem can be. Stories tend to 'grow tails' in the retelling until we are left with a deep sense of unease about whether we are in any way able to reconstruct the original version.

The claim is often made that there are some oral traditions that were preserved with a remarkable degree of accuracy over the centuries. While it is true that some people are indeed capable of prodigious feats of memory, we should be very careful to make claims for anything approaching flawless transmission and perfect recall when it comes to oral traditions.

Perhaps the most remarkable surviving oral traditions are the classic Hindu epics (the Mahabharata and the Ramayana). There are many examples of people being able to recite large parts of these huge epics from memory. In fact, the memorization of these key Sanskrit texts[38] is seen as a sacred obligation by many Hindus and there have been large numbers of specialists who dedicated their entire lives to memorizing and retelling these epics. Some of these reciters have been shown to have memorized more than a million words. Yet, even this elaborate system dedicated to the preservation of an oral tradition have not prevented the occurrence of significant variations between different versions of the epics.[39] These variations can typically be traced to certain regions of India or to specific groups within Indian society. It can, considering this, be argued that the epics reached their definitive form only when a more-or-less general consensus (still elusive as far as some Indian scholars are concerned) was reached based on a written-down version of the traditions.

The example of the Hindu epics should serve as a salutary warning to anyone making the claim that anything approaching flawless transmission of oral traditions is possible. This goal will be doubly elusive in settings where there is not an established procedure for passing on oral traditions (as is the case with the Hindu epics). If formal memorization still leaves us with variations and ambiguities, this will be all the more the case if we are simply dealing with stories retold from generation to generation around the campfire.

Considering this, most historians will treat written-down oral accounts pointing to a period in the distant past with extreme caution. They would ideally like to see such sources validated by other kinds of evidence, especially well attested primary documentary sources from the period in question.

1.5. The Islamic Sources under the Lens

The time has now come to pull some of the threads discussed above together by critically examining the standard sources for Islamic history.

The first thing that strikes the historical researcher when it comes to the generally accepted source material for Muslim history is how small the pool is that authors writing about the earliest years of Islam draw from. Whether we are talking about books written hundreds of years ago[40] or some of the slick biographies of Muhammad produced by the likes of John Esposito[41] or Karen Armstrong[42], they are all based on the same narrow collection of historical sources.

This means that mainstream research into early Islamic history is essentially a sterile enterprise, since virtually no additional information is allowed to intrude into the carefully guarded circle of canonical sources. The result is that, among those who limit themselves to these sources, essentially nothing new is being said and historical writing has degenerated into a desperate attempt to find innovative ways to say the very same things that Muslim scholars have been saying for ages. One of the key messages of this book is that it does not have to be this way. Applying sound principles of historical research can revolutionize our understanding of Islamic origins.

An important feature of the traditional source pool for Islamic history has already been identified, but is worth discussing in more detail. This is the fact that it consists mainly of documents claiming to be the written records of oral retellings stretching back to the time of Muhammad. The written records, however, date from much later (typically 200-300 years after-the-fact). In other words, and this vitally important to grasp: *Standard Islamic history rests mostly on secondary sources claiming to be based on oral primary source evidence.*

Therefore, the most basic question that we should ask of the Islamic sources is whether the claim of accurate oral transmission up to the point of a written record being created can be sustained. Unfortunately, many historians of the earliest years of Islam are not asking this question. Instead they tend to treat these secondary sources as if their reliability and authenticity have been established once and for all. This is, as we shall see, far from the case.

We will now proceed to look at some of the sources traditionally mustered in support of traditional Islamic historical accounts with a view to assessing their usefulness as building blocks for constructing an accurate historical picture. The obvious place to start is with the document at the heart of Islam, the Qur'an itself.

1.5.1. The Qur'an as a Historical Source

Most non-Muslims assume that they can, should they be so inclined, pick up the Qur'an and learn all they need to know about the early history of Islam. This is simply not the case. The Qur'an is remarkably de-contextualized. Very few individuals, place names or historical events are mentioned. For example, the word Mecca occurs exactly once in the Qur'an (Qur'an 48:24)[43] and the name Muhammad, as opposed to indirect references, a mere three times (Qur'an 33:40[44], 47:2[45] and 48:29).[46] When you look up these references, it quickly becomes clear that they all make general statements and are of no use in terms of discovering the true history of either Mecca or Muhammad. The Qur'an could in a sense have been written at any time or any place for all the historical information that it provides.

The extent to which the Qur'an is deficient in the area of geographical and historical references is quite staggering. It contains just shy of 150,000 words in Arabic. Only 65 of these words are references to specific locations. The figure of 65 is further reduced when we consider that several of these markers occur more than once and are, therefore, counted several times within the total. In fact, there are only 9 unique location references within the entire book.[47] To put it in another way, you must read on average 2,229 words in the Qur'an before encountering a reference to a location. A useful point of comparison is the Gospels (Matthew, Mark, Luke and John) in the Christian New Testament, all of which contain about ten times more location references than the Qur'an, with the Gospel of Mark referencing a location on average once every 200 words.[48]

Early Muslim scholars tried to solve the problem of the de-contextualized nature of the Qur'an by writing voluminously on the supposed origins of every chapter in the book. This so-called 'Occasions of Revelation' (*Asbāb al-nuzūl*) literature[49] divides the chapters of the Qur'an into different periods: Early Meccan, Intermediate Meccan, Late Meccan and Medinan. These divisions correspond to the biography of Muhammad as it is traditionally presented.

The main problem with the 'Occasions of Revelation' literature (a problem we will encounter again and again during this discussion of sources) is that all attempts to provide context for the Qur'an were written generations after the book was supposedly revealed. They are therefore open to the charge of being back-projections from another place and time (200 years into the future, in fact) to the time of the prophet. The suspicion that this is what happened is further confirmed by the fact that there are often several precisely contradictory contexts provided in different books. Without reliable contemporary eyewitness testimony or documents, it is impossible to choose between these different versions of events.

1.5.2. The *Hadiths* to the Rescue?

If you visit the study of any Muslim scholar, you are likely to find huge collections of beautifully bound books purporting to contain authentic traditions of the acts and sayings of Muhammad. They are *hadith* collections containing many individual *hadiths* (the word *hadith* literally means 'report' in Arabic, but is more commonly translated as 'tradition'). *Hadiths* generally consist of two parts. The 'chain of transmission' (or *isnad*) refers to the authorities who reported the *hadith*, supposedly right back to the time of the Muhammad.[50] A typical *isnad* will read like this: "I heard from A, who heard from B, who heard from C, who heard from E, who heard from F that the prophet did such and such a thing". The second part of the *hadith* then contains the text of the act or saying that is being reported.

This sounds like a very neat and reliable system, except for the fact that there are literally hundreds of thousands of *hadiths* floating around, often containing directly contradictory descriptions and teachings.[51] It is easy to work out why this would be the case. If someone in a later era wanted to bolster his argument on an issue, it would be the easiest thing possible to invent a saying of the prophet in support of that position. This will work well until your opponent gets the same idea. This is apparently exactly what happened and the result was utter chaos. By the mid-850's CE tens of thousands of *hadiths*, many profoundly at odds with each other, but all claiming to go right back to Muhammad were circulating in the Muslim world.[52] Muslim scholars of past generations tried to get around this problem by researching the supposed reliability of different *hadiths* and classifying them as *sahih* (authentic or sound), *hasan* (good) and *da'if* (weak).

Over time, whole collections of *hadiths* were compiled in order to provide the faithful with easy access to the more reliable traditions. Within Sunni Islam, six of these collections eventually came to be regarded as the most reliable[53]:

- Sahih Bukhari compiled by Imam Bukhari (died 870 CE)

- Sahih Muslim compiled by Muslim bin al *Hajj*aj (died 875 CE)

- Sunan al-Sughra compiled by Al-Nasa'i (died 915 CE)

- Sunan Abu Dawood compiled by Abu Dawood (died 888 CE)

- Jami al-Tirmidhi compiled by Al-Tirmidhi (died 892 CE)

- Sunan ibn Majah compiled by Ibn Majah (died 887 CE)

The first two collections (Sahih Bukhari and Sahih Muslim) are especially important, and their contents are regarded as generally sound by most Sunni Muslims.[54]

Shi'a Muslims do not accept the same collections as the Sunnis do. Within Shi'a Islam, the so-called 'Four Books' are regarded as the most reliable.[55] These are:

- Kitab al-Kafi compiled by Muhammad ibn Ya'qub al-Kulayni (died 941 CE)

- Man la yahduruhu al-Faqih compiled by Muhammad ibn Ali ibn-e Babuyeh (died 991 CE)

- Al-Tahdhib and Al-Istibsar compiled by Abu Jafar Muhammad Ibn Hassan Tusi (died 1067 CE)

It is hard to overstate the importance of the *hadiths* in constructing Islamic faith and practice. If it were not for the *hadiths*, Muslims would have no textual basis for key aspects of Islam. For example, without the *hadiths*, Muslims would not know the words of the *Shahada* (Confession of Faith)[56], how to perform the *Hajj* (Pilgrimage)[57] and how often to pray.[58] While it is true that there are small groups who follow 'Qur'an Only' Islam[59], they are generally regarded as apostates by both Sunni and Shi'a. The scholars of both these groups agree that Islam is impossible to follow without referencing the *hadiths*.

The importance of the *hadiths* as sources for the beliefs, practices and history of Islam seems to indicate that they can be regarded as ultra-reliable documents dating from the very beginning of Islam. This is evidently not the case. To substantiate this claim, we simply have to look at the death dates given for the compilers of the major Sunni and Shi'a *hadith* collections above, while keeping in mind that Islamic tradition states that Muhammad died in the year 632 CE. It will immediately be obvious that these compilers all lived roughly 200-400 years after the time of Muhammad. This means that we are asked to accept the historicity of documents that supposedly circulated orally for *six to seven generations* before being committed to paper. To put that in perspective, a modern equivalent would be for someone to go to Europe and collect oral traditions on the last days of Napoleon and the Battle of Waterloo (which happened almost exactly 200 years ago) and publish it as the definitive version of those events.

The main problem with extended oral retellings of events or circumstances is obviously that the potential for corruption of, or additions to, the original content is tremendous. In fact, Muslim scholars agree that there were many spurious *hadiths* around[60], to the extent that only about 3-4 % were accepted in the canonical *hadith* collections.[61] Even with these, there are huge problems.

There is straightforward evidence that many people struggled to memorize the Qur'an for a single generation (with many chapters or verses found only with single individuals)[62], yet we are asked to believe that thousands of traditions survived flawlessly across seven generations. In this regard the so-called *isnads* (chains of transmission) create more problems than they solve. The earliest *hadiths* appeared without them until they were suddenly 'discovered' to lend authority to certain *hadiths*.[63] This means that we are asked to believe that *isnad* and *hadith* existed in isolation until they were somehow magically brought together.

There are, furthermore, many examples of supposedly sound (*sahih*) *hadiths* in the canonical collections that directly contradict each other. You have, for example, separate and contradictory collections accepted by the Sunni and Shi'a.[64] What clearer evidence for the unreliability of the *hadiths* can you ask for than the fact that the two major divisions of Islam both have access to collections that support their positions to a tee? Beyond this, we even find that irreconcilable contradictions occur within individual collections. This leads to the absurd situation that two traditions both regarded as *sahih* (sound) and in the same collection will profoundly disagree with each other. We see, for example, that there is a *hadith* in Sahih Bukhari (by far the most respected Sunni collection) that states that Muhammad performed only one ablution before praying (1:4:159)[65], the very next *hadith* states that he did so twice (1:4:160)[66] only to be contradicted by the next one (1:4:161) where it states that it should be done three times.[67] So much for the supposed accuracy and soundness of the oral traditions that we find in the *hadith* collections.

There is another factor that casts serious doubts on the value of the *hadiths* as historical sources. This is the simple fact that many of them are absurd in the extreme, being filled with fanciful tales supposedly associated with Muhammad. They tend to portray Muhammad as the greatest miracle worker who ever lived[68] despite the fact that the Qur'an makes it clear that Muhammad was not a miracle worker but a 'warner' (cf. Qur'an 13:7).[69] This kind of over-the-top elaboration on the life of a historical figure is, of course, exactly what we would expect from tales that grew in the telling over the centuries, but their presence certainly does nothing to increase confidence in the *hadiths* as historically reliable records of the life and teachings of Muhammad.

In considering the reliability of the *hadiths*, we also have to consider why a literate people would need a vast amount of oral traditions to preserve their history. It is true that Muslim tradition states that Muhammad was illiterate (although legitimate questions can be asked about whether this was in fact the case[70]), but many of his followers clearly were not. This fact is specifically acknowledged in the Islamic tradition which states that some of the early Muslims were tasked to act as secretaries for Muhammad[71] and others to help with the compilation of the written form of the Qur'an after his death.[72] This raises a few crucial questions:

- Why would a people who counted many excellent scribes among their number rely *exclusively* on oral retellings to preserve something as important as the historical memory of their prophet?

- Why, furthermore, would they keep this peculiar practice up for two hundred years, especially given the risk that these precious memories could be corrupted or lost?

- If the *hadiths* were such an important part of the legacy of Muhammad, why are references to them glaring by their absence in the attested historical record? Why do the earliest Muslim rulers, for example, not reference them on their inscriptions, correspondence or legal rulings?

The only conclusion that we can come to is that they did not reference them because they did not know they existed. A very strange position for those who supposedly succeeded Muhammad as the leaders of the faithful (and who were thus supposed to emulate his example as found in the *hadiths*) to be in.

It may, lastly, be worthwhile to ask a profound theological question from within the Muslim tradition itself: Why do the *hadiths* exist at all if the Qur'an is indeed a 'detailed record' (Qur'an 6:114)[73] from which 'nothing is omitted' (Qur'an 6:38)?[74] These verses, and others like them, make it clear that the Qur'an is a sufficient guide for faith and conduct. The Qur'an, therefore, does not contain a single direct command related to the collection and memorization of a secondary source like the *hadiths*. This fact places yet another massive question mark over the reliability of the *hadith* collections. We are asked to believe that thousands upon thousands of people independently undertook the mammoth task of *hadith* memorization despite the absence of any encouragement whatsoever from Allah or Muhammad to do so.

It should be obvious from the above that the official explanation behind the composition of the *hadiths* is exceedingly hard to credit and this significantly increases the suspicion that they were simply invented at a later date to serve the political agendas of future generations of Muslim leaders. All of which must necessarily lead to significant doubts about their reliability as sources that could contribute anything of value to the process of reconstructing the early history of Islam.

1.5.3. Biographies of Muhammad

Muhammad is, of course, the major human figure in the religion of Islam. It would therefore be only natural for Muslims to want to find out everything that they can about him. This market is well served by a variety of biographies purporting to fill in every detail of the life of the Islamic prophet. There is just one problem with this whole enterprise. Not even one of the biographies of Muhammad can be viewed as a primary source as all of them date from a much later period.

The most famous and earliest biography of Muhammad of which we have a written record is the *Sirat Rasul Allah* (Biography of the Apostle of Allah)[75] by Muhammad ibn Ishaq ibn Yasār (often known simply as Ibn Ishaq) who lived from 704-770 CE. It is instructive to focus on his birth and death dates. The author of the earliest biography of Muhammad in written form was born a full 70 years after the date traditionally given for the death of Muhammad and probably started work on his famous biography more than 100 years after Muhammad's death. It should, furthermore, be noted that we do not have the actual book, but only references and extended quotes from later biographers like Ibn Hisham (who died in 833 CE, almost exactly 200 years after Muhammad).[76] It is very significant, when it comes to assessing Ibn Hisham's passing on of Ibn Ishaq's writings, that the later author is quite upfront about the fact that he did not simply transmit Ibn Ishaq's material as he found it. He instead seems to have exercised a significant level of editorial control. Or as he put it: "...confining myself to the prophet's biography and omitting some of the things which Ibn Ishaq has recorded in this book in which there is no mention of the apostle and about which the Quran says nothing and which are not relevant to anything in this book or an explanation of it or evidence for it; poems which he quotes that no authority on poetry whom I have met knows of; things which it is disgraceful to discuss; matters which would distress certain people; and such reports as al-Bakka'i told me he could not accept as trustworthy - all these things I have omitted. But God willing I shall give a full account of everything else so far as it is known and trustworthy tradition is available."[77] Hardly the kind of statement designed to inspire ringing confidence that we are dealing with a pristinely preserved historical tradition.

We must conclude, then, that even the most revered of Muhammad's biographies is hamstrung by the twin impediments of being chronologically far removed from its subject and serious questions about whether its contents were reliably transmitted.

Several other works (besides those by Ibn Ishaq and Ibn Hisham) are sometimes cited as more reliable biographies of the prophet, especially by those who dislike some of the elements of the biography as related by Ibn Ishaq. These include works ascribed to Urwah ibn Zubayr[78] (died 712 CE) and Aban bin Uthman bin Affan[79] (died 723 CE). The problem with these claimants (as, in fact, with the biography of Ibn Ishaq itself) is that the originals were lost and all that we have are references to these works written down generations after their authors died. Again, the potential for textual corruption and putting 'words into the mouth' of these figures is immense. To put it bluntly, *claiming* an ancient pedigree is not the same as actually *proving* an ancient pedigree. This principle is confirmed by countless forgeries of historical documents that have been unearthed over the years. Thus, as with so much of the Islamic historical record, the claims regarding alternatives to Ibn Ishaq should be taken with a healthy pinch of salt.

When we analyze the contents of the earliest prophetic biographies, certain problems emerge almost immediately:

- The contents of several of the biographies are, firstly, significantly at odds with the teachings of the Qur'an. There are many examples of this, but the divergence between the Qur'an and the biographies of the prophet on the issue of miracles is perhaps most striking.[80] In the Qur'an, Allah repeatedly refuses requests for miracles by stating that Muhammad is simply 'a warner' (cf. Qur'an 13:7)[81] Based on this, we would have to say that the Qur'anic Muhammad was not a miracle worker (except for the supposed miracle of the Qur'an itself and the dubiously attested 'splitting of the moon'[82]). The picture presented in Muhammad's biographies is rather more spectacular. Muhammad seems to have performed miracles aplenty. Water flows from his fingertips[83], he pops eyeballs back into the eye sockets of injured people causing them to work better than before[84] and multiplies food for his followers.[85] The list goes on and

34

on. The austere non-miracle working figure of the Qur'an has now been transformed into a prolific 'wonderworker'.

- A curious fact about the biographies of Muhammad is that the later the biography is (in terms of the date that it was written), the more detailed it tends to be. Later generations of writers seemingly had access to a wealth of detail that entirely escaped earlier biographers.[86] This is strange to say the least. Where did all this new information, never before committed to paper, suddenly come from hundreds of years after Muhammad's death? What we see here is a clear example of legend creation and myth making in action.

- One of the strongest arguments against the accuracy of the biographies of Muhammad is that they are all based on the 'wrong' calendar. In Ibn Ishaq (and later biographies), the dates when certain events occurred are scrupulously recorded. This may seem like a very commendable commitment to accuracy until you realize that every third year has an entire month missing. The context of this is that the traditional account tells us that the Islamic lunar calendar replaced the pre-Islamic pagan calendar in 629 CE.[87] The pagan calendar had a leap month every three years to keep pace with the solar calendar. The Islamic calendar does not have this leap month[88] and is thus 11 days shorter than solar-based calendars. The year 629 CE (when the pagan calendar was replaced) was 19 years since Muhammad claimed to have received his first revelation. In the intervening period, he lived through six leap months, claiming to be a prophet, before the Islamic calendar was adopted. Yet of all the thousands upon thousands of events recorded of his prophetic ministry, *not a single one takes place during a leap month*. One can only conclude, on the basis of this, that the traditions in Ibn Ishaq were created at a time when all knowledge of how the previous calendar worked was lost.[89] Date selection was, therefore, arbitrary and not based on any well-preserved tradition. This suspicion is further strengthened by the fact that many of the major events of Muhammad's life are placed on exactly the same day (Monday) and date (12 Rabi Al Awwal) in different years.[90]

In addition to the issues discussed above, we haven't even touched on the errors, absurdities and inconsistencies in these biographies. Despite this, Ibn Ishaq and those who followed him are widely accepted by Muslims as giving a reliable picture of the life of Muhammad. Even those who are embarrassed by Ibn Ishaq still return to his work for the only available historical references to some of the widely-accepted events in Muhammad's life. While there are claims that some biographies are more accurate, no early copies of these exist. The reader will have to agree on the basis of the above, that the traditional biography of Muhammad is built on an exceedingly shaky foundation.

1.5.4. Early Islamic Historical Texts and Their Legacy

At about the same time when the *hadith* collections were being compiled, some early historians took it upon themselves to systematize the material contained in the sources above into histories of the earliest years of Islam. There are many examples of such works emerging from the mid 850's CE (i.e. 200 years after the death of Muhammad). The most famous of these early Muslim histories is 'The History of the Prophets and the Kings' by Muhammad ibn Jarir al-Tabari (839-923 CE).[91] This book, often simply known as the Tarikh al-Tabari (History of Tabari), is a monumental work and is still immensely influential as one of the fountainheads of Muslim history writing.[92]

How exactly did Al Tabari write his history? Did he engage in meticulous primary source research in order to reconstruct the time of Muhammad and the subsequent Arab Conquests as accurately as possible? Not quite. Al Tabari's method (a method also used by the many who followed in his footsteps) was essentially to collate material that he believed to be surviving oral traditions and to present this with as little commentary as possible. The Tarikh Al Tabari is, therefore, simply a series of narrations presented in a more-or-less chronological order.[93] What is more, Al-Tabari's version of history was highly partisan, designed to bolster the legitimacy Islam's second ruling dynasty, the Abbasids.[94] It is a distinct possibility, when history is 'weaponized' like this that ideological point scoring will trump a commitment to historical accuracy. The suspicion that this is exactly what happened can be confirmed through the many instances where Al-Tabari's confident claims about the speed, nature and make-up of the Arab Conquests are comprehensively contradicted by contemporary sources.

By giving preference to supposedly ancient yet highly partisan oral traditions as the bedrock of Islamic history, Al Tabari (widely regarded as one of the most important theologians and historians of the early Islamic period) established a very significant precedent. He accepted without question that the biography of Ibn Ishaq and the 'sound *hadiths*' were indeed reliable and directly connected to the time of Muhammad. This established these 'secondary sources claiming to be primary sources' as unassailable authorities in the eyes of many who followed Al Tabari's lead. In the process, the very significant questions outlined above about the reliability of the transmission of the oral traditions were essentially ignored and the *hadiths*, Ibn Ishaq's biography and some other later traditions were enshrined as reliable source material. The uncritical acceptance of these sources is still the default position of traditional Muslim historiography.[95]

1.5.5. The Current State of Play: A Puzzling Lack of Critical Engagement

One can perhaps understand why Muslim historians would accept without question the historiographical tradition established by Ibn Hisham, Al Tabari and others, since it so significantly underpins traditional understandings of Islam. What is rather puzzling, however, is the readiness of many Western scholars to fall into line. Pick up just about any introductory text on Islamic history prescribed at Western universities and you will find essentially a standard retelling of the narratives first penned by Ibn Ishaq, Al Tabari and other Muslim historians following in their wake.[96] References to actual contemporary primary sources will, by contrast, be conspicuous by their absence.

What is particularly ironic is that this uncritical acceptance of sources that would normally be laughed out of court, or dismissed as 'legendary material' when applied to any other period (or religion), is occurring at universities and research institutions where revisionist projects questioning various other 'accepted histories' will often be actively encouraged.

The ignoring of accepted standards for historical enquiry when it comes to the history of Islam, including by Western scholars, has a long history. Even a figure as illustrious as Edward Gibbon (1737-1794) in his majestic 'Decline and Fall of the Roman Empire' confessed to neglecting to rigorously examine the sources for Islamic history. He prefaces his discussion of Muslim history with this rather startling but eminently honest statement: "I am ignorant, and I am careless, of the blind mythology of the Barbarians: of the local deities, of the stars, the air, and the earth, of their sex or titles, their attributes or subordination."[97]

While few modern historians would be willing to own up quite so flippantly to being careless in checking out their sources, we evidently have not progressed too far from Gibbon's supreme indifference to the idea of investigating the reliability of the sources supporting the standard Islamic account. In fact, scholars who dare to embark on critical investigations of early Islamic history are often vilified and ostracized for threatening accepted orthodoxy.

Instead we are loudly called upon by the guardians of the traditional view to continue to believe that hundreds of literate people independently undertook the mammoth task memorizing a vast oral tradition despite the absence of any encouragement whatsoever from their God or his prophet to do so. We are also asked to believe that while engaged in this essentially pointless project (why did they not simply commit their precious memories of the prophet to paper?), Muslim leaders also apparently took great care to never so much as mention the existence of this supposedly authoritative oral tradition. Even as a basis for the laws that they were devising for their expanding empire. Not to put too fine a point on it: the standard narrative underpinning Islamic history stretches credulity beyond breaking point, even before we begin to investigate possible alternative sources for reconstructing the history of the beginning of Arab dominance in the Middle East.

There are many reasons behind the reluctance of many within the academic establishment to going beyond regurgitating the same supposed certainties (bereft of solid primary source evidence) when discussing the history of early Islam. An awareness of the fate of critics of Islamic orthodoxy almost certainly plays a part (which is, by the way, also why several scholars working in this area use pseudonyms).[98] There is also the well-established fact that many Islamic and Middle Eastern Studies departments in the West are generously supported by Islamic governments[99] and other entities who have a vested interest in perpetuating the teaching of the orthodox narrative that have become so deeply embedded in the teaching of Islamic history.

There is, lastly, the belief that that the classic Islamic sources are essentially all that we have to work with. In other words, so the thinking goes, we must accept the standard Islamic sources, otherwise the period in question will be a blank canvas. This is simply not the case. There are many other sources we can turn to, many of them *bona fide* primary sources. It is to these possible alternative sources that we now turn.

1.6. Not So Silent After All: Finding Alternative Sources

Traditional Muslim historiography tends to emphasize the idea that pre-Islamic Arabia contained very little of worth.[100] If we accept the idea that all was darkness, ignorance and barbarity, then it follows logically that very little must have survived as far as historical sources from this period goes. The problem is, however, that the Muslim characterization of Arabia before Muhammad as nothing more than a wasteland filled with ignorance is a grotesque misrepresentation. Ancient and sophisticated cultures flourished in this part of the world.[101] Many of these cultures and societies left deep and multi-faceted layers of historical evidence. One can understand why Muslim scholars, wishing to maintain a firm belief in an Islam that owes precisely nothing to what came before, insist that pre-Islamic Arabia was a cultural and political wasteland. This belief can, however, only be maintained in the teeth of overwhelming evidence to the contrary. Much of this evidence is contained in the many documents touching directly on life in the Arabian Peninsula that survived from the 5th to the 7th centuries.

The richness of the pre-Islamic historical record is partially due to the fact that the Arabian Peninsula was firmly tied into contemporary international trade networks. Where money is involved, which is invariably the case with trade, a documentary trail inevitably follows. This principle was as true in the ancient world as it is today. There are, therefore, an abundance of documents relating to trade in the Arabian Peninsula that historians can consult.

Add to this the fact that the Romans and Persians enlisted Arab tribes to fight their wars for them and, therefore, kept obsessively detailed records (many of which survive) of the places and tribes of Arabia and you have a veritable feast of primary source documents to choose from when it comes to the history of this part of the world. Sources that the historian of early Islam can draw on include:

- *Correspondence:* By the time of late-antiquity, letter writing has long been accepted as a vital part of long distance communication and much can be learned about the world from which they originated by reading letters surviving from this period.

- *Trade route descriptions and maps:* Those crossing the Arabian Desert obviously had to have some idea of where to go and what to expect on route. There are several surviving trade route descriptions that take in the area that we are interested in (sometimes at a level of detail that could almost be regarded as obsessive).[102] Occasionally these descriptions included rudimentary maps.

- *Formal Geographical Descriptions:* Over the course of this book we will meet a range of ancient authors who went to great pains to provide their readers with accurate information on the ancient Near East. They include Herodotus, Diodorus Siculus, Strabo, Pliny[103] and many others. We will also have occasion to consult works that provided geographical information for official use. Since both the Roman and Sassanian (Persian) empires enlisted Arab tribes to fight on their behalf, the two world-powers of Late Antiquity had a keen interest in Arab lands. We can, therefore, draw upon both Roman and Persian official descriptions for more information on this part of the world. This type of document is often referred to as a 'gazetteer', i.e. a kind of geographical dictionary that describes the features, population and other important features of a particular territory

- *Christian, Jewish and Persian Chronicles:* Contrary to Muslim claims, Arabia was not merely a pagan wasteland before the coming of Islam. There were significant communities of Christian, Jews and Zoroastrians living both in Arabia and on its edges. Members of these communities wrote about their experiences (sometimes in formal chronicles, at other times more informally)[104] both before the coming of Islam and during the Arab conquest. By reading these sources, we can get a rich and varied picture of the period we are studying.

- *Artifacts:* Perhaps the most important artifacts from this period are coins. The study of coins (formally known as numismatics) can be of tremendous help in reconstructing the history of a period. Particularly since coins tend to be very closely associated with the exercise of political and military power.

- *Archeology:* The period that we are studying left some very significant archeological traces. The opposite is true as well. There can sometimes be an utterly surprising lack of archaeological traces where we might reasonably expect them to be.

There are, in summary, no lack of verifiable primary sources from the period and places intimately associated with the early years of Islam and the subsequent Arab conquest. It is just that these sources are steadfastly ignored by those wedded to the traditional account of Islam's origins. We are, in fact, left with a rejection of actual primary sources in favor of much later secondary sources (albeit ones claiming to be based on primary oral traditions).

One of the basic approaches underlying this book will be to do everything possible to rely on as wide a range of sources as can be found. Particular attention will be paid to previously neglected primary sources. This will not only help us to evaluate the claims made about the reliability of the oral tradition contained in the *hadiths*, Ibn Ishaq, Al-Tabari and others, it may also open our eyes to an entirely different world from the one presented so confidently in these canonical sources.

It is worth emphasizing again that care will be taken to fully reference all sources taken from the list above when they are referred to. By consulting the endnotes, the reader will, therefore, be able to ascertain whether these sources are being used in an accurate and historically responsible manner.

1.7. Chapter Summary

Islamic history is strongly contested, suggesting a high likelihood that the historical record was manipulated to serve and strengthen later partisan political positions.

Interaction with primary sources represents the gold standard of historical research. However, the standard Islamic account rests on secondary sources mostly compiled about two to three centuries after the events they claim to describe.

These secondary sources claim to be a written record of reliable oral traditions stretching back to the time of Muhammad. There are, however, several serious objections to the idea that oral traditions in general, and these in particular, could have been flawlessly preserved.

Many of those working on the early history of Islam neglect to practice rigorous source criticism on the classic sources generally used for this purpose, choosing to accept them on face-value. This is an inconsistent (given the vigorous investigation into the reliability of the sources underpinning other periods) and unscientific approach.

There are, contrary to popular belief, a vast range of non-Islamic primary sources that we can draw upon to reconstruct the history of the Arabian Peninsula in the 6th - 8th centuries CE.

2.

The Incredible Vanishing City: Mecca and Pre-Islamic Arabia

*T*he classic Islamic sources tell us **that the ancient city of Mecca was a site of immense spiritual and economic importance.** However, by the time Muhammad was born (570 CE) it was adrift in a sea of paganism and barbarity that enveloped the entire Arabian Peninsula. Muhammad was a member of one of the most important tribes of Mecca, the Quraysh, and received a call from God to act as his prophet in a cave just outside the city. Acting upon this call, Muhammad received a series of revelations over a period of about twenty years, right up to his death in 632 CE. These revelations form what we now know as the Qur'an. After Muhammad's death, his followers burst out of the Arabian Peninsula in the name of Islam and conquered the Persian and much of the Eastern Roman Empire. The coming of Islam established the Muslim religion, with the message of Muhammad and the city of Mecca at its center, as the pre-eminent belief system from Egypt to Persia within 100 years of the death of the prophet.

2.1. The Centrality of the 'Mother of all Cities'

There is an obvious starting point for any discussion about the origins of Islam: the city of Mecca. It would, in fact, be hard to overstate the importance of Mecca within Islam, both in terms of Muslim history and the present practice of the Muslim religion.

Here are just some of the beliefs associated with Mecca by Islamic teaching, all of which serves to illustrate its unchallenged supremacy as the 'City at the Center of the World':

- Mecca supposedly stands at the spot where Adam and Eve settled after being expelled from the Garden of Eden. Muslim tradition further holds that the black stone that is kissed by Muslim pilgrims during the *Hajj* was first brought to the city by Adam himself. Its supposed association with Adam and Eve is believed to be the reason behind the city's title as the 'Mother of all Cities' (Qur'an 42:7).[105]

- It is, furthermore, believed that Abraham, the 'father of the faithful', spent a significant amount of time in Mecca. He is also credited with the construction (or restoration after Noah's flood, according to some traditions) of the *Ka'aba*, the cube shaped building in the middle of the city that is the focus of Muslim pilgrimage and in which the abovementioned black stone is embedded (cf. Qur'an 2:127).[106]

- The fame of this most glorious of cities was not only due to the vital role that it supposedly played in the lives of Biblical figures. Much is made in Muslim historical accounts of its inhabitants 'losing their way' to the extent that Mecca eventually became established at the heart of Arabian pagan worship[107], a position that it held until Muhammad finally cleared it of all traces of idolatry.[108] So entrenched, in fact, was its position as a center of inveterate paganism that Muslims believe that many of the earlier chapters of the Qur'an were specifically revealed to convince the idolaters in the city to change their wicked ways.

- The status of Mecca was supposedly further enhanced by the fact that it was one of the pre-eminent trading centers of Arabia. Some would even go so far as claiming that the city occupied a magnificent strategic position on the crossroads of two trans-Arabian trade routes.[109] Meccan traders used this fact to establish themselves as a significant presence wherever trade took place in the Middle East.[110]

44

- For many Muslims, the supreme glory of Mecca is the fact that Muhammad was born in the city.[111] Not only this, he spent a significant period of his life there and experienced his greatest moment of triumph when he conquered the city in the name of Allah a few years before his death.[112]

- Mecca became the focal-point of Islamic worship during Muhammad's lifetime when believers were instructed to offer their prayers in the direction of the *Ka'aba* at its center (cf. Qur'an 2:142-143).[113] Today all mosques in the world are oriented towards Mecca and more than a billion Muslims offer their daily prayers towards this city in the middle of Arabian Desert.

- Mecca also occupies a place at the heart of the so-called '5 Pillars of Islam'[114] the central religious obligations of the Muslim religion. Participating in the *Hajj*, or pilgrimage to Mecca, is expected of every able-bodied Muslim, who can afford it, at least once in his/her lifetime.

Given the absolutely central role of Mecca within Islam, it comes of something as a surprise that there is very little, if any, indication in primary sources dating from the period of Islam's origins that the city even existed before the time of Muhammad. This is certainly a rather shocking statement, but its truth will be confirmed in the upcoming examination of the evidence (or rather lack thereof) for the pre-Islamic existence of Mecca.

2.2. Najran: A Case Study

Before focusing on the history of Mecca, it may be quite instructive to take a detour to a rather less famous and illustrious city as a reference point.

The city of Najran is in the southwestern corner of modern Saudi Arabia about 400 miles from Mecca as the crow flies. Najran is hardly known outside of the Arabia Peninsula and is therefore right at the other end of the scale in terms of name recognition from Mecca. According to the traditional Muslim account, it has always been this way. Najran, if mentioned at all, is referred to in passing, while Mecca is presented as being at the heart of the history of the Arabian Peninsula, and in fact the world.

We would, considering the above, logically expect that the historical evidence for the pre-Islamic existence of Mecca will be orders of magnitude more substantial than what is available for Najran.

The evidence relating to the pre-history of Mecca will be presented over the course of the rest of this chapter. As a point of comparison, let us have a look at what is known about pre-Islamic Najran based on contemporary primary sources. As you read through these points, keep in mind that Najran is about 400 miles south of Mecca, so it is much further from the parts of the world where most of our surviving documentary records from this period originated. Yet another reason, alongside its relative insignificance, why we might expect that there will be much less available historical evidence related to Najran. Let us now see if this is, in fact, the case.

The first thing to note is that Najran sits on deep layers of archeology, with a wide range of inscriptions reaching back centuries before the Islamic era having been uncovered there.[115] It is also mentioned in the writings of Strabo (64 BCE - 24 CE). He was a resident of the Roman province of Asia Minor and gained renown as a geographer, historian and philosopher. His life coincided with a time of significant imperial expansion for the Roman Empire and he acts as a great defender of the idea of the empire in his writings. His most famous work was his *Geographica* (Geography) in which he attempted to provide a descriptive history of most known people and places of his time. As such, this book ranks as one of the fullest descriptions of the physical and political state of the world at the dawn of the Christian era. Strabo includes extensive material on the Arabian Peninsula (a part of the world very important to the Romans because of the trade in spices and aromatics). Much of Strabo's knowledge of the Arabian interior came from a perilous southward journey along the central Arabian trade route by a Roman General named Aelius Gallus. Here is the reference to Najran in Strabo: "The next country which he traversed belonged to nomads and most of it was truly desert; and it was called Ararenê; and its king was Sabos; and in passing through this country, through parts that had no roads, he spent fifty days, arriving at the city of the Negrana (Najran) and at a country which was both peaceable and fertile."[116] The 'truly desert' part of Strabo's description refers to the area where the modern city of Mecca is located. Yet, even though tiny villages are mentioned, it is not even referred to in passing. How on earth could such a supposedly splendid city be totally missed by an army desperately in need of supplies and rest? Instead the first city they encounter on their southward journey through central Arabia is Najran.

Writing about half a century after Strabo, Pliny the Elder (23-79 CE), one of the most celebrated authors of Roman antiquity, also mentioned Najran. While recounting the aforementioned expedition by Gallus, Pliny stated: "Aelius Gallus, a member of the Equestrian order, is the sole person who has hitherto carried the Roman arms into these lands, for Caius Cæsar, the son of Augustus, only had a distant view of Arabia. In his expedition, Gallus destroyed the following towns, the names of which are not given by the authors who had written before his time, Negrana (Najran), Nestum, Nesca, Masugum, Caminacum, Labecia, and Mariva the above-mentioned, six miles in circumference, as also Caripeta, the furthest point of his expedition."[117]

Perhaps the most famous geographer of the ancient world was Claudius Ptolemy (100 - 170 CE). His 'Geographies' provides us with one of the most complete pictures of the geography of the then known world. Ptolemy identifies six cities in Arabia worthy of the title 'metropolis' and Najran is included in this list.[118]

In addition to being explicitly mentioned by the three giants of Roman geographical writing (Strabo, Pliny and Potlemy), Najran is also mentioned in a wide variety of trade and other geographical descriptions of this era.[119] It is, furthermore, mentioned in several religious texts dealing with the coming of Judaism[120] and Christianity[121] to this part of the Arabian Peninsula.

Perhaps the most famous episode in the history of Najran was the martyrdom (in 524 CE) of the local Christian Bishop, Aretas, and much of his flock were martyred at the hands of the last king of the Himyarite

Kingdom Yusuf As'ar Dhu Nuwas.[122] The martyrs of Najran briefly gained worldwide fame and may even be mentioned in the Qur'an (85:4-8).[123] Aretas is still recognized as a saint by both the Eastern Orthodox and the Roman Catholic Church.[124]

This section has barely scratched the surface as far as historical references to the relatively unimportant and obscure city of Najran is concerned. Today, and in Muslim historiography, it pales in comparison with Mecca, its much more famous northern neighbor in terms of its importance. Yet when it comes to evidence confirming their ancient existence, the comparison between the two can only be described as deeply embarrassing and puzzling if you are a devout Muslim.

2.3. Investigating the Evidence for the Ancient Existence of Mecca

It must be stated from the outset that the title of this section is something of a misnomer because if its contents were limited to actual pre-Islamic historical evidence for the ancient existence of Mecca, there would be nothing here. To put it as bluntly as possible: there is not a single shred of uncontested primary source evidence confirming the existence of an ancient city at the spot where the modern city of Mecca is located.

This may seem, at first glance, like a very bold and startling claim, and one that is likely to be profoundly disruptive to the faith of devout Muslims. The facts, however, speak for themselves. Mecca is not mentioned in any correspondence, travel description or gazetteer (geographical dictionary) or any other type of historical source before the 8th century. In fact, the first references to Mecca all occur more than a century after the date commonly given for the death of Muhammad, with the oldest mention of the city dating from 741 CE (i.e. 109 years after Muhammad's death) where it is referred to in a document known as the 'Continuatio Byzantia Arabica'.[125]

A common response to the easily verifiable fact of Mecca's absence from the pre-Islamic historical record is to claim that this period of the history of Arabia is so shrouded in mystery that the problem of the absence of sources is a general one, rather than being limited to Mecca. In other words, Mecca is absent because the entire history of the period and area is simply a blank page. The discussion above of the sources providing us with a rich and varied history of Najran should, however, go some way towards dispelling any notion that the historical record for pre-Islamic Arabia consists of empty nothingness. If it is so relatively easy to find a multitude of sources for Najran, it should logically be orders of magnitude easier to find such sources for Mecca (if it did, in fact, exist).

Besides Najran, we can also point to detailed historical records for many other towns and cities dotted up and down the Arabian Peninsula. These include Yathrib (later Medina, 'second city' of Islam), Sana'a and Petra. We can even, perhaps most interestingly for our purposes, point to detailed sources confirming the pre-Islamic existence of the city of Ta'if.[126] At 70 miles from Islam's holy city, Ta'if is practically on modern Mecca's doorstep. It is presented in the Islamic record as very much in the shadow of its much more illustrious neighbor. We would be justified in thinking, considering this, that there would be plenty of sources from which to reconstruct the pre-Islamic history of Mecca with scanty evidence for Ta'if. Instead we have much to draw upon for Ta'if and precisely nothing for Mecca.

The gaping hole in the historical record where references to Mecca should be (if the traditional Islamic account is to be believed) is nothing short of astounding. This is the city at the heart of Islam, the supposed mother of all cities. A city that was a major trading hub and religious center. Yet, as Patricia Crone points out in her seminal work 'Meccan Trade and the Rise of Islam': "Greek trading documents refer to the towns of Ta'if (Southeast of Mecca), Yathrib (later Medina), Kaybar, but never Mecca!" We must wait, as mentioned above, for a full 109 years after the traditional death date of Muhammad for the first mention of Mecca to appear (in a document dating from 741 CE)[127] and more than another century (i.e. around 900 CE) after that for the city to be shown on a map.[128]

Mecca's complete absence from the pre-Islamic historical record is not the only question that could be asked about the place of this supposedly ancient site within Islamic history. There are also significant doubts about whether descriptions of the holy city of Islam in the Qur'an and *hadiths* correlate with the physical features of the city of Mecca. This is a topic to which we shall return to in depth later.

The silence of the ancient sources about Mecca is certainly deeply embarrassing to those Muslim scholars who are aware of this issue and many of them have tried very hard to prove we can indeed find Mecca in ancient documents if we just look hard enough. Over the next few pages this claim will be tested by turning to historical sources dealing with ancient Arabia in an attempt to unearth even a single pre-Islamic reference to the city of Mecca.

2.3.1. Mecca and its Near Neighbors

I realize that claiming that Mecca is absent from the ancient historical record is not the same as proving that this is the case. The purpose of this section is, therefore, to thoroughly investigate the ancient documentary and archeological record as it applies to pre-Islamic Arabia. In the process, several instances where we would logically expect to find references to a city supposedly as important and well-connected as Mecca will be pointed out.

Before we begin, it is important to note that ancient Arabia is an absolute treasure trove for the historical researcher. The reason behind this is that documents, artifacts and archaeological evidence survive best in dry conditions. Thus, the ultra-dry conditions prevailing on much of the Arabian Peninsula means that a wealth of historical evidence survived into the modern era. Modern Mecca is, furthermore, located in one of the driest parts of the peninsula, which means that evidence from there have an even better chance at survival.

The extraordinary longevity of historical evidence from this part of the world means that we are able reconstruct lists of rulers for several of the small kingdoms bordering the region where modern Mecca is located to as far back as ten centuries before the Christian era. This is nothing short of remarkable. There are often significant gaps in the lists of rulers of earlier incarnations of the modern European nations and other entities in the post-Roman period. It is, for example, not possible to draw up a definitive and uncontested primary source based list of popes back to the first century.[129] Yet we can trace the king-lists of several insignificant Arabian territories back for millennia into deep antiquity.[130] It should, therefore, once again be emphasized that a lack of sources is not an insurmountable problem when we consider the history of the Arabian Peninsula. We are, if anything, confronted with an overwhelming array of historical records emanating from Arabia. The one thing that these records have in common is that *none of them ever mentions Mecca.*

A rundown of the historical evidence (or rather lack of evidence) for the claim that Mecca is absent from the historical record could very easily become tedious to the non-historian. I will, therefore, keep the discussion of this vitally critical issue as brief and non-technical as possible. As always full references will be provided for those readers who would like to look at the sources cited in more detail. The way in which this discussion will be approached is by starting with the Hejaz (the region where Mecca is located) then working our way clockwise around the regions of the Arabian Peninsula with a focus on the areas that are directly adjacent to the location of the modern city of Mecca. In the process, we will be able to have a good look at the state of the records relating to these neighboring regions in the pre-Islamic era, and their links with the region where Mecca is located.

The Hejaz: The Hejaz is the region of western central Arabia where the modern city of Mecca is located. It is, even by desert standards, an exceptionally dry part of the world and there is therefore very little archeological evidence pointing to any ancient civilization ever existing here. What human habitation there was, was largely confined to scattered oases. The sparseness of the archeological record for the central Hejaz stands completely at odds with traditional Islamic historiography which, of course, places a great and glorious city at the heart of this region. This tradition also states that a tribal confederation known as the Thamud controlled the Hejaz as the dominant power in this region in the pre-Islamic era. The Qur'an makes much of the Thamudic past of the Hejaz (it devotes

24 of its 65 geographical references to the Thamud). Yet a very significant anomaly arises when we compare actual pre-Islamic archeological and documentary evidence with the confident assertions of later Muslim historians. The available evidence points to the Thamud having controlled an area hundreds of miles to the north of the central Hejaz.[131] If we remove the Thamud (as a North Arabian power) from the equation as far as the history of the Hejaz is concerned, there is precious little left. Both the documentary and archeological record confirm what logic would dictate anyway: no great city or civilization ever flourished here in one of the driest regions on the planet.

North of Mecca: The Qedarite Kingdom and the Kingdom of Nabataea. In this section, we will briefly profile two ancient political entities that existed north of the present location of Mecca. The first is the ancient kingdom named Qedar[132], centered on the area immediately east of the Red Sea that reached its zenith between the 8th and 4th centuries BCE. Because of the strategic position it occupied, the Qedarite kingdom featured prominently in the world of ancient geopolitics and it is mentioned frequently in Hebrew[133], Assyrian and Greek sources. Many of these references refer to its dominance over Arabia and the important role that Qedar played in controlling parts of the trans-Arabian spice and incense trade. It is possible, from the records, to list specific cities and towns (i.e. Qedar, Dedan, Teima, and Dumah) that stood at the heart of Qedarite political life. Absent from any record unearthed relating to these localities and the Qedarite Kingdom more generally are any references to Mecca or trade with the Meccans, although a city supposedly as important as Mecca must have loomed large in Qedarite strategic, political and economic calculations.

If we wind the clock back a bit closer to the Islamic period, we will encounter the great Kingdom of Nabataea as the dominant force in the northern part of the Arabian Peninsula and the northern Hejaz from about the 2nd century BCE to 106 CE (when it was annexed by the Romans).[134] The Nabataeans may not have very high name-recognition today, but they were once the rulers of one the greatest empires that Arabia had ever known. The remains of their capital, Petra, eloquently testifies to the wealth and influence of this ancient Arabian kingdom. The historical record related to Nabataea is very rich and historians can reconstruct king-lists dating back to the 2nd century BCE.[135] We, furthermore, have a detailed picture of the wars that they were engaged in and the extent of their trading relations. This last fact is particularly important because the historical record shows that the Nabataeans for several centuries controlled the northern end of the trading routes that the ancient city of Mecca was supposed to have been located on. Yet despite this fact, Mecca is not mentioned a single time in any inscription or other record linked to Nabataean political influence or trade. Think for a moment how extraordinary this is. There is solid evidence for Nabataean trade links with cities and territories up and down the peninsula[136] and even further afield (e.g. Ethiopia and the Roman province of Syria). Yet, glaringly absent is any mention of what was supposedly the most important city in all of Arabia.

East of Mecca: The Kingdom of Kindah. The Kingdom of Kindah was based around its capital Dhu-Kahilum about 500 miles east of Mecca and came to prominence just before the start of the Islamic era. Once again, its history is well documented.[137] We can trace the areas that it controlled and there are records of several of its kings and their dealings with the Kingdom of Himyar to the south (see below) and conflict with the Lakhmids to the north. Again, no records have been found detailing any relations between the Kindites and a city known as Mecca, even though it would have been practically on their doorstep.

South of Mecca: The Kingdom of Himyar. One of the Arabian pre-Islamic entities for which we have the most extensive records is the Kingdom of Himyar (110 BCE – 525 CE). This was the name given to a kingdom ruling over large parts of what is now Yemen and southern Saudi Arabia (and even at times Ethiopia). This kingdom was preceded as the dominant force of South Arabia by the equally well attested Kingdom of Saba. The Kingdom of Himyar survived right up to the dawn of the Islamic area, until it was finally subjugated by the ruler of Aksum (Ethiopia) with the help of the Romans. What makes Himyar particularly interesting is that several of its rulers, including its last king, were Jewish.[138] This is a fact that we will return to later in this book. We have prodigious amounts of source material available with which to reconstruct Himyarite history.[139] This includes not only detailed chronicles describing the lives of the kings, but many surviving inscriptions on buildings and dams dotted throughout southern Arabia.[140] Whereas the Nabataeans controlled the northern end of the trans-Arabian trade route, the Himyarites controlled the southern end. What follows should be totally familiar by now. Even though the Himyarites left many records and sent countless trading caravans right through the area where Mecca is supposed to have been, it never rates so much as a mention in any of their records. This is particularly interesting given the fact that many other settlements, some of them only tiny way-stations in mid-Arabia, are mentioned (including the city of Ta'if about 70 miles from Mecca) in Himyarite records.

West of Mecca: Nubia, Aksum and Ethiopia. Tracing a line due west from Mecca one will soon encounter the Red Sea. This was a lively maritime trade route as is amply documented in the historical record. Once again, any mention in trade descriptions of a supposedly wealthy and ancient city just inland from the waters of this vital trade passage is conspicuous by its absence. On the other side of the Red Sea, there existed thriving African civilizations that traded extensively with the Arabs. The Red Sea coast of Africa was at various times controlled by the Nubian Kingdom, the Kingdom of Aksum and the Ethiopian Empire. Not a single mention of Mecca can be found in the records of any of these ancient kingdoms.[141]

We have now completed a circuit around the site where Mecca is located today. To the north lays Nabataea, to the south Himyar, to the east Kindah and to the west (across the Red Sea) various African kingdoms. Not only did these kingdoms exist right next to the region of Arabia where Mecca is located, some of them actually occupied it at different stages of their history. It would be logical to expect that the writings and inscription of these civilizations would be brimful with references to Mecca as it would have been a very close and important neighbor (if the Islamic accounts are to be believed). Instead we are confronted with absolute silence as far as the fabled 'mother of all cities' is concerned. To put it as simply as possible: If Mecca existed in ancient times, the scribes and kings of Arabia and Northeast Africa would have noticed. They clearly did not. It is entirely absent from the historical record and implications of this should be abundantly obvious.

To draw an analogy, the silence of the Arabian documentary and archaeological record regarding Mecca would be akin to studying the early medieval records of Naples, Florence, Venice, Pisa, Genoa and Milan and not finding even a single mention of the city of Rome. It simply beggars belief that Mecca could have existed as the most important city of mid-Arabia and then not make it into any kind of historical record.

2.3.2. Mecca and Ancient Imperial Records

In the previous section, we had a look at cities, kingdoms and civilizations that existed within striking distance of the current location of Mecca. We found that the scribes of these entities were entirely unaware of the great city supposedly right on their doorstep. We now turn to the records of some of the great empires of the ancient world. Several of these empires had a significant level of interest in the Arabian Peninsula. The reason for this can be found in the place that the peninsula occupied between some of the most important political configurations of the ancient world. Exerting some level of control over Arabia was an attractive proposition because it would give whoever controlled it access to trade routes and natural resources.

Another very significant reason for the importance of Central-Arabia applies specifically to the Sassanians (Persians) and Romans. Arabia was very much on the frontline between the two great empires of Late Antiquity and whoever controlled the peninsula would be able to use it as a jumping-off point for an attack on the enemy. Whoever controlled Arabia could also better secure its borders and use the region as a recruitment ground for tribal mercenaries to fight in their wars.

The imperial powers we will be discussing here were in some ways globe spanning enterprises and the amount of source material associated with them is vast. There are, therefore, plenty of specific places where historians can go looking for evidence for the ancient existence of Mecca. The empires that will be profiled below are as follows:

- Babylonian
- Assyrian
- Persian
- Hellenistic (Greek)
- Roman

Arabia and the Babylonian Empire: The term 'Babylonian Empire' is a bit of a misnomer as there are several entities that can lay claim to this title and that controlled large parts of the Middle East for more than a millennium. For our purposes the most important manifestation of Babylonian interests in Arabia came right towards the end of the Babylonian era. One of the Babylonian kings, Nabonidus (reigned 556-539 BCE), left his empire under the control of one of his sons, Belshazzar, and proceeded to conquer much of Arabia.[142] He eventually set up his Arabian headquarters in a city called Teima (about 500 miles from the location of modern Mecca as the crow flies). From there he continued his conquests southwards, eventually gaining control of the most important cities of the Arabian interior including Dedan, Khaybar and Yathrib (later renamed Medina). These conquests are described in detail in the so-called 'Haran Inscriptions of Nabonidus', the 'Verse Account of Nabonidus' and the 'Babylonian Royal Chronicles'. By consulting these documents, we can reconstruct a detailed record of his conquests and movements. These conquests would have given him control of the all-important trade routes through the Arabian interior. Although even some small settlements are mentioned, there is not a single reference to the city that Muslim sources assure us was the most important city in Arabia since time immemorial. This is particularly baffling given that it was clearly the intention of Nabonidus to control Central-Arabia. Such a move would have been strenuously resisted by the military might of the Meccans (if they in fact existed).

Arabia and the Assyrian Empire: The military might and lust for the empire of the Assyrian rulers (centered on what is now Northern Iraq) was legendary and their conquests regularly took them all over the Middle East and deep into Arabia. They were also some of the best record-keepers in the ancient world, so we are once again faced with an abundance rather than a lack of sources to draw from. A prominent part of the archaeological record for ancient Assyria are the many steles (stone pillars containing carved inscriptions) that several of the Assyrian emperors erected to broadcast their achievements during their reign. Prominently displayed on these steles were records of the conquests of the Assyrian rulers and the nations paying tribute to them. The steles are particularly valuable for our purposes as they typically list conquests and tribute paying nations in regional order. We can therefore use them to reconstruct the geo-political make-up of the Middle East during the reigns of different Assyrian rulers. Arabia is mentioned with regularity in the records of Shalmaneser III (reigned 858-824 BCE)[143], Sargon II (reigned 721-705 BCE)[144], Sennacherib (reigned 704-681 BCE)[145] and Assurbanipal (668-627 BCE).[146] In all their records, some of which provide minutely detailed lists of the tribes, cities and towns of Arabia, Mecca is once again conspicuous by its absence.

Arabia and the Persian Empire: A discussion of the Roman and Persian Empires is particularly important when it comes to possible evidence for the pre-Islamic existence of Mecca, since these were the political entities that were directly affected by the emergence of Islam and the subsequent Arab conquests. To put it plainly, if anyone would have noticed the existence of a place called Mecca in the Arabian interior, it would have been the leaders of the two great powers of Late Antiquity. Once again, we have extensive records of Persian conquests. During the later stages of the existence of the Persian Empire (when it was known as the Sassanian Empire, 224 – 651 CE), it was in perpetual conflict with the (Eastern) Roman Empire. Arabia was of immense strategic importance in this conflict. A quick look at a map will confirm why this was so. Firstly, Arabia represented a kind of soft underbelly as far as the Persians were concerned. If the Romans could somehow manage to launch a flanking movement through the Arabian Desert, they could hit the Persians in areas where their defenses were not up-to-scratch. The Sassanians had, secondly, to contend with massive manpower needs in order to pursue their military campaigns against the Romans and other enemies. Keeping the Arabian frontier safe and recruiting as many mercenaries from there as possible was, therefore, a pressing priority for any Persian emperor. These policies were pursued with such vigor that entire cities populated by Arab tribes in league with the Persians sprung up in the immediate pre-Islamic period. The largest and most influential of these cities was Hira, headquarters of the Lakhmids, an Arab tribe that policed the desert on behalf of the Sassanians.[147] All of this activity inevitably led to the creation of detailed Persian records dealing with realities on-the-ground in Arabia.[148] Several examples can be cited of exhaustive descriptions of the Arabian interior. This included discussion of tribes that inhabited it. This was particularly important for the Persians as they were constantly looking for tribes to recruit to their cause. It is, in light of this, once again exceedingly curious that we do not find a single mention in any Persian document of the *Quraysh*. According to the traditional Islamic account, the *Quraysh* (the tribe to which Muhammad supposedly belonged) was one of the most important tribes of Arabia. It should go without saying by now that there is also not a single mention of the supposed seat of power of the *Quraysh*, the fabled 'mother of all cities', Mecca.

Arabia and the Hellenistic Empire(s): There would at first glance not seem to be any connection between Greece[149] and Arabia, were not it not for the fact that Alexander the Great conquered vast swathes of land (including parts of Arabia itself). After the death of the great conqueror, his empire was divided between his generals. Two of these Hellenistic successor states (the Ptolemaic and Seleucid Empires) bordered Arabia at different times during their history and would, therefore, logically have had some dealings with a city of the stature that Islamic history claims Mecca enjoyed. Instead there is nothing in their records that indicate that the rulers of these states were even remotely aware of the existence of a great metropolis in Arabia. It is also very significant that the great Greek historian Herodotus (484 – 425 BCE), who attempted to provide his readers with a thorough immersion in the history of the world as he knew it, also makes no mention of the 'mother of all cities' when describing Arabia.[150] Mecca is, furthermore, equally absent from the monumental 'Universal History' of the later Greek historian Diodorus Siculus (90 – 30 BCE).[151]

Arabia and the Roman Empire: It is sometimes easy to forget that Arabia was a direct neighbor to the Roman Empire for many centuries. The Roman province of Syria was much larger than the current country by the same name and took in the modern countries of Israel, Jordan, Lebanon and of course modern Syria itself. These territories are located right on the northern edge of the Arabian Peninsula. In addition to this, the Romans were intensely interested in the southern parts of the peninsula as it controlled the lower reaches of the routes that were such an important part of Roman trade. We have, for example, detailed records of Roman involvement (through their support of the Kingdom of Aksum, centered on modern Ethiopia and Eritrea) in the downfall of the Southern Arabian Kingdom of Himyar in the mid 6th century CE.[152] Returning to the north, the position of the Romans was like that of the Persians. They too had to keep their Arabian frontier safe and recruited Arab tribes to fight in their wars. They even created several garrison cities occupied by loyal Arab tribes. To help commanders on the ground navigate the complex realities of Arabian politics, the Roman authorities regularly published descriptions of the region that included detailed records of the tribes, cities and resources of different areas. Many of these records survived into the modern era and they have been invaluable in reconstructing an accurate picture of Arabia before the rise of Islam. By rights these documents should be exceptionally rich sources of information on pre-Islamic Mecca and especially the tribe that supposedly dominated it, the *Quraysh*. Yet all that we hear is total silence. Mecca is absent from records that record even tiny hamlets and insignificant little tribes. This absence is even more baffling in light of the Muslim claim that one of Muhammad's ancestors entered into a formal alliance with the Romans.[153] Needless to say, no record of a central-Arabian ally called the *Quraysh* exist in Roman records. When it comes to the Roman geographers and historians, the silence continues. Mecca is absent from the writings of the trio of great Roman geographers, namely Strabo (64 BCE - 24 CE), Pliny the Elder (23-79 CE) and Ptolemy (100 – 170 CE).[154] In addition to the great geographers, Mecca also does not appear in the writings of any Roman historian. Its absence in the writings of two later Roman authors is particularly striking and telling. Amianus Marcellinus (330 – 400 CE)[155], one of the most important late-Roman historians spent much of his time describing Roman campaigns in Persia. He frequently touched on the Roman presence in Arabia, yet he seems to have been entirely unaware of the existence of a great city in the interior. Right on the dawn of the Islamic age we encounter Procopius of Caesarea (500-564 CE). He was a native of Palestine and would, therefore, have known Arabia well. In fact, his 'History of the Wars' includes a rich and full description of western Arabia (without any mention of Mecca).[156]

2.3.3. Mecca as a great trading city?

Even those with a very sketchy knowledge of Islamic history will know that Mecca was supposed to have been one of the most important trading cities of the ancient Middle East. However, if you have read this far, you would probably be entitled to raise an eyebrow at this claim. Surely such a rich and fabled trading hub would have made it onto the historical record? Besides this obvious point, there are several other reasons that cast doubt on the claim that there was a trading city called Mecca in the middle of the Arabian Desert during the time when Muhammad was supposed to have lived.

- *Trans-Arabian overland trade was effectively at a standstill by the 6th Century CE:* Patricia Crone in her ground-breaking work 'Meccan Trade and the Rise of Islam' points out that there would have been few commodities for Meccan traders to trade in by the 6th century as trans-Arabian overland trade had essentially collapsed by this time. This trade was heavily dependent on the transport of incense from Southern Arabia to the Roman province of Syria and beyond. The collapse of paganism in the Roman Empire (the rituals associated with Roman gods required prodigious amounts of incense) coupled with political instability effectively put an end to the incense trade. This leaves spices and other items imported from India as possible objects of trade. Crone points out, however, that these commodities were typically transported via sea-routes (i.e. through the Persian Gulf or the Red Sea) instead of making use of the slow and dangerous route through the center of the Arabian Peninsula. If we remove spices and incense out of the equation, we are essentially left with low-value commodities (e.g. dates, animal hides and salt) as possible candidates for trans-Arabian trade. It would indeed be remarkable if the Romans and Persians imported such heavy and relatively abundant goods over large distances and at great cost given that they would have had cheaper, and arguably better quality, sources of these materials available much closer at hand. As Crone asks: "... what commodity was available in Arabia that could be transported such a distance, through such an inhospitable environment, and still be sold at a profit large enough to support the growth of a city in a peripheral site bereft of natural resources?"[157] So even if Mecca was a great trading city in earlier ages it could not have been a trading hub by the time of Muhammad's birth (as claimed by Muslim tradition). It will, however, become clear from the rest of this section that even the claim that it played a vital part in earlier Arabian trade cannot be sustained.

A trade route through Mecca would have necessitated a costly and pointless detour. If you plot the major trans-Arabian trade routes as detailed in ancient sources, it will quickly become clear that they bypassed Mecca entirely. The reason for this is readily apparent. The route obviously followed the straightest and easiest route across the peninsula. When it comes to the general area of Mecca, the most important site was the ancient oasis of Ta'if where traders could stop, rest, and get fodder for their camels. The fact that Ta'if was a major stop is abundantly attested to in the ancient records. If Mecca was on the route, we must believe that traders left Ta'if for a 140-mile round trip up a narrow valley to visit Mecca, only to re-join the established route at more or less the same place they left from. Such a detour would have taken several days and would therefore have been very expensive in terms of time, energy and wasted resources. Why time and money conscious traders would have embarked on such a clearly unnecessary detour is left entirely unexplained by the promoters of the traditional view. Here is the basic question that those who want to uphold this traditional view must answer according to Patricia Crone: "Mecca was a barren place, and barren places do not make natural halts, and least of all when they are found at a short distance from famously green environments. Why should caravans have made a steep descent to the barren valley of Mecca when they could have stopped at Ta'if."[158]

These commonsense arguments are sometimes countered by the claim that Mecca was in the heart of Arabia and that trade caravans were, therefore, bound to pass by it. A simple look at a map will show that this is not the case. As Richard Bulliet memorably put it: "...only by the most tortured

map reading can it (Mecca) be described as at a natural crossroads between a north-south route and an east-west one."[159]

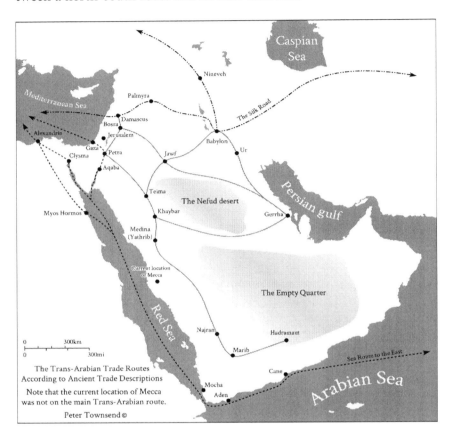

The Trans-Arabian Trade Routes
According to Ancient Trade Descriptions

Note that the current location of Mecca
was not on the main Trans-Arabian route.

Peter Townsend ©

Mecca is absent from ancient trade descriptions. We have many surviving trade descriptions from the ancient world that we can consult. We
can add to this correspondence and other forms of writing in which the
Trans-Arabian trade were referred to. By using such sources, we can reconstruct a very detailed picture of pre-Islamic trans-Arabian trade.[160]
Even to the point of identifying the role that tiny settlements played in
this trade. Trade descriptions would go into significant levels of detail
as to which commodities could be sourced where, what people are likely
to buy in various places and where provisions might be obtained.[161] Yet,
the supposed 'trading hub' of the Arabian Peninsula (according to the

Islamic account) is entirely absent from these descriptions. A contemporary equivalent would be to write a description of trading centers in modern Arabia without once referring to the city of Dubai.

There are no references to Meccan traders in ancient literature. Ancient people were no different from us when it came to being curious about the cultures and habits of strangers. This kind of curiosity would certainly have been enhanced when the profit motive was introduced into the equation. There are many surviving descriptions of diverse groups of traders (Syrians, Persians, Nabataeans etc.) to help those dealing with them to understand what 'makes them tick' and how they did business. According to the Islamic account, Meccan traders worked the Trans-Arabian route and traded deep into the Roman province of Syria. Yet we search in vain for any description of, or even passing reference to, Meccan traders plying the trade routes of late-antiquity.[162]

It should be clear, based on the evidence presented above, that it is highly unlikely that a major trans-Arabian trading center existed at the location of the modern city of Mecca. This represents a direct and fundamental challenge to the accepted Islamic historical account. Another role that this account ascribes to Mecca is that it was a major religious hub for the entire Arabian Peninsula. It is to this claim that we turn next.

2.3.4. Mecca as an Ancient Religious Center?

Given the current centrality of Mecca in Islamic worship (all Muslim prayers offered anywhere in the world are offered towards Mecca), it would seem almost logical and inevitable that it has always been a place of immense religious importance. This is indeed the claim that Islamic history has consistently made. According to the traditional account, Mecca is a place of fabulous antiquity. They claim that Adam spent time here (some accounts even have him building the *Ka'aba*)[163] as did Abraham, a major figure in the Hebrew Bible as well as in Christian tradition.[164] In fact, a major part of the Muslim Pilgrimage rests on the story of Abraham's concubine Hagar attempting to find sustenance for her son Ishmael after they were turned out by Abraham. Muslim scholars claim that Mecca went backwards very fast after the heady days of Abraham's residence and that by the time of Muhammad's birth, it was firmly established as the most important center for pagan worship on the Arabian Peninsula. Once again, there are significant objections that can be raised when it comes to these claims. These include the following:

Mecca does not appear in ancient records as a site of religious importance. We have many historical sources from which to construct a picture of religion in pre-Islamic Arabia. Mecca is not mentioned in a single one of them. We read, for example, of places like Mamre (at the northern edge of Arabia)[165] and Ma'rib (the ancient Sabean capital)[166] that were fabled as places where Arabs came to pray and worship. Another such site was the capital of the Nabataeans, Petra.[167] Once again, we do not find any record at all of large numbers of Arabs travelling to Western Arabia to worship at a shrine at the location of the modern city of Mecca. As with so much of Islamic history, the records that state that Mecca was a place of pilgrimage post-dates the time of Muhammad by about two hundred years.

The Islamic historical accounts on Mecca do not align with what we know about Arab religious practices. There are several sources that we can use to reconstruct Arab religious practices before Islam (this will be discussed in more detail in Section 3.1.1). Arab religion in the central part of the peninsula tended to be heavily pagan (outside of Jewish and Christian enclaves). As such it was focused on the worship of nature deities (i.e. gods of the sun, moon, stars etc.).[168] The worship of these gods often happened on a rather unorganized level as their devotees were nomadic Arabic tribespeople. With nomads, religious devotion can necessarily not be focused on fixed temples or meeting places. This fact represents a powerful counter-argument to the idea that Mecca acted as a religious center at the heart of the Arabian Peninsula. Furthermore, where large communal gatherings of pagan Arabs occurred it would typically be during so-called 'sacred months' (an idea that made its way into Islamic tradition as well).[169] During such sacred months, the Arab tribes, who were perpetually at war with each other, entered a temporary truce in order to trade and engage in the worship of the gods.[170] For such truces to be honored, the large 'worship events' during the sacred months had to take place on neutral ground (i.e. territory not controlled by a single tribe). The reason for this should be obvious. By consecrating 'no man's land' for worship, all the tribes would be in the same strategic position, thus decreasing the temptation to break the truce. It would also turn the defiling of such neutral ground by engaging in violence into a major sin. Let's apply these ideas to the Islamic view of Mecca before the coming of Islam. One thing that the accepted tradition emphasizes very strongly is the claim that Mecca before the birth of Muhammad was under the control of a specific tribe, the *Quraysh*.[171] This fact alone would disqualify Mecca as a religious site for the nomadic Arab tribes, as going there to worship would not be going to 'no man's land', but rather an entry into hostile territory.

Abraham in Arabia? The Biblical figure of Abraham is obviously a major presence within both Judaism and Christianity, and scholars associated with these faiths have spent millennia reflecting on his life and movements as it is presented in the Hebrew Bible. In none of these reflections up to the time of Muhammad was there ever any suggestion that he spent a significant part of his life in Arabia. With the coming of Islam (i.e. millennia after the dates associated with Abraham's life), we suddenly see claims that Mecca was a major focus for Abraham's activities.[172] The obvious first question that must be asked is how the many scholars who across the centuries obsessed over even the tiniest details of Abraham's movements happened to miss this? A simple look at a map will also raise significant questions. Abraham's recorded movements covered an arc from Mesopotamia to Canaan (roughly equivalent to the area covered by the modern state of Israel) and Egypt. To go from there to the middle of Arabia would require a 750-mile trip, mostly through empty desert and we are entitled to ask why on earth Abraham undertook such a journey and why this epic expedition did not leave any trace on the earliest records dealing with his life. The close connection between the coming of Islam and Abraham would, in light of this, only make sense if the foundational events of Islam took place much further to the North where memories of the patriarch persisted.

So, was Mecca an ancient center of worship (either Arab Pagan or Abrahamic)? Once again, the evidence that a city in the middle of Arabia fulfilled such a role is slim to nonexistent.

2.3.5. Could Ptolemy's 'Macoraba' be Mecca?

We now turn to claims sometimes made by Muslim scholars regarding possible pre-Islamic references to Mecca. The two most common candidates are a reference to a place called Macoraba in the writings of Ptolemy and a reference to 'Baka' in the Hebrew Bible. The fact that these, highly dubious, references are the best that the 'counsel for the defense' can come up with speaks volumes.

Ptolemy (110-170 CE) was a Roman writer who in his 'Geographies' attempted to provide a description of much of the world of his time. In the pages of this work Ptolemy refers to a place called Macoraba and calls it a 'famous temple of the Arabs'. Edward Gibbon in his 'Decline and Fall of the Roman Empire' (1776) assumed that this referred to Mecca, but did not look into the matter, as he cheerfully admitted his total lack of knowledge of Arabia: "I am ignorant, and I am careless, of the blind mythology of the Barbarians."[173] Even so, on the basis of this 'careless' 18th century conjecture, Muslim apologists have ever since built a towering edifice.

Fortunately, we do not have to follow Gibbon in his ignorance. *The Geographies* is obviously an immensely important historical document as it allows scholars to construct an accurate geographical, strategic and political picture of the Roman Empire and the regions bordering it. Such reconstructions are made easier by the fact that in drawing up his geographical descriptions, Ptolemy used a systematic approach This means that town and cities in the same region are described in ways that indicated their proximity. This makes obvious sense as any other method of organization in this 'word atlas' would have left the reader hopelessly confused.

Teams of scholars have pored over Ptolemy's descriptions and have, in the process, been able to turn Ptolemy's word pictures in *The Geographies* into something more user friendly by plotting his locations on a map. There are, therefore, works wherein you can look up detailed grid references for all the places that Ptolemy referred to.[174]

When we consult these sources, it quickly becomes clear that 'Macoraba' could not have been anywhere near the location of Mecca. It is, furthermore, necessary to move through such spectacular linguistic gymnastics to get from 'Macoraba' to 'Mecca' that serious scholars generally give this theory short shrift. As Patricia Crone states in her ground-breaking study 'Meccan Trade and the Rise of Islam': "The plain truth is that the name of Macoraba has nothing to do with that of Mecca, and that the location indicated by Ptolemy for Macoraba in no way dictates identification of the two."[175]

2.3.6. Psalm 84, 'The Valley of Baka' and Mecca

The next possible candidate for an ancient mention of Mecca that we have is a reference to the 'valley of Baka' in Psalm 84 in the Hebrew Bible. For this to be considered a legitimate reference to Mecca, we would have to agree that a place called Bakka in the Qur'an (3:96-97) is, in fact, a reference to Mecca.

One can see why believing Muslims would want the reference in this passage to be about Mecca[176] when we read what this text actually says: "The first House (of worship) appointed for men was that at Bakka: Full of blessing and of guidance for all kinds of beings: In it are clear signs [such as] the standing place of Abraham. And whoever enters it shall be safe. And [due] to Allah from the people is a pilgrimage to the House - for whoever is able to find thereto a way. But whoever disbelieves - then indeed, Allah is free from need of the worlds."[177]

Again, for the claim that the Hebrew Bible refers to Mecca here to be sustained, the following statements will have to be true: 1) That when the Qur'an refers to 'Bakka', it is in fact a reference to Mecca and 2) That, upon analysis of the Psalm, there can be no doubt that it refers to a city in the middle of the Arabian Desert.

We will spend some more time later on discussing the first question, i.e. whether the 'House of Worship' mentioned in Qur'an 3:39 refers to Mecca. Let us for the moment, however, accept the Muslim claim that Bakka refers to Mecca at face value and ask the question if Psalm 84 could, in fact, be referring to a city located in the middle of the Arabian Peninsula.

As we begin to answer this question it is worth quoting the relevant Psalm in full:

(1) How lovely is your dwelling place, Lord Almighty!

(2) My soul yearns, even faints, for the courts of the Lord; my heart and my flesh cry out for the living God.

(3) Even the sparrow has found a home, and the swallow a nest for herself, where she may have her young— place near your altar, Lord Almighty, my King and my God.

(4) Blessed are those who dwell in your house, they are ever praising you.

(5) Blessed are those whose strength is in you, whose hearts are set on pilgrimage.

(6) As they pass through **the Valley of Baka,** they make it a place of springs; the autumn rains also cover it with pools.

(7) They go from strength to strength, till each appears before God in Zion.

(8) Hear my prayer, Lord God Almighty, listen to me, God of Jacob.

(9) Look on our shield, O God; look with favor on your anointed one.

(10) Better is one day in your court than a thousand elsewhere; I would rather be a doorkeeper in the house of my God than dwell in the tents of the wicked.

(11) For the Lord God is a sun and shield; the Lord bestows favor and honor; no good thing does he withhold from those whose walk is blameless.

(12) Lord Almighty, blessed is the one who trusts in you.

Before we get into an analysis of this Psalm and its supposed link to Mecca, it is interesting to note a striking double standard at work when Muslim apologists make claims based on the Jewish and Christian Scriptures. The standard line from Muslim scholars is that both the Hebrew Bible and the Christian New Testament are completely unreliable. This is because, so they claim, copyist errors and deliberate falsification of manuscripts mean that we now have only corrupt versions, that are worlds away from the originals, left. It is, in light of this, rather odd that one of only two possible candidates for a pre-Islamic reference to Mecca comes from the Hebrew Bible. Are we to understand that the Biblical text was reliably transmitted in cases where it supports Islamic positions, but that it is corrupt in instances where it challenges Islamic positions? A clear case of an attempt to 'have your cake and eat it too'.

Let us now analyze the Psalm itself with a view to determine whether it could, in fact, contain a reference to Mecca.

The first thing that should immediately be obvious is that this text deals with pilgrimage to Jerusalem. The following verses are clear references to the Jewish temple that took center-stage in Jerusalem: 'your dwelling place, Lord Almighty' (v. 1), 'a place near your altar, Lord Almighty, my King and my God' (v. 3), 'those who dwell in your house' (v. 4). After setting the scene in the describing the glories and benefits of the temple, the author introduces the theme of pilgrimage: 'Blessed are those whose strength is in you, whose hearts are set on pilgrimage' (v. 5). There can be no doubt whatsoever about the destination of the pilgrims: 'They go from strength to strength, till each appears before God in Zion.' (v.7) The word Zion was originally a reference to a hill just outside Jerusalem, but over time the word simply came to be a synonym for Jerusalem itself.[178] This is a usage that we commonly find in the Psalms and the rest of the Hebrew Bible. One example of this is the following famous line expressing the longing of the Hebrew exiles for Jerusalem: "By the rivers of Babylon we sat and wept when we remembered Zion" (Psalm 137:1).

To summarize: Psalm 84 speaks eloquently of the joys of going to Jerusalem 'to appear before the Lord' at his temple. Let us now consider the reference to Baka in light of this: "As they pass through the Valley of Baka, they make it a place of springs; the autumn rains also cover it with pools." (v. 6) It should be clear from this that the valley of Baka' was a place that the Jerusalem-bound pilgrims passed through.[179] Could this have been Mecca? This is highly unlikely for the following reasons:

- The destination of the pilgrims could not be anywhere but Jerusalem. They are going to Zion after all.

- It is made clear that they are not on pilgrimage to Baka; it is merely a valley that they pass through.

- Zion (Jerusalem) is about 750 miles from the modern location of Mecca. Passing through Mecca on the way to the temple from other parts of Israel would, therefore, require a staggering 1500-mile detour through empty desert. There is no evidence anywhere in Jewish literature of pilgrims ever engaging on such an epic, not to mention punishing, journey as part of the pilgrimage process.

- The 'valley of Baka' is portrayed as a place with plenty of water: "they make it a place of springs; the autumn rains also cover it with pools" (v. 5) If there was ever a description particularly ill-suited to Mecca, located as it is in the middle of a baking desert, this is it.

- Hebrew scholars propose an interesting explanation for the reference to the 'Valley of Baka', namely that that it refers to a valley full of Balsam (Baka) trees or that it is a metaphorical reference to tears being turned into joy as pilgrims approached Jerusalem.[180] Baka (Balsam) trees often weep when they are cut and references to them could be seen as shorthand for the shedding of tears.[181] The link with the Baka (Balsam) tree inherent in this interpretation essentially rules out treeless Mecca.

It should be clear from the discussion of the references to 'Macoraba' (in Ptolemy) and 'Baka' (in Psalm 84) that the claims that both or either of these are instances of pre-Islamic mentions of Mecca cannot be sustained without a willing suspension of disbelief. Even if some of the points made above could perhaps be debated further, there is no way at all that any fair-minded observer can see these references as incontrovertible evidence of Mecca's ancient pedigree.

We are thus right back at a very familiar problem. While there is ample source material confirming the ancient existence of cities and even towns up and down the Arabian Peninsula, the best that can be done for Mecca are two references that cannot withstand even basic critical scrutiny. Contrast this with, for example, the abundance of historical data that we can quote when discussing Najran, a city that most people outside of Arabia have probably never even heard of.

2.4. Chapter Summary

- It would be hard to overstate the importance of Mecca in Muslim belief and practice. Muslims believe that Allah revealed himself to Muhammad in a cave near this Arabian city and all believing Muslims dream about going there on pilgrimage at least once in their lives.

- Despite the importance of Mecca within Islamic historical sources (which were first committed to paper generations after Muhammad was supposed to have lived), there is no historical evidence that a major city existed at the location of the modern city of Mecca in ancient times.

- When we study the inscriptions, documents and archaeological evidence produced by Mecca's Arab near-neighbors and the imperial powers that dominated the ancient Near-East (Babylonian, Assyrian, Persian and Roman), we do not find a single reference to Mecca. This despite the fact that we can produce historical evidence trails for even relatively insignificant Arabian cities.

- Mecca could not have been the great trading center described in Islamic history because the trans-Arabian trade in incense had collapsed by the 6th century, while the spice trade with the East was focused on sea routes through the Red Sea and Persian Gulf.

This leaves only low-value commodities (e.g. animal hides, salt and dates) as potential tradable goods. The high cost of transport and the fact that the great empires had cheaper sources of these goods nearer to hand make it highly unlikely that anyone from central Arabia would have engaged in long distance trade in them.

- The location of the modern city of Mecca is nowhere near the well-attested Trans-Arabian trade route and visiting the city would have required traders to embark on a tortuous, expensive and point-less detour (since they could resupply at Ta'if, about 70 miles from Mecca).

- Mecca could not have been an ancient religious center as Islamic sources show it as being under the control of a specific tribe (the *Quraysh*). The nomadic Arabs held their 'sacred month' ritual in places that were not under the control of specific tribes. There is, furthermore, no evidence (besides the 7th century CE Muslim claim) that the Biblical figure of Abraham ever set foot in central Arabia.

- The two candidates often proposed by Muslim scholars as pre-Is-lamic references to Mecca (Ptolemy's 'Macoraba' and the Valley of Baka in Psalm 84) cannot withstand even a basic level of scrutiny.

All of the above must be deeply troubling for devout Muslims as it places profound question marks over the version of history that they have been taught to believe. The disconnect between official Muslim history and 'on the ground' realities should prompt us to have a close look at what alternative sources tell us about issues, questions and ideologies that an-imated the world from which Islam sprang. This is where we turn next.

3.

Setting the Scene: The Arabian Peninsula at the Dawn of Islam

*T*he classic Islamic sources tell us that the ancient city of Mecca was a site of immense spiritual and economic importance. **However, by the time Muhammad was born (570 CE), it was adrift in a sea of paganism and barbarity that enveloped the entire Arabian Peninsula.** *Muhammad was a member of one of the most important tribes of Mecca, the Quraysh, and received a call from God to act as his prophet in a cave just outside the city. Acting upon this call, Muhammad received a series of revelations over a period of about twenty years, right up to his death in 632 CE. These revelations form what we now know as the Qur'an. After Muhammad's death, his followers burst out of the Arabian Peninsula in the name of Islam and conquered the Persian and much of the Eastern Roman Empire. The coming of Islam established the Muslim religion, with the message of Muhammad and the city of Mecca at its center, as the pre-eminent belief system from Egypt to Persia within 100 years of the death of the prophet.*

The standard way in which Muslim sources refer to Mecca in the immediate pre-Islamic period is to state that it was in the grip of the 'Time of Ignorance' (*Jahiliya*).¹⁸² Ironically another standard description is that of emptiness. What is in view here is obviously not the emptiness of the historical record that we discussed in the previous chapter, but rather a deep spiritual emptiness. In other words, traditional Muslim historiography paints Central-Western Arabia as a spiritual and intellectual wasteland.

It is easy to work out why Muslim scholars would want to emphasize this theme. A very common strategy to bolster the prestige of the prophet is to claim that Muhammad burst upon the scene as a bolt from the blue. For this to be true, it must be believed that he learned precisely nothing from followers of other religions (particularly Christianity and Judaism). There must, also, not have been significant other civilizations in the neighborhood so that Muhammad had no one from whom to glean the arts of warfare, diplomacy and statecraft. It would, therefore, make sense to de-populate the Islamic historical record as far as the followers of the other Abrahamic religions and significant political entities is concerned.

The purpose of this chapter is to examine whether this version of the origins of Islam corresponds to reality by researching the actual historical record in order to reconstruct a picture of the Arabian Peninsula in late antiquity. What will quickly become clear is that the standard Islamic view pointing to deep isolation and insularity cannot be sustained. Arabia was home to rich and varied cultures, and followers of a variety of religions were found here during the age of the rise of Islam.

Our explorations will begin with a look at the Arabian religious scene. In the process, we will discuss the three major religions that dominated Arabia during this period (namely Animism, Judaism and Christianity). From here the discussion will move on to political realities through an examination of Arab tribal nomadism and Roman and Persian influence.

3.1. The Religious Make-Up of the Arabian Peninsula at the Dawn of Islam

3.1.1. Arabian Paganism

A study of Arabian paganism as it existed in late antiquity must inevitably raise questions about the nature of the seedbed from which Islam sprang, as the 'paganism' that we are confronted with in the Qur'an does not necessarily immediately evoke an inveterately pagan context.

The form of paganism practiced in the immediate pre-Islamic period should perhaps properly be described as Animism. This is the belief, common in premodern societies, that natural phenomena and certain physical objects are endued with (literally 'animated' with) spiritual power. The beliefs of the nomadic Arabs therefore centered very much on things that would have been very familiar to them: the sun, the moon, stars and certain sacred places and animals.[183] These natural features were then associated with a staggeringly large pantheon of gods. As is often the case with animistic belief systems, this was not a religion of fixed temples and highly elaborate rituals. There are, however, a few unique features of Arabian paganism that are worth pointing out.

The first of these features has already been referred to. The central part of the peninsula was populated by nomadic tribes who were often at war with one another. Once a year during the so-called 'sacred month' they would, however, cease their hostilities and gather at a predetermined place to engage in religious worship.[184] One of the biggest taboos within the society was to violate the truce of the sacred month and attack other tribes while it was in force. This prohibition was even referenced in the Qur'an (9:36).[185]

The sites where 'sacred month' worship was offered were not necessarily permanent sacred spaces. Their most important quality was that they could be considered 'neutral ground' where none of the tribes had the upper hand. This fact contributed to the sanctity of the spot in the sense that it ensured that members of different tribes could go about their religious observances without fear of molestation.[186]

Another interesting feature of Arab pagan worship before the coming of Islam is the emphasis that was placed on alcohol in many of the rituals.[187] Another was an affinity for female deities. Some of these (goddesses known as Al-Lat, Manat and Al-Uzza), in fact, played a significant role in one of the most infamous episodes in the textual history of the Qur'an, namely the revelation of the so-called 'Satanic Verses'.[188] In addition, the area around Mecca was supposedly also associated with the worship of a god known as Hubal.[189] There is, however, no contemporary primary source or archeological evidence to confirm widespread pagan worship at the location of the modern city of Mecca.

While 'sacred spaces during sacred months' seems to have been the pattern for most of the nomadic tribes in central Arabia, there is clear evidence that pagan Arabs who lived more settled lifestyles (i.e. on the edges of the Roman and Persian Empires) had correspondingly more settled worship practices. It is, therefore, possible to point to some more fixed worship spaces like those at Petra[190], Mamre[191] and Marib.[192]

It would be highly unusual if the pagans living on the borderlands of Arabia did not adopt at least some of the beliefs and practices of neighboring societies. This kind of mixing of belief systems (a process referred to as 'syncretism') is often a feature of communities straddling what might be termed 'spiritual fault lines'. The obvious question that arises from this is whether the pagans that Muhammad encountered were what might be termed traditionalists (i.e. those practicing the kind of paganism associated with nomadic central Arabian tribes) or people whose paganism had somehow been modified by belief systems that they interacted with due to proximity to other traditions. It is almost certainly the latter (i.e. that the Arab paganism that Muhammad encountered was deeply syncretistic in nature).[193] This may seem like a rather academic point, but it is vital in helping us to understand the context of the Qur'an and the early history of Islam. Consider the following picture that emerges from the Qur'an of the religious practices of the pagan Meccans:

- Muhammad's opponents at Mecca are often called the '*mushrikun*' (polytheists). However, we find not a single indication in the Qur'an that they were worshipping named pagan deities. Instead they are being castigated for offering what might be termed 'deficient worship' to the one true God and of devoting misdirected attention to angels.[194] The specific charge that is most consistently leveled at them is that they regularly added 'partners' to God (cf. Qur'an 10:105[195] and 12:106[196]). This could very well be a classic description of a syncretistic belief system in the sense that elements of belief that would seem entirely incompatible in the eyes of the purists are added together. This is such an important point that it is worth repeating: the main charge of the Qur'an against Muhammad's opponents is not that they regularly engaged in the worship of named false gods, but rather that they corrupted the worship of the one true God.

- We, secondly, see that the Qur'an assumes a great deal of familiarity with the ways of the God that Muhammad is proclaiming (i.e. the God proclaimed in the Hebrew Bible).[197] Why this would be true for dyed-in-the-wool pagans living in the middle of the Arabian Desert is left unexplained. What is even more intriguing is that the Qur'an places the activities of his opponents in the area where key Biblical events took place. For example, it reinforces a point about the rebellion of Lot's wives by stating that the '*mushrikun*' passes by the place where this happened on a daily basis (Qur'an 37:133-138).[198] We, again, have to ask the question as to why people who are supposed to dwell in the middle of the Arabian Desert regularly pass by a location that is hundreds of miles to the north.

- The *mushrikun* are, lastly, portrayed as crop (Qu'ran 6:99)[199] and livestock farmers. They are, for example, taken to task for 'cutting the ears' of their livestock (see Qur'an 4:119).[200] if there is any place on earth that is entirely unsuitable to crop cultivation and livestock farming it is the baking hot Arabian Desert. This is one of the driest places on earth and is entirely unsuitable for farming. There is, therefore, not a single bit of archeological evidence of large scale farming in the area around modern Mecca. The implication should be obvious. *Either the Meccan pagans addressed in the Qur'an could not have been farmers or, if they were farmers, they could not have lived in Mecca.*

What should be rather obvious from the above is that the standard Muslim narrative of the straightforward conflict between Muslim monotheists and classically polytheistic Meccan pagans is difficult to sustain in the light of the text of the Qur'an. The Qur'anic data may, in fact, point to a rather different point of origin. This is a theme that we will return to several times in the pages that follow.

3.1.2. Judaism in the Arabian Peninsula

Within the standard Islamic account, it is strongly emphasized that the Arabs were inveterate pagans and that Muhammad was the very first prophet to bring the message of monotheism to them (cf. Qur'an 6:154-146).[201] Within this framework, steps had to be taken by whoever wrote the standard Muslim histories to keep the record clear of influential Christians and Jews. Otherwise it could be argued that such people played an important role in the development of Islamic theology. One way of achieving this outcome was through claims that Muhammad had very little in-depth (in terms of the exchange of ideas) contact with Christians and Jews. In fact, within official Islamic historical sources Christians and Jews are often merely 'stock characters' whose only role in the narrative seems to have been to recognize Muhammad as a prophet and then disappear off stage. One famous and momentous example of this is the portrayal of the conversion of a rabbi named Abdullah bin Salam who allegedly said: "When I heard about the apostle I knew by his description, name, and the time at which he appeared that he was the one we were waiting for, and I rejoiced greatly thereat, though I kept silent about it until the apostle came to Medina".[202] Ibn Ishaq goes on to relate that bin Salam sought sanctuary with the Muslims as the "The Jews are a nation of liars" and they would deny that he was their leader if they knew about his conversion. After questioning the Jewish community and having them confirm that Bin Salam was indeed a respected rabbi, the Muslims called upon their new convert to reveal himself and exhort his former co-religionists to follow in his wake. He did so in the following terms: "O Jews, fear God and accept what He has sent you. For by God you know that he is the apostle of God. You will find him described in your Torah and even named. I testify that he is the apostle of God, I believe in him, I hold him to be true, and I acknowledge him. They accused me of lying and reviled me. Then I reminded the apostle that I had said they would do this, for they were a treacherous, lying, and evil people."[203]

Aside from the obvious fact that narrations like this, filled with anti-Jewish slurs as they are, would go on to have a hugely negative impact on Muslim-Jewish relations they also represent a rather simplistic dismissal of the religious complexities of Arabia around the time of Muhammad.

They seem to communicate 'Yes there were Jews, but they were few and far between and all the good ones converted to Islam at the earliest opportunity'.

However, a closer reading of the Qur'an and *hadiths* will immediately make it clear that things are not nearly as simple as this. These documents are deeply preoccupied (one might even say obsessed) with a dialogue, sometimes peaceful and respectful and, at other times decidedly not, with Christian and Jews. It would, in light of this, be exceedingly odd if the earliest Muslims were not in regular contact with followers of these religions who did not become Muslim. Why go to all the trouble of formally disputing with people if they are entirely absent from your part of the world?

The reality is that we have ample evidence that sophisticated and long-lived Jewish communities existed over the length and breadth of the Arabian Peninsula.[204] This is not only true as far as its northern borderlands is concerned (this would be expected given its proximity to the Jewish heartlands), but even all the way down to the southern edge of the region.

The political entity that dominated southern Arabia in the era before the coming of Islam was the Kingdom of Himyar, which was roughly equivalent to the modern country of Yemen. It should come as a remarkable discovery for someone thinking of early Judaism as a faith centered largely on the Mediterranean basin that several of the kings of Himyar were Jewish.[205] In fact the last Himyarite king, Yusuf At-Ar Yafar (also known as Du Nuas), could plausibly lay claim to being one of the last Jewish monarchs ruling anywhere on earth.[206]

The fall of the Himyarite Kingdom certainly did not mean the end of Judaism in southern Arabia. In fact, the Jewish community survived the coming of Islam by many centuries. The effective end-point of this community was only reached in 1948 with the establishment of the State of Israel to which most Yemeni Jewish people eventually migrated.[207]

Another piece of evidence to confirm the strength of Judaism in southern Arabia comes from a rather interesting quarter, namely Ethiopia.

Ethiopian Christianity shares many characteristics with Egyptian (Coptic) Christianity. In fact, for centuries the Ethiopian church was led by bishops imported from Egypt. It is very interesting to note that Ethiopian Christianity differs from Coptic Christianity on one crucial point: its deep affinity for practices that can be traced back to Judaism.[208] Thus we see that many Ethiopian Christians observe the Jewish Sabbath, keep strict dietary laws and practice circumcision. In fact, some Ethiopians went beyond selective observance of Jewish practices to full-blown acceptance of Judaism.[209] Most members of the Ethiopian Jewish community eventually migrated to Israel.

So where did this substantial level of Jewish influence in Africa come from? Clearly not from Christian Egypt (to the north) or from animistic tribes to the east and south. The obvious answer is the Arabian Peninsula. It is only a short hop across Red Sea from Ethiopia to the Arabian Peninsula and trade and other links between the two regions were many and varied. This is even confirmed by the Islamic historical record through the fact that Muhammad supposedly sent some of his early followers to live under the protection of the Negus (Emperor) of Ethiopia in order to escape persecution in Mecca.[210]

If South Arabian Judaism was so vibrant and influential that it influenced beliefs on another continent, it would be rather silly to assume that it had no impact in the rest of Arabia itself. So, while it is most likely that Islam was deeply influenced by Jewish people living on the borderlands of the Roman Empire, Jewish influence would still be virtually impossible to avoid even if Islam originated much further to the south, as the traditional Islamic historical account claims.

3.1.3. Christianity in the Arabian Peninsula

When it comes to Christianity, the Islamic historical tradition also takes great pains to emphasize that Muhammad had very little contact with Christians and that the part of the Arabian Peninsula where the Qur'an was supposedly revealed was largely free from any Christian presence. In fact, for the Christian equivalent of Muhammad's recognition by the

Jewish rabbi, he had to travel all the way to Syria according to official accounts. The tradition has him going to Syria as a boy, there to be recognized as a future prophet by the monk Bahira who said that the child displayed the 'mark of prophethood' (although it is not explained exactly what this means).[211] In an interesting development, given the passage dealing with his recognition by a rabbi above, the monk cautions Muhammad's uncle to shield him from the Jews who would surely try to kill him should they find out that he will grow up to be a prophet. [212]

A glaring inconsistency in the historical tradition can be found in the fact that this encounter with Bahira must have meant (if it did indeed happen) that Muhammad grew up with the conviction and belief that he would become a prophet in adulthood. Yet, the traditions dealing with his first revelation uniformly present him as entirely bewildered by the experience, to the point that he even suspected that he was demon possessed.[213] This is an exceedingly odd reaction for someone who supposedly grew up with the belief that his life's calling was to be a prophet. In light of this, the story of Bahira can be dismissed for what it is, a dramatic 'just so' story written many years after the life of Muhammad to uphold both the belief that Muhammad was recognized by Christians from a very early age while at the same time very conveniently placing this Christian in Syria (i.e. too far away from Mecca for the monk to have any continuing influence on Muhammad). The parallels with the story of the Jewish rabbi recognizing Muhammad is striking. In that case the rabbi dies almost immediately after recognizing Muhammad as a prophet. In both cases the message is: Muhammad was recognized by leaders of both the Christian and Jewish communities, but they could not have had any influence over his teachings.

As with the Jewish example, the reality of just how deeply Christianity could have influenced the development of Islam is a world away from this rather simplistic dismissal of the possibility of sustained Christian influence.

The first and most basic response to any question about the presence of Christianity in the Arabian Peninsula would, of course, be to look at the available documentary and archeological data. When this is done for the northern and southern parts of the peninsula, the evidence for a very significant level of Christian influence is overwhelming. In the north this is only to be expected since it bordered the Roman Empire, which was quite forceful in its expression of Christian commitment at this point in history. This does not mean that Christian influence somehow petered out completely the further south you went. As the story of the persecution of Christian believers in Najran illustrate (see Section 2.2), strong Christian communities could be found hundreds of miles south of the location of the modern city of Mecca.

What is perhaps most surprising is that more and more evidence is turning up to prove that even the Hejaz played host to significant numbers of Christians long before the coming of Islam. In fact, recent archeological excavations in Saudi Arabia unearthed the oldest example of Arabic script yet discovered and it was written by a Christian. It simply reads 'Thabwan Son of Malik' and is accompanied by a cross.[214] It has long been known that Arabic script developed from the writing system used by the Nabataeans. Discoveries like these are adding an interesting piece to the puzzle by showing that at least some of those who took this script southward were Christians.

In other words, many of the arguments presented above about the undeniable influence that Judaism exerted on the early development of Islam can be repeated in the case of Christianity. As with Judaism, the Qur'an keeps up an incessant dialogue with aspects of Christian doctrines. In the process, it denies the divinity of Christ[215], the Trinity[216] and even that Jesus died on a cross.[217] Again, we are entitled to ask why this would be such a major theme in a book that was revealed in a part of the world where Christianity was supposedly largely absent?

We can furthermore, once again, point to several instances where the Qur'an contains significant borrowings from Christian sources. What is, however, deeply interesting is the fact that these sources do not tend to be documents that modern Christians would regard as orthodox and authoritative. Several references to the life of Jesus in the Qur'an are, for example, taken from the 'Arabic Gospel of the Infancy of the Savior'.[218] This inclusion of apocryphal Christian sources is quite interesting and should, at the very least, leave us with the suspicion that the compilers of the Qur'an had significant levels of contact with Christians who existed beyond the mainstream of Christian belief and practice as it eventually came to be defined.

This suspicion is all but confirmed by the fact that the Qur'an gets some key Christian doctrines dead wrong, at least from the perspective of modern Christians. The most significant example of this happening is the Qur'an's identification of Mary (the mother of Jesus) as part of the Trinity.[219] There are, of course, Christian traditions (most notably Roman Catholicism) that greatly honor Mary, but any notion that she is somehow a member of the godhead would be regarded as blasphemous even by them.[220]

Not only is the Qur'an wrong on key Christian doctrines, it also has a rather interesting name for Christians, namely *Nasara* (or Nazarenes). This name, which references the place (Nazareth) where Jesus spent his childhood[221] was never popular among mainstream Christians.[222] This is probably because it may be seen to place too much emphasis on the humanity of Jesus. It is, in fact, in modern Arabic still an exclusively Muslim usage in the sense that it is not used by Arab Christians to refer to themselves, they tend to use the term 'Masihi'. This is essentially a direct cognate of the English term Christian (the word Christian is derived from the Greek translation of Messiah i.e. '*Christos*'). Why then the use of the rather peculiar term '*Nasara*' in the Qur'an?

It is quite possible that in this term and in the doctrines that the Qur'an ascribes to Christians, we find confirmation that the authors did not only have contact with Christians, but that they learned what they knew about Christianity from non-orthodox Christians who must have had a presence wherever it was that the Qur'an was composed. This group used a specific name (*Nasara*) to refer to themselves and may have held to doctrines (e.g. the membership of Mary in the Trinity) that would have put them significantly at odds with other Christians. One school of thought is that '*Nasara*' was a synonym for a heterodox Christian group known as the Ebionites.[223] Given the doctrines ascribed to the *Nasara* in the Qur'an, this would make sense since the Ebionites can be said to have been the most Jewish of the early Christian sects in terms of their insistence on keeping the commandments contained in the Hebrew Bible and their open skepticism regarding the divinity of Christ.[224]

It is not hard to work out why groups like the Nazarenes/Ebionites would have existed on the borderlands of the Roman Empire or even deeper into the desert. By the 6th century, the major Christological[225] debates were largely settled as far as the orthodox party was concerned. The orthodox consensus was that Christ should be worshiped as the eternal Son of God (settled at the Council of Nicaea, 325 CE)[226] and that he had two natures, human and divine, that came together in one person (settled at the Council of Chalcedon, 451 CE).[227] Christians who disagreed with these propositions, or even how they should be interpreted would have found the Eastern Roman Empire (ruled from Constantinople) a particularly inhospitable place. By the early 6th century, some Roman emperors came to regard themselves as active guardians of Christian orthodoxy.[228] In practice, this sometimes meant that those who disagreed with imperial Christology were hounded out of the empire. Within this context, it would make perfect sense that non-traditional Christian communities flourished on the edges of the Roman Empire. Many Christians (quite possibly the Ebionites/Nazarenes among them) who did not feel comfortable with the decisions reached at Nicaea or Chalcedon most probably simply uprooted themselves and moved to areas that were not fully under Roman jurisdiction so that they could practice their faith in relative freedom.

We should at the very least consider the possibility that whoever wrote the Qur'an had significant levels of contact with such a non-orthodox Christian community and that the results of these interactions found its way into the pages of the supposedly divine revelation. If this was indeed the case it provides us with just one of many instances where it can be showed how the Qur'an was very much a product of the world and of the age out of which it arose.

3.2. The Arabian Geopolitical Scene at the Dawn of Islam

We now turn our attention to the political realities on the Arabian Peninsula during the immediate pre-Islamic period. Once again, we will begin with what is familiar as far as the traditional Islamic historical account is concerned before moving on to some wider realities that were bound to influence the early development of Islam. This means that the starting point will be Arab tribalism before the focus is widened to include Roman and Persian involvement in the area.

3.2.1. Arab Tribalism

The official Islamic sources dealing with the political environment before the advent of Islam frames the discussion almost entirely in the context of Arab tribalism. While this ignores the reality that there were many urban Arabs for whom tribal ties were perhaps not that strong it does reflect an important insight about pre-Islamic Arabia.

Arabian society was, and to a certain extent still is, intensely tribal. In the pre-Islamic period, this tribalism was most clearly displayed in fierce loyalty to one's own and a deep mistrust and enmity towards outsiders.[229] This mistrust often led to open conflict between different tribal bands. It seems that the Arabs did not need many excuses to fight, but where reasons can be discerned, feuds often centered on women, perceived insults and camels or other possessions.[230] Since the interior of the Arabian Peninsula was incapable of supporting a large population before the advent of modern technology, most conflicts would fortunately have been between small war bands rather than between large armies. We would, in this sense, probably be well-advised to speak about inter-tribal skirmishes instead of wars. These skirmishes ceased, as we have seen, during the so-called sacred months during which energy was devoted to religious observance, trade and matchmaking.[231]

As if a society where it often seemed to be a 'war of all against all' was not complex enough, it should be remembered that much of the above was occurring with everyone on the move. Nomadism is often part of the reality of desert life as tribes move around in search of scarce resources. There are, in fact, still nomadic tribes (now often referred to as Bedouin) in this part of the world.[232]

If any leader could manage to unite the Arab tribes, he would have a formidable fighting force at his disposal. The Arab tribes would provide such a leader with men used to almost constant warfare, able to live off the land and for whom the rigors of being constantly on the move would simply have been a fact of life. This leader would, however, also have had to deal with what would have been a basic fact of life in any Arab tribal coalition: endemic disunity.[233]

Armies made up of members who are used to normally fighting each other are not stable, as soldiers will tend to turn on each other at the slightest sign of misfortune, idleness or mutual provocation. This basic reality is even acknowledged in the Islamic historical record where ample reference is made to serious conflicts within the armies of Islam and it was supposedly only the genius of Muhammad that turned them into a unified fighting force.[234] These inter-Muslim conflicts contributed, among other things, to the enduring Sunni/Shia split.[235]

While the disunity that eventually developed within the Muslim camp is widely acknowledged by Muslim sources, it could be that these sources do not go far enough. Could it, in fact, be that the Arab tribes were never united, not even under the banner of Muhammad? If this was the case, we must take a fresh look at the Muslim conquests with their rather neat narrative of a unified fighting force with the name of the prophet on their lips bursting from the Arabian Peninsula to take on and defeat the Roman and Persian empires. This is a line of enquiry that we will return to later.

We will now continue our discussion of political realities on the Arabian Peninsula by focusing on the two great empires of the age namely the Roman and then the Persian.

3.2.2. The Roman Empire and the Arabian Peninsula

References to the Roman Empire will for most people conjure up images of the Colosseum, togas and villas in the Italian countryside. However, although the Roman Empire that we encounter in 7th century Arabia certainly has its roots in Rome, the Eternal City, it was not based there anymore. It was the Emperor Constantine (272-337 CE) who decided to move the capital of the empire from Rome to a city that he rather modestly named after himself: Constantinople.[236] This city, now known as Istanbul, sits at the meeting place of Europe and Asia in a superb strategic location. It also achieved the objectives that Constantine had in making the bold move to permanently rule the Roman Empire from a place other than Rome. These can be summarized as follows: to bring the imperial administration closer to the majority of the imperial population (concentrated in Asia-Minor), to bring the bulk of Roman fighting strength closer to what Roman emperors of the era would have viewed as the ultimate geopolitical fault line (the border with Persia) and to escape the chronic instability due to barbarian incursions that was already beginning to plague the European borders of the empire and even Italy itself.

The removal of the imperial administration from the city of Rome effectively removed it from global power-politics for many centuries. The city could, in fact, not manage to resist the repeated barbarian incursions into Italy and in 410 CE it succumbed to Alaric the Goth.[237] It should by now be clear that this much-vaunted 'Fall of Rome' was not in any way also 'The Fall of the Roman Empire'. The Roman imperial administration was by this stage safely ensconced in Constantinople and the fall of Rome could merely be regarded as the loss of just another imperial city (albeit one of immense symbolic importance). Rome's loss of status as the imperial capital and its subsequent conquest by the Goths effectively ended the influence of this ancient city in the Middle East. It would only again play any role in the region in an indirect but very significant way through the influence of the papacy in the calling and supporting of the Crusades from 1095 CE onward[238].

It is crucial to remember that the end of Rome as a political player did not mean the end of Roman power itself. The Roman Empire would continue to exist in one form or another for more than a millennium after the fall of Rome. It only finally succumbed to the Ottoman Sultan Mehmet II in 1453.[239] Historians sometimes refer to this continuing Roman Empire based in Constantinople as the 'Eastern Roman Empire' or as the 'Byzantine Empire' (the settlement that existed at the site of Constantinople before Constantine decided to locate his capital there was known as Byzantium).[240] It is, of course, this expression of Roman Imperial rule that we encounter in the context of the rise of Islam. There are, as we shall see, several reasons why the Byzantines took a particularly keen interest in Arabia.

The strategic importance of the Arabian Peninsula from the perspective of the Byzantines can largely be ascribed to its proximity to the Roman provinces of Syria and Judea. Syria for the Romans was much more extensive than what we would today refer to as Syria.[241] It included Israel, Palestine, Jordan, Lebanon and of course Syria itself.[242] This was one of the richest provinces of the Empire and it also contained one of the most important cities in the Empire, Antioch. Syria was also directly adjacent to the 'breadbasket' of the Roman Empire, Egypt.[243] Add to this the fact that Syria historically acted as the northern terminus for the trans-Arabian trade routes and it becomes clear why it was regarded as one of the jewels in the imperial crown.

It goes without saying that the borders of such an important asset would have to be very carefully protected which in this case meant that potentially hostile forces in Arabia, directly to the south, had to be pacified or contained. The fact that Syria was vulnerable from attacks launched from Arabia was brutally reinforced in 252 CE[244] and 540 CE[245] when the Persians used Arabia as a launch pad for successful attacks on Roman territory. Any Roman governor surveying once prosperous Antioch after the Persian Emperor Khusro II comprehensively sacked it in 540 CE[246] would have had the urgent need for a strategic defense policy to deal with possible threats from Arabia brutally driven home.

This brings us to the key geopolitical reality of the Middle East in late antiquity: it was often the stage of a massive game of power-politics between the Persian and Roman Empires.[247] This was a conflict that dragged out over centuries and that resulted in stunning victories and massive setbacks for both parties as they both managed at certain stages to drive deep into each other's territories. Often such attacks would have a full-frontal character with the armies of these two behemoths simply marching across their shared border, a shifting line now to be found in the far-east of Turkey and the west of Iraq. Some strategic thinkers on both sides, however, realized that flanking attacks through Arabia could be just as effective. This pulled Arabia right into the heart of the most important conflict of the age. The importance of this fact for the development of Islam simply cannot be overstated.

Far from being a rustic backwater that no one much cared about, Arabia was a part of the world that the Romans and Persians both studied, mapped and obsessed about.[248] One response to the instability of the Arabian frontier was followed by both the Romans and Persians and has already been referred to. This was the recruitment of Arab tribesmen to act as mercenaries to help pacify the border and even to fight in offensive campaigns in enemy territory. To this end huge networks of patronage sprung up as different Arab tribes were enrolled on opposing sides of this conflict (e.g. the Lakhmids on the side of the Persians[249] and the Ghassanids on the side of the Romans[250]). We have already noted how strange it is considering the above that we find not a single reference in any Roman or Persian document mentioning the *Quraysh*, the powerful central-Arabian tribe to which Muhammad was supposed to have belonged.

It is very illuminating to read the Qur'an and *hadiths* in the light of the Roman-Persian wars. When we do, it quickly becomes clear that the community being addressed had sympathies, probably induced through monetary compensation, towards the Roman cause. We see, for example, that there is a tradition that an ancestor of Muhammad, Qusay, entered into an agreement with a Roman general.[251] Quite astonishingly, we even find the Roman-Persian conflict reflected in the pages of the Qur'an itself. The Qur'an contains precious few references to specific names, places and events, but whoever wrote it chose to include this enigmatic line: "The Romans have been defeated in the lowest land, but after their defeat they will soon be victorious. Within three to nine years. The decision of the matter, before and after, is with Allah." (Quran 30:2-4)[252] This is most likely a reference to the Roman defeat to the Persians in 613-614 CE but why, out of all the possible earthshaking events of the age, does the Qur'an choose to include just this single reference to the great Empires of the day? Could the reason for this be that the fortunes of the original audience of the Qur'an were intimately bound up with that of the Roman Empire? If so, the original recipients of the Qur'an may have included *foederati* (i.e. members of tribes that were allied to the Romans).[253] Some scholars even suggest that the term *Quraysh* is a corruption of the Syro-Aramaic verbal root (*qras* 'to gather').[254] This would make perfect sense within the context as it would denote, not a specific tribe, but those Arabs who gathered (*qras*) to join with the Romans (i.e. Arab *Foederati*)

The possibility that the Qur'an's audience were allied to the Romans must at the very least be seriously considered. How else are we to explain the reassurance given to them that the Romans will eventually be victorious (Qur'an 30:2-4)? This may also partially explain the success of the eventual Arab conquests. As the Roman Empire entered a period of slow-bleed due to the relentless nature of the conflict with Persia it would have become more and more difficult for Roman generals to pay their mercenaries. These mercenaries would also have been keenly aware of, and ready to pounce at, the first sign of weakness of their former paymasters.

All of the above, and this is probably beginning to sound a bit like a constant refrain, suggests that the intended audience for the Qur'an may not have been located in the middle of the Arabian Desert (where they would be in a strategically unimportant position), but right on the borderlands of the Roman Empire where the Arab Roman allies were overwhelmingly concentrated.

3.2.3. The Persian Empire and the Arabian Peninsula

Much of what needs to be said about the influence of the Persian Empire in the Arabian Peninsula has, in a sense, already been said during our discussion of the Roman Empire above. The Persian Empire was in many ways the mirror image of the Roman Empire[255], but also its eternal and sworn enemy.

The policies that the Persian Empire (also known as the Sassanian Empire in the immediate pre-Islamic period) followed towards the Arabian Peninsula was remarkably like that of the Romans, except that they were probably even more convinced of the strategic importance of this part of the world. This is because Persian rulers twice used the strategy of passing through Arab lands to strike at parts of the Roman Empire (in 252 and 540 CE). Persian emperors must, therefore, have lived with the terrible awareness that what they did during war could also be done to them in return. They were, therefore, if anything even more deeply committed to keeping their Arabian borderlands safe by using Arab mercenaries. The Sassanian-sponsored desert city of Hira, populated by the Lakhmids (Arab allies of the Persians)[256] was renowned for hosting some of the most ferocious warriors on the planet as well as for providing outlets for the fleshly enjoyments of such warriors.[257]

It perhaps need not be repeated here that the Persians clearly had never heard of the Meccans or the *Quraysh*, this despite their deep involvement in Arab tribal affairs.

The recipients of the Qur'an were probably more inclined to support the Roman cause (they were supposed to rejoice in a future Roman victory after all). This does not mean, however, that Persia had no influence on the development of Islam and the Qur'an. For while the Persians had evidently never heard of the Meccans, whoever wrote the Qur'an certainly knew about the Persians. For while they are not directly mentioned in the Qur'an (as are the Romans), Persian ideas and entities do make an appearance. The most obvious place where this can be seen is in the multitude of Persian loan-words that made their way into the Qur'an.[258] Another intriguing possibility can be found in the Qur'anic recognition of the religion of the Sabians as a legitimate revelation from Allah (Qur'an 2:62, 5:69 and 22:17). Several hypotheses as to what 'Sabianism' refers to have been advanced and the theory that it was a religion of Persian origin (also known as Mandeanism) is one of the strongest contenders.[259]

Having said all of this, it is probably fair to say that the most profound Persian influence on Islam occurred long after the life of Muhammad and after the Persian Empire had, in fact, been destroyed by the Arab conquests. This was due to fact that many of the Persians who were converting to Islam in later centuries brought with them beliefs and ideas that had very little to do with the preaching of a desert prophet, but that drew deeply from the ancient Persian religion known as Zoroastrianism[260] (this is a topic we shall return to later).

3.3. Chapter Summary

- The classic Islamic accounts claim that the Qur'an was revealed in a place awash in paganism and entirely isolated from other religious ideas (e.g. Judaism and Christianity) and political realities (e.g. the conflict between Rome and Persia).

- The idea of 'Arab Isolation' was aggressively promoted by early Muslim scholars to ensure that the claim could not be made that Islam 'borrowed' from other belief systems or political systems. This view can, however, be challenged on several levels.

- While there is indeed solid evidence for the practice of animism and for enduring patterns of tribal nomadism there is also solid evidence for the presence in Arabia of many other belief systems that could potentially profoundly influence the early development of Islam.

- Jewish communities existed up-and-down Arabia. In fact, one of the last Jewish monarchs anywhere on earth reigned in southern Arabia. The Jewish presence in Arabia is clearly reflected in the Qur'an with several of its chapters containing material that was lifted from Jewish sources.

- Many Christians lived beyond the borders of the Roman Empire. In fact, Christians who for, whatever reason, were unwilling to sign up to standard definitions of Christian orthodoxy may have preferred to live in places like Arabia where they would be free from imperial persecution designed to bring them back into line. It is quite possible that Muhammad, or whoever wrote the Qur'an, had contact with such a group. This is evident in the non-standard way

(*Nasara*) in which the Qur'an refers to Christians and the fact that it attacks doctrines (e.g. that Mary is part of the Trinity) that is not part of orthodox Christianity.

- The Roman Empire, in the form of the Eastern or Byzantine Empire, had a keen strategic interest in the Arabian borderlands next to their province of Syria. One strategy that they utilized to keep the frontier safe was to employ Arab mercenaries to act on their behalf. The Muslim historical tradition states that the Meccans entered such an alliance with the Romans. The Qur'an also, very strangely for a book with vanishingly few references to specific contemporary events, prophecies a future victory for the Romans. This would only be significant for the Arab readers if their lot was somehow intertwined with that of Rome. All of this suggest a location much further north than Mecca as the Romans would have wanted their allies to act on their behalf on their borders and not in the middle of an empty desert.

- Like the Romans the Persians were also keenly aware of the strategic importance of the Arabian Peninsula. They, therefore, essentially mirrored the Roman strategy by enlisting Arab tribes to act as their proxies on the borders of their empire. The Persian influence on Islam can be seen in the recognition of the Sabian religion as divinely inspired but would actually be much more profound long after the death of Muhammad when ex-Zoroastrians brought much of their worldview and practices into Islam.

It should be evident, after reviewing the contents of this chapter, that the classic Islamic idea of a place called Mecca existing in a sea of paganism and entirely isolated from wider geopolitical realities cannot be sustained. There is indeed ample evidence of significant levels of Jewish and Christian influence in the pages of the Qur'an. It is, furthermore, the case that deep Persian and Roman involvement in the Arabian Peninsula raises the question of 'how' (rather than 'if?') the original recipients of the Qur'an were affected by the clash of the superpowers of late antiquity. The most plausible answers to these questions, once again, raise troubling questions about the reliability of the standard Muslim accounts dealing with the early history of Islam. In the next chapter, we will tackle some of these questions head-on by attempting to pinpoint a possible location for the events related in the Qur'an and *hadiths*.

4.

Where did Islam Originate?
Examining the Islamic Sources

*T*he classic Islamic sources tell us that the ancient city of Mecca was a site of immense spiritual and economic importance. However, by the time Muhammad was born (570 CE), it was adrift in a sea of paganism and barbarity that enveloped the entire Arabian Peninsula. **Muhammad was a member of one of the most important tribes of Mecca, the Quraysh, and received a call from God to act as his prophet in a cave just outside the city.** *Acting upon this call Muhammad received a series of revelations over a period of about twenty years, right up to his death in 632 CE. These revelations form what we now know as the Qur'an. After Muhammad's death, his followers burst out of the Arabian Peninsula in the name of Islam and conquered the Persian and much of the Eastern Roman Empire. The coming of Islam established the Muslim religion, with the message of Muhammad and the city of Mecca at its center, as the pre-eminent belief system from Egypt to Persia within 100 years of the death of the prophet.*

The time has now come to bring some of the themes addressed thus far together by focusing on the location of the first recipients of the Qur'an. Or to put it another way: was Mecca the original 'holy city' of Islam?

Most Muslims would probably dismiss the raising of questions of this nature as bordering on the ridiculous as there is no doubt in their minds that someone named Muhammad lived and preached at the location of the modern city of Mecca.

If you have read this far, you will probably be aware that things are not quite as simple as this. In fact, this chapter will show that Muslim beliefs about Mecca are almost certainly mistaken. This is a matter of no small importance. If it can be proved that the Qur'an was not revealed at the location of the modern city of Mecca, it will shake the foundations of the entire Islamic historical tradition. More than this, given the importance of history in the formulation of Muslim belief and practice, it will bring the truth of Islam itself into question. It is, therefore, a matter far too important to simply take on blind faith.

4.1. Geographical Clues in the Qur'an

By now one of the basic problems of Muslim history as traditionally presented should be starkly apparent. On the one hand, we have confident Islamic historical accounts (committed to paper at least 200 years after the death of Muhammad) claiming to tell us exactly what happened in Mecca during this period. On the other hand, we have the realities that we focused on so far namely that there is no incontrovertible evidence that Mecca even existed in 570 CE (the year commonly given for the birth of Muhammad), let alone that it was an important trading or religious center. So how are we to square this circle?

One possible approach would be to compare the documents revered by Muslims themselves (i.e. the Qur'an, sound *hadiths* and classical histories) with verifiable historical and geographical data. The next few pages will, therefore, focus on the geographical indicators in the Qur'an and *hadiths* and compare them with on-the-ground realities. When historians analyze documents in this way, they will typically look for both direct and indirect geographical references. It may be useful to briefly explain what we mean by this.

Direct geographical references refer to named cities, towns, regions, mountains, rivers, tribes etc. that can help researchers to place a document in a specific location. In most cases this is a very straightforward process (e.g. few historians will doubt the writings of Tacitus[261] originated and describes life in Rome since the geographical references all 'check out'). Sometimes, however, direct references can indicate the fact that an author was not familiar with a specific area that he claims to describe. For example, a historical document that places Athens on the Italian Peninsula or that describes a day-long journey between Constantinople and Jerusalem (impossible before the advent of air travel) is bound to raise questions about whether the author was, in fact, familiar with the time and place that he is seeking to describe.

Indirect geographical references are in-text mentions of features from which we can infer some geographical insights. If, for example, I read a book describing icebergs, glaciers and husky teams pulling sleds across frozen landscapes, I can make a fair guess that it is not set at the equator. Such indirect clues are often invaluable in piecing together the origins of a document where its place of origin is different from what is claimed. An artistic analogy would be the many Renaissance era paintings that supposedly evoke ancient Israel, but in which all the characters look like they've just stepped off the streets of Florence. In such cases you would have to be rather silly to claim that these paintings were painted on-site in Jerusalem. In the same way, a document can claim to be from a certain place, region or country, while all the indirect geographical references make it clear that this is highly unlikely.

If we apply the idea of direct and indirect geographical references to the history of Islam, we note that the Qur'an contains precious few geographical markers (i.e. direct geographical references). The *hadiths*, on the other hand, contain copious amounts of direct geographical references. In this case, however, the problem is that they tend not to align with the geographical realities on the ground in Arabia (several examples of this phenomenon will be noted later in the chapter). The task of the researcher in a case such as this must be to examine the available evidence to construct a picture that is as accurate as possible given the available evidence.

'Examining the available evidence' obviously does not mean that the standard Islamic account can simply be accepted. Instead we will be engaging in a bit of textual sleuthing to answer some basic questions related to the contents of key Islamic historical documents. The most important of these questions will relate to the place and date of composition of these documents. Specifically, if they are connected to 7th century Mecca in any fundamental sense? This question is particularly important given the fact that our discussion up to this point revealed the fact that there is a complete lack of evidence that such a place even existed.

Just to recap, the earliest documentary reference to Mecca appears in the Apocalypse of Pseudo Methodius in the Continuato Byzantia Arabica, dating from 741 CE.[262] This is more than a hundred years after Muhammad was supposed to have died. The earliest inclusion of Mecca on a map dates from around 900 CE. We would, therefore, be more than justified in being highly skeptical of the classical account as we embark on researching the question of whether the original holy city of Islam was, in fact, located at the place towards which millions of Muslims pray every day.

An obvious way to enter into this discussion is to take a slightly lateral approach by looking at the clues that we can glean from sources like the Qur'an and *hadiths* that might give us contextual indicators that could help us locate their place of origin. The problem is, however, that the Qur'an contains very few names, places, dates or other direct markers that could help us place it within a specific time and place. The task of the historian will, therefore, in this case be rather difficult in the sense that it will require an extremely detailed reading of the text to pick up clues to a context that may not be immediately obvious. In other words, very careful attention should be paid to indirect forms of evidence. One of the most important forms of indirect geographical markers is language and this is where our exploration will begin.

4.1.1. Linguistic Clues Relating to the Origins of the Qur'an

The first and the most basic fact that we must take note of when we attempt to investigate the origins of the Qur'an is that it was written in Arabic. This may seem like the most obvious statement possible, but there is something self-conscious and odd about the way in which the Qur'an talks about its character as an Arabic book.

The author of the Qur'an makes several statements reassuring readers that the Qur'an comes to them in 'pure Arabic'.[263] While it is easy to read such a statement as a mere rhetorical device the critical reader will immediately sit up and take notice. If the author felt it necessary to make a statement about the purity of the Qur'an's Arabic, it stands to reason that at least some people must have criticized its use of Arabic. If this is not the case, the statement would be entirely redundant, on a par with Shakespeare including the line 'Remember this document is written in excellent English' in his plays.

At this point the reader may wonder why we are talking about language when the focus is supposed to be on geography. Simply because language, and the different ways that it is used in different locations, can be a very important geographical marker. The use and the influence of neighboring languages can often help linguists to pinpoint the origins of documents to very narrowly defined ranges. Vocabulary and other language facets can also help scholars to accurately date documents.[264] It turns out, that in this case, language is one the most important pieces of evidence that we have. This is because, whoever wrote the Qur'an was right to be concerned about how the Arabic that it contains will be received. It is, in fact, very far from the 'pure Arabic' that it claims to contain.

Most Muslims would regard the idea that the Qur'an was not written in 'pure Arabic' as preposterous. Especially given the prominence that Arabic enjoys within the world of Islam and of how the Qur'an is perceived to be the gold standard of the Arabic language. The problem with this, however, is that it is a logical fallacy to assume that just because Qur'anic Arabic eventually became enshrined as the standard form of classical Arabic, it has always been regarded as such. In fact, there is very little evidence that Arabic in the form that it appears in the Qur'an had even been fully developed by the beginning of the 7th century when the book was written.

Also, the current status of a language does not necessarily align with ancient realities. We can, in fact, point to many cases where a certain variant or regional dialect become the standard form of a language, thus displacing equally venerable and perhaps even purer versions of the language.

Thus, the standard German of today is largely based on the Saxon dialect of Martin Luther[265] and standard French on the Parisian dialect[266] (a dialect that would have been virtually incomprehensible to many people living in other parts of France before the era of mass communication). We should, therefore, be very careful of interpreting the current unassailable position of Qur'anic Arabic as indicating that it has always been regarded as the purest possible expression of the Arabic language. If anything, its protest that it is indeed 'pure Arabic' (cf. Qur'an 16:103) should indicate that this was far from a settled conviction among those who heard it for the first time.

Let us now turn to the pages of the Qur'an itself with a view to find linguistic clues with geographical relevance. It has, firstly, often been pointed out that the Qur'an contains several glaring grammatical errors,[267] thus indicating that its composer was not entirely confident in using complex forms of the Arabic language. A high level linguistic analysis of whether this is, in fact, the case lies beyond the scope of this book, but is at the very least interesting to note that the suspicion exists. Far more interesting for our purposes (i.e. looking for linguistic clues with geographical implications) is the presence of many hundreds of foreign (i.e. non-Arabic) words in the Qur'an.

The following is a partial list of 'loan words' from other languages that occur in the Qur'an:

- Persian: *Ara'ik*, 18:31 (couches); *ghassaqan*, 78:25 (pus); *jinn*, 51:56, (spiritual being halfway between humanity and angels); *sijjil*, 105:4 (baked clay)
- Pahlavi: *Firdaws*, 18:107 (paradise); *huri*, 55:72, (this refers to the beautiful women that Muslim men will receive in paradise); *maqalid*, 39:63, (keys); *suradiq*, 18:28 (pavilion); *zanjabil*, 76:17 (ginger)
- Greek: *Injil*, 3:48 (Gospel)
- Hebrew: *Jahannan*, 8:36 (hell); *ma'un*, 107:7 (charity); *sabt*, 27:124 (Sabbath); *sakina*, 2:248 (Shekinah, a reference to the glorious presence of God)
- Ethiopian: *Mishkat*, 24:35 (niche)
- Coptic (Egyptian): *Tabut*, 2:247 (ark)

The presence of these words is immensely important as it speaks quite eloquently against the idea that the Qur'an was somehow the product of a sheltered and isolated desert environment. For foreign words to be incorporated into the way you use your own language, you must obviously be in contact with the foreigners who speak that language. You would, for example, be far more likely to find Spanish loan words in the English spoken in New Mexico than in the English of the Scottish Highlands. Analyzing loan-words can, therefore, be very useful in pinpointing the origins of a document.

All the above raises the obvious question: which non-Arabic language had the greatest influence on the Arabic used in the Qur'an? It turns out that this is Syriac.[268] Syriac does not have immediate name recognition among most modern Westerners, but it was a hugely important language in its day, being the *lingua-franca* of the Roman Province of Syria and well into what is now the eastern part of Turkey.[269] It was, as such, very widely spoken. A version of this language, Aramaic, was in fact most likely spoken by Jesus.

Syriac contributes many of the non-Arabic loan words to the Qur'an. These include: Allah, 1:1 (*Ilah* in Syriac); *Adn*, 9:72 (Eden) *Fir'awn*, 73:15 (Pharaoh); *Sura*, 9:124 (chapter); *taghut*, 2:257 (idols); *zakat*, 21:110 (alms). It is, however, quite possible that Syriac played an even more significant role than simply being a word contributor.

One of the greatest challenges in gleaning meaning from the Qur'an is the fact that some words, phrases and even entire verses defy all attempts at interpretation. This brings us to a startling but credible theory, namely, that parts of the Qur'an were originally not written in Arabic at all but in Syriac.[270]

The original Arabic of the Qur'an was written without vowels (much like Modern Hebrew). It could, therefore, be that the wrong vowels were eventually added, obscuring the true meaning of the words. To illustrate: If you have a language that does not write vowels, and you read the word 'ct', the vowels that you add, either in your mind or on paper, can make a huge difference. It can, for example, become:

- Cat
- Cot
- Cut

You can usually tell which vowel to use by taking the context into account. Modern Hebrew would again be a good example of how this is done. What happens however if you do not know the original context or cannot go back to the sources as is the case with the Qur'an? The German linguist Cristoph Luxenberg, who studied many of the unintelligible riddles of the Qur'an, believes the solution is to remove the classical Arabic vowel sets and replace them with Syriac vowel sets. His thesis is expounded in his book 'A Syro-Aramaic Reading of the Koran: A Contribution to Decoding the Text of the Koran'.[271]

By taking away the Arabic vowels (added according to Muslim tradition by Al-Hajjaj Ibn Yusuf Al-Thakafi, 660-714 CE[272]) and replacing them with Syro-Aramaic vowels, Luxenberg can show how many obscure passages can suddenly be rendered perfectly understandable, thus indicating that they were originally written in Syriac and not in Arabic. One of his most famous conclusions is that the *huris* (white eyed virgins) awaiting the faithful in paradise (Qur'an 44:54, 52:20, 55:72, 56:22) refer to grapes or raisins.[273] This is consistent with earlier Christian texts in which grapes are associated with paradise. If Luxenberg is correct, some martyrs for the cause of Allah may be in for a rude shock.

The fun that has been had with the 'grapes for martyrs' claim should not, however, distract from Luxenberg's serious and very carefully researched conclusion: it is impossible to fully understand the Qur'an without taking Syriac influence into account.[274]

This leads us to a logical conclusion. Syriac was spoken throughout the Roman province of Syria and its borderlands from the time when Syria became an imperial province[275] to its conquest by the Arabs. The Qur'an must, therefore, have originated in this part of the world instead of hundreds of miles away in the middle of the Arabian Desert where Syriac influence would have been negligible. Why this is so should be obvious. For this level of linguistic cross-fertilization to take place, the author of the

Qur'an would have to have been in daily contact with speakers of Syriac and for an Arabic speaker only the Syrian borderlands (or the province of Syria itself) would have provided such conditions.

The influence of Syriac on the Qur'an's Arabic could also explain its extreme touchiness about the purity of the language in its pages. The claims made in this regard may have been a direct response to Arabs further to the south who reacted negatively to what they must have seen as the 'corruption' of their language through the incorporation of Syriac influences.

4.1.2. Geographical References in the Qur'an

The Qur'an is a remarkably de-contextualized work in the sense that whoever wrote it seems to have deliberately eliminated references to contemporary events, people and geographical locations from its pages. Comparisons between other roughly contemporary religious documents are quite enlightening. The Jewish and Christian Scriptures contain as many as ten times more geographical references when compared to the Qur'an.[276] This is a quite intriguing and one cannot help but wonder why this would be so. Given what we have seen this far, one possibility that should be considered is that there may have been a deliberate attempt to purge the pages of the Qur'an of potentially troubling geographical references that would have cast doubt on the claim that it originated in the middle of the Arabian Desert.

If there had been an attempt to 'scrub' the Qur'an of references to locations that could help us to locate its place of composition, they were not completely successful. In a remarkable book entitled 'Qur'anic Geography' author Dan Gibson analyses the 'surviving' geographical references in the Qur'an. According to Gibson there are only 65 definite such references (roughly only one every second chapter).[277]

In determining the importance of these references, it is important to remember that local context will inevitably 'seep into' a document. An American colonist in Massachusetts during the 17th century would, for example, be much more likely to regularly refer to places like Boston,

Plymouth, Northampton and Cambridge than to settlements in colonial Virginia. In terms of the population, we will once again expect many more references to local Indian tribes than to those who lived further to the south. By plotting such references on a map, scholars are often able to quite accurately determine where a document originated.

Of the 65 geographical references in the Qur'an no less than 54 are references to three tribes. They are The People of 'Ad (23 References), The People of Thamud (24 References) and the Midianites (7 References). When we plot the references on a map, it quickly becomes clear that they are all clustered hundreds of miles to the north of Mecca (i.e. Northern Arabia).

In fact, the Qur'an contains vanishingly few references to settlements further to the south, where the modern city of Mecca is located. This is very odd indeed and must, once again, inevitably raise the question of how the classical accounts of Islam's origins could possibly be accurate if the Qur'an does not even so much as acknowledge the immediate geographical context of the modern city of Mecca? One possible response is the fact that Mecca is at least mentioned in the Qur'an and that this must somehow validate the position given to it by Muslim faith and practice. Let us, therefore, now turn to the Qur'anic references to Mecca and its possible position as Islam's original holy city.

4.1.3. Mecca in the Qur'an

When it comes to tracing the role that Mecca plays in the Qur'an, the first thing that strikes the reader as very strange is that the supposed 'mother of cities' is mentioned by name exactly once in the Qur'an and even this single reference is highly problematic from the perspective of the classical account. Here is the verse in question: "And it is He Who has restrained their hands from you and your hands from them in the midst of Makka, after that He gave you the victory over them. And Allah sees well all that ye do." (Qur'an 48:24)[278]

The problem, from the perspective of the classical Islamic historical accounts, is that this reference is so general that it can, in fact, be anywhere.

The Qur'an is, therefore, not very helpful of settling the matter as to whether it had its origins in the middle of the Arabian Desert. Most Muslim scholars would obviously protest vigorously at such a statement and will in response perhaps proceed to produce their trump card. A reference to a place called Bakka, which they associate with Mecca, where there is a clear indication that it was the location of a place dedicated to the worship of Allah.

4.1.4. Bakka, Mecca and the Possibility of an Alternative Focus for Early Muslim worship

We have already encountered references to Bakka in relation to the Muslim claim that a reference to a place called 'The Valley of Baka' (note the slightly different spelling) in Psalm 84 of the Hebrew Bible is a reference to Mecca (Section 2.3.6). While this claim can be very safely dismissed on the basis of a textual analysis of the psalm, the larger claim of the identification of Mecca with Bakka still has to be addressed.

The Qur'anic verse dealing with Bakka reads as follows: "The first House (of worship) appointed for men was that at Bakka: Full of blessing and of guidance for all kinds of beings," (Qur'an 3:96).[279] One can easily see why believing Muslims would immediately want to make the claim that this is a reference to Mecca. In fact, some translations of the Qur'an dispense with the term 'Bakka' altogether and simply render the phrase 'Valley of Mecca' in translation.[280] They justify this linguistic sleight of hand by claiming that Bakka is an ancient alternative name for Mecca. The only problem with this claim is obviously that there is no evidence for the ancient existence of Mecca, let alone for any alternative names. This identification was simply made because it was necessary in the context of Islamic beliefs. As FE Peters memorably said: "The Quran mentions that the 'first house was established for mankind at Bakka' which left the medieval commentators little choice but to identify Bakka with Makka (Mecca), though no one was quite sure why."[281]

In the end Muslim scholars will have to concede that the reason behind the identification between Bakka as Mecca is theological (and not based on literary, historical or geographical evidence). Bakka, so the argument goes, is such an important center for the worship of Allah according to the Qur'an that the term simply *must be* a synonym for Mecca. However, wishing something was so is not a very useful yardstick for determining actual historical truth so it is imperative that we probe a little deeper.

It cannot be emphasized too strongly that there is nothing whatsoever in the Qur'anic reference to Bakka that absolutely necessitates its identification with Mecca. The 'house of God' that it refers to can be anywhere. It is vitally important that we avoid reading present realities back into ancient documents and that we at least consider alternative interpretations.[282] Millions of modern Muslims pray towards the middle of the Arabian Desert. This does not conclusively prove, however, that the 'House' towards which Allah directed his followers to pray in the Qur'an (after changing the direction from an orientation towards Jerusalem) has always been located at this spot. Most modern Muslims would reject the notion that they are misdirecting their prayers with scorn. However, the absence of Mecca from the historical record, the consistent indications of the proximity of the earliest Muslims to the Syrian borderlands and some very compelling archeological evidence (more on this later) combine to make this a very convincing thesis.

4.1.5. Indirect Geographical References in the Qur'an

It would be foolish to think that a document without direct geographical references do not contain any geographical clues at all. The environment in which any document is written is bound to leave some marks on the text. We have already seen how this is the case with the kind of Arabic used in the Qur'an. There are, however, also many non-linguistic clues that can help us to locate the original location of the Qur'anic text. Many of these have been mentioned earlier in the book, but it would be good to systematically list them here as part of the developing argument:

- Muhammad's enemies are often referred to as the '*mushrikun*' (polytheists). While this may seem to indicate a certain penchant for idolatry, it is not at all clear that they were out-and-out pagans. The

Qur'an's gripe against them was rather that they worshipped the one true God in the wrong way (cf. Qur'an 10:105[283] and 12:106[284]). Why the author of the Qur'an thinks it proper to castigate people who were supposed to be entirely isolated from other belief-systems for not properly worshipping the Abrahamic God is left unexplained. The reality is that this kind of syncretism would be much more likely to develop in frontier societies where there is sustained contact between different belief systems.

- The *mushrikun* are, furthermore, portrayed as crop and livestock farmers. In fact, some of the sins for which they are taken to task deals with how they treated their animals (i.e. not invoking a prayer upon slaughter and clipping the ears of livestock, see Qur'an 4:119[285]). It is left unexplained why 'ear clipping' is such a heinous sin. What should be beyond any doubt, however, is that the people thus accused could not have lived in Mecca, as livestock farming would have been a total impossibility in the arid interior of the Arabian Peninsula. What is true for livestock farming is even more applicable to arable farming. There is no way that the crops of the *mushrikun* i.e. grapes, grain, olives and pomegranates (Qu'ran 6:99)[286] could have flourished in Mecca. As Douglas Gibson points out: "The presence of trees and plants in ancient times can be easily tested by the presence of spores and pollens in undisturbed ancient soil. To date there is no record of trees having ever existed in ancient Mecca."[287]

- It is, furthermore, interesting to note that the author of the Qur'an assumes that the *mushrikun* would be familiar with the geography of Palestine. After discussing the story of Lot's wife (who according to the Biblical account was turned into a stone pillar for looking back as God destroyed Sodom and Gomorra), the Qur'an states that those who are being warned pass by the pillar every day (Qur'an 37:133-138).[288] Why this would be true of people who supposedly inhabited a region hundreds of miles to the south is not explained. It would, however, make perfect sense if the recipients of the text lived on the Syrian borderlands.

- It is stated in the Qur'an that the city in which Muhammad delivered his prophecies lies between two mountains. Muslim tradition also states that Hagar, Abraham's concubine, ran between these mountains (known as Al-Safa and Al-Marwah) as she looked for water for her son Ishmael after they were turned out by the patriarch Abraham. Apparently, these mountains were so impressive that they could be seen as 'signs from Allah': "Surely the Safa and the Marwa are among the signs appointed by Allah; so whoever makes a pilgrimage to the House or pays a visit (to it), there is no blame on him if he goes round them both; and whoever does good spontaneously, then surely Allah is Grateful, Knowing." (Qur'an 2:158)[289] Even a very cursory look at the geography of Mecca will confirm that this does not correspond with reality on the ground (i.e. there are no high mountains in or near the center of Mecca). The Muslim guardians of Mecca attempted to remedy this rather embarrassing fact by declaring two low rises, that are not even worthy of being called hills, to be the mountains referred to in the Qur'an. Just how ridiculous this is, is proved by the fact that these two 'mountains' are now fully enclosed in the mosque complex (with the *Ka'aba* at its center) that dominates modern Mecca.[290] The mind boggles at the idea that anyone would think that it is appropriate to refer to a mound of earth and rocks that can be covered by a building, and not a very high building at that, as a mountain.

The evidence is compelling. Even despite the 'cleansing' of the Qur'an of geographical references, those that we do find (both direct and indirect) make it highly unlikely that the original audience lived at the location of the modern city of Mecca. Muslim scholars may respond to this by stating that the *hadiths* clearly and unambiguously place many of the crucial events of Muhammad's life in Mecca. Thus supplying, or so these scholars claim, the evidence for a Meccan origin that is so glaringly absent from the Qur'an. It is, therefore, to the geographical references contained in the *hadiths* that we turn next.

4.2. Geographical References in the *Hadiths*

The origins of the *hadiths* as well as the question of their historical reliability have already been discussed. These questions are particularly relevant when it comes to the usefulness of the *hadiths* in terms of providing
definitive confirmation of the geographical location of the early life and
ministry of Muhammad. To fully investigate this issue, it may be necessary to briefly recap some remarks made earlier about the reliability of the
hadiths before looking at geographical markers that we can find in them.

4.2.1. The Reliability of the *Hadiths* Revisited

It is not necessary to repeat everything that has been said earlier about
the reliability of the *hadiths,* but it is important to keep the following in
mind as we consider the geographical markers in the *hadiths*:

- The *hadiths* were committed to paper 250-400 years after the life
  of Muhammad.
- This means that 7 or more generations of narrators had to flawlessly
  transmit these traditions, despite any command from Allah to do
  so.
- Significant levels of corruption occurred during the transmission
  process. This is confirmed by the fact that many supposedly 'sound'
  hadiths contradict each other. In other words, either the contents
  of the *hadiths* were tampered with or they were not transmitted
  accurately.
- We find that later *hadiths* tend to be much more detailed than earlier ones and that many *hadiths* contain information that does not
  fit in with the supposed context (central Arabia) of the narrations.

It would, in light of the above, be extremely foolhardy to simply accept
the statements in the *hadiths* related to Mecca at face value. It would be
far better to take a critical look at the *hadiths* to look for geographical clues
related to the place they are describing (supposedly Mecca) and the place
where these documents were written. This is where we will turn next.

4.2.2. The Holy City of Islam in the *Hadiths* and Classical Sources

While there are very few geographical references in the Qur'an, the exact opposite is true of the *hadiths* and classical sources (e.g. Ibn-Ishaq's 'Sira' and Al-Tabari's 'History of the Prophets and Kings').[291] They abound with references to specific places and even details associated with those places. It should, therefore, be the simplest thing possible to reconstruct an accurate picture of Mecca during the life of Muhammad by bringing the details from a range of *hadiths* and classical sources together. It will very quickly become clear that things are not nearly as simple as this. This might have been suspected, given what we know about the historical evidence related to Mecca.

The central problem with the geography presented in the *hadiths* is that while it claims to locate events in Mecca, the authors (or narrators) clearly had no idea of the *actual* geography of central Arabia. In other words, descriptions of events taking place in and around Mecca have very little bearing to realities on the ground in that part of the world. There is, in fact, a distinct feeling that what is described would fit much better in other geographical contexts. This raises an important question: could the original holy city of Islam have been located in a totally different location? This would indeed explain why so many *hadiths* feel utterly out of place in Mecca.

Examples of the phenomenon of Mecca not quite 'fitting' the geography presented in the *hadiths* and classical sources can be multiplied, but the following should suffice:

- In the *hadiths,* the holy city of Islam is consistently described as being in a wide valley[292] with a stream running through the middle of it.[293] The center of Mecca is located on a flat plain and does not have a river or stream flowing through it.

- According to *hadiths* and classical sources, the original holy city of Islam was surrounded by high mountains. These mountains crowded in close to the city and some of them seemed to have been considerable peaks. In fact, Ibn Ishaq describes a battle inside the holy city of Islam that people observed from the slopes of a high mountain.[294] The problem here is that the nearest high mountain is more than 3 kilometers away from the center of modern Mecca, too far away to observe the minute details of a battle with the naked eye. The city is indeed signally lacking in the mountain department. This is a significant issue as one of the foundational stories of Islam is the tale of how Abrahams's concubine Hagar ran between the mountains of Safa and Marwah near Islam's holy city in search of water for her son Ishmael.[295] In the tales depicting her ordeal, the mountain peaks are depicted as very high with a valley between them.[296] They were so substantial that they housed shrines to different idols before the coming of Islam.[297] They must also have been some distance from each other as there are plenty of *hadiths* that describe people being completely exhausted in attempting to journey between them. Safa was, furthermore, so high that it was used as a military observation point.[298] As has been pointed out in the previous section, modern Muslims must convince themselves that two low rises entirely enclosed inside a mosque complex are the 'mountains' of Safa and Marwah. These two 'hills' are only 1500 feet apart. So close, in fact, that modern Muslim pilgrims move between them seven times in a single day as part of the *Hajj*.[299] Most of them probably do this without breaking much of a sweat since the 'mountains' are so close to each other. It need not be emphasized how deeply at odds this picture is with the majestic descriptions in the *hadiths* of the high peaks of Safa and Marwah in Islam's original holy city.

- The *hadiths* are full of statements like the following: "When the Prophet came to Mecca he entered from its *higher side* and left from its *lower side*. (Sahih Bukhari Vol. 2, Book 26, *Hadith* 647)[300] There are many other references to the 'higher' and 'lower' side of Islam's holy city in the *hadith* and the classical sources.[301] These references must be entirely perplexing for modern Muslim as the center of Mecca is located on a low flat plain with no identifiable upper and lower entrance routes. It was, furthermore, possible to enter the holy city of Islam through a narrow and rocky route through the mountains, as in the following example: "Allah's Apostle used to enter Mecca from the high *thaniya* and used to leave Mecca from the low *thaniya*. (Sahih Bukhari Vol. 2, Book 26, *Hadith* 646)[302] A '*thaniya*' is a narrow mountain pass and there are, again, many references stating that there was a higher and lower one that could be used to enter or exit the holy city of Islam. By now, it should not be surprising to note that there is absolutely nothing in the geography of the modern city of Mecca that corresponds with this striking and unique topographical detail.

- According to the *hadiths* and classical sources, the soil of the holy city of Islam consisted of clay and loam and had cultivated fields.[303] It was furthermore home to grasslands, trees[304] and grapevines[305]. According to Ibn Ishaq there were, in fact, so many trees that a clearance project had to be undertaken in the *Ka'aba* area.[306] None of this corresponds with the modern location of Mecca in one of the most barren spots on earth. Soil studies have, furthermore, confirmed that Mecca has never played host to anything remotely approaching the vibrant horticultural environment described in the sources (abundant plant life would have left unmistakable traces like seeds and organic material in the soil).[307]

- The traditional accounts contain several descriptions of what would be impossible journeys (if the holy city of Islam was indeed located at the modern location of Mecca). There are numerous examples of messages passing between northern cities (e.g. Damascus) and the holy city in a matter of days, instead of the many weeks that would normally be required for a round-trip between Syria and the location of Mecca (over 860 miles, one-way, through baking desert).[308]

- There are several examples of people entering the holy city of Islam from the 'wrong side' if this city was indeed Mecca. If you, for example, travel from Medina you would enter Mecca from the north (as it is located to the north of the location of Mecca). Yet we consistently see travelers from Medina entering the holy city from the south. The same principle applies in the reverse as well. We note from Al-Tabari that when the *Quraysh* attacked Medina, they always did so from the north[309]. This does not make sense at all as they would have been resident to the south if they lived at the location of Mecca. So, either ancient Arabian travelers and armies had a penchant for taking pointless and dangerous detours (circling a city before attacking it does not do much for the element of surprise), or the original holy city of Islam must have been to the north of Medina. This would make an entrance from the south, and attacks on Medina from the north, entirely logical.[310]

- There are many cases in the *hadiths* describing how some of Muhammad's henchmen used the proceeds from their military exploits to buy extensive property holdings in Syria.[311] This immediately raises the question: Why on earth would someone living 800 miles away buy a property in Syria? In the world of late antiquity, this kind of long distance property transactions, with 'barbarians' buying land inside the Roman Empire, would have been unheard of. This was a time when people were simply not secure in the possession of their property and the only way to maintain security of tenure was to be close enough to your property so that you can defend it and thus ensure that your rights were not transgressed. So, why would so many of Muhammad's followers have thrown basic common sense to the wind and buy properties in a place where it could be easily expropriated? Could it be that these inhabitants of the holy city of Islam may have been much closer to Syria than what the modern location of Mecca would lead us to believe?

It should by now be clear that reviewing the geographical data related to the original holy city of Islam leaves us with more questions than answers. One overwhelming impression that we are left with is that the location of the modern city of Mecca is a very bad 'fit' for what it is being described. This is not yet the right moment to engage in speculation as to exactly where this city may have been located, but it seems obvious that we can at least begin to narrow down the options. This is because the available evidence so consistently point to Islam having had its origins far to the north of Mecca. In fact, probably right on the doorstep of the Roman Empire in northern Arabia.

4.2.3. Geographical Clues Related to Place of Composition of the *Hadiths*

Mention has already been made of the fact that its place of composition inevitably leaves traces in the text of any document. The *hadiths* and classical Muslim historical sources are obviously not exempt from this general principle. So, in placing these sources under the microscope, we can glean much about the context in which they were written. As will become clear, the evidence that such an investigation will uncover must definitively put to rest any notion that the canonical historical accounts are the products of a somehow flawlessly preserved oral tradition. It will also show how Islam as it developed was very much a product of the prevailing worldviews of a region that is worlds away from central Arabia.

Even the official records concede that during the initial phase of the Arab conquests, the political center of gravity was located in Syria with Damascus as the de-facto capital of the spreading Arab empire under the Umayyad Dynasty (661-750 CE).[312] This very fact adds yet another question to the discussion about the actual place of origin of Islam: why, if Mecca was literally at the center of the Muslim universe, did it not act as the center of Islamic political and religious power? The most likely answer to this question is probably the simple fact that we cannot even be sure that it existed at this stage of history. Be this as it may, for about the first century after Muhammad, Arab political power was solidly anchored in Syria and certainly not in central Arabia.[313]

Muslim political power did not remain centered on Damascus though. The defeat of the Umayyads, the dynasty that controlled Damascus and for about a century the succession to Muhammad, by their arch-rivals the Abbasids[314] meant that Muslim political power shifted further east to heartlands of the former Persian Empire. It was here that the Abbasids established Baghdad as their capital city.[315] The Persian Empire had succumbed to Arabs more than a century before the victory of the Abbasids, but this did not mean that every single person living in its former territories were now Muslim. Rates of conversion were fairly low and this meant that many of the people of Mesopotamia[316] (i.e. the 'Land between the Rivers', the Tigris and Euphrates) still persisted in their pre-Islamic beliefs. This is evidenced by the fact that major centers of both Jewish and Zoroastrian scholarship and worship remained influential until long after the Arab conquest.

It can, in fact, be conclusively demonstrated that late-antique Mesopotamian manifestations of Judaism and Zoroastrianism profoundly influenced Islam in its final form. In the process, it can also be shown that many of the *hadiths* were not the product of Arabia, but rather of the erstwhile Persian heartlands. If this is true, and it would be hard to argue otherwise, then the *hadiths* can tell us very little indeed about Arabia during the lifetime of Muhammad and much more about the way in which Islam reached its final form in Mesopotamia about 300 years later. It would, therefore, be appropriate to proceed to briefly document the extent to which Islam was influenced by Mesopotamian Zoroastrianism and Judaism.

4.2.4. Zoroastrianism and the Rise of Islam

Zoroastrianism, although much reduced today, was one of the most important religions of the ancient world.[317] It was recognized as the official court-religion in Persia before the Persian Empire fell to the Arab invaders. After the fall of Persia, the Zoroastrian worldview and belief system did not simply disappear among those who eventually converted to Islam. This fact was pointed out by contemporary writers who stated that the Zoroastrians who accepted Islam in many ways continued with their previous beliefs and practices by importing it into their lives as newly minted Muslims.[318] Here are some of the ways in which Zoroastrian beliefs and practices made their way into the *hadiths*:

Zoroastrianism was unique among ancient religions in that it contained a strong legal tradition that called for the death penalty for apostates (i.e. those who left the religion).[319] Demands for such executions would have been particularly shrill during the period of the Islamic takeover of Persia as desperate Zoroastrian priests tried to prevent their followers from 'crossing over' to Islam.[320] This is not the position of the Qur'an. It merely states that apostates could expect a terrible fate in the hereafter.[321] Yet, there are several *hadiths* that takes the Zoroastrian line (i.e. that apostates should be killed). For example: "Whoever discards his Islamic religion, then kill him." (Sahih Bukhari Vol. 4, Book 52, *Hadith* 260)[322] The ruling that apostates should be executed, even though it goes beyond Qur'anic teaching, has official status in all Islamic legal schools (although they differ in terms of the strictness with which it should be applied). Given where the *hadiths* were finally formalized (Mesopotamia), it seems undeniable that this is an instance of a Zoroastrian position being adopted as Islamic.

Another, rather amusing, area of influence is in the area of dental health. Keeping your teeth clean was a positive obsession in Zoroastrianism and religious scholars advocated that a special stick should be used as a toothbrush for this purpose.[323] Using a stick to clean your teeth was almost certainly not part of ancient Arabian Desert culture. There would, for starters, be the significant problem of accessing a sufficient supply of sticks in the middle of one of the driest places on earth. Yet there are many *hadiths* describing Muhammad's scrupulous attention to keeping his teeth clean with a stick (known as a '*siwak*'), just as a devout Zoroastrian would.[324] It is rather amusing to reflect on the fact that the millions of Muslims around the world who use specially packaged sticks to 'religiously' (!) clean their teeth may be following a practice initiated by the priests of a different religion.

The third area of Persian/Zoroastrian influence is one that has caused misery to Muslim women since the time that the *hadiths* were written down. This is the insistence of some *hadiths* that Muhammad had his wives wear full face veils when out in public. This is not mandated in the Qur'an where Muslim women are only counseled to cover their bosoms (Qur'an 24:31).[325] While there is no explicit indication in the *hadiths* that Muslim women should veil their faces, they do show that the faces of Muhammad's wives were veiled. This is enough for many Muslim men who regard the fact that the prophet is supposed to be an 'excellent example' (cf. Qur'an 33:21)[326] as decisive and, therefore, also insist that their wives cover their faces. When we examine this practice more closely it quickly becomes clear that this was not an ancient Arab custom, but there is evidence that the wives of Persian noblemen were required to cover their faces.[327] It is not hard to work out what happened. Since the *hadiths* portray Muhammad as a ruler, it would have been only natural for Persian authors of *hadiths* to transplant a practice that they associated with the wives of rulers to Muhammad's wives (see, for example, Sunan Abi Dawud Book 10 *Hadith* 1829).[328]

These are just three of the most obvious ways in which Zoroastrianism and ancient Persia left their mark on the *hadiths*, and thus on the practice of Islam. There is, however, another religion that quite possibly exerted an even more profound influence. This is Judaism, and specifically the form of Judaism practiced in Mesopotamia.

4.2.5. Mesopotamian Judaism and its Influence of Islam

The reason that Mesopotamia came to play such a significant role in the development of Judaism is inextricably linked to the Jewish experience of exile. Jewish people were exiled from their homeland in two great waves. During the first wave many of the members of the ten northern tribes of Israel were exiled to Assyria in 722 BCE. In 586 BCE, it was the turn of the members of the two southern tribes to face exile, this time to Babylon. So it came to be that 'the land between the rivers' became home to a significant Jewish population. While there were efforts to repatriate many of the exiles, especially under the Persians, it was by no means the case that all Jewish people eventually returned to Israel.

Those who remained behind, while still cherishing the memory of their Promised Land, set about to formulate the rules and principles for practicing their faith and surviving as a Jewish community in exile. This led to a flowering of Jewish culture, largely guided by scholars known as rabbis. These Mesopotamian rabbis were responsible for formulating a vast number of legal principles guiding the correct practice of Judaism.

Anyone with even a passing familiarity with Judaism will be aware of the Talmud. The Talmud can be described as a series of laws, legal rulings and commentaries on the Hebrew Bible with a particular emphasis on the Torah (the first five books of the Hebrew Bible). The central concept behind the compilation of the Talmud was the idea that God did not only reveal his 'written law' to Moses at Mt Sinai, but that he also entrusted an 'oral law' (Mishnah) to him at the same time.[329] This oral law was not be written down, but was to be passed on orally from generation to generation until some point in the future when it would finally be committed to writing.[330] This concept should sound instantly familiar to anyone who is aware of the official explanation for how the *hadiths* came into existence.

What does all of this have to do with Mesopotamia and ultimately with Islam? Simply the fact that it was in Mesopotamia (and specifically at the great rabbinical schools of Sura and Pumbedita) where the Jewish rabbis labored to give the Talmud its final form by committing the oral law to paper and commenting on it.[331] In fact, the name which is given to the most important Talmud collection (i.e. the 'Babylonian Talmud') still reflects its origins in the 'land between the rivers'.[332]

Definitively committing the oral law to writing was obviously a very difficult exercise and the rabbis had to somehow make sure that they were not importing additional information into what they believed to be an ancient tradition. To guard against this, they took to citing authorities supposedly stretching back all the way to Moses to confirm the versions of the Oral Law that they were writing down.[333] It is no exaggeration to state that Judaism as it exists today is, in large part, a product of the labors of these rabbis to systematize and formalize the Jewish legal system on the back of traditions that they claimed rested on a direct oral link to Moses and Sinai.[334]

It is fascinating to note that all of this activity took place in the very region (i.e. Mesopotamia) where the Islamic legal tradition would also eventually take its final shape.[335] In fact, the Talmud would still be taught in the rabbinical schools of Sura and Pumbedita for a long time after the completion of the Islamic conquest.[336] It is, therefore, certainly not beyond the realms of possibility that Islamic scholars looked with envy at the process of establishing present belief and practice on ancient authority through the use of venerable oral traditions.[337] It could even be that some Jewish scholars converted to Islam and brought with them their legal training and their propensity to emphasize ancient oral traditions in the formulating of theological and legal positions.

It seems obvious that the *hadiths* with their chains of transmission (*isnads*) borrowed more than a little from the concept of the Mishna (Oral Law) as a body of knowledge supposedly transmitted throughout the centuries by a series of narrators.[338] To claim that they somehow arose independently and that they are, in fact, reliable transmissions of what Muhammad said and did is to willfully ignore the fact that the *hadiths* arose in exactly the place where Jewish scholars had for centuries been engaged in exactly the same exercise with regards to their own faith.[339] Jewish influence is, furthermore, confirmed in the contents and nature of several of the *hadiths*.

Perhaps the most striking instance of the influence of Jewish laws on the *hadiths* is to be found in the area of legal punishments for adultery. The Qur'an states that adulterous spouses should be sentenced to house arrest and admonished (Qur'an 4:15 and 24:2). Yet when we consult the rulings of the Islamic legal schools, they make it clear that the punishment for adultery is death by stoning. Why is this? Simply because there are several *hadiths* that command this punishment (cf. Sahih Bukhari Book 65 *Hadith* 4556).[340] This is in line with ancient Jewish laws and is most probably an example of the Jewish legal tradition[341] that made its way into Islam through the influence of the Mesopotamian rabbis. It is clear that those who formulated the *hadiths* were very sensitive to the charge that they were departing from the teaching of the Qur'an to the point that they even invented a *hadith* to state that a verse commanding stoning for adultery was once part of the Qur'an, but that it was lost (Sahih Bukhari Volume 8, Book 82, *Hadith* 816).[342]

There are many other areas where the influence of Mesopotamian Rabbinical Judaism can be discerned in the Qur'an. These include the adoption of slightly modified versions of Jewish dietary laws and rules for maintaining ritual purity.

These instances are only the tip of the iceberg as far as the influence of rabbinical teaching on Islam is concerned. The presence of these clear areas of

influence combine with the instances of Zoroastrian influence to definitively anchor many *hadiths* to Mesopotamia in an age (roughly 850-1000
CE), long after the death of the person whose life they claim to describe.

4.3. Chapter Summary

- Linguistic analysis is one of the most important tools that can be
  used to determine the location where a specific document was written. When such an analysis is performed on the Qur'an, it quickly
  emerges that it is full of loan-words from a wide variety of sources.
  This would be rather odd if the Qur'an sprang from the isolation
  of the Arabian Desert. It is, furthermore, particularly important
  to note that the language that seems to have influenced the Qur'an
  the most is Syriac. This means that it must have been composed in
  close proximity to the Roman province of Syria.

- There are precious few geographical markers in the Qur'an and
  the single reference to Mecca is so vague that it cannot be used to
  provide a fix on the location of Islam's holy city.

- The other geographic references in the Qur'an are all concentrated
  in northern Arabia and not in the west-central area of the Arabian
  Peninsula (where the modern city of Mecca is located).

- There are many indirect geographical clues that indicate that the
  Qur'an could not have been directed at people living in the middle of the Arabian Desert. These include references to arable and
  livestock farming and the assumption of familiarity with concepts
  and locations associated with Abrahamic religion.

- Given the evidence presented thus far in this book, references to
  the 'House at Bakka' in the Qur'an cannot automatically be assumed to refer to Mecca.

- Many *hadiths* do not seem to be based on an intimate knowledge
  of the area around Mecca. This is manifested in glaring descriptive

mistakes and the inclusion of events (e.g. very short journeys from northern Arabia to Islam's holy city) that would be physically impossible if this holy city was located at the modern location of Mecca.

• Many of the geographical impossibilities and absurdities in the *hadiths* are immediately resolved if we propose a location of Islam's first holy city far to the north of Mecca.

• The deep unfamiliarity of many *hadiths* with the geography of the area around Mecca is not only due to a likely north Arabian location for the early years of Islam, this is also because they were mainly written down several centuries later in Mesopotamia.

• The fact that many *hadiths* that were written down in Mesopotamia had a profound influence on the final form of Islam. This is clearly visible in the considerable number of Zoroastrian and Jewish beliefs and practices that were included in the *hadiths* and continues to exert significant influence over the contemporary practice of Islam.

It would be easy to dismiss one or two indications that Islam's original holy city was not located in Mecca, but much further north as interesting outliers. The fact is, however, that wherever we turn (historical analysis, linguistic analysis, geographical analysis etc.) the results that we get back all lead to the same conclusion: Islam, as presented in the Qur'an and *hadiths*, could simply not have originated in the middle of the Arabian Desert. This means that the accepted Islamic historical account has much to answer for. It was constructed either in ignorance or in a willful attempt to deceive the faithful, but it simply does not correspond in any way to actual historical and geographical realities. This means that every aspect of the story that they are telling must inevitably be suspect. Over the next few chapters we will take a critical look at three of these aspects: a) The history of Muhammad b) The origins of the Qur'an and c) The history of the post-Muhammad period.

5.

Finding Muhammad behind the Shadows

*T*he classic Islamic sources tell us that the ancient city of Mecca was a
site of immense spiritual and economic importance. However, by the
time Muhammad was born (570 CE), it was adrift in a sea of paganism and barbarity that enveloped the entire Arabian Peninsula. Muhammad was a member of one of the most important tribes of Mecca, the Quraysh,
and received a call from God to act as his prophet in a cave just outside the
city. **Acting upon this call Muhammad received a series of revelations over
a period of about twenty years, right up to his death in 632 CE.** These revelations form what we now know as the Qur'an. After Muhammad's death,
his followers burst out of the Arabian Peninsula in the name of Islam and conquered the Persian and much of the Eastern Roman Empire. The coming of
Islam established the Muslim religion, with the message of Muhammad and
the city of Mecca at its center, as the pre-eminent belief system from Egypt to
Persia within 100 years of the death of the prophet.

5.1. In Search of the Historical Muhammad

The purpose of this chapter is to discuss the documented historical record
regarding Muhammad. The problem is, however, that there is precious
little to go on. The first incontestable Arabic reference to Muhammad on
any inscription dates from as late as 691 CE or sixty years after he was

supposed to have died.[343] There are some hazy earlier Arabic references to a charismatic leader of the community, but before 691 CE he is never called Muhammad. The name does crop up in some non-Arabic documents, but some of the details associated with this leader are, as we shall see, fundamentally at odds with the Muhammad of the Islamic tradition.

It is hard to overstate how strange the absence of Muhammad from the historical record is. Muhammad is everywhere in the fully developed Islamic tradition. He is even at the heart of the *Shahada*, the Muslim confession of faith: "I testify that there is no God but God and *Muhammad is the messenger of God*."[344] This is supposed to have been the words on the banners of the conquering Arab armies. This is the person whom they were supposedly following in everything from conducting warfare to teeth brushing techniques.[345]

Yet, despite the overwhelming later prominence of Muhammad, not a single contemporary Arabic writer seems to have heard of him before sixty years had elapsed after the date given for his death. This was sixty years during which the Persian, and half of the Roman Empire, were overrun by warriors supposedly taking him as their supreme example. How strange then that none of the multitude of contemporary authors describing the Arab conquest confirm the details modern Muslims would regard as basic elements of Muhammad's biography.

Our task will, considering the massive discrepancy between the Islamic tradition and actual historical evidence, once again be to investigate what the available evidence can tell us about the one whom Muslims believe to be embodiment of Allah's ideal for humankind (Qur'an 33:21). Our first port of call must be to assess the usefulness of the Qur'an and *hadiths* in terms of providing us with an accurate picture of the life of Muhammad.

5.2. Muhammad in the Qur'an

What immediately strikes the observant reader looking for traces of Muhammad in the Qur'an is how few times he is mentioned by name in its pages. There are exactly four (possibly five) direct references to him. His name is, therefore, far less prominent than those of Moses (136 times), Abraham (69 times), Mary (34 times, the only woman mentioned in the Qur'an) and Jesus (25 times, with many more indirect references).

The relative absence of mentions of Muhammad in the Qur'an should give us pause for thought as to the likelihood that it will be possible to get an accurate historical picture of him in its pages. While thus acknowledging that it will be a difficult task, let us now look at the Qur'anic references to him to see what picture we can form of the 'historical Muhammad' by reading Islam's holy book:

- "Muhammad is no more than a messenger: many were the messengers that passed away before him. If he died or were slain, will ye then Turn back on your heels? If any did turn back on his heels, not the least harm will he do to Allah; but Allah (on the other hand) will swiftly reward those who (serve Him) with gratitude." (Qur'an 3:144).[346] Here we learn that Muhammad was a messenger that stands in some kind of 'prophetic' tradition ('Many were the messengers that passed away before him.').

- "Muhammad is not the father of any of your men, but (he is) the Messenger of Allah, and the Seal of the Prophets: and Allah has full knowledge of all things." (Qur'an 33:40)[347] In this verse we find an affirmation of his prophetic ministry, but the verse goes further than the previous one in stating that he is the 'seal of the prophets', in other words no other prophets will follow him.

- "But those who believe and work deeds of righteousness, and believe in the (Revelation) sent down to Muhammad - for it is the Truth from their Lord, He will remove from them their ills and improve their condition" (Qur'an 47:2).[348] This is yet another affirmation of the prophetic ministry of Muhammad and the importance of holding to the revelation 'sent down to him'.

- "Muhammad is the messenger of Allah; and those who are with him are strong against Unbelievers, (but) compassionate amongst each other." (Qur'an 48.29).[349] This verse can perhaps be seen as confirming Muhammad's role as a military leader as it speaks of his followers being 'strong against the unbelievers'.

- "And remember, Jesus, the son of Mary, said: "O Children of Israel! I am the messenger of Allah (sent) to you, confirming the Law (which came) before me, and giving Glad Tidings of a Messenger to come after me, whose name shall be Ahmad." But when he came to them with Clear Signs, they said, "this is evident sorcery!" (Qur'an 61:6)[350] The name Ahmad is generally seen as a variant of the name of Muhammad so Muslim people would accept this verse as one of the five mentions of Muhammad in the Qur'an. There are, however, some who question whether this should be the case. Be this as it may, if we do accept this verse to be about Muhammad, it establishes the idea that the coming Muhammad was predicted by Jesus. This has led Muslim scholars on a quest to try and find, rather unsuccessfully it must be said, references to Muhammad in the Christian Gospels.

The verses above represent the sum total of direct references to the name of Muhammad in the Qur'an. There are, however, some other verses that use titles (most commonly 'Messenger of Allah') to refer to him. The most important among these is probably the verse that establishes Muhammad as an excellent example for those who hope to inherit eternal life (Qur'an 33:21). This verse is usually given as a justification for the compilation of the *hadiths* dealing with the acts and teachings of Muhammad as it would be hard to follow someone's example if you do not know what that example was.

Other verses emphasize the deep connection between Muhammad and the Qur'an and insist that what the messenger is relating is not merely 'tales of the ancients', but a fresh and legitimate revelation from God (Qur'an 68:15).[351] We also sense evident discomfort over the fact that the prophet is merely a warner and not a miracle worker. When pressed for a miracle Allah insists that 'the book' is the only miracle associated with Muhammad (Qur'an 29:50-51).[352]

An interesting, and deeply troubling, aspect of the verses establishing Muhammad's status as a messenger of God is the fact that certain parts of the Qur'an seem to be directly designed (or have been altered) to serve the needs, and whims, of a particular individual or group. Many of these verses are directly linked to certain incidents described in the *hadiths* and are used to grant Muhammad 'special permissions' and to exonerate him for actions that could be interpreted in a negative light. It is for this reason that they are often known as the 'Convenient Revelations'.[353] The following are some incidents described in the *hadiths* and how they are linked to specific verses associated with Muhammad in the Qur'an[354]:

- In Qu'ran 4:3[355] it is revealed that Muslims could marry up to four wives. For a variety of reasons, Muhammad wanted to marry more than four women. In response, Allah sent down a revelation that stated that the limit of four is only for ordinary Muslims. He told Muhammad that he could marry as many wives as he liked. It is made very clear that this privilege is "...for you only, not for the rest of the believers" (Qur'an 33:50).[356]

- In the same verse cited above (Qur'an 4:3), it is stated that those with multiple wives should treat them all equally. Muhammad experienced this to be a too difficult burden, especially as he began to develop favorites among his wives. Again, Allah stepped in and absolved him of the requirement to treat his wives equally, essentially telling the prophet that he could treat his wives as he wished and that he could 'postpone' and 'receive' them according to his own desires (Qur'an 33:51).[357]

- The story of the marriage between Muhammad and Zainab, who was the wife of his adopted son Zaid, is another occasion where Allah (or more likely later editors) used the Qur'an to help Muhammad out of a very tight spot. According to Muslim tradition, Muhammad went to the house of Zaid to look for him one evening. Upon arriving there, he found Zainab in a state of semi-undress. Muhammad rushed away, but it seems that from this moment the desire to marry Zainab began to consume him. Zaid, who obviously saw how the wind was blowing, divorced her, so that Muhammad could marry her. This caused a great deal of grumbling among his followers, many of whom regarded his actions as tantamount to incest. However,

apparently Allah immediately stepped in with another special revelation, making it clear that when adopted sons are 'done' with their
wives, their adopted fathers may marry them and that whoever questions this ruling, questions Allah, (Qur'an 33:37).[358]

- On another occasion, Muhammad had sex with a slave (Mary the
  Copt) whom he had not married yet. The wife (Hafsa) whose turn
  it was to have Muhammad with her that night furiously object-
  ed. Muhammad promised not to touch Mary again if Hafsa kept
  quiet. She did not keep quiet, however, and a scandal ensued. Ever
  faithful, Allah steps in to smooth things over (Qur'an 66:1-5). He
  begins: "O Prophet! Why do you ban (for yourself) that which God
  has made lawful to you..." (Qur'an 66:1)[359] and goes on to say that
  Muhammad is not bound by his oaths. The two ladies in question
  get a severe tongue lashing from Allah who tells them that they
  had better toe the line or else Muhammad may yet divorce all his
  wives and marry more obedient ones.

- In Sahih Bukhari, the most respected Sunni *hadith* collection, we
  read of the following exchange: "There was revealed: 'Not equal are
  those believers who sit (at home) and those who strive and fight in
  the Cause of Allah.' (4.95) The Prophet said, "Call Zaid for me and
  let him bring the board, the inkpot and the scapula bone (or the
  scapula bone and the ink pot)."' Then he said, "Write: 'Not equal
  are those Believers who sit," and at that time 'Amr bin Um Mak-
  tum, the blind man, was sitting behind the Prophet . He said, "O
  Allah's Apostle! What is your order For me (as regards the above
  Verse) as I am a blind man?" So, instead of the above Verse, the
  following Verse was revealed: "Not equal are those believers who
  sit (at home) except those who are disabled (by injury or are blind
  or lame etc.) and those who strive and fight in the cause of Allah,"
  (4.95) (Sahih Bukhari Vol. 6, Book 61, *Hadith* 512).[360] Here, we have
  an example of how Allah's supposedly eternal word was changed in
  a flash as a result of Muhammad wanting to accommodate one of
  his disabled followers. While his motivation may be praiseworthy,
  this playing loose-and-fast with Allah's word to fit in with what
  Muhammad (or later editors) wanted is quite instructive.

- During the so-called Battle of the Trench, Muhammad ordered some of his followers to dig a deep trench around Medina. This was obviously very hard work and some of the men went absent without leave. This greatly irritated Muhammad. Sure enough, Allah again comes through and makes it clear that those who want to leave the work can only do so with Muhammad's explicit permission (Qur'an 24:62).[361]

It is worth stressing how remarkable these convenient revelations are. Some of the key aspects of Islamic faith and practice, such as how to pray, how to make the pilgrimage and how to confess your faith, are not to be found in the Qur'an. Muslims have instead to turn to the *hadiths* for these crucial bits of information. On the other hand, the 'Eternal Qur'an' is filled with verses clearly aimed at smoothing things over for just one single person. Perhaps, the last word in this regard belongs to Aisha (Muhammad's favorite wife according to the Islamic tradition), who responded as follows to the revelation that Muhammad can marry as many women as he wished: "I feel that your Lord hastens in fulfilling your wishes and desires," (Sahih Bukhari Volume 6 Book 60 *Hadith* 311).[362]

The, justified, suspicion that parts of the Qur'an were revealed to suit a specific agenda is perhaps one of the clearest pieces of evidence that we have for a later origin of parts of the book. It is easy to establish that some verses were intended to serve the rather idiosyncratic needs (the desire for many wives, the desire to marry daughters-in-law, the desire for obedient wives etc.) of one person or a group of persons. Establishing that this person, or group, lived in the middle of the Arabian Desert is another matter altogether.

In light of the above we can summarize the Qur'anic data about Muhammad in the following way: "Muhammad was predicted by Jesus and stood in a long line of messengers from God to act as a prophet or messenger. The revelations that he transmitted should be obeyed and his example should be followed. It is possible that he was involved in acts of belligerence against unbelievers. After him there can be no other prophet." When we move to verses where titles (rather than the name Muhammad) is used, we see that he enjoyed extraordinary favor in the eyes of

Allah to the extent that he 'revealed' certain parts of the Qur'an specifically to meet his needs.

The above really is it as far as gleaning biographical details of Muhammad in the Qur'an is concerned. Any fair-minded reader would have to agree that this adds very little in terms of the actual historical Muhammad and what he said and did. Perhaps the *hadiths* can provide us with a fuller picture?

5.3. Muhammad in the *Hadiths* and Traditional Sources

We now turn to the *hadiths* and the canonical sources to see whether we can glean some verifiable historical information about Muhammad from the many traditions revered by Muslims as a major source of information about their prophet. This section will be divided into three parts: Muhammad the prophet, Muhammad and his family, and lastly Muhammad as a military leader.

Before we launch into this information, it should be noted that there are tens of thousands of *hadiths* claiming to describe aspects of Muhammad's life.[363] What follows here will, therefore, obviously only be a summary of the details contained in the main *hadith* collections. It is, however, an accurate summary and interested readers are invited to verify that the relevant *hadiths* were correctly cited by consulting the endnotes (where they are included in full).

It is, also, worth repeating that the *hadiths* were written down many generations after the time of Muhammad and that there is clear evidence of traditions being invented, added or borrowed from non-Islamic sources. The problems associated with using the *hadiths* as historical sources have already been discussed. They can be summarized by stating that the *hadiths*:

- Place events in a city for which there is no actual historical evidence.

- Contradict the Qur'an on many issues (e.g. Muhammad being a miracle worker and the punishment for adultery).

- Show clear traces of inter-Muslim conflict (e.g. Sunni and Shi'a *hadiths* give a very different picture of Muhammad's wishes as far as succession is concerned).

- Often directly contradict each other.

- Regularly reflect the worldview of a later time (800-1000 CE) and a different location (mostly Mesopotamia).

We should, considering the above, be very suspicious of these traditions in terms of historical accuracy and reliability. Let us, nevertheless, do our best to see whether anything can be recovered from them as far as a picture of the historical Muhammad is concerned.

5.3.1. Muhammad as a Prophet

The fact that Muslims revere Muhammad as a prophet is obviously so fundamental to Islam that even most non-Muslims would be able to cite this as a core Muslim belief. It is, therefore, no surprise that many of the *hadiths* focus on the prophetic calling and ministry of Muhammad. Ibn Ishaq states that Muhammad's family recognized that they had a prophet in their midst.[364] Incidents where his future greatness is predicted by 'those who should know' (e.g. a Syrian monk and a Jewish leader) are also related.[365]

When it comes to his prophetic ministry itself the initial emphasis is on his calling by Allah in a cave outside Mecca. The *hadiths* paint this as a time of intense mental anguish as Muhammad struggled to discern whether this calling was truly from Allah (Sahih Bukhari Volume 1 Book 1 *Hadith* 3).[366] The status of Muhammad is, however, supposedly decisively confirmed by the many miracles that he performs. Water flows from his fingertips[367], he pops eyeballs back into the eyes of injured people causing them to work better than before and plates of food sing his praises.[368] The list goes on and on. His prophethood is also confirmed by many tales of people who are utterly convinced of his status and who convert on-the-spot after meeting him.[369]

There are several significant problems with these accounts from an historical perspective, including the following:

- The *hadiths* dealing with Muhammad's birth and childhood bear striking similarities to Christian nativity stories complete with an 'Annunciation' and statements about the future glory of the child. Such statements about Muhammad are entirely absent from the Qur'an, but plentiful in the *hadiths* and the canonical historical sources. It is, therefore, possible to cite these *hadiths* as yet more examples of ways in which other religious traditions influenced the development of Islam.[370]

- The way in which Muhammad's prophetic ministry is presented should cause any believing Muslim deep concern. Several examples can be cited of failed prophecies[371] and strangely there is even a *hadith* that seems to suggest that Muhammad was rejected by Allah for presuming to prophesy things that he was not instructed to.[372]

- The issue of whether Muhammad performed miracles provides us with perhaps the greatest disconnect between the Qur'an (which is emphatic that Muhammad is merely a non-miracle working 'warner')[373] and the *hadiths* in which a string of miracles is ascribed to him. It is not hard to work out what happened here. The further we move from historical events, the more time there is for additions to the historical record. This would explain why the authors of the *hadiths* seemingly had access to so much material that went well beyond Qur'anic teaching. A significant amount of this 'new' material must have been invented with the specific aim of bolstering Muhammad's claims to prophetic legitimacy by endowing him with miracle working powers.

It can, in summary be stated that an analysis of the 'prophetic' material in the *hadiths* provides us with very little to work with as far as reconstructing an accurate picture of who this person was and what he taught. It does, however, provide us with an abundance of evidence that later generations of Muslims enthusiastically added to the record to promote specific convictions about their 'prophet'.

5.3.2. Muhammad's Family Life and Relationships

The *hadiths* and classical Islamic sources are unanimous that Muhammad hailed from Mecca and that he was a member of a tribe known as the *Quraysh*. In terms of his early life and ministry he was, therefore, supposedly embedded in a complex web of relationships in this part of the world. This is, of course, rather problematic given that there is no pre-Islamic evidence for this city or tribe even existing until long after the death of Muhammad. Leaving this aside for a moment, we can still glean much about what later generations wanted the world to know about the family life of the prophet of Islam. When we have a close look at the picture thus presented it quickly becomes clear that data back-projected onto the life of Muhammad was consistently used as a way of reinforcing certain key ideas about life, morality and sources of authority within the Muslim community.

In his childhood years his uncle, Abu Talib, one of the senior members of the *Quraysh* was the greatest early influence on Muhammad's life.[374] He would eventually get married to Khadija, a rich widow, and she was to be his only wife as long as she lived.[375] She was also one of the earliest supporters of the Muhammad's prophetic claims.[376]

After Khadija's death, Muhammad embraced polygamy with a vengeance and many *hadiths* deal with his multiple marriages (13 in total according to the most widely accepted count)[377] and the domestic squabbles that resulted.

Unfortunately, one of these marriages was to a six-year-old girl, Aisha.[378] This marriage was consummated when she was nine years old.[379] This fact, combined with the idea that Muhammad is recommended as an excellent example (Qur'an 33:21) would have devastating consequences for generations of young girls across the Muslim world.

Perhaps the most famous incident in Muhammad's deeply troubled home life as related by the *hadiths* was his marriage to the wife (Zainab) of his adopted son Zaid[380] (The details of this incident was related above as part of the discussion of Muhammad's 'convenient revelations'). The way in which Muhammad's conduct was portrayed here had the potential to cause a huge scandal as Arab culture had a high view of adoption and Muhammad's actions could, therefore, be seen as tantamount to incest.[381] The Qur'anic revelation that essentially invalidates any notion of formal adoption can therefore be seen as a very effective way of getting Muhammad off the hook for what many traditional Arabs would have seen as reprehensible behavior.[382] It is likely, however, that there is something much more significant going on here. Arab lines of succession were patrilineal (i.e. through the father's line) and only boys were included. The 'demotion' of Zaid from his status as a full member of Muhammad's family (through adoption) is very significant within this context. Through this action he (or any later descendant) lost any claim that he might have had of being Muhammad's successor.

The scotching of any political ambitions Zaid may have had leads us straight into another aspect of Muhammad's home life: the fate of his natural children. According to tradition, Muhammad fathered seven children, three sons and four daughters. Sunni's and Shi'as will disagree about the legitimacy of some of the daughters[383], but it is the sons that should concern us here. They were: Qasim ibn Muhammad (598 – 600 or 601 CE), Abd-Allah ibn Muhammad (d. 615 CE) and Ibrahim ibn Muhammad (630-631 CE).

Two things should immediately strike us as curious. The first is how few children there were.[384] Many *hadiths* testify to Muhammad's extremely healthy sexual appetites.[385] Yet over decades of regular sexual relations with his 13 wives in an age before contraception only 7 children were born.[386] Infertility clearly wasn't the issue here as a son was born to him as late as two years before his death. The second issue is that none of the boys survived infancy. This is certainly not impossible, but it should be honestly acknowledged that this is an exceedingly convenient fact for those who would like to deny Muhammad's descendants political power and influence.

To summarize and draw a few conclusions: when it comes to Muhammad's home and family life, we see a significant amount of very convenient traditions from the perspective of those who would like to legitimize certain practices (e.g. polygamy and sadly also child-marriage). There are also compelling reasons to suspect that political considerations related to the succession to Muhammad were inserted into the tradition. This is already apparent in the Qur'an itself where it is declared that Muhammad is not the 'father of any of your men' (Qur'an 33:40).[387]

The locking out of any possible descendant of Muhammad (whether natural or through adoption) from political power in the Muslim world is then made iron-clad in the *hadiths* through the insertion of traditions that have Muhammad's sons die in their infancy[388] and statements invalidating adoption (see above). This did not eliminate conflicts in this area (as the continuing Sunni/Shi'a split eloquently confirms)[389], but it did at least go some way towards dampening possible claims by those who would otherwise have had an almost unassailable claim to leadership of the community (i.e. being the sons or linear descendants of Muhammad).

So once again, we see very strong indications of later dynastic struggles being read back into the time of Muhammad, while it is very unlikely that these traditions tell us anything of substance about actual events in Western Arabia.

5.3.3. Muhammad as a War Leader

The third major theme that we can observe in the *hadiths* as far as the portrayal of Muhammad is concerned is his intense involvement with warfare. In fact, when we trace his biography from the time that he relocated to Medina, Islamic tradition has him engaging in warfare with almost every single neighboring tribe and city that he came into contact with.[390] This eventually culminated, according to the tradition, in the subjugation of a significant part of the lower Arabian Peninsula by the time of his death.[391]

A significant aspect of the portrayal of Muhammad as a war leader is the fact that he is not only presented as a great strategist[392] but also as someone who was not afraid of shedding blood and getting his hands dirty in pursuit of his war aims. In fact, the portrayal of Muhammad the warlord in the *hadiths* is nothing short of alarming. Here are just some of the actions that he engaged in according to the *hadiths* and classical Islamic sources:

- He ordered raids (*razzias*) on caravans (and took part in several) in order to steal their contents and to sell people for ransom.[393]

- He forced several of his enemies (e.g. Abu Sufyan) to accept his prophethood or be executed.[394]

- He 'married', and had sex with, a woman on the same day that her husband, father, brother and most of her family were slaughtered by his followers.[395]

- He was present and did nothing to stop an act of genocide when his followers slaughtered disarmed male members of the Banu Qurayzah (Jewish) tribe after they refused to embrace Islam[396] and he received 'divine sanction' for it (Qur'an 33:25-26).

- He ordered the assassination of several people who were critical of him (e.g. the poets Asma bint Marwan[397] and Abu Afak).[398]

- He ordered the torture of Kinana al-Rabi with a red-hot iron to 'encourage' him to reveal the whereabouts of a hidden treasure.[399]

- He broke a treaty (the treaty of Hudabiyyah), which committed him to live in peace with the people of Mecca.[400] Again he conveniently receives a 'revelation' justifying his actions (Qur'an 60:10).[401]

- He allowed his followers to rape captive women.[402]

- He consistently taught that warfare for the sake of Allah is the highest duty that a Muslim can perform.[403]

- He taught that those who abandon Islam should be executed.[404]

- He actively encouraged his followers to lie for the sake of the spread of Islam, especially in the context of warfare.[405]

The picture presented above is nothing short of horrifying and deeply embarrassing to some Muslims who want to claim that the version of Islam followed by groups like ISIS deviates from the example of Muhammad as presented in Muslim historical sources. In fact, so-called 'radical' groups claim that they are following the words and actions of the 'excellent example' (Qur'an 33:21) to the letter. The legacy of this example is obviously still with us today and merits a separate discussion (for this see my book *'Nothing to do with Islam? – Investigating the West's Most Dangerous Blind Spot)*[406], but our focus for now should be on the historical implications of the thoroughly reprehensible way in which Muhammad is portrayed in the *hadiths* and the rest of the historical tradition.

On the one hand Muhammad's almost incessant involvement in warfare provides us with the rare opportunity to cross-reference the claims that are being made with actual recorded history since it can be safely assumed that battles that forever changed, or so it is claimed, the political configuration of the Arabian Peninsula would leave at least some mark on recorded history. This angle of investigation will be more fully pursued below.

For the moment, it is instructive to once again note the origins of the *hadiths* 200-300 years after the events that they claim to describe. Origins that are rooted in a time of intense conflict within the Muslim community as well as of Muslim military expansion. In such a setting, it would be only natural to attempt to rally the troops involved in contemporary conflicts by pointing to the intensely belligerent example of the one person Muslim people are supposed to emulate if they desire a good outcome on the Day of Judgment. In this way, the prophet could be used as a prime asset in terms of building morale and drumming up fighting spirit and hatred towards the enemy. The temptation to invent ever more bloodthirsty traditions to 'keep the swords sharp' must have been overwhelming.

It should be clear that this temptation was not, in fact, resisted and we can once again confidently state that we have later conflicts to thank (blame?) for the extremely warlike Muhammad that emerges from the pages of the *hadiths*.

5.3.4. Cross Referencing Key Events from Muhammad's Biography with Recorded History

There are, as mentioned above, elements of Muhammad's biography that were bound to have been noticed by the outside world, had they actually taken place. By checking these incidents against actual recorded history, we can come to certain conclusions as far as the accuracy of the biography of Muhammad as presented in the classical Islam tradition is concerned.

Many events or incidents could possibly have been selected for inclusion in this section, but the four discussed below provide a good representative sample and are also the most likely to have made it into wider history.

The Battle of Badr: The Battle of Badr is one of the most celebrated events in Muslim history. It is also one of the military skirmishes associated with Muslim history for which the highest level of detail is provided in Islamic sources. According to these sources, it took place on Tuesday, 13 March 624 CE (17 Ramadan, 2 AH in the Islamic calendar).[407] The reason for its importance can be found in the fact that it was the first major victory for the Muslim army after the *hijra* (Muhammad's flight to Mecca).[408] Its central place in Muslim historiography is underscored by the fact that Muslim scholars believe that it is discussed at length in the Qur'an (8:38-48). Ibn Ishaq went as far as including the full battle order in his biography of Muhammad.[409] He would also consistently identify someone as a veteran of Badr, if he had occasion to refer to such a person later in his narrative. In short, if there was any battle associated with the career of Muhammad that would have registered outside the Muslim community, this would have been it. It would have sent a very clear signal to both traders and political rulers that there was a 'new kid on the block' who could significantly impact their religious and political relationships with the greatest city, so it is claimed, of the Arabian Peninsula. Yet, just as there are no pre-Islamic mentions of Mecca, there is also not a single outside reference to this most momentous of battles fought by the people of Mecca against Muhammad. The only place where we can read of this battle is in the Qur'an, the *hadith* collections, Ibn Ishaq's biography of Muhammad and later Muslim historical sources. In other words, this supposedly world changing battle is only ever mentioned in Muslim sources. Nowhere else.

Muhammad's Visit to Jerusalem: Media commentators often breathlessly declare that Jerusalem is the 'third holiest city of Islam'.[410] Few of them stop to ask what this special status is based on. If the question is asked, Muslim theologians will invariably point to the visit paid by Muhammad to the city.[411] A visit that is supposedly magnificently commemorated by the Dome of the Rock.[412] This sounds very promising from a historical perspective. The presence of the central human figure of Islam in a well-connected city like Jerusalem might give us some verifiable links to Muhammad. By the 7th century the importance of Jerusalem as central to the claims of Christianity was amply supported by the Eastern Roman Empire and the city was visited by thousands of pilgrims every year.[413] Many of these pilgrims wrote about their experiences and it is, therefore, not inconceivable that a visit by such a towering figure as Muhammad might have left some literary trace. However, when we consult the descriptions of Muhammad's visit any hope of connecting Muhammad's time in Jerusalem with the historical record immediately disappears. According to the Qur'an (17:1)[414] Muhammad journeyed to the 'farthest mosque'. The modern name of the mosque located on the Temple Mount (*Masjid Al-Aqsa*) translate as 'The Farthest Mosque', but it is crucial to remember that the location of 'the farthest mosque' is never identified as Jerusalem in the Qur'an or *hadiths*. In fact, Jerusalem is not referred to directly in the Qur'an at all. This name is, therefore, reflective of later theological developments. In fact, the existence of a mosque in Jerusalem during Muhammad's lifetime seems highly unlikely as there is absolutely no indication of this in the extremely well developed historical tradition dealing with Jerusalem. Secondly, the traditions make it clear that Muhammad's never physically left his home on the night in question. The wife whom he spent the evening with testified that he was in his bed the whole time.[415] Add the claim that Muhammad was transported on the wings of a winged horse, called Buraq,[416] for part of his journey and it becomes clear that we have entered a realm where regular principles of historical enquiry cease to be of any use.

The Massacre of the Banu Qurayza: The massacre of the men of the Jewish tribe of the Banu Qurayza (which supposedly occurred in 629 CE) is very well known to many modern Muslims[417] and the tale is prominent in the classical sources of Islam.[418] In fact, the memory of this event is often invoked in anti-Jewish statements by modern jihadists. More moderate Muslim people, on the other hand, are deeply embarrassed by these events and employ a variety of 'They deserved it' defenses in order to exonerate their prophet for what essentially amounts to an act of genocide.[419] It is not necessary to repeat the full account of what happened here, but in summary we can say that Muhammad was present when hundreds of unarmed Jewish men (and boys who reached the age of puberty, determined by checking for pubic hair) were killed in response to what was perceived as their betrayal of Muhammad. Some traditions even have Muhammad actively participating in the massacre. What is significant in terms of the present discussion is that this action was not aimed at another Arab tribe, but against the Jewish community. In other words, hundreds of members of perhaps the most literate and best-connected community of late antiquity died in this massacre.[420] We can, considering this, expect that the massacre of the Banu Qurayza would have left deep traces on the historical record as news of an event like this would have spread like wildfire throughout the Jewish diaspora. A point of comparison is the massacre of Christians in Najran about a century earlier, news of which reached deep into Europe and Asia (see Section 2.2). We do, in fact, have ample evidence of other anti-Jewish actions and the sensation they caused in Jewish communities around the world.[421] Yet, we once again see no mention in any Jewish text that survived from this period of a massacre of this scale that occurred on the Arabian Peninsula.

Muhammad's 'Documents': Those attempting to link the person of Muhammad with the verifiable historical record sometimes point to certain documents dictated by him (he was illiterate according to Islamic tradition). The three most famous ones are: 1) The so-called 'Constitution of Medina' 2) Muhammad's Final Sermon and 3) A document offering protection to the monks of the St Catherine's monastery in Sinai. In assessing the historical reliability of these documents, we immediately encounter a problem that has been highlighted multiple times already. The records of these documents are found within Islamic sources themselves and they may therefore have been subject to all of the processes of retroactive tradition formation that evidently played such a significant part in the compilation of the *hadith* collections. Thus, if totally independent (i.e. mentions in the contemporary non-Muslim primary source record) corroboration of the existence of these documents cannot be produced, they will have to be regarded in the same light as the rest of the highly questionable Islamic historical tradition.

- In the case of the Constitution of Medina[422], it may very well have been that Muslim sources adapted an existing document that detailed an attempt to reach some kind of settlement between the Jewish and Arab tribes at the oasis of Medina (unlike Mecca there is ample historical evidence for the pre-Islamic existence of Medina and for the fact that it was home to a large Jewish population).[423] There is, however, no definitive evidence outside of the Islamic tradition linking the terms of the settlement to a person named Muhammad. In fact, even the name given to the document was only formalized many centuries after Muhammad was supposed to have lived.[424]

- As far as Muhammad's final sermon is concerned,[425] this is simply part of the accepted Islamic tradition and no mention of this sermon is found in any non-Islamic source. It is, therefore, useless as a non-Islamic reference point confirming elements of the Islamic historical tradition.

- The supposed letter of Muhammad to the monks of St Catherine's Monastery on the Sinai Peninsula is an interesting case. In the letter Muhammad extends his protection to this monastery.[426] The sanctity of this promise is attested to, rather charmingly, by what is claimed to be an imprint of his hand. There are several problems with this document however. Firstly, according to the Islamic tradition, Muslim armies did not conquer the Sinai Peninsula until after Muhammad's death.[427] An offer of protection during his lifetime would, therefore, have been entirely redundant since he did not have forces active in the area according to the tradition. This document is, therefore, probably a very crafty forgery by the monks of the monastery to ensure that their institution would not be attacked when Sinai did come under Muslim attack later. As such it takes its place among a host of forged charter-type documents designed to safeguard the rights of monasteries and other religious buildings.[428]

5.3.5. Muhammad in Contemporary Arabic Sources

Up to this point the focus was on what the Islamic sources themselves have to say about the human figure at the center of Islam. It should be clear from what was presented that the picture of Muhammad that emerge from these sources is confused, contradictory and shows strong evidence of politically motivated back-projection.

Whoever Muhammad was, we simply cannot reach an accurate estimation of him and his ministry from these sources.[429] We cannot, in fact, even conclusively conclude that he existed. It is highly likely that some charismatic religious figure operated in the Arabic and Syriac[430] speaking world in this period, but a huge historical chasm separates this figure from the fully developed 'Seal of the Prophets' so revered by Muslims around the world today.

One way to fill in this historical chasm is to, once again, do what any responsible historian should do right at the outset, namely to consult the earliest sources that have come down to us. Obviously not the Qur'an, *hadiths*, biographies and traditions discussed above, but actual contemporary primary sources. When we consult these primary sources we immediately encounter, instead of the 'full light of history', a murky darkness.[431]

We have already noted that one aspect of this darkness is the fact that the first references to Muhammad written in Arabic (supposedly his own language) only arrive on the scene during the early 690's CE, with a few coins and the famous inscription on the Dome of the Rock in Jerusalem.[432] This is very strange indeed especially given the all-pervasiveness of the formula 'I testify that there is no God but God and Muhammad is the Messenger of God' in fully developed Islam.[433] However this formulation, or any other reference to Muhammad in fact, is simply not present in *any piece of Arabic writing* until sixty years had elapsed since the date on which he supposedly died.

The absence of Muhammad from the early Arabic written record must be profoundly perplexing for those who are committed to upholding a traditional understanding of Islam's origins. Many Arabs were deeply literate, they followed a religion based on a book after all, yet none of them seems to have gotten around to writing down the name of their prophet until almost 60 years after his supposed death date. The stark reality is that the early Arabic historical record presents us with a gaping void as far as the identity of Muhammad is concerned. We, therefore, have to turn our attention to non-Arabic sources in an attempt to fill in the blanks.

5.3.6. Muhammad in Contemporary Non-Arabic Sources

The Arab conquests that occurred from the middle of the 7th century CE involved heavily populated and highly cultured areas.[434] This means that the conquests would be widely commented on, in writing, by those being conquered. Many documents arising from this moment in history survived into the present.[435] It is among such sources, i.e. the earliest primary source descriptions of the Arab conquest, that we are likely to encounter authentic testimonies regarding the existence and activities of Muhammad.

The thing that immediately strikes one upon opening these contemporary testimonies is the complete absence of references to Islam or the Qur'an. Those sitting down to write about their experiences obviously knew that the Arabs were muscling in on their territories, but are somehow completely silent about the supposed main motivation of the conquerors (namely that they are doing it for God and his prophet).[436] Think for a moment how remarkable this is. We are in the habit of referring to the 'Early Muslim Conquests' after the time of the prophet. However, to those being conquered, there was nothing obviously and recognizably 'Muslim' about what was happening. They certainly also did not believe that they were being conquered in the name of a specific prophet.

So, the first thing that should be noted about the picture that emerges from the primary sources is not what we actually find in them, but rather what is absent. There is a deafening silence when it comes to issues, events and persons that stand at the heart of the later Islamic historical tradition.

Secondly it should be acknowledged that there are a handful of contemporary primary sources related to the early years of the Arab conquest that touches on the presence of an influential Arab leader among the incomers. However, when we look closely at these sources they create more problems (from the perspective of traditional Islamic historiography) than they solve.[437]

Perhaps the most neglected group of sources are those written in Syriac: the most widely spoken language in the Roman province of Syria and its borderlands. These documents are the closest, both in terms of geographical distance and chronologically, to the events of the early Arab conquests.[438] Yet many historians figuratively rush past them to concentrate on the much later Arabic tradition. It is in the Syriac documents that we find the first mention of someone known as Muhammad who is associated with the Arab conquests and battles against the Romans.[439] What is striking, however, is that there is no indication that he was a religious leader in the earliest Syriac documents. While we can obviously not expect the Syriac authors to fully understand all the religious motivations of their conquerors, this still seems like an exceedingly curious omission. Because of this omission, these documents add virtually nothing to our understanding of the historical Muhammad beyond the idea that his name was associated with the period of conquest. When we read conquest era documents in other languages, the picture becomes even more confused.

The *Doctrina Jacobi* was a Greek Christian text written between 634 and 640 CE.[440] This is one of the earliest documents that came down to us in which some of the elements of the Arab conquest are described and it, therefore, merits our careful attention. A key passage reads: "And they were saying that the prophet had appeared, coming with the Saracens, and that he was proclaiming the advent of the anointed one, the Christ who was to come. I, having arrived at Sykamina, stopped by a certain old man well-versed in scriptures, and I said to him: "What can you tell me about the prophet who has appeared with the Saracens?" He replied, groaning deeply: "He is false, for the prophets do not come armed with a sword. Truly they are works of anarchy being committed today and I fear that the first Christ to come, whom the Christians worship, was the one sent by God and we instead are preparing to receive the Antichrist. Indeed, Isaiah said that the Jews would retain a perverted and hardened heart until all the earth should be devastated.

But you go, master Abraham, and find out about the prophet who has appeared." So I, Abraham, inquired and heard from those who had met him that there was no truth to be found in the so-called prophet, only the shedding of men's blood. He says also that he has the keys of paradise, which is incredible (i.e. 'unbelievable')".[441]

A few details immediately catch the attention of the reader. It is, firstly, the case that the prophet of the Saracens (i.e. the Arab invaders) is presented as still being alive, despite this text having been written some years after Muhammad supposedly died. Secondly, the prophet of the Arabs seems to be proclaiming some version of Christianity, note especially the references that he foreshadowed the Christ who was to come and that he has the keys of paradise. So whoever this prophet was, his actions and beliefs clearly do not correspond to the traditional accounts of Muhammad's life and ministry.

The next significant reference to a charismatic Arab leader can be found in the Armenian Chronicle (written around 660-670 CE). This chronicle is attributed to a bishop named Sebeos.[442] He refers to a figure named 'Mahmet' and it is safe to assume that he is the same military leader referenced in the earlier Syriac documents.[443] Even so, the picture presented of Muhammad is, once again, significantly at odds with the traditional Islamic account. It depicts Muhammad as being in league with the Jews right up to the end of his life and furthermore, implies that Arabs and Jews are still (by 660-670 CE) the closest of allies.[444] According to standard Islamic history, Muhammad broke off all relationships with the Jewish people in the 620s CE, and the Qur'an even calls the Jews the "worst enemies of the Muslims" (Qur'an 5:82). The chronicle, one of the most detailed discussions that we have of the Arab conquests, once again contains not a single reference to Islam, Muslims or the Qur'an. Instead, we once again encounter a vague, ill-defined Arab monotheism.

We must wait for the writings of John of Damascus (676-749 CE), writing in the middle of the 8th century, for a Christian description of Islam that more-or-less aligns with what we recognize as key modern Muslim beliefs but even at this late stage, it seems clear that the developing religion of the Arabs is still in flux.[445]

Whoever the martial leader of the early non-Arabic documents was, there is precious little to connect him with the 'Muhammad of Faith' revered by more than a billion Muslims today. This 'Muhammad of Faith' suddenly appears on the Dome of the Rock in Jerusalem in 691 CE. Once this name makes its appearance in Arabic, a towering theological edifice is quickly constructed on the rather meager details we can glean from earlier sources (namely that a military leader named Muhammad was active during the Arab conquests). Why and how this happened will be discussed in more detail in Section 8.6.

5.4. Chapter Summary

- It is extremely difficult to construct an accurate picture of the 'historical Muhammad' from the sources available to us. He is mentioned by name only a few times in the Qur'an and upon reading the relevant verses, we are left with material that is mainly theological (in the sense that it deals with his role as a prophet called by God). There is, therefore, very little that we can use to construct an accurate picture of his life.

- When it comes to the *hadiths,* we find an abundance of material supposedly dealing with even the minutest details of Muhammad's life. The problem is, however, that these so-called traditions were written down hundreds of years after Muhammad supposedly lived. This means that there were many opportunities for corruption and additions to occur. That this, in fact, happened can be clearly seen in the inclusion of many miracle stories. Many traditions also seem to have been invented to serve the needs of a particular individual (or groups of individuals) by giving divine sanction for certain practices (e.g. traditions that validate the taking of booty in warfare).

- There are tens of thousands, often contradictory, *hadiths* claiming to provide an accurate picture of the life of Muhammad. If we stick to those that are regarded as sound by Muslim scholars themselves, we are left with an image of Muhammad as 1) Extremely warlike

2) Having a very complicated family life and 3) A prophet with a direct hotline to God. It should, once again, be emphasized that these details emerge hundreds of years after his life and are not based on contemporary historical data.

- One possible way to confirm some aspects of the biography of Muhammad as presented in the official Islamic accounts would be to cross-reference some of the prominent events that they relate with contemporary accounts. Upon doing this we find that even supposedly earth-shattering events (e.g. The Battle of Badr and the massacre of the Jews of the Banu Qurayza) did not raise so much as a ripple in contemporary historical sources, leading to a very strong suspicion that they never happened.

- When we turn to contemporary historical sources for direct references to Muhammad, we find that it took about 60 years after he supposedly died for him to be mentioned in any Arabic text. This is a staggering absence given the eventual ubiquity of the phrase *'I testify that there is no God but God and that Muhammad is the Messenger of God'* within fully developed Islam. Some non-Arabic sources do contain possible earlier references to Muhammad, but the picture that they paint is confused and differs in several key essentials from the Muhammad we find in the official Islamic tradition.

6.

The Qur'an: Proof of Islam's Origin Narrative?

*T*he classic Islamic sources tell us that the ancient city of Mecca was a site of immense spiritual and economic importance. However, by the time Muhammad was born (570 CE), it was adrift in a sea of paganism and barbarity that enveloped the entire Arabian Peninsula. Muhammad was a member of one of the most important tribes of Mecca, the Quraysh, and received a call from God to act as his prophet in a cave just outside the city. Acting upon this call, Muhammad received a series of revelations over a period of about twenty years, right up to his death in 632 CE. **These revelations form what we now know as the Qur'an.** After Muhammad's death, his followers burst out of the Arabian Peninsula in the name of Islam and conquered the Persian and much of the Eastern Roman Empire. The coming of Islam established the Muslim religion, with the message of Muhammad and the city of Mecca at its center, as the pre-eminent belief system from Egypt to Persia within 100 years of the death of the prophet.

6.1. Examining the Official Account of Qur'anic Origins

Some readers may respond to the points so far made in this book by stating that we at least have the Qur'an as a fixed point confirming the early history of Islam. It obviously exists and is undeniably ancient. Is it not all that we need to confirm the early history of Islam? The answer to this question would obviously depend on whether we can prove: 1) That the Qur'an existed during the time when Muhammad supposedly lived, and 2) That it came down to us unchanged since then.

Muslim scholars would obviously answer both questions above in the affirmative. They believe that the Qur'an came down to us in a completely reliable way in an unbroken line from the time of the prophet.[446] In other words, so they claim, the words you are listening to when a modern Muslim recites the Qur'an are the same as the words recited by Muhammad upon receiving the first revelations from Allah. Surely this must serve as the ultimate confirmation of the truth of the Islamic historical accounts? Or does it?

The official Islamic version of how the Qur'an came down to us provides a detailed explanation of how the 'perfect Qur'an' was preserved. The Qur'an was supposedly 'revealed' between 610-632 CE while Muhammad was active as a prophet. Upon receiving an individual revelation, Muhammad entrusted its contents to his followers, many of whom memorized every such utterance by heart. In addition to memorization, some of the revelations were also written down on a wide variety of materials.[447] The death of Muhammad obviously meant the end of new revelations as it is made clear in the Qur'an that he was to be the final prophet sent to humankind. According to the traditional Islamic account, Muslims continued to have access to the Qur'an through those who have memorized it and also through the many written fragments in circulation. Sunni *hadith* collections credit Zaid ibn Thabit[448] (610-660 CE), one of the companions of the prophet (and supposedly someone who memorized the entire Qur'an) with the collection of the various scattered fragments of the book into a single entity.

In his work of collection, Zaid acted on the instructions of the first Caliph, Abu Bakr (reigned 632-634 CE).[449] Abu Bakr had to overcome Zaid's deep reluctance in two areas. Zaid was firstly overwhelmed by the fact that the project would be immensely difficult because of the many scattered fragments of the Qur'an in existence. Zaid claimed that it would have been easier to move a mountain than to bring these fragments together. He secondly hesitated to do something which even Muhammad himself did not attempt. Abu Bakr eventually persuaded Zaid that it was 'a good thing to be done', and so he started the work. Despite Zaid's best efforts, some uncertainty about the exact composition of the Qur'an remained after this initial compilation of the text.

An exceedingly curious aspect of the narration dealing with this earliest compilation of the Qur'an is the extreme reluctance of Zaid to undertake the task. Was it not supposedly the case that there were many people, including himself, who flawlessly memorized the entire Qur'an? If this was indeed the case, compiling the written text could not have been easier. He simply had to gather the memorizers together and have them recite the entire book. Yet, we see that Zaid had to search high and low, even including material written on palm stalks and 'thin white stones' in his final compilation. So even in the official narrative strong hints remain that the process of Qur'anic compilation was not nearly as straightforward as later generations came to believe.

Despite Zaid's best efforts, his compilation did not definitively settle the questions about the Qur'anic text. The standard Muslim historical accounts credit the third Caliph named Uthman (reigned 644-656 CE) with the final standardization of the text of the Qur'an in the year 652 CE. According to Islamic tradition, Uthman collected all the divergent copies of the text, selected one (with the help of Zaid and others), and had all the others burned. Uthman's role in the compiling of the Qur'anic text is so foundational to the traditional Muslim understanding of the origins of their holy text that it is worth quoting the *hadith* in which these events are related in full: "Hudhaifa bin Al-Yaman came to Uthman at the time when the people of Sham and the people of Iraq were Waging war to conquer Arminya and Adharbijan. Hudhaifa was afraid of their (the people of Sham and Iraq) differences in the recitation of the Qur'an, so he said to 'Uthman, "O chief of the Believers! Save this nation before they differ about the Book (Quran) as Jews and the Christians did before." So 'Uthman sent a message to Hafsa saying, "Send us the manuscripts of the Qur'an so that we may compile the Qur'anic materials in perfect copies and return the manuscripts to you." Hafsa sent it to 'Uthman. 'Uthman then ordered Zaid bin Thabit, 'Abdullah bin AzZubair, Said bin Al-As and 'AbdurRahman bin Harith bin Hisham to rewrite the manuscripts in perfect copies. 'Uthman said to the three *Qurayshi* men, "In case you disagree with Zaid bin Thabit on any point in the Qur'an, then write it in the dialect of *Quraysh*, the Qur'an was revealed in their tongue." They did so, and when they had written many copies, 'Uthman returned the original manuscripts to Hafsa. 'Uthman sent to every Muslim province one copy of what they had copied, and ordered that all the other Qur'anic materials, whether written in fragmentary manuscripts or whole copies, be burnt."[450]

The above is, to be sure, a very edifying and satisfying version of events if you are a devout Muslim, but there are several reasons to believe that it represents nothing more than wishful thinking on the part of later Muslim scholars. Even in the *hadiths* dealing with these events, some doubts are already evident. For example: "Zaid ibn Thabit added, "A Verse from Surat Ahzab was missed by me when we copied the Qur'an and I used to hear Allah's Apostle reciting it. So we searched for it and found it with Khuzaima bin Thabit Al-Ansari. (That Verse was): 'Among the Believers are men who have been true in their covenant with Allah' (33:23)".[451] The purpose of the rest of the next section is to look at statements like these and follow them wherever they lead. In the process, we will hopefully be able to determine whether the traditional account can survive any level of critical scrutiny.

6.2. The Traditional Account of Qur'anic Origins under Scrutiny

If the *hadiths* related in the previous section (about the Qur'anic compilations under Zaid and Uthman) are indeed accurate and based on solid historical evidence, then it would confirm much of what Muslims believe about how the Qur'an came into being. It should, however, immediately be stated that they suffer from the very same credibility problem as all other *hadiths*, namely that they were written down hundreds of years after the events they claim to describe. It could therefore be that they simply back-project certain convictions about the origins of the Qur'an from a distant point in the future onto the time of Muhammad and the caliphs.

In the case of the *hadiths* dealing with the origins the Qur'an, we can, in fact, prove the charge of back projection through something as simple as the use of paper. We consistently see references to copies of the Qur'an being written down on paper.[452] The only problem is that paper was not in use in the Arabian Peninsula in the 7th century CE. Paper making only reached the Arabian Peninsula by the 9th century.[453] Before this, documents were written on papyrus or animal skins. Paper was, however, in use in Mesopotamia two hundred years later when many *hadiths* were written down in this part of the world. It is easy to see how what was familiar in one location and age was seamlessly (and anachronistically) transported to another place and age (i.e. from 9th century Mesopotamia to 7th century Arabia in this instance).[454]

Add to the above the fact that we do not find a single reference to the Qur'an in accounts of the Arab conquests. Those who were being conquered by the Arabs were seemingly blissfully unaware that the actions of their conquerors were guided by a written revelation from God. In fact, the first datable references to the Qur'an comes from as late as the middle of the 8th century (i.e. a hundred years after Muhammad died according to Islamic tradition).[455] This provides us with more than enough grounds to be profoundly skeptical of the Muslim belief that the text of the Qur'an was standardized under Uthman. Let us, however, now move from external considerations to the process described in the Zaid and Uthman *hadiths*.

Firstly, the very existence of these *hadiths* makes it clear that the first attempt at compiling a definitive text of the Qur'an was unsuccessful, since Uthman had to repeat the entire process again. Evidently the differences between the different manuscripts were so significant (i.e. more than merely minor copying errors) that a second thorough standardization had to be attempted.

The basic assumption behind the codification of the text seems to have been the belief that some people had all of the Qur'an memorized. In fact, both the *hadiths* detailing the codification under Zaid and Uthman state that the reason for the project was that many of those who committed the text to memory were passing away. We would assume, in light of this, that the best way to preserve the text would simply be to gather the surviving 'memorizers' and write down the text as recited by them. The picture is, however, rather more complex. It is, firstly, interesting to note that there are several *hadiths* in which Muhammad himself admitted to forgetting parts of the Qur'an.[456] This is a troubling snippet of information from an Islamic point of view. Muhammad was supposed to have been the only person who had access to the original revelation. If he forgot parts of it, it would have been impossible to reliably verify the accuracy of the text. So it can hardly be said that the process of Qur'an memorization got off to a flying start.

To make matters worse, the *hadiths* state that with both the codifications under Zaid and Uthman, verses remembered only by a *single person* were included.[457] This should immediately raise questions about the belief that the Qur'an was preserved perfectly in the memories of the faithful. Why did all the other Muslims not memorize these verses? If the Qur'an was indeed in the memories of many of the faithful (including that of Zaid), this would never have happened.

The 'single verse' incidents illustrate how relatively easy it would have been to insert material into the Qur'an. It seems that the memory of a single person was enough to warrant inclusion in the final text. It is hard to imagine a less stringent criterion for the inclusion of a statement into the Qur'an. One that would be very tempting for those involved in intense sectarian conflict to use. What better way could there be to legitimize your position than by 'remembering' a verse of the Qur'an in which the prophet supports your position to a tee?[458]

We also have to wonder about how and why the project to finally codify the text of the Qur'an took place under Uthman. There is no suggestion that he was a scholar of the Qur'an or that he had the document memorized. Instead he makes some rather arbitrary choices by selecting the manuscripts held by one of Muhammad's widows, Hafsa and preferring the *Quraysh* dialect over all others.[459] Uthman, furthermore, certainly followed a rather crude, not to say destructive, approach to textual codification by having all divergent copies burned.[460] This cannot but leave a lingering question in the minds of Muslims. What if the compilers made a mistake by selecting a wrong version and the actual 'words of Allah' ended up in the fire? Be that as it may, the Uthmanic codification speaks eloquently of the utter failure of previous efforts to get Muslims to agree on a text for the Qur'an and comprehensively debunks the idea that the Qur'an that Muslims read today rests on the perfect memories of the earliest followers of the prophet.

The one thing that the codification that supposedly happened under Uthman does is to provide us with an historical line in the sand as far as the compilation of the Qur'an is concerned. The events related above supposedly happened in 652 CE.[461] The accepted tradition states emphatically that afterwards the Muslim community had access to *only a single version* of the Qur'an (as the rest had been burned). This official version was sent to the capitals of the Muslim provinces where it was presumably copied by the scribes for the use of the faithful. By 652 CE these capitals would have included the following cities: Aden, Alexandria, Baghdad, Basra, Cairo, Damascus, Herat and Nishapur.[462] These cities were places where learning flourished and where many scribes plied their trade. We should, therefore, be able to find traces of the Qur'anic manuscripts sent to them in the historical record. If not the original manuscripts, then at the very least some copies made from them. It goes without saying that such copies should align very closely, if not perfectly, with the Qur'an that millions of modern Muslims base their faith on. How could it be otherwise? Muslim tradition steadfastly maintains that Uthman's compilation was the last word in the textual history of the Qur'an and that the text has not been changed at all since then.

Our next port of call should, considering the above, be to delve a little bit into the discipline of textual criticism. In its formal sense, this does not refer to commentary (or criticism) on the contents of ancient texts themselves, but rather to an investigation of how such texts came into existence and how accurately they have been transmitted since then.[463] The stock in trade of the textual critic is, therefore, the comparison of different copies of ancient texts (generally referred to as 'manuscripts') in order to arrive at some conclusions as to the content and shape of the original.

In this case the 'original' that we want to be looking at will be the Uthmanic Text (652 CE) and the main question that we should ask is simply how closely subsequent manuscripts aligned with each other and, therefore, with their supposed 'mother manuscript' (i.e. The Uthmanic text). As we do so please remember, once again, that the traditional Muslim account sets the bar incredibly high as far as this is concerned. According to the official version of events, the Uthmanic text set the standard that all Qur'ans slavishly followed since then. To put it another way, it is firmly believed that when a modern Muslim picks up the Qur'an today he is reading the exact same words that were standardized under Uthman. Or is he?

6.3. A Text Critical Investigation of the Qur'anic Text

In this section we will be looking at the Qur'anic text from a text critical perspective. This will entail investigating both the officially recognized textual lineage of the Qur'anic text (i.e. The Uthmanic tradition) as well as some other traditions that may do much to illuminate the process through which the Qur'an came into being.

Before embarking on this investigation, it may be useful to begin by using the Qur'anic text used by modern Muslims as a reference point. It may come as a surprise to some readers that the version of the Qur'an on which modern Muslims base their faith dates from as late as 1924.[464] It was formalized in Cairo and is, therefore, known as the 'Cairo Text'. This text came into being under the auspices of the Egyptian government, who wanted to produce a definitive version of the so-called 'Hafs' reading of the Qur'an in order to combat the confusion resulting from the fact that a variety of different readings were in use. The text, published on 10 July 1924 (and slightly modified in 1936) has since become the standard Qur'anic text for most of the Muslim world and it is therefore reprinted tens of millions of times per year. It is, for example, the basis of the text printed at the 'King Fahd Complex for the Printing of the Holy Qur'an' in Medina[465] which can produce 30 million copies of the Qur'an per year. The text printed at this complex is known as the King Fahd *Mushaf*.[466] It is the version of the Qur'an that is familiar to millions upon millions of Muslims around the world and we will refer to it regularly over the course of this chapter.[467]

It is interesting to note that the driving force behind the creation of the Cairo text was exactly what also motivated Abu Bakr and later Uthman to undertake the project of producing a standard text. As Gabriel Said Reynolds explains: "...the Egyptian government was motivated to begin the project that would lead to the Cairo Qur'an edition due to the variations (or "errors," as an appendix to the Cairo edition describes them) found in the Qur'anic texts that they had been importing for state schools. In response, the government destroyed a large number of such texts by sinking them in the Nile River and issued its own text. The Cairo project thus followed in the spirit of the caliph 'Uthman, and the governor al-Hajjaj b. Yusuf (d. 95/714), who are reported to have destroyed competing versions and distributed their own text of the Qur'an in the first Islamic century."[468]

The very existence of the Cairo Text means that many Muslims living before 1924 used a different Qur'an from what modern Muslims are reading and reciting. In fact, we can point to many other very different textual traditions in wide use before 1924 (e.g. the *Kufan* text).[469] Some modern Muslims will quickly respond that the Cairo text only smoothed over some discrepancies between different textual traditions and that these changes have no theological implications. This assertion can be challenged on several levels, but the fact that a major revision of the text was necessary should raise serious doubts about the 'Uthman settled it' school of Qur'anic textual criticism because if the text was indeed 'settled' no further revision would be necessary. Even so, many differences can be cited between the Cairo Text, other contemporary versions and especially the supposedly very early Uthmanic texts.[470]

It should also be noted that, although very popular, the *Hafs* tradition (as embodied in the Cairo Text) is not the only Qur'anic textual tradition followed in the contemporary Muslim world. In some Muslim countries, different traditions (e.g. the *Warsh, Qalun* and *al-Duri* traditions)[471] are in widespread use. These textual traditions are known as *qira'at* (literally 'readings') in Arabic and supposedly refers to the way in which the texts were recited by different persons in the distant past. However, they contain marked differences that go way beyond the style of recitation. We sometimes even encounter differences between the objects of verbs between the traditions.[472]

Even more troubling, from a Sunni Muslim perspective, are the Qur'an's circulated by some Shi'a groups that contain two extra chapters (*Suras*). Some Shi'a scholars claim that these chapters (known *as Sura al-Nurayn* and *Sura al-Wilaya*) were left out of the Qur'an during Uthman's standardization of the text.[473]

All of the above should go some way towards dispelling the notion that there is some kind of unbroken 'golden thread' stretching all the way from the Qur'an that modern Muslim people read to the time of Muhammad.

6.3.1. Investigating the Earliest Qur'anic Manuscripts (the Uthmanic *Mushafs*)

Let us now turn to the supposed Uthmanic texts, themselves. Muslim scholars justify their belief in the reliability of the Uthmanic tradition (and therefore a very early codification of the Qur'anic text) by pointing to a series of texts believed to be very ancient manuscripts (known as '*Mushafs*' in Arabic), which are supposedly copies of the Uthmanic text. In fact, it is even claimed that one such manuscript (the Topkapi manuscript)[474] was Caliph Uthman's personal copy of the Qur'an. This certainly seems very promising from a Muslim perspective. If these manuscripts can indeed be shown to date from the mid 600's CE and if they correlate with each other, it will definitively point to an ancient 'mother text' upon which they are all based. It would also do much to validate the rest of Muslim history as it will provide us with tangible links to the earliest years of Islam. Much will therefore depend on the question of the authenticity of the Uthmanic *Mushafs*.

It should in light of the above not be surprising to find that the so-called Uthmanic *Mushafs* have been subjected to intense scholarly scrutiny over the years. In fact, many devout Muslim scholars have worked on these texts, eager for the chance to firmly authenticate part of the Islamic tradition. It turns out, however, that the overwhelming consensus of the academics who analyzed these texts is that none of them can remotely be described as dating from the time of Uthman.

As mentioned, the most famous of the so-called Uthmanic manuscripts is the Topkapi Manuscript (so called because it is housed in the former Topkapi Palace, former residence of the Ottoman Sultan in Istanbul).[475] It is almost an article of faith for many devout Muslims that this manuscript used to be the personal Qur'an of the Caliph Uthman. This idea is, however, dismissed out of hand by two high-profile Turkish scholars who spent years studying some of the oldest Qur'an manuscripts in existence. This is their verdict on the Topkapi Manuscript:

- Prof Ekmeleddian Ishangolu: "Judging from its illumination, the Topkapi Mushaf dates neither from the period when the *Mushafs* of the Caliph Uthman were written nor from the time when copies based on those *Mushafs* were written."[476]

- Dr Tayyar Altikulac: "Even though we would like to publish this sacred text as the *Mushaf* of Caliph Uthman, our research indicated that it was neither the private *Mushaf* of Caliph Uthman, nor one of the *Mushafs* he sent to various centers."[477]

Another famous manuscript about which claims are made regarding its ancient origins is the so-called Samarqand Qur'an (housed in the Hast Imam Library in Tashkent, Uzbekistan).[478] Careful analysis of the text of this copy of the Qur'an, once again, proves that it is not nearly as ancient as is generally believed. This is Dr Altikulac's emphatic answer to the question as to whether this manuscript could perhaps be traced back all the way to Uthman: "[There are] six reasons why it could not be so, including almost no discipline of spelling, different ways of writing the same word, scribal mistakes, copyists' mistakes, written by a scribe who had no writing experience, and later added signs after verses. In conclusion, we can say that the Tashkent [Sammarqand] *Mushaf* was neither the *Mushaf*, which Caliph Uthman was reading when he was martyred, nor any one of the *Mushafs* that he sent to various centers, nor the copy that was kept in Medina for the benefit of the people"[479]

Many other famous manuscripts could be added to the list of supposedly ancient Qur'ans that go right back to the time of Uthman (e.g. the Istanbul *Mushaf*, the Cairo Al-Husayni manuscript and the Petropolitanus manuscript housed in Paris[480] etc.) but it can be shown in every case that they had their origins long after the time of Uthman. It should come as no surprise, given the convoluted Qur'anic codification process described in the *hadiths*, that the supposedly ancient *Mushafs* so deeply revered by Muslim scholars simply add more confusion to the textual history of the Qur'an. In short, instead of anchoring the origins of the Qur'an squarely in the mid-7th century Arabian Desert, these manuscripts merely confirm that the Qur'an is a creation of another time and place.

6.3.2. Divergence within the Accepted Textual Tradition

It can be confidently stated (as I do above) that none of the supposedly ancient Qur'ans (e.g. the Topkapi or Samarqand[481] manuscripts) that are often held up as Uthmanic can be shown to date from the mid-7th century. However, let us assume, for the sake of argument that this was not the case. That these texts are, in fact, reliable records of the earliest Qur'anic textual tradition. Would this assumption solve anything in terms of confirming the traditional Muslim historical account (including the idea that the Qur'an was accurately transmitted and preserved)? Actually the reverse is true. The acceptance of the accuracy of the ancient manuscripts would, in fact, create more problems than it would solve from the perspective of a modern Muslim. This is because it can be shown that these manuscripts differ markedly from each other and from the Qur'ans that modern Muslims use every day.[482]

There are, for example, many instances where entire verses from the older manuscripts are absent from the Cairo 1924 text being used today.[483] In addition to this, hundreds of minor differences between the individual ancient manuscripts and the modern text can be pointed out.[484]

What is perhaps most interesting, and most damaging from an Islamic perspective, is that it can be shown that many of the oldest manuscripts have been tampered with. In his groundbreaking research on the oldest

Qur'anic texts, Dr. Dan Brubaker highlights the following observable changes in the Qur'anic textual tradition: "Insertions (additions to the text between letters, above lines or in margins), erasures (intentional removals of texts from a page), erasures overwritten (writing covering an erasure), overwriting without apparent erasure (altering of a text without an erasure), covering (horizontal strips covering a text), and covering overwritten (which is writing over the top of horizontal strip covering). Brunaker observes that the earliest Qur'ans: "...show few signs of meticulous conformity to a standard, an odd fact indeed considering the care that Muslim historical accounts attribute to the standardization campaign of the caliph Uthman prior to 36 AH/656 AD."[485]

Brubaker maintains that the hundreds of alterations that he documented can only be explained by later generations of Muslim scholars attempting to go back to 'correct' these early manuscripts to be more in line with a later textual tradition. This project was a total failure (as many differences remain) and furthermore illustrate the fact that it is utterly impossible to speak of an impeccable Qur'anic textual tradition stretching all the way back to the time of the prophet.[486]

6.3.3. The Sana'a Qur'an and the Uthmanic Tradition

An interesting opportunity to cross-reference the Uthmanic *hadith* about the codification of the Qur'anic text with hard evidence is presented by the so-called Sana'a Qur'an. Whereas the recently discovered Birmingham Folios (discussed below) are just that, a few pages, the Sana'a Qur'an is a much more substantial collection, part of which can be quite definitively dated to the 7th century.

In 1972, some workmen were clearing out a storage area in the Great Mosque of Sana'a in Yemen. In the process, they discovered some manuscripts of the Qur'an. It was quickly realized that the manuscripts were very ancient and the Yemeni authorities called for outside help in order to assess and restore them.[487] One of the scholars who was intimately involved with this project was the German Islamicist Dr. Gerd Puin.[488] He and other scholars established that the Sana'a manuscript is a palimpsest. In other words, a manuscript that contains two layers.[489] An 'upper text' that is visible and a 'lower text' over which the upper text was written and that can be accessed through a special technique (X-ray fluorescence imaging). The lower text has been dated to the middle of the 7th century and the upper text to the beginning of the 8th century. Between them, both texts contain large portions of what is now chapters 2, 9, 12, 19 and 37 of the Qur'an.

Scholars have determined that the style of writing of both texts (in terms of the way letters are shaped) can be traced to the Arabian Peninsula, making it an even more important find than other ancient Qur'ans (e.g. the one in the Topkapi Palace in Istanbul and the so-called Tashkent Qur'an) that were copied in locations outside of Arabia.

The interesting thing about the Sana'a Qur'an is that both the upper and lower texts differ significantly from the text supposedly selected by Uthman and used by Muslims today. Puin notes unconventional verse orders, textual variations and non-standard orthography. All of this should raise some fundamental questions about the idea that the text of the Qur'an was fixed by the time of the third Caliph. Here we have portions of the Qur'an found in one of the most important mosques of the Arabian Peninsula, part of which can be definitively dated to after the supposed standardization of the text of the Qur'an, that do not align with the standard text.[490] To put it bluntly, arguably the oldest fragments of the Qur'an that we have differ markedly from the Qur'an that millions of Muslims read and recite every single day.[491]

6.3.4. What about the Birmingham Folios?

In 2015, it was breathlessly announced by the media that the oldest copy yet of the Qur'an had been discovered in Birmingham, England.[492] Media reports assured readers that the text could have belonged to one of the companions of the prophet himself as initial Carbon 14 dating indicated that it dates from 650's CE.[493] If that is all you heard about the so-called 'Birmingham Folios' you would assume that they provide powerful confirmation of the traditional Islamic account of Qur'anic origins. Things are, however, not nearly as simple as this.

Most readers will be familiar with the use of Carbon 14 dating (this is where the deterioration in a certain type of carbon molecule is measured in order ascertain the age of an object containing carbon). While this is sometimes used in textual dating, it can typically not be used to give a definitive reading on when a text was produced. The reason for this is certainly applicable to ancient Qur'anic manuscripts. Many of these manuscripts (and this includes the Birmingham Folios) were written on animal skins. This means that a manuscript may have been written on animal skin that belonged to an animal that was killed decades before ink was first applied to its leather. This was a widespread practice as skins were precious and often scraped and re-used multiple times.[494] Unless a way can be found to reliably test the age of the ink (this is very hard to do as it has obviously seeped into the writing surface), there will always be questions about the Carbon 14 dates assigned to documents based on animal skin.

To make matters even more complex, some laboratories which ran follow-up tests on the folios really threw the cat among the pigeons by claiming that the text predates the time of Muhammad.[495] This could, of course, be due to the 'dating ink vs. dating the writing surface' problem described above, but it does show the problems associated with relying solely on Carbon 14 dating in the case of ancient documents. Be that as it may, an early date (i.e. pre-Muhammad) would be fatal to the entire Islamic theological edifice as it will point to parts of the Qur'an being around before supposedly being 'revealed' to Muhammad.

As it turns out, this is exactly the area where the discovery of Birmingham Folios, received with such joy in the Muslim world, could be yet another nail in the coffin of the traditional Islamic understanding of how their holy book came into being. To see why this is the case, we must turn from the uncertain world of Carbon 14 dating to analyzing the text itself. As the name indicates the Birmingham Folios contain only a few pages (i.e. folios) from what is believed to be the Qur'an. They are, therefore, nowhere near to being a complete Qur'anic manuscript. The first thing to note is that the text on these pages do not align perfectly with the Qur'an currently in use by Muslims. It is orthographically different, especially in the fact that it leaves out the Arabic letter '*alif*'. Its verse divisions are also substantially different from the Cairo 1924 text in use today.[496]

When one takes a closer look at the passages that appear on the folios, a rather startling fact emerges: the folios contain material that is quite obviously derived from earlier sources. The Birmingham Folios contain Suras 18:17-31 and 19:91-20:40. The verses from chapter 18 tell a story about some youths who fell asleep in a cave because they were being persecuted for their faith. They are preserved by God and wake up after many years to changed circumstances. This is a straight plagiarization of the Orthodox folk tale known as the 'Seven Sleepers of Ephesus' (see Section 6.4.4.).[497] Chapter 19:98 is strongly related to the Proto-Evangelium of James and the Gospel of Pseudo-Matthew. The section from Sura 20 is a retelling of the Biblical story of Moses. As Joseph Hoffman says: "These are some of the most obviously derivative sections of the entire Qur'an – stories which the Qur'an cannibalizes without attribution, increasing the likelihood that what we may have is not the Qur'an at all but fragments of stories that were eventually incorporated into the Qur'an at a later period."[498]

In other words, far from confirming the Muslim understanding of the early history of the Qur'an, the Birmingham Folios does the exact opposite. It instead confirms that whoever compiled the Qur'an made extensive use of pre-existing materials. Thus, forcefully challenging the pious idea that it was transmitted fully formed into the mind of Muhammad by the Angel Gabriel himself. As Wesley Huff says: "...the Birmingham Qur'an remains problematic for many believing Muslims as it challenges the Qur'anic assertions of being perfect, preserved, and unchanged. Even if the dating proves to be completely wrong, the find would still highlight the reality of textual variants that, according to Islamic literature, simply should not be there. It would point very concretely to there never being one preserved or complete text of the Qur'an throughout its history."[499]

6.3.5. The *Hadiths* on Qur'anic Completeness

In this chapter thus far, we have looked at the fact that the compilation of the Qur'an was a much messier and more complicated process than the one described in the story of Uthman's compilation. Confirmation that the process of bringing the Qur'an together often led to significant levels of conflict within the early Muslim community is provided by an unlikely source: the *hadiths*. We find, for example, traditions that claim that both Muhammad's favorite wife (Aisha) and the second caliph (Umar) testified that a verse was removed from the Qur'an in error.

Aisha was the source of countless *hadiths* and her status as a person to whom the prophet was very close means that many contentious traditions were placed in her mouth.[500] In one such tradition, she stated that the Qur'an was indeed altered in a most surprising way: "The verse of stoning and of suckling an adult ten times were revealed, and they were (written) on a paper and kept under my bed. When the Messenger of Allah expired and we were preoccupied with his death, a goat entered and ate away the paper."[501] The fact that the Qur'an once contained a verse decreeing that adulterers should be stoned is confirmed by no less an authority than Muhammad's successor as the Commander of the Faithful, Umar (reigned 634-644 CE): "Allah sent Muhammad with the Truth and revealed the Holy Book to him, and among what Allah revealed, was the Verse of the Rajam, the stoning of married persons."[502] He also confirms that it was the practice of Muhammad to stone adulterers.[503] This is still the *shari'a* punishment even though the Qur'an does not decree it.[504] So it seems that Islamic law follows a practice that was once included in the Qur'an but cannot be found in its pages anymore.

The disappearance of the 'Verse of the Stoning' raises some troubling questions for believing Muslims. The most fundamental of these is the fact that we have these 'sound *hadiths*' vigorously disputing the current shape of the Qur'an. At the very least that should tell us that there must have been some epic battles about what should make it into the Qur'an and that long after the time of Uthman, some people still had not made their peace with their favorite passages being excluded.

6.3.6. The Crucifixion Verse: Evidence of a Later Addition?

One of the key differences between the Christian and Muslim views of Jesus Christ is a sharp disagreement about the crucifixion of Jesus. While the Christian Gospels are unanimous that he died after being crucified, the Qur'an denies the crucifixion in the strongest terms possible: "They (the Jews) boasted we killed Christ Jesus the Son of Mary but verily they killed him not, nor did they crucify him." (Qur'an 4:157)[505]

This verse has obviously been a massive bone of contention between the two faiths and has been endlessly debated. The purpose of this section is not to enter into this debate, but to show that this verse was almost certainly a later addition to the Qur'an. Thus, providing another piece of evidence for the self-evident truth that the Qur'an simply did not exist in the form that it does today at the end of Muhammad's life. The claim that this verse is a later addition is strongly confirmed by the fact that it is entirely absent from the earlier stages of the developing Islamic tradition.

The Dome of the Rock in Jerusalem was constructed in 691 CE by the Caliph Abd Al Malik (646-705 CE), quite specifically to act as a visual statement of the errors of Christianity from an Islamic perspective.[506] There are verses on the Inner Ambulatory denying the Trinity, the idea that Christ is the Son of God and that call Christians misguided. The presence of this visual statement in the heart of Jerusalem, the place where Christianity emerged, must have been a strong reminder to believing Muslims to completely reject the Christian version of the events surrounding the life of Jesus.[507] It was also a calculated snub directed at the Christian believers of Jerusalem.[508] Now, what would these Christian believers regard as the most important event ever to have happened in Jerusalem? Given the attention paid to this in the Gospels, the answer should be obvious: the crucifixion. Yet, there is one verse that is conspicuous by its absence in the Dome of the Rock's repudiation of Christianity: Qur'an 4:157 cannot be found on any of the original inscriptions of the Dome of the Rock.

The Qur'an is, furthermore, one of the most commented on books in history. Visit any Islamic library and you will see many commentaries on the sacred text so deeply revered by Muslims. Some of these commentaries will have something akin to canonical status in the sense that they are part of the official Islamic theological tradition (known as *Taqlid*). When we pick up these 'official' commentaries, we find them commenting in detail on all the verses of the Qur'an. Well, almost all of them. There is one verse that is conspicuous by its absence: Qur'an 4:157.[509] Think for a moment why this would be the case? It cannot be because this verse has no theological importance. Instead one may consider it as one of the most theologically loaded verses in the Qur'an given its importance for the way in which the followers of Islam are supposed to view Christianity. In fact, many modern Muslims take their cue from this verse as teaching them to absolutely detest the cross. The only possible explanation as to why this verse is absent from the commentaries should be blindingly obvious. It could only have been excluded because the verse in question was not part of the Qur'an at the time when the commentaries were compiled.

6.4. How did the Qur'an Come into Being?

Let us pause for a moment to take stock and recall some of the points made earlier in this chapter. Again and again we saw that considerable doubt can be cast on the official narratives of Qur'anic origins.

- None of the earliest members of the conquered societies who wrote about the Arab conquest had any inkling that their conquerors possessed a holy book, let alone that it was called the Qur'an.

- Archeological finds like the Sana'a Qur'an proves that the text of the Qur'an was still fluid long after it was supposed to have been standardized.

- One of the earliest records that we have of some of the verses of the Qur'an on an inscription can be found on the Dome of the Rock in Jerusalem (built 691 CE). This date is obviously long after Uthman supposedly standardized the Qur'an and yet we see that its inscriptions differ markedly from the Qur'an we have today.[510]

As late as the 730's CE (i.e. 100 years after Muhammad supposedly died), the Christian theologian John of Damascus (676-749 CE) wrote about the sacred scriptures of the Muslims as being a collection of texts rather than a single document. Also, when we analyze John's arguments against Islam, it quickly becomes clear that he had access to only parts of what would now be regarded as the 'full' Qur'an.[511] We would do well to remember that John was a senior official at the Umayyad court and he is writing specifically to equip Christians to respond to the practices and belief system of Islam as he experienced it every day of his life. A life lived at the heart of Muslim power. John of Damascus, therefore, provides us with a precious and informed snapshot of the state of Islam towards the middle of the 8th century. One of the clearest conclusions that we can draw from this snapshot was that the Qur'an was, even at this very late stage, a document that was still in flux. All of this serves to cast significant doubt on traditional versions of the compilation process of the Qur'an, making it almost certain that it emerged in its present form long after the death of Muhammad.

The above points should lead us inescapably to the conclusion that the Qur'an is not a composition that emerged fully formed from the Arabian Desert during the mid-7th century. How do we then account for its compilation? It can be shown that several streams flowed into the Qur'an and that these were then compiled to form a single, not always coherent and consistent, whole.

The idea that the Qur'an 'borrowed' from several sources is, of course, a blasphemous proposition for any believing Muslim. It is a fundamental Muslim belief that the Qur'an is the very Word of Allah and that it, therefore, does not contain human sources. Some orthodox Muslims go so far as to claim that the Qur'an is eternal and that a perfect copy has always been preserved with Allah in heaven. Yet even in the text of the Qur'an itself there is a sense of unease about its origins. Allah, for example, is made to say: "When Our Signs are rehearsed to them, they say: 'We have heard this (before): if we wished, we could say (words) like these: these are nothing but tales of the ancients.'" (Qur'an 8:31[512] see also Qu'ran 6:25[513])

It turns out that this charge is surprisingly accurate since we are not only able to show that the Qur'an does indeed contain 'tales of the ancients', we are also able to show exactly which 'ancients' were used in the compilation of the Qur'anic text. They include the following:

6.4.1. Syrian Christian Material

One of the major themes so far addressed in this work is the close and undeniable link between many of the documents of early Islam and the Syro-Arabian borderlands. It should come as no surprise, therefore, to discover that this part of the world also left clear traces in the Qur'an. These traces can be found in proper names, religious terms, commonly used words, orthography (i.e. the spelling system adopted in the Qur'an), the construction of sentences and foreign historical references.[514] It should be noted, however, that Syriac influence on the Qur'an goes well beyond the provision of much of the linguistic substratum on which the Qur'an is built. In fact (as pointed out in Section 4.1.1) some parts of the Qur'an only begin to make sense when it is assumed that certain passages started life not as some divine word spoken into the heart of Muhammad, but as Syriac Christian liturgical texts.[515] Much of the scholarly work in this area has been done by Christoph Luxenberg in his book 'A Syro-Aramaic Reading of the Koran'.[516] In this ground breaking work Luxenberg lists several examples (complete with convincing and highly technical proofs) of Syriac texts that were essentially plagiarized by the Qur'an.[517]

6.4.2. Jewish Writings

Given the proximity of the environment from which the Qur'an sprang to significant Jewish population centers, it should come as no surprise that there are many parts of the Qur'an that can be traced back directly to Jewish writings. The following are some examples:

- Qur'an 21:51-70[518] (in which Abraham takes issue with his father's idolatry) is an almost exact retelling of an illustration on the dangers of idolatry first penned by a Jewish Rabbi (Rabbi Hiyya) that is retold in the Midrash Rabba.[519] This story was not regarded as inspired or authoritative (and is therefore not part of the Jewish or Christian Scriptures). Instead it can simply be seen as a meditation on the dangers of worshiping idols. Yet, it is accepted wholesale into the Qur'an as part of Allah's eternal word. It should be noted that this story definitely predates the coming of Islam because its interpretation of Abraham's reaction to idolatry, is discussed by the Christian Scholar Jerome (died 420 CE).[520] It is also mentioned in the Jewish 'Book of Jubilees' (of which the oldest copy dates from around the beginning of the 2nd century CE) and in the Babylonian Talmud. It is possible to show how the author or compiler of this part of the Qur'an copied this story almost word-for-word.[521]

- Qur'an 5:30-35[522] (in which a raven shows Cain how to bury his dead brother) has a long pedigree in Jewish folklore. It is told in a collection of Jewish myths and fables known as the Pirke Rabbi Eliezer[523], which is part of the Midrash (in turn a part of the Talmud). In the Midrash, it is Adam who is recorded as burying Abel's body, but otherwise the stories are the same. This difference is consistent with the oral retelling of a well-known story, which is probably how the Qur'anic authors came to hear it. The Jewish link to this part of the Qur'an is proven beyond a doubt by the verse that follows the 'burial lesson' by the raven. It states: "On that account: We ordained for the Children of Israel that if any one slew a person - unless it be for murder or for spreading mischief in the land - it would be as if he slew the whole people: and if any one saved a life, it would be as if he saved the life of the whole people." (Qur'an 5:32)[524] On face value this is a very strange claim to make. What has the raven to do with the killing or sparing of many people? Yet, the Qur'an says that this injunction is instituted 'on that account' i.e. because of what happened with the raven. The connection is obscure to say the least. Yet, when the Midrash (the original source of this story) is consulted, everything falls into place. This is how the Midrash Sanhedrin comments on this text: "We find it said in the case of Cain who murdered his brother. 'The voice of thy brother's bloods crieth,'" (Genesis 4:10). It is not blood here in the singular, but blood in the plural, that is, his own blood and the blood of his seed. Man was created single in order to show him that he who kills a single individual, it shall be reckoned that he has slain the whole race, but to him who preserves the life of a single individual it is counted that he hath preserved the whole race." (Misnah Sanhedrin 4:5)[525] Suddenly everything makes sense. Not only did the compilers of the Qur'an plagiarize an ancient Jewish tale, they also elevated the commentary of a Jewish Rabbi on this incident to the very word of Allah.

- Quran 27:20-40[526] (which tells the story of Solomon and the Queen of Sheba) copies another much older Jewish manuscript, namely the Second Targum of Esther (Targum Sheni).[527] Even a superficial comparison of these two texts will make it abundantly clear that the Qur'anic version can only be described as straight plagiarism.

6.4.3. Extra-Biblical Christian Gospels

In addition to Jewish material, there are also many examples where a Christian substratum to the Qur'an can be identified. We have already noted the heavy reliance of the Qur'anic text on Syriac Christian materials. There is, however, also another major source of Christian influence. This does not come from the canonical gospels (Matthew, Mark, Luke and John). Instead the authors or compilers of Islam's holy text seems to have had access to a cache of apocryphal Christian material. Some examples include the following:

- Quran 19:29-31[528] and 3:46[529] claim that Jesus could speak while he was still in the cradle. This is not something that we find in the canonical Christian gospels. It does, however, occur in a later apocryphal (extra-Biblical) gospel. This is how the 'Arabic Gospel of the Infancy of the Savior'[530] (written at the beginning of the 5th century) speaks of Jesus in the cradle: "We find what follows in the book of Joseph the high priest, who lived in the time of Christ. Some say that he is Caiaphas. He has said that Jesus spoke, and, indeed, when He was lying in His cradle said to Mary His mother: I am Jesus, the Son of God, the Logos, whom thou hast brought forth, as the Angel Gabriel announced to thee; and my Father has sent me for the salvation of the world."[531] Whoever wrote this part of the Qur'an was clearly unaware of the actual origins of this story, i.e. that it does not appear in the canonical Christian Gospels, and is therefore willing to grant it exalted status as the Word of Allah.

- Qur'an 3:49[532] and 5:110[533] both describe how Jesus was able to breathe life into clay birds that he made. This is, once again, not part of the canonical Gospels, but it also comes from the Arabic Gospel of the Infancy of the Savior.[534] This is how this extra-Biblical Gospel relates this story: "And when the Lord Jesus was seven years of age, he was on a certain day with other boys, his companions about the same age. Who at play made clay into several shapes, namely, asses, oxen, birds, and other figures. Each boasting of his work and endeavoring to exceed the rest. Then the Lord Jesus said to the boys, I will command these figures which I have made to walk. And immediately they moved, and when he commanded them to return, they returned. He had also made the figures of birds and sparrows, which, when he commanded to fly, did fly, and when he commanded to stand still, did stand still; and if he gave them meat and drink, they did eat and drink. When at length the boys went away and related these things to their parents, their fathers said to them, Take heed, children, for the future, of his company, for he is a sorcerer; shun and avoid him, and from now on never play with him."[535] What we have here is, once again, the elevation of a story told among the Christians of the Arabian Peninsula to divinely inspired status.

- Perhaps the most startling case of borrowing by Muhammad was from the infancy narratives of the Buddha. The Qur'an tells a story about Allah instructing Mary, giving birth under a tree[536], to eat a few dates from branches that bent towards her while she was overcome with labor pains during the birth of Jesus (Qur'an 19:22-26)[537] These details are lifted from various accounts about the birth of the Buddha (including Nidanakatha Jatakam and Cariya-Pitakim,[538] both included in the Pali Canon, the most authoritative collection of Buddhist texts). The stories seem to have reached the compilers of the Qur'an through their old favorite, The Arabic Gospel of the Infancy of the Savior.[539]

6.4.4. Stories, Legends and Myths

Qur'an 18:10-22[540] tells the story of some young people who were prevented from hearing false doctrine while being shut up (and asleep) in a cave for many centuries. This story shows remarkable similarities to the Orthodox folk tale of the 'Seven Sleepers of Ephesus' and is clearly based on it.[541] The author of this part of the Qur'an was, however, very unclear on some of the details, including the exact number of the sleepers. He, therefore, includes this statement in his retelling of the story: "(Some) say they were three, the dog being the fourth among them; (others) say they were five, the dog being the sixth- doubtfully guessing at the unknown; (yet others) say they were seven, the dog being the eighth. Say thou: "My Lord knoweth best their number; it is but few that know their (real case)." Enter not, therefore, into controversies concerning them, except on a matter that is clear, nor consult any of them about (the affair of) the Sleepers." (Qur'an 18:22)[542]

This confusion about the number of 'sleepers' is powerful confirmation that this is a story borrowed from somewhere else that was perhaps only half-remembered. Isn't Allah supposed to be the author of this book? If so, why does he not simply tell the readers how many sleepers there were? Instead we are faced with a narrator who is uncertain about the exact details of the story and admits as much.

There are many other instances where we can show that the compilers of the Qur'an drew deeply on the folklore of the ancient Near East. We can, for example, find traces of the Epic of Gilgamesh[543], the legend of Gog and Magog[544] and the exploits of Alexander the Great[545] in its pages.

6.4.5. Zoroastrian Influence

Besides these clear cases of plagiarism from Jewish and Christian sources, there are also several instances where we can point to Zoroastrian (the ancient Persian religion) origins for some Qur'anic and Islamic concepts. These include the following:

- The '99 Names of Allah' are probably derived from the names of Ahura Mazda[546] (chief 'good God' in Zoroastrianism) not only in terms of the concept, but also in terms of some of the individual names. Many of these seem to have been lifted straight out of the Avesta (one of the key scriptures of the Zoroastrian religion).[547]

- The use of *'Bismillah* al Rahman al Rahim" (In the Name of Allah the Most Gracious, the Most Compassionate), the formula that begins every Sura (chapter) of the Qur'an[548] copies a Zoroastrian work called the Dasatir I Asmani.[549] This book begins each of its fifteen chapters with the following formula: "In the name of God, the Giver, the Forgiver, the Merciful, the Just"[550]

- Foundational to the Muslim doctrine of salvation is the *sirat mustaqim*, most often translated as the 'straight path' (a concept that is foundational to the first chapter of the Qur'an).[551] This term is sometimes used in relation to a razor thin bridge over hell that believers will have to cross before they can reach paradise.[552] This is copied from an ancient Pahlavi book called the Dinkart.[553]

- Qur'an 52:20 promises the (male) faithful: "They will recline (with ease) on Thrones (of dignity) arranged in ranks; and We shall join them to Companions, with beautiful big and lustrous eyes."[554] These women (called *huris* in Arabic)[555] are derived from the *hurust* of Zoroastrian belief.[556]

6.4.6 The Compilation and Editing of the Qur'anic Text

The many strands that were weaved into the Qur'an, in addition to the fact that it took more than a century after the supposed death of Muhammad for it to be regarded as the 'holy book' of a religion called Islam, should immediately alert us to the fact that it must have come into existence through a long and complicated process. As such it cannot in any way be used to confirm the accuracy of the traditional Islamic historical accounts (including accounts of where the Qur'an came from). The most that we can say is that the Qur'an was systematized from a mass of material (Christian, Jewish, Zoroastrian and legendary) into the single book that we have today. This was a process that took a considerable time. As we have seen, as late as the 730's CE John of Damascus (living at the heart of the Muslim empire) still regarded the Qur'an as collection of separate documents and not as a single book.

The exact process of how the systemization of the Qur'anic text occurred will probably forever be obscured by the mists of time. We can, however, take an educated guess as to the identity of an individual who was probably involved in the earliest stages of this process. This role is even confirmed by the Islamic traditions themselves. Al-Hajjaj Ibn Yusuf Al-Thakafi (660-714 CE) was an important early Muslim teacher and leader[557] who rose to become the governor of Baghdad.[558] He taught Arabic at Ta'if before embarking on a public career.[559] As a recognized master of the Arabic language, he was well placed to undertake a project to make the Qur'an more intelligible. Most of his changes had to do with the adding of diacritical marks to enhance the readability of the text. He certainly went beyond tinkering on the sidelines however. It is said that he added more than 1000 *alifs* (the first letter of the Arabic alphabet) to the text of the Qur'an. Interestingly a tradition is preserved where it is stated that Al-Hajjaj made no fewer than 11 changes to the actual text of the Qur'an.[560] Muslim apologists naturally attempt to cast doubt on the accuracy of this tradition, but it is instructive to note its existence.[561] It is clear from this that at least some of the compilers of the *hadiths* thought that changing the Qur'an was a perfectly acceptable thing to do, to the point of including a description of such changes in a *hadith* collection (the *hadith* collection of Abu Dawood in this case[562]). As such, we can say that at least some memory of the complex process of how the Qur'an came into being survived. The reasons behind this complexity will become clear in the final two chapters of this book.

6.5. Chapter Summary

- The purpose of this chapter was to evaluate whether the Qur'an can be used to provide a solid marker in terms of validating some of the key aspects of the traditional Islamic historical accounts. Particular attention was paid to the generally accepted narrative of Qur'anic origins namely that the Caliph Uthman did Islam the immense service of collecting a variety of divergent readings, choosing an authoritative version, and publishing it as the definitive record of Allah's word to humanity.

- The first and most basic problem with the traditional account of how the Qur'an came into being is the simple fact that this was committed to paper more than 200 years after the events that it described supposedly occurred. In fact, it took about a century after the traditional death-date (632 CE) of Muhammad for the Qur'an to emerge onto the world stage.

- When we subject the text of the Qur'an as we now have it to a text critical evaluation we see that the constantly repeated Islamic mantra that the book was 'Never changed, never altered' is little short of laughable. A comparison between the Cairo Text (used by modern Muslims) and earlier Qur'anic manuscripts reveals a vast number of changes, additions, corrections and other editorial interventions.

- The fact that serious questions can be asked about the textual history of the Qur'an can also be confirmed by looking at some of the very earliest Qur'anic texts, the Birmingham Folios and the Sana'a Qur'an. The first is filled with examples of earlier material from a variety of sources that made it into the Qur'an and the second is a post-Uthmanic Qur'an that differs markedly from the supposedly once-and-for-all definitive edition promulgated by Uthman.

- While the Qur'an does contain some original Arabic material, it is also, as we have seen, filled with much that was plagiarized from other sources. These range from Syriac Christian material, pseudo-Gospels, Jewish writings, folk tales and even Zoroastrian theological concepts. All of this confirms what should be obvious to the attentive and historically aware reader. Rather than a work authored by a single author (divine or human), the Qur'an is almost certainly composite work that reflects the complex theological, ideological, cultural and linguistic melting pot from which it emerged.

7.

The Post-Muhammad Period: Muslim Conquest and Victory?

*T*he classic Islamic sources tell us that the ancient city of Mecca was a site of immense spiritual and economic importance. However, by the time Muhammad was born (570 CE), it was adrift in a sea of paganism and barbarity that enveloped the entire Arabian Peninsula. Muhammad was a member of one of the most important tribes of Mecca, the Quraysh, and received a call from God to act as his prophet in a cave just outside the city. Acting upon this call, Muhammad received a series of revelations over a period of about twenty years, right up to his death in 632 CE. These revelations form what we now know as the Qur'an. **After Muhammad's death, his followers burst out of the Arabian Peninsula in the name of Islam and conquered the Persian and much of the Eastern Roman Empire. The coming of Islam established the Muslim religion, with the message of Muhammad and the city of Mecca at its center, as the pre-eminent belief system from Egypt to Persia within 100 years of the death of the prophet.**

For the sake of clarity, it may be good, in this case, to expand our introductory paragraph a little to include some extra information about what the standard Islamic view entails.

It is believed that by the death of Muhammad the tribes of central Arabia had abandoned paganism and that they united under the banner of Muhammad and Islam. They then proceeded, under the command of four 'rightly guided

179

caliphs' to mount a lightning-fast advance of Muslim armies into both the Roman and Persian Empires. Within a few short years, both these empires would be dealt devastating blows (a fatal blow in the case of the Persian Empire) by the Muslim forces who very quickly established the domination of Islam over public religious life. Religious zeal is consistently portrayed as the most significant motivating factors behind the conquests. In short, the conquerors were conquering in the name of Islam.

7.1. Muslim or Arab Conquest?

Historical sources dealing with the middle of 7th century are unanimous that the Middle East was shaken by a significant political realignment during this period. We see, in short order, the displacement of the 'Great Powers' of the day (i.e. Rome and Persia) by Arab tribes and later the emergence of Arab-led dynasties (i.e. the Umayyad and Abbasid Empires). Unlike many of the other so-called historical facts associated with the early years of Islam, the Arab conquests are well attested to historically. A multitude of primary sources can be cited to show that they did, in fact, occur and that they profoundly disrupted what many people thought of as the settled order of the world.[563] The question of how these conquests occurred, and what they were motivated by, are obviously of immense interest for our purposes.

The first thing that we need to note is that no one thought of calling the Arab invaders 'Muslims'. In fact, the first documented reference to the term Muslim only appears on the 'Dome of the Rock' (constructed in 691 CE), sixty years after the date traditionally given for the death of Muhammad.[564] Prior this the Arabs were simply referred to as such (i.e. their ethnic or linguistic identity was emphasized).[565] When they were not referred to as Arabs, those who discussed the conquerors used words denoting their identity as migrants (*Magaritai*[566] in Greek and *Mahgraye*[567] in Syriac). An Arabic version of this term is *Mujahirou*n (i.e. those who participated in a *hijra* or migration).[568] The reason behind this term could be the fact that Arabs were coming in from central Arabia to settle Syria, Palestine and northern Arabia. This filled the vacuum left by super-power weakness. It seems, in light of this, that the most important fact that people, including they themselves, noticed about the Arabs was that they were 'incomers', not their religious identity.

Some other names were also used for the Arabs, these include *Hagarenes*[569] and *Saracens*.[570] It is quite evident, therefore, that those who wrote about the Arab conquests had no shortage of titles with which to refer to the Arab invaders. Yet the name given to them by the traditional Islamic historical accounts (i.e. 'Muslims') is *entirely absent* from the primary source record for the first six decades of these conquests.

The era of conquest brings us into a time when Muslim forces supposedly grappled with two of the most powerful entities of late-antiquity. This means that it should theoretically be possible to cross-reference Muslim accounts with Syriac[571], Persian[572], Roman[573] and other records. It is, once again, baffling to note that this is rarely done. As with the traditions dealing with the earliest years of Islam, so with the conquest period, Muslim accounts (committed to paper hundreds of years after-the-fact) are mostly accepted without question. Just how wrong-headed this approach is will become clear through the course of this chapter as it will be shown that on point after point, the Muslim accounts are contradicted by contemporary historical sources. It is to some of these sources that we now turn.

7.2. Non-Arab Writings on the Arab Conquests

Muslims sources dealing with the Arab conquests were committed to paper more than 200 years after the events they supposedly describe. They can, therefore, in no way be regarded as the earliest documentary evidence related to the origins of Islam and the Arab conquest. There are, however, many other well-attested documents that describe this period of the Arab conquest. This is because the Arabs conquered territories (including Egypt, Syria and Persia) where literacy was firmly established among the elites. We can, therefore, turn to the writings of the conquered societies to gain a contemporary perspective on the conquest. It should, by now, not be surprising to find that these sources paint a very different picture of the early origins of Islam from the one presented in the traditional Islamic accounts.

This section will profile some of the most important and accurately sourced early documents that discuss the Arab conquests. The basic question that will be addressed is, once again, whether these documents support the idea that Islam emerged fully formed from the Arabian Desert in the 630's CE. It will quickly become apparent that they do not.

Some of the most important non-Arabic documents discussing the conquests are presented below.

The *Doctrina Jacobi* (written between 634 and 640 CE) is a Greek Christian tract.[574] It is perhaps the earliest document that came down to us in which some of the elements of the Arab conquest are described in some detail. A key passage reads: "And they were saying that the prophet had appeared, coming with the Saracens, and that he was proclaiming the advent of the anointed one, the Christ who was to come. I, having arrived at Sykamina, stopped by a certain old man well-versed in scriptures, and I said to him: "What can you tell me about the prophet who has appeared with the Saracens?" He replied, groaning deeply: "He is false, for the prophets do not come armed with a sword. Truly they are works of anarchy being committed today and I fear that the first Christ to come, whom the Christians worship, was the one sent by God and we instead are preparing to receive the Antichrist. Indeed, Isaiah said that the Jews would retain a perverted and hardened heart until all the earth should be devastated. But you go, master Abraham, and find out about the prophet who has appeared." So I, Abraham, inquired and heard from those who had met him that there was no truth to be found in the so-called prophet, only the shedding of men's blood. He says also that he has the keys of paradise, which is incredible (i.e. 'unbelievable')."[575]

There are, as mentioned earlier, a few details that immediately catch the attention of the reader. It is, firstly, the case that the prophet of the Saracens (i.e. the Arab invaders) is presented as still being alive, despite this text having been written at least two years after Muhammad supposedly died. Secondly, the prophet of the Arabs seems to be proclaiming some version of Christianity, note especially the references that he foreshadowed the Christ who was to come and that he has the keys of paradise. So whoever this prophet was, his actions and beliefs clearly do not correspond with the traditional account of who Muhammad was.

Sophronius (died 639 CE) was the Patriarch (senior Christian religious leader) of Jerusalem during the Arab invasion.[576] He wrote at length about the plight of the Christian community in Jerusalem under the Arabs and portrays the fall of Jerusalem as part of the judgment of God on a community that strayed from His ways.[577] His accounts are interesting both in terms of how the invaders are portrayed and in terms of what is absent from his description of events. Traditional Muslim versions of the history of the capture of Jerusalem by the Arabs state that they were particularly magnanimous and treated the Christian population with the greatest respect.[578] This is certainly not the perspective of the patriarch. He portrays the Arab invasion as an utter calamity and describes their conduct in the bleakest and darkest of terms. Far from respecting the Christians, it seems the Saracens (as he habitually refers to the Arab invaders) even went as far as pulling down churches.[579] This is significantly at odds with the way Muslim sources would later come to interpret these events. What is perhaps more significant for our purposes is the fact that Islam is entirely absent from the descriptions of the Patriarch. He calls the Saracens 'godless' and 'Fighters against God', but there is no indication in any of these writings that the Arabs had a specific prophet, a specific book or a specific religion called Islam. This is a remarkable omission, given the traditional Muslim account of these events. It is even more so because Sophronius is writing to strengthen his community and to help them to withstand the pressures that the Arabs are applying against them. In this context, it would have made perfect sense to address features of the religious beliefs of the Arabs in order to equip his flock to better interact with them. Yet, in none of the writings of Sophronius that have come down to us is there any indication whatsoever that such a thing as Islam even existed. This is utterly remarkable because it comes from a source who was an eyewitness to the conquest and who lived cheek-by-jowl with the Arabs over an extended period.

The Armenian Chronicle (written around 660-670 CE) is attributed to an Armenian bishop named Sebeos.[580] Here, finally, we have a reliably sourced reference to Muhammad (called 'Mahmet' in the chronicle), a full thirty years after he was supposed to have died. Even so, the picture presented of Muhammad is, once again, significantly at odds with the traditional Islamic account. It depicts Muhammad as being in alliance with the Jews right up to the end of his life and furthermore, implies that Arabs and Jews are still (by 660-670 CE) the closest of friends. According to standard Islamic history, Muhammad broke off all relationships with the Jews in the 620's CE, and the Qur'an even calls Jews the "worst enemies of the Muslims." (Qur'an 5:82)[581] The chronicle, one of the most detailed discussions that we have of the Arab conquests, once again contains not a single reference to Islam, Muslims or the Qur'an. Instead, we once again encounter a vague, ill-defined Arab monotheism.

By 730 CE, the Christian theologian John of Damascus, living at the heart of the Islamic Empire, wrote a polemic work against Islam.[582] He identified certain key elements that we would now recognize as being in line with how Islam developed. But even at this late stage it seems that certain aspects of Islam were still very fluid. John, for example, had no idea of the existence of a single work called the Qur'an and instead seems to regard the Muslims as possessing separate writings which they base their faith on.[583] This occurred more than a century after the Qur'an was supposed to have been compiled and standardized.

7.3. The Missing Caliphs

This brief survey of non-Muslim sources writing about the Arab conquests should, at the very least, cause us to be rather suspicious when it comes to the reliability of the much later officially accepted Islamic descriptions of this period. These suspicions will be strongly confirmed when we search for the names of the Caliphs in the historical record. Muslims believe that Muhammad was followed by a series of Caliphs (literally 'successors').[584] The first four of these are known as the 'Rightly Guided Ones' (or 'Rashidun')[585] and the period of their rule is still viewed by many Muslims as a vanished golden age. According to the official version of Sunni Muslim history, these Caliphs ruled for the following periods:

- Abu Bakr: 632-634 CE
- Umar ibn al-Khattab: 634-644 CE
- Uthman ibn 'Affan: 644-656 CE
- 'Ali ibn Abi Talib: 656-661 CE[586]

If the absence of Muhammad from the wider historical record is puzzling, it is doubly the case for these leaders. It could perhaps be argued that Muhammad never ventured outside of the Arabian Peninsula (except for a mythical 'night journey' to Jerusalem)[587] after taking up the mantle of leadership of the Muslim community. In the case of the men listed above, however, Muslim history tells us that they had a stunning impact on the wider world.

Abu Bakr supposedly launched the early conquests as Muslim armies started to threaten the Persian and Roman empires.[588] Umar was at the head of these armies as they conquered first Jerusalem[589] and then the Sassanian (Persian) Empire[590] and he thus became the ruler of one of the most important political entities of late antiquity. Under Uthman the wide-ranging conquests continued (albeit at a slower pace) and he is pictured as a man with enough political control to standardize the text of the Qur'an over a vast area.[591] Ali, who would go on to become the major figure within Shi'a Islam, stood at the center of the first Islamic Civil War (known as the 'Fitna')[592], a conflict that supposedly tore the Islamic world apart and that had stunning repercussions in terms of the political stability of the areas ruled over by Islam.

In short, the official Islamic record paints the 'Rightly Guided Caliphs' as giants on the geopolitical stage of their day. Yet, as with Muhammed, they are absent from the primary source record dealing with this period. We must wait for documents (especially the histories of Muhammad Al-Tabari, 839-923 CE and Ibn Kathir, 1300-1372 CE) that were written hundreds of years after their supposedly glorious exploits to even learn of their existence.[593] Think for a moment how utterly implausible this is. We have primary source evidence for even the minutest engagements in the back-and-forth wars between the Romans and Persians.[594] Yet the person who supposedly finally brought Persian Empire to its knees (Umar ibn al-Khattab) is never so much as mentioned in the contemporary primary source record. This simply beggars belief.

The first of the Arab caliphs to definitively appear in traceable archaeological records is not one of the four 'Rightly Guided' ones, but a ruler named Muawiya. He was the first leader of the Umayyad Caliphate and acted as

Caliph from (661-680 CE).[595] The only problem, from a Muslim perspective at least, is that Muawiya is not presented as a Muslim ruler at all. As we will see below, an inscription on a dam near Ta'if (in modern-day Saudi Arabia) built around 678 CE simply calls him 'The Commander of the Faithful'.[596] No mention whatsoever is made to Mecca, to Muhammad or to the Qur'an. This is very surprising considering the subsequent insistence on the Islamic confession of faith on all official documents and inscriptions.[597]

7.4. Misdirected Mosques

One of the basic facts that most people know about Islam is that Muslims pray while facing Mecca.[598] Muslims believe that this is mandated in the Qur'an where Allah instructs the faithful to pray in the direction of the 'sacred mosque' (cf. Qur'an 2:142-145, 149-150).[599] Muslim commentators on this text are unanimous that this can only refer to the mosque (with the *Ka'aba* at its center) in Mecca that is still the focus of all Muslim prayer.[600] Since this statement is in the Qur'an itself, and is dated to 624 CE by Muslim scholars, we can assume that all mosques built during the Islamic conquests would have had *qiblas* (prayer directions) pointing towards Mecca. The problem, from an Islamic perspective, is that this is simply not the case. Many ancient mosques have been excavated and the floor plans of the oldest among them do not align with an orientation towards Mecca. Here are some examples of the oldest mosques in the Islamic world and their alignments:

- The Al-Aqsa Mosque, Jerusalem (built 709 CE). This is one of the oldest and most important mosques in the Islamic world.[601] However, instead of towards Mecca it points to 169.23 degrees (i.e. towards the south of the modern country of Jordan).[602]

- Wasit, Iraq (built 702 CE)[603]: This mosque should be oriented to the southwest (in order to point at Mecca). Instead it is oriented towards a spot between Jerusalem and Mecca.[604]

- Kufa, Iraq (supposedly built in 670 CE)[605]: Kufa is northeast of Mecca so one would expect the mosque to be oriented to the southwest. Instead it is oriented to the West.

- Fustat (now part of Cairo, built in 714-719 CE): This mosque was supposedly built by the Islamic conqueror of Egypt, Amr ibn al-Aas.[606] Mosques in this part of Egypt must be oriented to the southeast if one is to pray towards Mecca. Yet the original orientation of the Fustat mosque was almost due east.[607]

- The above is only the tip of the iceberg as far the issue of mosque misalignment is concerned. In his excellent work entitled 'Qur'anic Geography', author Douglas Gibson lists page after page of ancient mosques[608] along with satellite photos showing their original alignment. The list of mosques whose *qiblas* did not face Mecca reads like a 'Who's Who' of ancient Islamic architecture and includes buildings in: Quangzhou, China[609] (reputedly built in 630 CE); Ba'albek, Lebanon[610] (700 CE); Sana'a, Yemen[611] (705 CE), Amman, Jordan[612] (700 CE) and Damascus, Syria (709 CE)[613].

In plotting the alignments of the mosques listed above, Gibson identifies a clear and undeniable pattern. The 'misalignments' of the oldest mosques were not random at all. Instead, all mosques built before the 8th century CE are oriented to a spot hundreds of miles north of current location of Mecca.[614] In addition to Gibson's work, we can also point to excavations of the palaces of Umayyad rulers. The Umayyads were the first Islamic dynasty according to Muslim historical accounts so we can expect their buildings to conform to Islamic ideals. Yet we see in the floor plans of their palaces in places like Humeina[615] (built 700 CE) and Amman[616] (built 710 CE) the same trend that we have already observed. Their prayer rooms are not oriented towards Mecca, but to a point much further north. This pattern is so consistent that it acts as a powerful confirmation of the theory that Islam's original holy city was probably located not in central Arabia, but in the Syro-Arabian borderlands of northwest Arabia.

Some Muslims respond to the undeniable fact that none of the earliest mosques pointed towards Mecca by stating that this is due to computational errors made by the original builders.[617] This stretches credulity beyond breaking point. The Arabs were renowned as some of the best navigators of Late Antiquity.[618] They were, after all the people who had to navigate the vast emptiness of central Arabia with nothing more than the stars as their guides.[619] Also, many of the misaligned mosques were to be found in very sophisticated and cultured cities (e.g. Sana'a, Cairo, Damascus and Jerusalem). If the Arabs could not accurately plot a direction, then there would have been plenty of people around to correct their mistakes. It is lastly, very important to once again emphasize that the misalignment of these early mosques was not random. Instead they all consistently point towards northwestern Arabia. So, if we are asked to believe that the early mosque builders made mistakes, we are surely entitled to ask in response why they all seemed to have made *exactly the same mistake* by all pointing their mosques at the same point in northern Arabia, hundreds of miles from Mecca.

It is important to note that we do not only have archeological evidence for the fact that post-conquest Muslims did not pray towards Mecca, but rather towards a point much further north. Plenty of literary evidence can be cited as well. There is, for example, an Islamic tradition that states that Amr ibn al Aas (Islamic conqueror of Egypt) prayed towards the east.[620] Also, in 705 CE the Christian chronicler Jacob of Edessa (modern Urfa in Turkey) wrote as follows about the practices of the Arab (he calls them Mahgraye[621]) in his part of the world: "So from all this it is clear that it is not to the south that the Jews and the Mahgraye here in the regions of Syria pray, but towards Jerusalem or the *Ka'aba*, the patriarchal place of their race."[622] Note that the mention of a Ka'ba here does not imply a reference to Mecca. There were many cube shaped buildings (i.e. *Ka'abas*) dotted across Arabia and many of them were the focus of worship.[623] It would stand to reason that such a structure would have been part of Islam's original holy city, wherever this was.

In his work on the early mosques Gibson identifies an interesting pattern. All mosques built in the 7th century and during the early 8th century point reliably towards northwestern Arabia. Between the years 725-822 CE confusion reigns with 12% of mosques pointing to northwestern Arabia, 50% towards Mecca and 38% running parallel to a line drawn between northwestern Arabia and Mecca.[624] This period corresponds with the second Islamic civil war and it can, therefore, be logically concluded that deep disagreements about the direction of prayer were part and parcel of this conflict. It is only when the Abbasid Dynasty[625] begins to firmly pacify areas previously hostile to their rule (i.e. from 822 CE onwards) that mosques begin to uniformly point towards Mecca. Thus, it took almost 200 years after the death of Muhammad to finally and formally standardize the direction of prayer towards the modern location of Mecca.

There are several theories as to where exactly the earliest mosques pointed to. Gibson makes a very strong and compelling case that the ancient Nabataean capital, Petra[626] (in modern day Jordan) was the original holy city of Islam and it is indeed the case that directional lines drawn from the earliest mosques all seem to converge in the general vicinity of Petra (more about the Petra hypothesis in Section 8.1). Others maintain that the direction of prayer was not changed away from Jerusalem until decades after Muhammad's death (thus contradicting an essential part of Islam's origin narrative).[627] Still others believe that there may have been a yet to be discovered shrine somewhere in northwestern Arabia.

The standardization of mosque prayer directions after 822 CE necessitated a lot of building work to bring earlier structures into line. This may be easy to do on the inside of such buildings (i.e. simply install a marker or niche on the wall in order to point people towards Mecca), but it is an entirely different matter when it comes to the entire building. Thus, the lopsided and misdirected nature (where people would face in a different direction from the one in which the building itself was oriented) of Islam's oldest mosques[628] bear eloquent testimony to a time when the faithful prayed towards a holy city that was at the opposite end of Arabia from where Mecca is located. This necessarily raises significant questions about the accuracy of traditional Muslim accounts of the period of Arab conquest and the insistence that the invaders were devout followers of a religion focused on the city of Mecca.

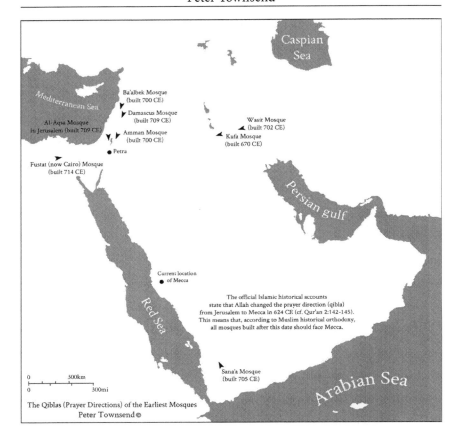

The Qiblas (Prayer Directions) of the Earliest Mosques
Peter Townsend ©

7.5. The Survival of Paganism

The traditional Islamic account states that paganism was eradicated in the Arabian Peninsula by the end of 632 CE (i.e. just after the death of Muhammad), and that after this date Islam was totally dominant with no pagan remnant to contend with.[629] Yet, there is plenty of evidence for the survival of paganism among the Arabs long after the last pagan tribe was supposed to have been defeated by Muslims. A Nestorian Christian Synod held in 676 CE[630] declared, for example, that believing women among the Arabs should avoid living with pagans. It then goes on to describe the practices of these pagans (including elaborate funeral ceremonies, that have no place in Islam), leaving us in no doubt that the reference here is to real pagans and that 'pagans' is not just a slur aimed at the Muslims.

Along the same lines, Athanasius II Patriarch of Antioch (683-686 CE) warns his flock to disassociate from the pagans (in an area where they are not supposed to be at all if the Islamic account is to be believed).[631] It is, again, clear that he refers to actual pagan practices (and not Islamic ones) as he mentions the strangulation of animals that are sacrificed by these pagans. Strangulation of animals is not something that is a feature of Islamic worship. These two examples, and others could be added, make it clear that paganism survived in the very areas where it was supposed to have been eradicated according to the Islamic account.

The clear evidence that paganism persisted in Arabia long after the Arab conquests is just one more example of how unreliable the standard Islamic traditions are and how little they correspond with the witness of contemporary sources.

7.6. The Early Umayyad Caliphate: Archaeological and Documentary Sources

It should be evident by now that serious questions can be asked about the idea that Islam emerged fully formed from the Arabian Desert to embark on the conquests for which it became famous. These questions, including whether we can talk about a 'Muslim Conquest' at all will only deepen when we consider the recorded histories of Islam's earliest ruling dynasties. The first of these dynasties were called the 'Umayyads'.

We have already noted above that the early Caliphs are absent from contemporary records. The first Arab ruler to definitively appear in the record was Muawiya ibn Abi Sufyan[632] (who reigned as Caliph from 661-680 CE). Muawiya is viewed as the founder of the Umayyad Caliphate[633] that dominated the Arab world from 661-750 CE. He was succeeded by the following rulers, all of whom are substantially present in the contemporary historical record:

- Yazid I (680 – 683)
- Muawiya II (683 – 684)
- Marwan I (684 – 685)
- Abd al-Malik (685 – 705)
- Al-Walid I (705 – 715)
- Sulayman (715 – 717)
- Umar II (717 – 720)
- Yazid II (720 – 724)
- Hisham (724 – 743)
- Al-Walid II (743 – 744)
- Yazid III (744)
- Ibrahim (744)
- Marwan II (744 – 750)

The rulers of the Umayyad dynasty all ruled from Damascus.[634] Their rule came to an end with the emergence of the Abbasid Caliphate (750 CE)[635], whereupon the capital of the Islamic empire was moved from Damascus to Baghdad.

The reign of the first three Umayyad Caliphs (Muawiya I, Yazid, and Muawiya II) is known as the Sufyanid Period (661-685 CE).[636] This was followed by the Marwanid Period (685-750 CE)[637] after Muawiya II died without an heir. These periods are so named because the rulers were supposedly descended from different companions of the prophet. It can be argued, however, that far more was at stake than a simple shift from one branch of a family to another. In fact, the shift from Sufyanid to Marwanid may involve nothing less than the birth of Islam itself.[638] This shift will be explored in more detail below. For the moment, it will be good to focus on what we can learn about the actual nature of early Umayyad rule (as opposed to the claims of later Islamic sources) from studying the documents, inscriptions and coins of this period.

The first thing to notice is the relative abundance of source material relating to the early Sufyanid Period that we can work with. This is curious to say the least. We have virtually no primary source material relating to Muhammad and the first four caliphs. Then it is as if there is just a sudden proliferation of historical material relating to the Umayyad rulers, even the earliest ones.[639] We are spoilt for choice when it comes to documents, coins and inscriptions referencing them. So, once again, we see that there is no lack of source material dealing with this period of history. What is lacking, is *material confirming the Islamic accounts* written down hundreds of years later.

What is particularly interesting for our purposes, when it comes to the primary source record related to the early Sufyanid period, is the total absence of references to Islam, the Qur'an or Muhammad[640] even in places where we would most expect to find them.

One of the earliest inscriptions associated with Muawiya is a dedication placed on a bathhouse in Gadara. This can be dated to the year 662 CE. It simply describes Muawiya as 'The Commander of the Faithful'.[641] He is not in any way linked to Islam. It refers instead to the Arab conquest (not the 'Islamic Conquest'). Most striking of all is the fact that this inscription is prefaced with a cross. This is surprising, to say the least, considering the later Islamic detestation of the cross.

Another very important inscription associated with Mu'awiya I can be found at Ta'if. It appears on the wall of a dam built in the year 678 CE[642] and reads as follows:

> This dam [belongs] to servant of God Mu'āwiya,
> Commander of the Faithful. 'Abdullāh b. Ṣakhr built it
> with the permission of Allāh, in the year fifty-eight.
> Allāh, pardon servant of God Mu'āwiya,
> Commander of the Faithful, and strengthen him, and make him victorious, and grant the
> Commander of the Faithful the enjoyment of it. 'Amr b. Ḥabbab wrote [it].[643]

The 'year fifty-eight' here refers to the beginning of the era of Arab dominance and this dating system is common in inscriptions from this period. Muslims would claim that this is the date of the '*hijra*' (i.e. Muhammad's flight from Mecca to Medina)[644], but there is obviously nothing in the actual historical record to support this assertion. Be that as it may, Ta'if is less than 100 miles from the modern location of Mecca (and unlike Mecca is amply attested to in the pre-Islamic historical record).[645] Yet even here, in the middle of the Arabian Desert, the supposed heartland of Muhammad and the *Quraysh* (his tribe), he is not mentioned at all. All that we see are generic references to God and to 'the faithful'. There is, in short, nothing Islamic about this inscription.

One of the most interesting areas of study when it comes to the early Su-fyanid period is in the field of numismatics.[646] Coins are regarded by historians as one of the most reliable types of evidence of the spread of the influence of a ruling class or ideology.[647] This is because coins are almost always produced by dominant authorities (or those seeking to become so). Such authorities typically used coins to make a claim for legitimacy and to define the basis of their reign. If the Arab conquests were Muslim in nature, we could therefore expect that the coins produced by the conquerors would bear inscriptions proclaiming Islam and its prophet as the basis of their rule. This is not the case at all with Sufyanid coins[648] and those seeking an affirmation of the traditional Islamic view of history are bound to be disappointed when the coins of the Arab conquest are studied.

The earliest coins associated with the Arab conquest (minted from 650-670 CE) simply bear the inscription "In the name of God" (*Bismillah*) or some variant.[649] Completely absent is the second part of the Islamic confession of faith "Muhammad is the messenger of God". We can, therefore, at the most ascribe a vague monotheism to the Arab conquerors. Any specific mention of Islam or Muhammad is absent.

A striking feature of the coins of the early Umayyad period is the fact that many of them contain crosses. One of the most interesting of these coins was probably minted in the 650s CE. The implications of this coin are troubling, to say the least, for pious Muslims and their view of the Arab conquests. It depicts a human figure with a crown alongside a cross[650]. The letters MUH (in Arabic) also appear on the coin. Some Muslim authors speculate that these letters should be extended to spell Muhammad. This, however, does not solve anything as far as the traditional Islamic account is concerned. Firstly, the depiction of Muhammad is obviously anathema to observant Muslims[651] yet, if this was indeed Muhammad, it seems the early Muslim rulers had no problems with making him appear on a coin. What is even more striking is the appearance of the cross. The Qur'an emphatically denies the crucifixion of Jesus Christ[652], so the cross would therefore be viewed as an expression of blasphemy by pious Muslims. Islamic history is, in fact, full of instances of the destruction of crosses and there is a tradition that states that Jesus will one day return to break all crosses.[653] Yet here we see a cross very prominently displayed on a coin minted by the Arab conquerors. There are some interesting possible explanations for this:

- The religion of the Arab conquerors may have been a vague monotheism[654] which left room for the adoration of the cross. If this is the case, this religion was worlds away from fully developed Islam.

- The figure on the coin may not be Muhammad at all but Jesus Christ instead (which would explain the cross). The name Muhammad can also be a title meaning 'The Praised One'[655], which could in this case possibly have been applied to Jesus.

Neither of these possible explanations correspond with the later orthodox view of Islamic history since both place the cross center-stage in the theology of the Arab conquerors. Such a concept directly contradicts Qur'an 4:157 (see section 6.3.6.) where it is emphatically stated that Jesus was not crucified.

It is hard to overstate the extent to which Islam and Islamic religious concepts are absent from the historical record related to the early Umayyad period. Some of the most interesting work in this area was done by Prof. Yehuda Nevo (1932-1992). He analyzed literally hundreds of rock inscriptions scattered across Arabia.[656] Nevo shows that there are some standard phrases that occur in both religious and non-religious inscriptions. The most important of these is the 'Bismillah' (In the Name of God) formula.[657] Note that this is generic in nature (i.e. there are no references made to Muhammad or Islam). The invoking of God without including any reference to Muhammad, even in religious inscriptions, for more than sixty years after the traditional date given for his death is hugely significant. Later Muslim religious writings are intensely focused on Muhammad with hundreds of traditions claiming to illuminate even the most mundane details of his life. Arabic documents, coins[658] and inscriptions[659] from the 690's CE onwards consistently add references to Muhammad to inscriptions invoking the name of God. Yet the Arabic inscriptions closest to his time do not mention him at all. *Not even once.* Therefore, whatever religion the earliest Arab rulers clung to, it was nothing like the fully developed Islam practiced today. Nevo contends that the Arab conquerors promoted a vague monotheism, but that this creed was: "… demonstrably not Islam, but [a creed] from which Islam could have developed."[660]

Many more examples can be added, but those listed above should suffice to convince us that it is highly questionable whether the Sufyanid rulers thought of themselves as followers of someone called Muhammad. As Patricia Crone says: "It is striking that such documentary evidence as survives from the Sufyanid period makes no mention of the messenger of God at all. The papyri do not refer to him. The Arabic inscriptions of the Arab-Sassanian coins only invoke Allah not his *rasul* (messenger)… Even the two surviving pre-Marwanid tombstones fail to mention the *rasul* (messenger) though both mention Allah; and the same is true of the Mu'awiya inscription at Ta'if. *In the Sufyanid period, apparently, the prophet had no publicly acknowledged role.*"[661]

To put it as bluntly as possible, the Muslim version of events, namely that the Arab conquests and early Arab rule were intimately associated with a fully developed religion known as Islam, rests only on the exceedingly shaky foundation of theologically motivated writings compiled centuries later. Nothing more.

The actual historical evidence related to the Sufyanid period is perhaps the reason why many Muslim scholars are deeply ambivalent about the Arab rulers of this period (the Shi'a especially so[662]). By examining their records, we see that these supposed 'Muslim' rulers left nothing to suggest that they read the Qur'an, revered Muhammad or followed a religion called Islam. It is also clearly the case that their base of operations and the center of their power was not in the middle of the Arabian Desert, but in Syria[663] and northwestern Arabia. The records associated with them, therefore, stand as a powerful corrective to standard Islamic historical orthodoxy.

7.7. Civil War, the Marwanids and the Emergence of Islam

While the Sufyanids, especially Muawiya, did much to expand Arab rule and could generally be regarded as competent rulers, it is by no means the case that their rule was universally welcomed across what we now refer to as the Middle East. They were, firstly, strongly opposed by those from whom the Shi'a movement would later draw its strength.[664] Also, in the vastness of the Arabian Desert others were beginning to preach a message about an austere desert prophet. One such leader, Ibn al Zubayr[665] (624-692 CE), even claimed to be a companion of this leader and opposed the Umayyads precisely because of this.[666] It, therefore, required a great deal of skill and leadership to keep the burgeoning Arab empire together. Even so, civil war and bloody conflict dogged the Umayyads throughout their reign. The Sufyanids tried to respond to this challenge by maintaining broad religious policies, hoping that they could unite as many people as possible around a vague and broad monotheism.[667] Marwanid rule (from 684 CE onwards), however, heralded an entirely new era and a centrally enforced religious policy. Because of this religious policy, we see the emergence of something we can begin to recognize as developing Islam.

The emergence of recognizably Islamic words, symbols and concepts was clearly not due to a slow process of development. In fact, it is almost overnight that we can begin to observe not only the insistence on the supreme importance of a person named Muhammad but also the official emphasis on his status as the 'Messenger of God'. This change is most strikingly reflected on documents through the so-called protocols with which they began. During the Sufyanid period, the standard protocol was simply 'In the Name of God' (*Bismillah*).[668] From about the early 690's the name of Muhammad (as the 'Messenger of God') began to be consistently added to the protocols on Arab documents.[669] The change is so striking that it can be likened to someone flicking a switch and affecting this change in an almost instantaneous manner. It is furthermore not only on documents that the change is observable. Muhammad's name suddenly appears on coins, milestones and inscriptions.[670] This is very surprising. Pre-690 CE Muhammad is absent from Arabic inscriptions and documents. After 690 he is simply everywhere. Why this change almost 60 years after he supposedly died? The most likely answer is that this was due to some centrally directed policy. This suspicion is confirmed when it emerges that the new formula caught on instantaneously in the centers of Umayyad power, while the traditional single-*Bismillah* ('In the name of God', without the reference to Muhammad) persisted for decades in more remote and inaccessible areas (e.g. the Negev desert) where Umayyad power could not be so effectively projected.[671]

7.8. The Dome of the Rock: Islam Finally Steps from the Shadows

One of the most significant changes during the Marwanid period happened during the reign of Abd al-Malik (caliph from 685 to 705 CE)[672]. Like the other Umayyad rulers, Abd al-Malik ruled from Damascus.[673] What marked his reign as different from that of earlier rulers is that he chose to decisively emphasize Arab identity.[674] This was something that his predecessors, reliant as they were on Syriac, and especially Greek speaking Christians and Jews to run their empire, did not do. It seems, however, that Abd Al-Malik felt that the only way to effectively respond to threats from the outside and to protect against being dominated by non-Arabs internally was to aggressively assert the Arab identity of the empire. In practice this meant that the official language of correspondence changed to Arabic (from Greek) almost overnight.[675] Coins with Arabic inscriptions were also minted for the first time on a large scale during his reign.[676]

Instituting a new language policy was one thing. That, however, still left the inconvenient fact that many of Abd al-Malik's subjects adhered to a variety of Christian confessions. He, therefore, evidently felt the need to also declare religious independence by asserting the primacy of the Arabs in the religious sphere. In practice this would entail the active and decisive repudiation of the religion of his greatest enemy, the Christian Eastern (Byzantine) Roman Emperor.[677]

The place where Abd Al-Malik chose to make his boldest religious statement was in the very city regarded by many Christians as the most sacred place on earth: Jerusalem. It was here that Abd Al-Malik constructed the remarkable building now universally known as the Dome of the Rock (completed in 691 CE).[678] It should be noted that the Dome of the Rock is not a mosque.[679] Nor is it primarily a monument to Muhammad's fabled 'night journey' from Jerusalem. There is not a single reference to this mythical event in the original inscriptions.[680] Instead it seems that part of its purpose was to present vehement anti-Christian rhetoric set in stone.[681] The following original inscriptions appear on the Inner-Ambulatory of the Dome of the Rock:

- There is no God but God. He is one. He has no associate. Say: He is God the One. God the eternally besought of all. He begetteth nor was begotten. And there is none comparable unto him. Muhammad is the Messenger of God. (Sura 112)

- People of the Scripture! Do not exaggerate in your religion, nor utter aught concerning Allah save the truth. The Messiah, Jesus son of Mary, was only a messenger of Allah and His word which He conveyed unto Mary and a Spirit from Him. So believe in Allah and His messengers and say not 'Three'. Cease, it will be better for you. Allah is the only One God. Far removed is it from His transcendent majesty that he should have a son. (Sura 4:171)

- Praise be to God who hath not taken unto Himself a son, and who hath no partner in the sovereignty, nor hath he any protecting friend through dependence (Sura 17:111)[682]

The first thing to notice about these inscriptions is that they differ markedly from the way in which these verses appear in the Qu'ran used by Muslims today[683]. So even though we are clearly dealing with a developing scriptural tradition here, there is no indication that it is a settled tradition. The second, striking feature is just how strongly anti-Christian the inscriptions are. It is almost as if Abd Al-Malik wanted to rub the noses of the Christian citizens of Jerusalem in his categorical rejection of their faith[684]. This is obviously a world away from the more conciliatory policies of the earlier Sufyanid rulers.

In addition to the anti-Christian polemic, the Dome of the Rock also contains a whole list of 'firsts'. These include:

- The first accurately datable occurrence of passages from the Qur'an on an inscription (although as seen above these are not in word-perfect agreement with the Qur'an Muslims use today).[685]

- Possibly the first incontestable Arabic reference to Muhammad.[686]

- The first expression of the sentiments expressed in the *Shahada* (i.e. the Muslim confession of faith: 'There is no God but God and Muhammad is the Messenger of God'). Although again the words are not exactly equivalent to those Muslims use today in their prayers.[687]

- The first reference to Islam and to Muslims.[688]

- The first explicit Muslim repudiation of the divinity of Jesus (see above).[689]

There are, in fact, so many firsts included in the inscriptions that the inescapable conclusion is that the Dome of the Rock heralds a radical new beginning in Arab religious sensibilities. This building, dating from 691 CE, is in fact where Islam finally announces itself to the world, six decades after Muhammad supposedly last walked the earth.

This is not the place to speculate as to exactly how and why this entirely new religion (albeit claiming much older origins) suddenly burst upon the scene. This will be the focus of the next chapter. Let it just for the moment be stated categorically that this is, in fact, what we are dealing with when we consider the Dome of the Rock: the announcing of a freshly minted Arab religion, custom designed to challenge the dominance of Christianity in Arabia, Syria and beyond.

7.9. Chapter Summary

- Islamic sources, committed to paper in in the 9th and 10th centuries, make the strongest possible connection between the Arab conquests of the mid-7th century and the rise of Islam. This version of events is, however, comprehensively contradicted by the available contemporary documentary and archeological evidence. In these sources, the conquests are never linked with a fully developed religion named Islam and the persons supposedly conquering the world for Islam (the four 'Rightly Guided Caliphs') are equally absent from the record.

- Muslim post-conquest accounts are furthermore contradicted by the fact that not a single 7th century mosque was oriented towards Mecca. Instead, mosques from this period consistently pointed towards northwestern Arabia. We also find clear indications of the survival of paganism in the Arabian Peninsula long after it was supposedly eradicated by the rise of Islam.

- Instead of Islam sweeping all before it, the contemporary record indicates that the first three Arab rulers (661-684 CE) who are reliably attested in the historical record (the so-called Sufyanids) followed a broad religious policy centered on a vague Arab monotheism (the standard opening protocol on their documents was simply 'In the Name of God'), which even left room for strongly Christian symbolism (cf. the appearance of the cross on their coins and inscriptions).

- A decisive change occurred under the so-called Marwanid rulers (from 684 CE onwards). These rulers were clearly intent on emphasizing and cementing the specifically Arab nature of their rule. This is evidenced in a decisive turn towards Arabic (instead of Greek in official documents) and the introduction, almost overnight, of a new protocol ('In the Name of God, Muhammad is the Messenger of God') which would become ubiquitous on Umayyad correspondence from 690 CE onwards.

201

- With the construction of the Dome of the Rock in Jerusalem under Caliph Abd Al-Malik in Jerusalem (691 CE), Islam as we now know it finally announces itself to the world. It stands as a decisive repudiation of Christianity and as a marker for a separate Islamic identity focused on someone named Muhammad. As such it contains the oldest Qur'anic inscriptions (although the inscriptions are somewhat different from the modern Qur'an) and the first references to Muhammad, Muslims and Islam in Arabic.

- Whatever the reasons behind the sudden emergence of Islam, there can be little doubt that it had its roots in the policies of Arab rulers who lived decades after Muhammad supposedly dominated the Arabian Peninsula. Some of the reasons behind why it was necessary to invent this new ideology will be presented in the next chapter.

8.

What Happened? Some Tentative Conclusions

Over the course of this book so far, we had a close look at the evidence for the traditional Islamic historical accounts and found that on point-after-point that the confident assertions of late 8th and 9th century Muslim writers about mid-7th century Arabia cannot survive critical scrutiny.

Just how stark the mismatch between official Islamic history and the actual historical record is can be illustrated by how the list of 'firsts' given below compares with the date traditionally given for Muhammad's birth and death (570 to 632 CE):

- The first use of material that would eventually form part of the Qur'an in inscriptions (although significantly these differ from the eventual text of the Qur'an): 691 CE (Dome of the Rock)[690]
- The first Arabic reference to Muhammad: 691 CE (Dome of the Rock)[691]
- The first appearance of 'Islam' and 'Muslims': 691 CE (Dome of the Rock)[692]
- The first non-Muslim reference to the Qur'an: 730's CE (John of Damascus)[693]
- The first reference to Mecca: 741 CE[694]
- The first biography of Muhammad: Around 750 CE[695]

- The first appearance of Mecca on a Map: 9th Century CE[696]
- The final formalization of the 'sound' *hadith* collections: 800-900 CE[697]

Some explanation for the vast discrepancy between Islamic accounts and the data presented in this book is clearly needed, and the time has come to briefly present some theories on the early history of Islam.

As stated earlier, this section should not be viewed as the most important part of this book. Too many responses to the fundamental questions that can be asked about Islamic history focus on poking holes on alternative theories without dealing with the fundamental issues. This response is based on a logical fallacy. Disproving B (e.g. Muhammad led an early religion known as Hagarism[698]) does not automatically prove A (the standard version of Islamic history is accurate). In other words, it should be possible to ask critical questions about the accepted version of Islamic history without having to posit an iron-clad alternative explanation. It is, of course, the case that asking critical questions might lead to conclusions that with justice, could be described as speculative. However, in this case the speculation will be based on a careful consideration of the surviving contemporary evidence instead of a reliance on questionable traditions dating from 200-300 years after the event.

It should be strongly emphasized that there is no good reason to simply succumb to the 'Last Man Standing' view of Islamic history. This is the assumption that the standard account is the best possible explanation that we are left with in the absence of other theories. The evidence presented thus far should convince any fair-minded reader that this position is not even close to tenable. The standard account is so hopelessly out of sync with actual historical realities that it would be far better to simply say 'We don't know exactly what happened' rather than having to accept a version of 'history' that is patently inaccurate.

Having said this, it is still possible to make a series of educated guesses when it comes to the early history of Islam. This is what will be presented below, as an attempt is made to describe the various influences that made their way into the eventual development of Islam. At the end of the chapter an alternative to the paragraph based on the traditional account that preceded each chapter will be provided.

Fully developed Islam can be likened to a rope woven from many strands. The best possible way to explain the nature of each of these strands is to indicate how they fit into the final product. This is what is proposed with this chapter. Almost all of what will be discussed will have been touched on earlier in this book. The idea here is to fit the data into a coherent narrative of the likely origins of Islam.

It would be anachronistic to refer to many of the early developments discussed below as 'Muslim' or 'Islamic' since these terms will only come into use right at the end of the 7th century. The earlier part of this tradition will therefore be referred to as 'proto-Islamic' until we come to the construction of the Dome of the Rock in 691 CE.

We begin our journey in the ancient Kingdom of Nabataea.

8.1. Nabataea: A Forgotten Kingdom Worth Remembering

We are so used to thinking of Arabic and Arab culture as a product of central Arabia that the whole question of Arab origins almost seems redundant. The fact is, however, that the single society that did most to shape early Arab culture was that of the northern Arabian Kingdom of the Nabataeans.[699] The history of this Kingdom goes all the way back to antiquity and there is strong evidence that the Nabataeans and the Hyksos (the Western Semites who conquered Egypt) were, in fact, the same people.[700] By simply having a look at the spectacular ruins of their capital Petra[701] we can clearly see that the Nabataeans, although largely forgotten today, were the guardians of one the most important cultures of the ancient Near East. They also, bequeathed a language, a way of writing and a religious vocabulary that would eventually be absorbed into Arabic and Arab culture[702]. Nabataean dominance of northern Arabia came to an end when the Romans conquered their kingdom in the 2nd century CE and established a province known and Roman Arabia or Arabia Petraea that lasted until the emergence of Arab dominance in the 7th century[703].

Whatever else we might say about the rise of Islam, we should begin by stating that it built on foundations laid by the Nabataeans. This is confirmed by the fact that a careful cross-referencing of all the geographical references in the Qur'an locates the audience that is being addressed squarely in the Nabataean lands and regions further north. We should, therefore, take Nabataean ideas and religious concepts seriously (See Section 4.1.2.)

It is not only in the realm of ideas, however, that Nabataea should grab the attention of anyone interested in the origins of Islam. It is remarkable how the Islamic traditions that feel so utterly out of place at the location of the modern city of Mecca seamlessly slot into the Nabataean lands and specifically into their capital city of Petra. Some examples:

- It cannot be proved that Mecca even existed in the 7th century. By this stage Petra had dominated the northern end of the Trans-Arabian trade route for centuries.[704]

- The Qur'an contains precious few geographical references, but the tribes and places that are referred to are clustered in northwestern Arabia, a region with Petra at its heart (See Section 4.1.2).

- The topographical details (a city in a deep valley surrounded by two high mountains) and agricultural references (a place of livestock and arable farming) in the Qur'an are wholly alien to the location of Mecca, but fits Petra to a tee.[705]

- Many *hadiths* fit much better into Petra than Mecca. For example, some physically impossible journeys become possible when you consider that they took place from northwestern Arabia rather than from hundreds of miles south (See Section 4.2.2.).

It can, considering the above, be plausibly proposed that at least some of the traditions that made their way into Islam started life in Nabataean lands and that a Nabataean location (most probably Petra itself) was the original 'holy city' or 'house' at Bakka referred to in the Qur'an and *hadiths*.

The best work in comparing geographical references in the Qur'an and *hadiths* to actual on-the-ground realities was done by the archeologist Douglas Gibson and described in his book 'Qur'anic Geography'[706], an absolute gem. An interesting observation made by Gibson is that there are virtually no references to Petra in the official Islamic historical records. This is almost as remarkable as the absence of Mecca from the earlier historical records. One only has to look at the remarkable surviving ruins of Petra to conclude that this was a hugely important city in its time. Yet, while later Islamic traditions go into obsessive detail as to how even small Arabian villages were captured by Muslim forces, Petra hardly rates a mention. Could it be that Muslim historians 'scrubbed' Petra from their version of events to avoid some rather uncomfortable questions?[707]

Not everyone is necessarily convinced by the Petra hypothesis, but it should, at the very least, be clear that the geographical and linguistic clues in the Qur'an and traditions (not to mention the orientation of 7th century mosques, see Section 7.4) all consistently point to a place of origin far to the north of the location of the modern city of Mecca.

It is worth remembering that the Nabataeans had an effective mechanism for the diffusion of their ideas, language, culture and religion as they controlled the northern end of the Trans-Arabian trade route[708]. This fact, unlike the historical fiction of a place called Mecca being at the center of this trade, is amply attested to in ancient records. This means that desert wanderers across the region, many of whom would have played some role in the trans-Arabian trade, could have picked up many practices, beliefs and even a language that would initially simply have been thought of as Nabataean, but that would later be one of the foundational streams that fed into Arabic.[709] Thus from an Islamic perspective, the word 'Arabic' serves the handy function of obscuring the true origins of the culture that their faiths rests on. Making it much easier to argue for a place of origin deep in the interior of the Arabian Peninsula.

8.2. Arabian Paganism as the Bedrock of Proto-Islam

Those who wrote the official Islamic historical accounts were scathing about the paganism that was prevalent among the Arabs before the coming of Islam. One must wonder, however, whether this is not a classic case of 'protesting too much'. The fact is that fully developed Islam retains many elements that can be traced directly to Arabian Paganism. These include the idea of pilgrimage during a 'sacred month'[710], a cube-shaped building (*ka'aba*) as a focus for worship[711] and a deep fear of (mostly) malevolent beings known as '*jinn*'.[712] These pagan holdovers can, in some ways, be viewed as part of the deepest substratum of proto-Islam with many other layers eventually being built on top of it.

An important observation to be made about the nature of the paganism that is in view in the Qur'an is that it cannot be effectively traced back to central Arabia where Mecca was supposed to have been located. Traces of many languages and cultures have been found in the Hejaz but nothing at all that would suggest that it was a focus of pagan worship[713]. We can, however, point to the way in which elements of a paganism that may have grown out of Nabataean religion and the beliefs of the Bedouin of the Negev are clearly reflected in elements of the Islamic tradition. This would, immediately, suggest something that we have encountered time-after-time in this volume. A likely place of origin for Islam that is hundreds of miles to the north of Mecca.

This is, once again, confirmed by the fact that, as we have seen, much of what is criticized as paganism in the Qur'an cannot be described as pagan idolatry in the classical sense. Instead the '*mushrikun*' (idolaters) can rather be described as people who 'Did Monotheism Wrong' by ascribing partners to God[714] (See Section 4.1.2.).

In fully developed Islam we are left with a strange mixture of classical Arabian paganism and monotheism. For classic paganism, we can point to surviving pagan elements in Islam (See Section 3.1.1). There are, however, other expressions of paganism (especially polytheism) that have been strongly repudiated. In other words, paganism was not wholly accepted or rejected. To students of comparative religion, this would indicate that the followers of Arabian paganism experienced a sustained encounter with some very different belief systems during the formative period of proto-Islam. Syncretism (i.e. the mixing of belief systems)[715] will often be the result in such cases. For the kind of contact that can result in syncretism to occur, it will obviously be necessary for two groups who hold to different beliefs to *have close contact with each other over an extended period.*[716] This level of proximity was probably achieved by a mass migration of desert Arabs to more settled lives in the Syro-Arabian borderlands.

8.3. The Arabs and the Superpowers

It is one thing to state that a mass-migration of Arabs into settled areas occurred, but quite another to explain why it happened and why it is important for the story that we are trying to tell. To explain this, it will be necessary to briefly focus on the state of the two superpowers that dominated the life of the region: Rome and Persia.

One of the basic insights when it comes to the study of migrations is that there are often *push factors* (i.e. factors that motivate people to want to leave their current environment) and *pull factors* (i.e. factors that attract people to a new environment) involved.[717] In the case of desert Arabs, it is not difficult to work out what the 'push factors' may have been. Life in the desert was often 'nasty, brutish and short', and marked by insecurity. People who are not able to cultivate their own crops and who were also subject to constant attempts to keep them away from scarce resources (e.g. wells and oases) cannot be blamed for yearning for a settled, secure life. A trace of this yearning survives in the Qur'an through its description of paradise as a garden with ever-flowing streams.[718]

The 'push factor' of wanting to leave a challenging environment for a more comfortable and settled one has, of course, motivated migration throughout the centuries. It is fair to say, however, that those in the settled environments are not always wildly enthusiastic about sharing their precious resources with others. Therefore, history is littered with references to invasions of settled areas by land hungry armies coming from less fortunate areas.[719] This seems to be what happened during the Arab conquests. As we have seen above, however, things are not nearly as simple as this. We simply do not find much evidence in the historical record of a large-scale invasion.[720] An alternative explanation is needed. One possibility is something that was rare, but certainly not unprecedented in history: namely that the 'invaders' were invited in.

This idea of 'invaders' coming in by invitation is not nearly as far-fetched as it may seem. We can point to several historical examples of peoples who came into territories in response to requests made by kings and empires who thought that they could use hired military muscle to strengthen their own positions. Quite often these 'hirelings' ended up as the overlords of the territory they were supposed to protect. The very name of the English language testifies to the reality of Germanic groups (e.g. the Angels and Saxons)[721] invited into what we now know as the British Isles to serve as mercenaries.[722] In the end, they obviously ended up staying a great deal longer than intended by those who thought that it was a good idea to issue the invitation in the first place.

There is, as we have seen, solid evidence of the Roman and Persian armies enlisting Arab tribes to act as '*foederati*' (lit. 'federated ones')[723] on both sides of the interminable conflict between them (See Section 3.2.2.) These tribes were settled in garrison cities from where they could defend the empire they were enlisted by and from where they could also launch attacks against the 'federated tribes' of the other side.[724] These garrison cities were most probably the first to which the ideal of '*hijra*' was applied. It was incumbent, so it was argued, to support your kinsfolk by coming in from the desert and to earn a living by supporting the reign of the imperial powers.

As they moved in from the desert to garrison cities and towns, the Arab tribes very quickly came into contact not only with the cultures of the imperial powers, but also with Christianity as the imperial religion of the Roman Empire. In fact, by the bringing together of so many people from a wide variety of backgrounds, these garrison cities would inevitably act as melting pots in which a variety of influences could bump against, and rub off on, each other. It is significant, in this regard, to note that Jabiya (the largest of the Arab garrison cities supported by Rome) had a thriving Christian church[725].

The hiring of mercenaries to protect the borders of the Roman Empire took place during a time of Roman military weakness. Political entities at the height of their power do not normally require 'outside help' to protect their territories. In fact, one of the greatest points of pride for the Roman people was the ability of the army to keep them safe and to police the borders of the empire. Hiring Arabs to do this work, therefore, represented something of a capitulation as they could be viewed as the very people that the border policies of the Empire were designed to keep out in the first place.

The weakness that brought on the fateful decision to 'bring in the Arabs' can in large part be ascribed to war weariness among the superpowers. The fact is that Arab ascendancy began at precisely the point when the two great powers of the day (the Roman and Persian Empires) fought each other to a standstill.[726] The epic conflict between these two great antagonists left both with empty treasuries and depleted armies during the early decades of the 7th century.

Examples of how the strained resources of the Roman Empire led to changes on the ground in Syria and Arabia can be multiplied. Part of the response seems to have been to simply abandon fortified border positions and to consolidate power further north in the heartlands of the Empire. Archeological investigations therefore testify to the large-scale abandonment of previously held forts and garrisons.[727] This must have caused a great deal of anxiety among the Roman-aligned Arab tribes. A wholesale Roman withdrawal would mean the end of their settled and secure lives. It is hugely significant, in light of this, that a 'nearby' Roman defeat (and the assurance that this will be reversed) is one of the very few contemporary historical references to have been included in the Qur'an: "The Romans have been defeated in the nearby land, but after their defeat they will soon be victorious. Within three to nine years. The decision of the matter, before and after, is with God." (Quran 30:2-4)[728]

If this verse of the Qur'an is anything to go by, there must have been a surviving tradition that the Arab tribes allied with Rome were very aware of how the wind was blowing in their corner of the world. This included a realization that Rome was finding it increasingly difficult to project its

211

power into the Syro-Arabian borderlands. In short, it must have dawned on them that these lands were ripe for the picking since they themselves (i.e. the Arab *'Foederati'*) were the only vestige of Roman power left.

Vacuums, including power vacuums, will have to be filled eventually and the way in which the Arabs stepped into the vacuum created by Roman weakness provides the context for one of the most foundational concepts in Muslim self-understanding: The *Hijra*.

8.4. A *'Hijra'*, But Not as You Know It

Muslim historiography makes much of the idea of *'hijra'*[729] (the word literally means 'flight' in Arabic, but eventually came to be understood as 'migration') and the Muslim calendar begins with the *'hijra'* of Muhammad from Mecca to Medina.[730] While there is not a smidgen of evidence for Muhammad's migration in the primary source record, it can be argued that the idea of migration is crucial to understanding the rise of Islam. In this case, however, the references are not to a migration that occurred wholly within the Arabian Peninsula. Instead it was a migration from a life in the desert into more settled areas in the Syro-Arabian Borderlands and the eventual formation of the migrants into a coherent and ultimately dominant military force.

In a ground-breaking article, Prof Patricia Crone[731] analyzed more than 50 references to *'hijra'* in the Muslim tradition and she concludes that it is closely associated with desert Arabs moving to garrison cities. There is, therefore, within the tradition a great deal of criticism leveled at Bedouin (i.e. nomadic desert Arabs) who refused to 'come in' from the desert or those who reverted to a nomadic lifestyle after becoming settled for a while. How stridently the calls to migrate could be can still be seen in Qur'an 4:97-100[732] where it is made clear that significant punishments awaited those who refused to throw in their lot with the migrants.

This period of history is impossible to understand apart from acknowledging the move among desert Arabs to step into the military vacuum resulting from Roman weakness. Hence the emphasis is not only on 'coming

212

in from the desert' but specifically into centers where Arab tribes could gain and maintain military power through 'sticking together' in garrison cities.[733] In this context, it easy to see why not migrating (or returning to the desert) carried such a negative connotation. It would have been viewed as tantamount to desertion. By abandoning your fellow Arabs, you left them in a weaker military position.[734]

So, what was the '*hijra*'? Considering the above, it can be argued that it represented the realization among desert Arabs that they could live settled and secure lives in formerly Roman territories if they could just manage to fortify themselves sufficiently in well-protected settlements.[735] As more and more of them began to exercise this option, the trickle became a flood that could retroactively be described as an '*invasion*' or '*conquest*' as the net-effect was to leave the Arabs in a politically dominant position.

This is confirmed when we read the descriptions of those being 'conquered'. It is evident from the historical record that they did not experience the initial stages of the Arab migration as something nearly as dramatic and ground-breaking as the swift, decisive and overwhelming victories described in the Islamic traditions.[736] The numbers involved would simply have been too small for that, with many contemporary descriptions describing Arab 'war bands' conducting raids instead of full-scale armies fighting battles.[737] It is also, as we have seen, the case that there is solid archeological and documentary evidence that Rome had by the 7th century largely abandoned its Arabian possessions.[738] So, the overblown 'How we Beat the Romans' narratives of Islamic history may well have to be replaced with the rather more mundane idea of scores of desert Arabs 'moving house' (or rather moving from tent to house) at the same time.

If the idea of a gradual migration is significantly at odds with the standard Islamic account that breathlessly recounts the *military* successes of the early Islamic conquests as nothing less than a miracle for the ages[739], it poses even more challenges on a *religious* level. The fact is that the Arab migrations were not nearly as 'Islamic' as is commonly supposed.[740] They were in fact rather incremental and were not obviously connected with a new religion called 'Islam', a prophet called Muhammad, or a book called the Qur'an by those who experienced them firsthand and wrote about

213

what they have seen.[741] In fact, perhaps the most persuasive confirmation of the 'migration instead of invasion' thesis can be seen in the fact that both Greek and Syriac writers used some version of the word 'migrant' (and never 'Muslim') to refer to the Arabs for most of the 7th century.[742]

Over time these migrants became politically dominant in the former Roman lands. Thus, the term 'conquest' in the Arab conquests should properly be viewed as not so much a military, but rather as a cultural victory. Even so, it was something much less than a total victory for the Arabs. When less sophisticated cultures encounter more settled and advanced societies they are often profoundly changed by the experience (even where the less sophisticated culture is politically dominant).[743] It is, therefore, in the intellectual, cultural and religious ferment of a border society that the origins of Islam must ultimately be sought.

Thus far in this chapter we have looked at the influence of Nabataean culture and religiosity, Arabian Paganism and the impact of Arab migration. Two of the further strands of influence that were eventually woven into Islam are very easily discerned and will even be picked up through a casual reading of the Qur'an. This is the impact of Judaism and Christianity. These will be discussed later in this chapter. Before we get there, however, it will be important to chart the influence of something that would perhaps be much less obvious to the casual observer, namely Syriac language and culture.

8.5. The Arab-Syriac Encounter

'Syriac' is often used as a catch-all term for Eastern Semitic languages that used to be widely spoken in the Roman Province of Syria and deep into Asia-Minor.[744] Perhaps the most famous of the Syriac languages is Aramaic, spoken in Palestine during the time of Christ.[745] The Syriac world spawned a unique culture and writing system. This persisted for centuries, despite Greek and Roman encroachment, and eventually dominance, in the core Syriac lands. At the time of the rise of Islam, varieties of Syriac were still widely spoken in territories now covered by Israel, Jordan, Lebanon, Syria and Eastern Turkey.[746]

When we analyze the Qur'an and traditions, it quickly becomes clear that the migration of Arabs did not only bring them into contact with Rome and Persia, but also in a profound way with Syriac culture and Syriac Christianity.[747] This, once again, confirms the thesis that the Qur'an and Islamic traditions had their origins hundreds of miles to the north of the Arabian Desert.

We have repeatedly seen just how profound and wide-ranging Syriac influence on the Qur'an[748] and Islam was, even to the point where it can be shown that parts of the Qur'an started life as Syriac Christian liturgies.[749] It can thus be argued that modern Muslims prostrating themselves for a fixed number of daily prayers[750] after hearing a call to prayer from a minaret[751] (likely modelled on the pillars of the wildly popular Syrian Stylites[752]) are not following the dictates of a desert prophet, but the rhythms of Syriac Christianity.

Many other examples, showcasing the true origins of Islam in the Syriac heartlands, can be cited (See Sections 4.2.3. and 6.4.1). These range from the simple fact that the first Arab capital was Damascus[753] (and certainly not a spot in the middle of the Arabian Desert) and that the victorious Arabs engaged in fevered property speculation within Syria[754] (something that would be entirely unexpected if their base of operations was located at the modern location of Mecca).

Much more fruitful work will probably be done in this area in the future. For the moment it is sufficient to state that it would be impossible to understand proto-Islam if its deep roots in Syriac culture, language and religiosity is ignored.

8.6 Proto-Islam and Judaism

By moving into the Syro-Arabian borderlands, the Arab migrants were guaranteed to encounter Jewish people who treasured age-old memories of the heroes of their faith. Of these, Abraham and Moses, wanderers like themselves, seems to have made the deepest impression on the Arabs.[755] This caused them to comment extensively on the Abrahamic and Mosaic traditions and appropriate much of it as their own.[756]

215

One part of this tradition that came to be especially valued was the identification of the Arab people as descendants of Abraham through Ishmael.[757] While it is true that this descent was not through the 'official' line (i.e. the one that could be traced through Isaac) this was still a thing to be treasured and placed the Arabs on an inside track as having favor in the eyes of the God of Abraham. The story of Moses and his confrontation with pharaoh also came to be highly valued by at least some Arabs. This is evident in the fact that it is repeatedly referenced and commented on in the Qur'an.[758] In particular, it seemed to have convinced some Arabs of the folly of idolatry as the clear superiority of monotheism is a major theme in these retellings.[759]

It could thus be argued that the initial encounter between the Arab migrants and Judaism resulted in many of the migrants being deeply drawn to the Jewish faith and to the idea of monotheism. The initial affinity between the Arabs and the Jews, so surprising in the light of 21st century geopolitical realities[760], are very well attested in the contemporary record.[761] In fact, some non-Arab traditions speak of the Jewish people and the Arabs being allied, decades after the bond between them was supposed to have been broken according to the official Islamic historical tradition.[762]

There was, however, also a counter-tradition that probably emerged from a later encounter between Islam and Judaism, namely the period under the Abbasid Caliphate, when Islam was being set up as an irreconcilable rival to Judaism.[763] The framers of the later *hadiths* could not get rid of the traditions speaking of an early affinity between proto-Islam and Judaism altogether but they did try to 'quarantine' these traditions by claiming that it lasted only for a fleeting moment in history.[764] This development will be explored more fully towards the end of the chapter, but let us note for the moment that proto-Islam was clearly deeply influenced by Judaism[765], even if the official record would have us believe that the Jewish people should be viewed as the mortal enemies of Islam almost from the very first encounter of these religions.

8.7. Proto-Islam and Near Eastern Christianities

The plural form of Christianity used above is not a grievous grammatical error, but was chosen deliberately. It refers to the reality that the Arab migrants who came in from the desert encountered various expressions of the Christian faith.[766] Some of which would have been viewed as mutually exclusive by their devotees.

There is unmistakable evidence from the Qur'an that the Arab migrants did not simply stand aloof from the debates between these various Christian groups. In fact, a significant part of the emerging proto-Islamic tradition can be viewed as a vigorous and deeply opinionated contribution to this inter-Christian conversation.[767]

Part of the evidence for the above statement can be found in the peculiar way in which some Qur'anic passages deal with idolatry. While the immediate assumption is that the idolaters in question were pagans (i.e. worshipers of idols), this is not necessarily borne out by the text. Instead, the primary accusation against the disbelievers is that they added 'partners to God'.[768] Add to this the repeated mentions of Christian figures in the Qur'an (Jesus is mentioned 25 times and Mary is literally the only woman named in its pages[769]) and an intriguing alternative identity for the disbelievers immediately presents itself. It could very well be that many passages of the Qur'an are staking out Christological positions by condemning those who held certain views of the nature of Christ as disbelievers.

A bit of background is needed at this point. Christology (reflection on the person and nature of Jesus Christ[770]) was one of the major preoccupations of the age and the source of much conflict between Christians.[771] The Christian church in the Roman Empire had to call council after council to deal with the question of whether Jesus was fully divine in response to an Egyptian Christian leader by the name of Arius who stated that Jesus was a created being who was later elevated to divine status.[772] After the majority of church leaders present at the Council of Nicea (325 CE)[773] issued a statement that affirmed the full divinity of Jesus the bitter conflict over this issue continued to simmer for many decades more before the debate moved to the question of the exact nature of Christ. The key dilemma in this second Christological conflict essentially boiled down to the following: if Christ was indeed fully divine, how are we to understand his human nature? Was he human as well as divine or should his evident humanity be understood in some other way. A further council of the church held at Chalcedon[774] (a suburb of Constantinople) in 451 CE hammered out a compromise statement stating that Christ was indeed both fully human and fully divine (i.e. two natures combined in one person).[775]

The Chalcedonian position, still officially accepted by the vast majority of Christians, left many deeply discontented groups in its wake, some of whom formally separated themselves from churches holding to this position.[776] Further refinements of the orthodox position added to those who saw themselves as deeply at odds with imperially supported Christianity. There were, for example, those who taught that the human nature of Jesus was totally dominated by his divine nature. They were known as Monophysites.[777] Monophysite Christians (from a combination of the Greek words 'monos' and 'physis' meaning 'one nature) tend to strongly emphasize the divinity of Jesus at the expense of his humanity. At the other end of the spectrum a group, known as Nestorians[778] after one of their early leaders, maintained that the two natures[779] of Jesus remained entirely separate. A favorite analogy of this group was that like oil and water does not mix, so the natures of Jesus remained separate (i.e. not unified in one person as stated at Chalcedon).

What does all of this have to do with the rise of Islam? Simply that the debate about what might seem like rarefied doctrines was exceptionally intense and even violent in the very areas the Arab migrants moved into. This was a part of the world in which Orthodox, Arian, Monophysite and Nestorian Christians regularly rubbed shoulders and in which vehement theological disagreements were part of daily life. Just how all-consuming these theological debates could be is perfectly summed up in a quotation attributed to Gregory of Nyssa (335-395 CE): "Everywhere, in the public squares, at crossroads, on the streets and lanes, people would stop you and discourse at random about the Trinity. If you asked something of a moneychanger, he would begin discussing the question of the Begotten and the Unbegotten. If you questioned a baker about the price of bread, he would answer that the Father is greater and the Son is subordinate to Him. If you went to take a bath, the bath attendant would tell you that in his opinion the Son simply comes from nothing."[780]

It could be argued that the Roman Province of Syria (and especially its largest city, Antioch[781]) was in many ways ground-zero for the Christological debates of the age. This should immediately cause anyone interested in the early history of Islam to sit up and take notice, especially given what we have already discovered about the profound influence that this part of the world had on the development of Islam.

It is crucial to remember that the settlements reached at Nicaea (and subsequent 'ecumenical councils') were in many ways imperially sponsored projects.[782] The Roman political class, therefore, had a significant stake in enforcing the edicts of these councils as a means of fostering religious unity within the empire.[783] The problem was, however, that many people were not remotely willing to take the enforcing of what they viewed as the 'Emperor's Religion'[784] (i.e. Nicaean and Chalcedonian orthodoxy) lying down. Two main strategies of resistance presented themselves. In some places, like Antioch, outward conformity was more-or-less maintained while divergent Christologies were kept alive in informal ways.[785] Other heterodox Christians simply removed themselves to places where the edicts of Nicaea and Chalcedon could not be easily enforced.[786] It should be obvious that the Syro-Arabian borderlands was such a place and quite an appealing one at that. It was close enough to Syria to maintain contact with the empire, but large parts of it were under tribal control so the emperor's writ on religious matters did not run there.[787]

When we read the Qur'an against this background, its intense focus on Jesus and much of its anti-Christian polemic makes perfect sense. To state a hypothesis: parts of proto-Islam most likely had its origins in an Arian Christian context. It also stood in opposition to another heterodox group known as the 'Nazarenes'. This is quite a mouthful so let us unpack it a bit.

Nicene Christianity holds that Jesus was fully divine and thus not a created being.[788] Arian Christianity, on the other hand, maintains that Jesus was indeed created ('There was a time when he was not' was a favorite saying of Arius).[789] The Council of Nicaea (325 CE) with its strong anti-Arian pronouncements did not mean the end of Arian Christianity. In fact, some of the post-Constantine emperors actively promoted Arianism.[790] By the 7th century Arianism was perhaps in a much weaker position, but it certainly persisted on the fringes of the Roman Empire.

It can be argued that the Qur'an contains extended passages that could be interpreted as Arian anti-Nicene polemic.[791] Even though it is stated that Jesus is a prophet (not necessarily a theme in Arian polemics), there are many statements in the Qur'an that come straight from the Arian playbook. Most significant of these is the special, but non-divine, status given to Jesus as one chosen and anointed by God ('Messiah' a favorite form of address for Jesus in the Qur'an literally means 'anointed one'[792]). He is portrayed as being born of a virgin[793], a miracle worker, a life giver, sinless and with God in heaven.[794] These exalted statements certainly place Jesus several steps above Muhammad who is portrayed as a non-miracle working 'messenger'[795], who died and was buried. On the other hand, Jesus is also presented as certainly not divine or eternal.[796] In fact, we can even find traces of the quintessential Arian statement, 'There was a time when he was not'[797] in the Qur'an: "Indeed, the example of Jesus to Allah is like that of Adam. He created him from dust; then He said to him, "Be," and he was," (Qur'an 3:59).[798]

In addition to staking out its claim for the truth of the Arian position, the developing Islamic tradition as embodied in the Qur'an also seems to lock polemical horns with a heterodox group which we may call the 'Nazarenes'. On the face of it, 'Nasara' seems to be simply the Arabic word for Christian.[799] There are, however, a few problems with the use of this word to describe Christianity. Modern Arab Christians rarely use this term to describe themselves.[800] In this they follow in the footsteps of generations of Christians in not using Nazareth (the place where Jesus grew up according to the Gospels[801]) as one of the primary markers of Christ's identity.[802] Firstly, we know almost nothing about the time that Jesus spent there. Secondly the New Testament itself makes it clear that a link with a place as backward and isolated as Nazareth is best avoided.[803] Could it, therefore, perhaps be that the 'Nasara' were not mainstream Christians after all, but another one of the many heterodox groups (possibly with links to a movement known as the Ebionites[804]) pushed beyond the borders of the empire by the emperor's religious policies? (See Section 3.1.1)

A closer reading of the doctrines held by the *Nasara* seems to bear this out. Whoever is being addressed in the passages where the *Nasara* is mentioned held to doctrines that were not a feature of more mainstream Christianity (Chalcedonian or otherwise). Perhaps most significant is the fact that they seemed to have elevated Mary to a position inside the Trinity.[805] This is not a doctrine that even the most enthusiastic Marian devotees would subscribe to, as the Trinity has always been defined as 'Father, Son and Holy Spirit'.[806] Could it, therefore, be that the Qur'an contains a conversation with a now vanished sect of Arabian Christianity that worshiped Mary as part of the godhead?[807]

Another intriguing possibility in terms of Christian influence on the Qur'an is found in the very name Muhammad itself. It has been plausibly suggested that Muhammad ('the praised one') could possibly be a title for Jesus instead of the name of another individual. This may seem rather far-fetched until we consider the ground-breaking analysis performed by Christoph Luxenburg in his 'Syro-Aramaic Reading of the Koran'.[808] He points out that many hard to understand passages of the Qur'an make perfect sense when they are returned to their original contexts as Christological and Eucharistic[809] statements. In this context, it may indeed be that the Qur'an contains hymns to Christ as the 'praised one'.

8.8. In Search of Identity

The time has now come to pause and take stock of the different strands woven into proto-Islam and to pose the question as to how the major dilemmas they presented could be addressed. This can be stated as follows:

From a close reading of the Qur'an, the Islamic traditions and Non-Muslim primary sources we can deduce that the earliest audience of the proto-Islamic tradition were recent Arab migrants from the desert who suddenly found themselves in an area where economic life was dominated by farming (both crop and livestock farming) and seafaring. They made the move into these areas not, in the first instance, as a conquering army, but as mercenaries invited in by the Romans to protect their interests in the region. The coming of the Arabs was therefore neither as rapid or 'Islamic' as is commonly supposed and was not associated with a new religion called 'Islam', a prophet called Muhammad or a book called the Qur'an by those who experienced these events firsthand and wrote about what they experienced. Instead, eventual Arab dominance relied mostly on incremental migration and the eventual realization that they could simply 'take over' from a weakened Roman Empire.

The Arab migrants brought with them a language, culture and pagan religious ideas shaped by the legacy of the Nabataean Kingdom and many of them would still have regarded some Nabataean sites (mostly notably Petra) as deeply sacred. Yet the area of the Syro-Arabian borderlands presented them with a smorgasbord of alternative religious and cultural options. This was an area where Biblical sites reminded everyone of ancient Abrahamic religion and stories from the Christian Gospels. Many of the Arab migrants were deeply attracted to the religious ideas they were encountering. Thus, we find that layers of Judaism, Christianity and Syriac culture are clearly discernable within the developing tradition.

The many layered, and often conflicting, identities being adopted by the Arab migrants posed a significant and seemingly intractable problem for the developing Arab state. While it was true that Arabs were coming into positions of political power the question could still be asked: *Which Arabs?* Who were supposed to guide society? The Arab pagans? The Arab Nicene Christians? The Arab Arian Christians? The Arab Jews? Those leading Arab society must have seen the many influences pulling at their kinsfolk as deeply threatening. It was taken as non-negotiable by many thinkers in late antiquity that any state without a unifying guiding ideology could not survive for long[810] and this was clearly something that the Arab migrants lacked.

There was, furthermore, the threat of divided loyalties. Who was to say, for example, that Arabs attracted to Judaism would not someday rather support their Jewish fellow believers, instead of their ethnic kin, in a possible future conflict? This issue was particularly pertinent and troubling when it came to Christianity. There can be no doubt that Nicene Christianity was extremely closely identified with the Roman Empire[811], especially given vigorous past efforts by the Romans to enforce Nicene orthodoxy in the very areas that the Arab migrants now called home.[812] Those Arabs who belonged to the 'Emperor's Religion'[813] would, therefore, have been regarded with deep unease by Arab political leaders. These leaders must have been kept awake at night by the thought that their Christian subjects could potentially act as the advance guard for a return of Roman power.

What the Arab leaders desperately needed was a single identity built on a narrative that would unite, rather than divide, the Arabs. A simple return to pre-migration paganism would have been out of the question given that many of the Arab incomers were by now deeply wedded to various monotheistic beliefs.[814] Enforcing paganism might, therefore, have sparked a more devastating rebellion than the one they were trying to forestall. A solution was needed that would allow for a recognition of the pagan past while judiciously adding elements of the monotheisms that were so enticing to many Arabs and then fusing all of this into a coherent whole.[815]

It was from this politically motivated desire for a unifying ideology, that could be assembled by using the building blocks of readily accessible beliefs and traditions, that Islam was eventually born. This process had three main phases (after the initial chaos of the immediate post-migration period). They may broadly be described as: a) The prescription of a broad Arab monotheism b) The sudden declaration of a decisive and hostile break from all precursor traditions and c) The final consolidation and formalization of the new religion thus formed. These phases can be more-or-less equated with the reign of the Sufyanid Umayyads (661-684 CE), the Marwanid Umayyds (684-750 CE) and the rise of the Abbasid Caliphate (from 750 CE onwards) respectively.

8.9. Muawiya and Pan-Arab Monotheism

Muawiya (who reigned as caliph from 661-680 CE) was, as we have seen, the first of the Muslim caliphs who is independently attested in the primary source record. The four caliphs (Abu Bakr, Umar, Uthman and Ali) that supposedly came before him share in the problem of much of early Islamic history, namely that they are not reliably present in the primary sources dating from the period in question.[816]

It is curious to realize that although he is the first Arab leader of whom we can trace a satisfactory profile (or perhaps because of it), Muawiya was deeply disliked by many of those who followed in his wake and even by modern Muslims (especially vociferously so by the Shi'a[817]). This is because he clearly did not conform to what later Muslim historians thought of as the ideal Muslim leader and he is pointedly not included in the list of 'rightly guided caliphs'.[818] Could this perhaps be because he represents the authentic development of proto-Islam, while the earlier four caliphs (of whom we do not have sufficiently compelling primary source confirmation that they even existed) were invented later to legitimize 9th century theological positions?

One of the things that most irritated later generations about Muawiya was that he clearly displayed an ecumenical spirit and seemed to have promoted a general Arab monotheism instead of a narrow creed focused on Muhammad and the Qur'an. In this we can see his response to the pressing question of how to forge a single Arab identity out of the divergent beliefs and traditions followed by the Arab migrants. The creed proposed by him seems to have been built on the general acknowledgement of the existence of only one God (the protocol used on documents from this period was simply 'In the Name of God').[819] He, furthermore, seemed willing to allow a role for Christ within the creed he was promoting (many of his inscriptions contain crosses).[820] His hope was perhaps to promote religious policies that were broad enough to keep a variety of his subjects happy through the fact that they could all project their beliefs onto the bare canvas he was presenting them with. One, therefore, searches in vain in documents or inscriptions from this era for exclusive Christian, Jewish or Pagan pronouncements made by the Arab rulers.

What is obviously also conspicuously absent is the Islamic confession of faith ('I testify that there is no God but God and Muhammad is the messenger of God')[821] or any policy promoting the beliefs articulated in it.

Muawiya and the Sufyanid rulers who followed him may have thought that that their 'Can't we All Just Get Along' approach to the question of Arab religious identity would provide the necessary space for believers of various stripes to settle down and practice their faith. Secure in the knowledge that the state will not interfere with them. There were, however, powerful forces that made the realization of the ideal of peaceful coexistence very unlikely. Perhaps most important among these was the fact that the Arabs were steadily increasing their territorial holdings, thus encountering an ever more bewildering array of beliefs and traditions.[822] This increased the pressure on them to formulate a unifying and internally consistent religious policy. Strongly related to this was the fact that religion can play a powerful rule in motivating those 'fighting for the cause'.[823] Muawiya's broad religious settlement would have been very unsatisfactory in this regard. If religious truth is so pliable that everyone is encouraged to consider themselves as believing much the same as everyone else, there will be little inclination to take up arms for the faith.

The final factor in the failure of Muawiya's attempts at consensus building was probably the unwillingness of many believers to have their treasured convictions reduced to just one option among many and the fact that several leaders responded to the outrage that they felt at the religious levelling they saw around them by actively rebelling against the state.[824]

They say that the road to hell is paved with good intentions. This is a lesson that Muawiya must have learned very thoroughly by the end of his life. He was probably very sincere in his promotion of an open and tolerant monotheism, but it was found wanting by many of his opponents as a means of rallying the troops and for forging a distinct Arab identity that they could carry with them as a unifying force on their far-flung conquests. More was needed, and the Arab state was in danger of tearing itself apart due to the actions of rebels who had very firm ideas of exactly what this 'more' should be.[825]

To restore peace in the fractious environment that was the result of Arab religious differences would take strong leadership and the presentation of a clearly defined religious standard that people could rally to. It was precisely this that the Marwanids proposed to offer.

8.10. The Marwanids and the Birth of Islam

By the end of the reign of the Sufyanids as Umayyad caliphs, the need for a unifying focus for Arab identity was as pressing as ever. It was also clear that a middle-of-the-road policy designed to keep everyone satisfied merely left discontent and rebellion in its wake.[826] The family that succeeded the Sufyanids at the center of the Umayyad state, known as the Marwanids[827], clearly decided that it would not be 'more of the same' as far as Arab religious policy was concerned. The answer that they, and especially their most famous early caliph Abd Al Malik, came up with was nothing less than a complete and decisive break with previous traditions. This was done through latching on to the idea of a charismatic Arab leader with a direct calling from God to shape unruly tribes into a nation.[828] Enter Muhammad.

In non-Arab writings dealing with the post-migration period we encounter some references to a charismatic Arab leader who played a role in the process of the Arabs eventually rising to dominance.[829] However, as we have seen, the picture is fairly confused as some elements that are being discussed in these writings do not easily gel with the Muslim view of Muhammad (e.g. that the leader in question was in league with the Jews as late as the 640's CE).

It seems, however, that the Marwanids thought that the 'charismatic Arab leader' tradition as very promising in providing the raw material from which a separate religion could be built.

How rapid the change to recognizing Muhammad as the 'Apostle of Allah' was can be seen in the fact that the first Arabic references to him appear almost overnight in the early 690's CE.[830] From this point onwards he is simply everywhere. The name 'Muhammad' suddenly appears as part of the protocols, on official correspondence and on inscriptions. There was thus a clear move away from merely invoking the name of Allah to also referencing Muhammad as the messenger of Allah.

We have repeatedly seen just how vitally important the Dome of the Rock was in announcing the coming of age of Arab religiosity (see Section 7.8). The Dome of the Rock not only represents the entry of Muhammad onto the world stage, almost 60 years after he supposedly breathed his last. It is also a thoroughgoing repudiation of orthodox Christianity with its emphasis on the divinity of Jesus. To top it all off, it announces the name of the new creed in whose name Christianity is rejected: Islam.

Thus, we now see all the building blocks in place for a specifically Arab belief system to which the migrants and their descendants could rally. At the heart of this was the enigmatic figure of Muhammad. This elevation of Muhammad was unprecedented to say the least: no Arab seems to have heard of him before the early 690's CE, but now they were assured that following his message was the way to God.

It is easy to see how placing Muhammad at the center of Marwanid religious policy could have led to some potentially positive outcomes from the perspective of the Arab rulers. If people could be made to believe the claims about the austere and persuasive prophet who spoke for God, they could be shaped into a community of faith over which the inventors and transmitters of the tradition would have almost total control.

One aspect of this control was related to the fact that the Arabs were involved in almost constant warfare in order to extend their reach or to shore up gains made previously. This meant that the 'perfect example' (cf. Qur'an 33:21) that they were creating had to be someone of a sufficiently warlike bent to inspire others to also take up arms.[831] Thus, the new prophet became a kind of divinely inspired recruiting sergeant who could help ensure that a steady stream of eager new recruits made it to the battlefield, and that they stayed motivated while there.[832] All of this explains why the later part of the Muhammad tradition is so laced with bloodlust and calls to arms. Once again, we see an example of the effective ideological use to which back-projected traditions could be put.

The centrality of Muhammad within the emerging Arab creed must inevitably have led to an almost insatiable thirst for information about him and so traditions claiming to shed light on his life began to proliferate.[833] The framers of these traditions drew upon snippets of information that had their origins firmly in the Syro-Arabian borderlands, added their own emphases, and presented this as an accurate record of the life and teachings of God's Messenger.[834]

The problem with the invention of traditions supposedly stretching back to the distant past is that it is a game that can be played by many people at once. Thus, anyone who invents a tradition will in some ways be at the mercy of whoever decides to invent a counter-tradition. The upshot of this was that the hoped-for peace associated with a unifying Arab religious narrative never materialized and the Marwanids continued to experience the vicious inter-Arab conflict that they so desperately hoped to prevent. They simply did not reckon with the fact that other leaders could step forward with the claim that they represented the authentic Muhammad tradition and that the Umayyads were usurpers who corrupted it.[835]

It can be argued that Abd Al Malik and his successors sowed the seeds for the destruction of their dynasty by creating a new religion to unify the Arabs under a single banner. By 750 CE, the Umayyads would be swept away by a dynasty that made the audacious claim that they were in fact the true followers of the Umayyads most enduring creation: Islam.[836] Before this happened, however, the Umayyads played what they must have believed to be a masterstroke. They sought to place their version of a unifying Arab religious tradition beyond the ability to question or amend it by quarantining it to the middle of the Arabian Desert.

8.11. Salvation in the Desert: Why it was Necessary to Invent Mecca

It is interesting to note that both major figures of the Umayyad era Muawiya I and Abd Al Malik were content to reign from Damascus as the center of Arab dominance.[837] If they did show any interest in the Arabian interior, it was as a place where Arab culture had some of its roots. Muawiya also made some low-key efforts to set up outposts of Umayyad influence in this region, most notably around Ta'if where he built a dam.[838] There is, however, no way that you could describe the Umayyads as a primarily central Arabian power. As for the location where the modern city of Mecca is located, it hardly needs repeating that it was completely unknown and unremarked on in the pre-Islamic historical record.

Yet, from the beginning of the 8th century CE onwards, a strange thing begins to happen. New mosques were being built pointing to the Hejaz (i.e. West-Central Arabia) and mosques that had previously been oriented much farther north were modified to do the same.[839] The resulting awkward placement of *qiblas* (prayer directions) in many of Islam's oldest mosques thus bears silent but eloquent testimony to a change of monumental proportions: the siting of Islam's holy city in a location that allowed the Umayyads to control the development of their newly minted religion.

We should be under no illusion that the southward move represents anything less than a total departure from previous Arab religious policies. In the early years of the migration and Arab dominance, the emphasis seems to have been on connecting the emerging Arab religion with pre-existing traditions in Syria and northern Arabia. It became clear very quickly, however, that this policy created significant problems in the way in which it divided Arabs along confessional lines. In what they must have believed to be a political and religious masterstroke the Arab rulers therefore decided to remove the focal point of their religion as far away as possible from the melting pot and ferment of religious ideas where it originated.

Headquartering their new religion in Syria or Northern Arabia would always leave the followers of Islam open to the charge that they plagiarized their ideas from Judaism, Christianity or pre-existing forms of Arab paganism.[840] In contrast to this, the Hejaz presented them with a blank canvas upon which they could paint their ideas about God and his prophet and to make the claim that their new revelation emerged fully formed into world, owing precisely nothing to what came before.

The Umayyads could, furthermore, exert full control over the site of their new religion by placing it in the middle of an empty desert over which

229

they held military sway. This was not the case in places like Damascus or Jerusalem. While they did have political control there, there were still plenty of believers of rival faiths around who could challenge their claims to be the inheritors of an authentic religious tradition. It is one thing, for example, to make a claim for religious supremacy in Jerusalem through the construction of the Dome of the Rock[841], but the very continuance of Christianity in this city[842] bore eloquent testimony that there were still plenty of people who did not find the bold statements on the sides of Abd Al Malik's masterpiece at all credible.

By placing the 'holy of holies' of their new religion far from prying eyes in the middle of the desert, the later Marwanid rulers neatly took care of this problem. At this early formation phase of the new religion very few people in the large cities controlled by the Umayyads would ever have been in the Hejaz (not to mention Mecca, which obviously only now begins to enter the historical record), so stories and traditions located there would simply have to be taken by faith. This was a useful contrast to a tradition set in, say, Jerusalem where those being confronted with the teachings of the new religion could cross-check its claims against realities on the ground.

Thus, it came to be that many of the traditions and proto-scriptures that were beginning to grow around the new Arab religious tradition were progressively wrenched from their North Arabian and Syrian places of origin and transferred lock, stock, and barrel to the newly minted holy city of the Arabs. Sometimes this wrenching may have been all too literal as there is evidence that the black stone in the side of the *ka'aba* in Mecca may have been brought there from a holy site much further north.[843]

We noted that the relocation of the focus of early Islam to Mecca created some patent absurdities. For example, the 'mountains' associated with Islam's holy city were obviously absent in Mecca so two very low hills were suddenly promoted to the status of mountains. They are, in fact, so low that they are housed inside the great mosque complex in Mecca.[844] This is just one example of how many of the early traditions surrounding Muhammad are such a terrible 'fit' for the environment, geography and conditions of the present location of Mecca. An analogy would be to take the fairy tales of the Grimm brothers with their brooding forests and north European lakes and set them on the African savanna. The stories will probably still make sense on some level, but something will not feel quite right. It is in this sense that the Muhammad traditions with their background of crop-based agriculture, valleys, ravines and mountains feel weirdly out of place in the desert heat of central Arabia.[845]

Even so, the advantages outlined above must have convinced the Arab rulers that the hard work of making the traditions 'fit' in a new, and in many was incompatible, context was a small price to pay for the advantage of starting from scratch in a place where they believed they could fully control the further development of their new religion. This still does not mean that everyone was equally enthusiastic about this literal about-face. We still see mosques constructed deep into the 8th century stubbornly maintaining their orientation to northern Arabia, even as others were being built facing Mecca.[846] This utter confusion would only be fully re-solved with the exertion of much stronger central control under the rule of the Abbasids (i.e. from 750 CE onwards). This coupled with the, by now, fading memories of alternative centers of Arab devotion meant that Mecca eventually became firmly entrenched as the primary physical focal point of Muslim devotion. A position that it obviously retains to this day.

8.12. The Creation of a Scriptural Tradition

We've noted throughout this chapter how several different strands went into the creation of what we now know as Islam. The early 8th century was not only the time when the focus of Arab devotion shifted decisively southwards (i.e. towards newly minted Mecca), it was also the age of the creation of a written tradition to serve as the foundation of the new faith.

A major part of the formalization of Arab religion under the banner of Islam was, of course, the creation of the Qur'an. It is, therefore, precise-ly from this period that we begin to see reliably datable fragments of the Qur'an turn up in the historical record. The compilation of the Qur'an is a process that probably took several decades and certainly did not result in a seamless whole.[847] How could this be otherwise given that so many diverse sources and agendas had to be harmonized? In fact, in the early years, there was still an awareness that developing Islam relied on several books. This was, for example, evident in the statements by John of Damascus (circa 730 CE) about the different Arab 'holy books' (which eventually became mere chapters of the Qur'an) as individual titles.[848]

The splicing together of a variety of traditions happened against the background of the fact that the early 8th century world was a very different place from that into which the early Arab migration occurred. For one thing, Arab expansionism was kicking into high gear and the main priority seems to have been to provide a firm and exclusive ideological basis for an Arab empire spanning several continents.[849] What better way to do this than to create a religious justification for it? The creation of Mecca was an attempt to provide a secure focus for the religion of the conquerors. This would not have been enough however. The written tradition also had to be shaped in ways that conformed to the needs of the age.

Perhaps chief among these needs was the necessity to establish the new Arab religion as much more than one truth among many, but instead as the very truth of God. This was achieved through the emergence of passages that made claims about the exclusive truth of Islam in the most strenuous terms possible. Gone were the earlier openness to other traditions as equally legitimate revelations of God. From now on it was going to be Islam or eternal damnation: "And whoever desires other than Islam as religion - never will it be accepted from him, and he, in the Hereafter, will be among the losers," (Qur'an 3:85).[850]

Another need was, as has already been mentioned, the pressing one of recruiting vast numbers of troops to spearhead the task of imperial expansion. This is the reason behind the warlike turn that the tradition now takes. We are shown how Muhammad sweeps everything before him and participates in what would today be described as a series of war crimes[851]. The overwhelming impression that this part of the tradition leaves one with is the idea that the end justifies the means and that total victory at any cost should be the goal of the community.

It is significant to note that orthodox Muslim scholars acknowledge that the most belligerent chapters of the Qur'an (like Chapter 9, the so-called 'Chapter of the Sword'[852]) are to be placed last in the Qur'an's chronological order of composition (or 'revelation' as they would have it). There is obviously no record of these chapters even existing before the early 8th century. It is, therefore, quite likely that these verses made their entrance at about the same time as the tradition that painted the emerging Muhammad figure as one of the most warlike figures ever to bestride the Arabian Peninsula.[853] These traditions were then superimposed, not always in a seamless way, on an older tradition showing the charismatic Arab leader as a visionary moral and religious reformer. It is, once again, fascinating to note that the idea that there are two very distinct parts of the Qur'an persists even in orthodox Islamic theology. Muslim scholars attempt to explain away the vast disconnect between the two Muhammad traditions by sorting them into earlier (Meccan) and later (Medinan) parts.[854] An unfortunate consequence of this is that 'Muhammad the Warrior' is the dominant tradition in classical Islam as later revelations are believed to supersede earlier passages where they differ.[855]

In addition to the very different types of material that were increasingly being pulled into the growing body of religious texts that would eventually become the Qur'an, there were also a wide variety of traditions that claimed to go right back to the time of the prophet (these would form the basis of the *hadith* collections). The problem with this way of forming a coherent historical tradition has already been identified. It seems as if literally hundreds of people with a wide array of religious and political persuasions simply invented traditions to support their positions and convictions.[856] And why not? The entire edifice was created from scratch anyway. What could the problem with adding a few novel layers of your own be?[857] The problem is, of course, that this way of forming a tradition was guaranteed to entrench discord and strife as Muslims with diametrically opposed positions sought to give divine sanction to them by calling on the prophet's words and example to vindicate and support them.

If Islam, the new Arab religion (which by now was beginning to attract ever larger groups of non-Arabs keen to join the ruling elite), had any hope of long term survival, some way had to be found to impose order on the swirling mass of traditions and to streamline them into a more-or-less coherent body of teaching. What was particularly needed was guidance and teaching on how this new faith was to be lived on a day-to-day level (i.e. when not striving for its military expansion).

To see how this happened we must shift our narrative to the part of the world now known as Iraq, under the Abbasids[858].

8.13. By the Rivers of Babylon: The Final Strand is Added

Even those with only a fleeting familiarity with Islam, as it eventually developed, will know that it has its own legal system known as *shari'a*. The development of a formal legal tradition represents the addition of a final layer of influence that culminated in the creation of Islam more-or-less as it exists today.

We should, once again, remember that although Mecca was supposedly the mother of all cities, it was never the capital of the emerging Arab empire (the reason for this is obviously that it probably did not even exist during the earliest years of the Arab empire). Even when the traditions around Muhammad and Mecca began to develop at the beginning of the 7th century, there was very little appetite to move the center of the Empire to this newly founded city. Instead two cities dominated the early centuries of Arab hegemony. They are Damascus and Baghdad[859] (with Jerusalem as the site of the Umayyad ruler Abd al Malik's 'Dome of the Rock' rating an honorable mention).

The reason for the move of the center of Arab power from Damascus to Baghdad was a dynastic shift that occurred in 750 CE. The Umayyads were displaced by the Abbasids[860], a dynasty that claimed to be more faithful adherents to the Arab religion invented by the Umayyads. This was a quite spectacular example of spiritual audacity, but it could be that aspects of Islam had been around for long enough that those who remembered the earlier forms of Arab monotheism were not around anymore to challenge this move. Be this as it may, the Abbasids quite explicitly based the legitimacy of their rule on their claim to be the authentic followers of Muhammad.[861]

One of the problems that the Abbasids faced was that their power base, with Baghdad as their capital[862], was geographically distant from the Arabian Desert and crucially also from the Syro-Arabian borderlands out of which the early monotheistic proto-Islamic tradition sprang. They instead called Mesopotamia, the 'land between the rivers' home. With the rise of Abbasid power, the political center of gravity of emerging Islam now moves into the former heartlands of the Persian Empire. Thus it was that while the earliest years of Islamic development occurred in or around former Roman territory, it found its final shape in a very different environment.[863]

This environment was home to some very sophisticated religious and cultural traditions that would go on to have a profound impact on Islam's development and specifically on the codification of Islamic law.[864] The two most important Mesopotamian religious traditions had one crucial thing in common. Both the Zoroastrian priests and the Jewish Rabbis of Mesopotamia claimed that they were the custodians of an ancient oral tradition that they were called to commit to writing.[865]

The efforts of the Zoroastrian priests have largely slipped from public consciousness in the West as most people are unlikely to be in regular contact with Zoroastrians, but the achievements of the Jewish rabbis are still very much with us. These rabbis, working in several centers along the Mesopotamian Rivers maintained that God did not only give a written copy of the law to Moses at Sinai. Equally important was the fact that the 'Oral Law' (Mishnah) was also entrusted to him at this time. In the centuries since then, it fell to people like them to continue to memorize and transmit this venerable tradition. By the time many Jewish people reached Babylon as exiles, it was decided to finally commit this tradition to paper and also to produce voluminous commentaries on it. Thus, we see the birth of the Babylonian Talmud, a collection of commentaries on what was believed to be ancient oral traditions.[866]

It is probably not coincidental that the Islamic legal traditions were produced in the exact same area where the Zoroastrian priests and Jewish Rabbis labored to shape the past in their own image through the formulation of supposedly ancient oral traditions.[867] It is, furthermore, striking to note how many of the Muslim legal traditions that emerged during this time precisely reflected Jewish legal priorities as reflected in the Mishnah and Talmud.[868]

These newly minted Islamic legal positions sometimes even go head-to-head with older layers of the emerging Islamic tradition by choosing to side with Jewish and Zoroastrian positions. Two examples of this trend should suffice. The Qur'an itself simply states that apostates (i.e. those who leave the religion) will have to answer to Allah in the hereafter.[869] In Zoroastrianism, however, the prescribed punishment for apostasy is death.[870] There are several Islamic traditions that emerged from this period which back-projects this exceedingly strict ruling right into the mouth of the Muhammad figure who supposedly founded the community in the 7th century Arabian Desert. He is made to say, in total agreement with the Zoroastrian position: 'If anyone changes his Islamic religion, then kill him'.[871]

The other example deals with adultery. Once again, the older layers of the emerging Islamic tradition prescribed relatively mild punishments (e.g. house arrest[872]) in such cases. However, the Mesopotamian rabbis took a much harder line by prescribing stoning as the appropriate punishment.[873] Once again, the Islamic legal tradition developing in Mesopotamia followed the rabbis. In this case there was evidently a great deal of embarrassment that the earlier tradition was being so blatantly ignored. To deal with this, several secondary traditions were invented (this time placed in the mouths of those who outlived the prophet). The second Caliph Umar is made to swear that the Qur'an once contained a verse prescribing stoning[874] and Muhammad's wife Aisha states that the absence of the verse mandating stoning from the Qur'an was due to a goat eating some papers with Qur'anic verses on them on the day Muhammad died.[875]

It can plausibly be argued that the incorporation of Jewish and Zoroastrian legal positions into Islam did not only occur in the same place where the earlier traditions emerged (Mesopotamia), but that many of the same people who labored on the earlier traditions also worked hard to make them part of Islam. It is likely that as Islam increased its authority and influence, some Zoroastrian priests[876] and Jewish rabbis[877] flocked to its standard. They quite probably did not only bring their own personal devotion, but also their extensive legal training and their deep experience of transforming the present by re-imagining the past through supposed oral traditions.

There is in some ways a deep irony here. While Islam was envisioned as a vehicle to legitimize Arab rule, it was given much of its final shape by non-Arab converts who brought their unique skills in weaponizing the past for present purposes to their new religion. In the process, the traditions they were inventing eventually placed tremendous pressure on the rulers who saw Islam as a tool for strengthening their rule. Both because the legal scholars de-emphasized Arab identity as the primary basis for authority (replacing this with strict adherence to Islamic law) and because they set themselves up as the primary guardians and interpreters of this law.

With the addition of the Jewish and Zoroastrian inspired legal tradition, the development of Islam into the fully developed religion that we know today was essentially complete. It should be obvious from what has gone before that this was only one strand that was added to many others. These include pre-Islamic Arab paganism, a vague monotheism centered on the Syro-Arabian borderlands and an invented tradition with an Arabian prophet from the distant past at its core. These strands were not at all woven together in a seamless fashion and some of the fault lines between them are still visible and active in modern Islam. We may be astounded by the many and varied influences that shaped Islam, but what we simply cannot and should not do is to ignore the way in which they fundamentally challenge the accepted narrative of Islam's origins.

8.14. Chapter Summary: An Attempt at an Updated History

The time has now come to update the statement that prefaced every chapter of this book. In light of the material presented in this chapter it can be posited that Islam developed in the following way:

"At the beginning of the 7ᵗʰ century a power vacuum existed in the Syrian borderlands due to the Roman and Persian armies fighting each other to a standstill. This area was also in the grip of intense sectarian conflict as diverse groups of Christians strongly opposed the decisions (on the divinity and nature of Christ) of the Councils of Nicaea and Chalcedon. As Roman imperial control broke down (both on the military and political levels), different Arab tribes migrated into this area, eventually becoming militarily dominant. Thus, the coming of Arab domination during 7ᵗʰ century appears not to have been religiously motivated, but was rather driven by a desire for land and political control. As Arab power was consolidated, a way had to be found to keep Arabs with different religious convictions politically unified. The Sufyanid Arab ruler Muawiya attempted to do this by adopting and promoting a bland monotheism that was so non-dogmatic that most of those Arabs following competing monotheisms could make their peace with it. This attempt at forging a broad religious consensus came to an end with the reign of the Marwanids through their very explicit repudiation of Nicaean Christianity (the religion of the Roman Empire). Even this break with the religion of Rome was not enough for many of the martially inclined Arabs, who saw the need for a religion that could sustain and motivate their endless wars against non–Arab entities. The response to this was the projection of an interpretation of what the ideal Arab warrior should be onto a figure named Muhammad who supposedly lived about six decades before in the middle of the Arabian Desert. A variety of scriptural and narrative traditions were invented to illuminate his life and to provide a holy text for the new religion. The development of Islam as a religion was finally completed in Mesopotamia under the Abbasid Empire. It was during this period that the supposedly ancient oral traditions dealing with the life of Muhammad were finally written down. Many of these traditions clearly had more to do with Jewish and Zoroastrian teachings than with life in 7ᵗʰ century Arabia and they supplied the emerging religion with its own legal tradition known as shari'a."

9.

Whereto from Here?

Tipping over sacred cows may well be the favorite pursuit of some historians who delight in the shock value produced by their questioning of the supposed certainties of history. However, the purpose behind writing this book was about much more than presenting an alternative view of history because it will ruffle a few feathers.

There is so much at stake when it comes to Islam and its role in the modern world that an accurate appraisal of its history is much more than merely an academic matter. Considering this, the conclusions reached in this work should ideally evoke the following responses:

9.1. Commit to Honest, In-Depth Research

If nothing else, the material presented in this book should bring us to the conclusion that the true history of Islam is likely to be worlds away from the 'open and shut' version presented by Islamic orthodoxy. Unfortunately, however, much of what passes for academic scholarship in the field of Islamic history are merely attempts to find creative ways to tell the same old story. It is time to break out of this closed loop and recognize that fundamental questions can and should be asked about the reliability of the sources upon which the traditional account is based.

There are, as you will no doubt be aware after reading this book, scholars asking searching questions along these lines, but they are all too easily dismissed as mavericks and revisionists by those in the mainstream Islamic Studies community whose pay-checks all too often depend on carefully toeing the party line. This needs to change. You may not be convinced by every single argument that was presented in this work, but hopefully you will be very aware by now that it is simply not the case that the version of Islamic history taught in mosques and other Islamic institutions is remotely all that there is to say about how Islam developed.

To simply ignore possible alternative histories because they do not align with Islamic orthodoxy is intellectually lazy and represents the surrendering of established principles of historical research to faith-based certainties.

Those scholars willing to reject the ridiculous notion that nothing more needs to be asked about the early years of Islam should be encouraged to pursue their research wherever this may lead. The stranglehold of the 'don't go there' approach so vigorously promoted by politically correct academia when it comes to anything to do with Islam must end. When this happens, we stand a good chance of seeing the unanswered questions still lingering in this field answered. If it doesn't, the Muslim faith will continue to enjoy the 'free pass' from serious questioning that has so effectively stifled conversations about anything Islamic over the past few decades.

9.2. Bring Questions about Islam's History into the Open

While research and academic work on Islamic origins are desperately needed, some significant changes should also occur on the popular level, specifically in the way Islam is treated by the media. A significant number of key Islamic doctrines rest squarely on the orthodox version of history. Muslim leaders, in fact, routinely demand adherence and respect for these doctrines precisely because they are supposedly ancient and therefore venerable.

But what if the events that demand our respect never happened? What if, to take but one example, pilgrimage to Mecca is not an ancient rite, but something that was invented long after the death of Muhammad to strengthen the political position of Arab leaders of a later generation? If this is the case, then all the week-long '*Hajj* Special Reports' produced by Muslim employees of Western media outlets[878] (non-Muslims are not allowed to enter Mecca) are more than a little redundant. Perhaps the time has come for the kind of searching questioning of supposed certainties that Christians, Jews and Hindus have long been accustomed to. When it comes to these faiths, new documentary discoveries and even wildly speculative hypotheses[879] are boldly proclaimed as earth shattering and ground breaking in the print and broadcast media (think for example of the amount of positive attention the revisionist 'Jesus Seminar'[880] enjoyed in the media).

What is needed is a level playing field, one where the claim that 'Islam emerged in the full light of history' is not simply accepted as axiomatic, but where probing questions are routinely asked and discussed. One reason why this is not the case is the pervasive culture of supposedly tolerant political correctness (which somehow decided to give shelter to one of the most intolerant creeds imaginable). Another is the simple fact that questioning aspects of Islamic teaching is attended by significant risks to life and limb. This leads to the next point: open criticism of Islam is a fraught and dangerous exercise, even in the 21st century West, and this needs to change.

9.3. Challenge the Culture of Fear

One of the reasons why questions surrounding the history of Islam are treated with kid gloves by both academia and the media is the fact that many of those who are able to ask hard questions are often deeply intimidated by the response of many in the Muslim community to even the mildest forms of questioning. Sadly, the inclination of some Muslim groups to respond to criticism by attempting to shut it up instead of interacting with it often extends all the way to a willingness to use violence for the sake of defending the supposed truth of Islam. Perhaps the most high-profile recent expression of this was the attack that targeted the offices of the satirical magazine Charlie Hebdo in Paris in 2015 for publishing cartoons of Muhammad.[881] However, it extends wider than high-profile acts of *jihad* terror. The objective of silencing all questioning of Islam is also achieved through threats of violence. Several of those who are challenging the traditional interpretations of the history of Islam are forced to work under pseudonyms after receiving death threats. Likewise, the UK Television Station Channel 4 had to cancel perhaps one of the only television programs of recent times to at least attempt to honestly assess the history of Islam after threats of violence that arose from within the Muslim community.[882]

This cannot be allowed to continue. If freedom of speech means anything, it must also include the right and the ability to question even the most deeply held beliefs of others. Attempts to curb our ability to speak freely about Islam should, therefore, be met with a refusal to be intimidated or silenced. This does not mean that we should seek to be obnoxious or unnecessarily argumentative. Instead we should strive for a world in which questions about issues like the history of Islam can be asked in a robust, informed and incisive manner. For this to happen media organizations should be strongly encouraged not to buckle under the pressure from Muslim groups. Any effort to silence critics of Islam through violence should be met with the full force of the law. My appeal to the reader, in this regard, is to speak freely and fearlessly about the challenges to Islamic certainties that you encountered in this book. If these ideas can reach critical mass, it will be ever harder for those who would shut us up through intimidation to be successful.

9.4. Use Historical Facts to Undermine Islam

The heading of this section may strike some people as slightly jarring. It is, however, my considered opinion that the classical Islamic doctrines have an overwhelmingly negative impact on communities where it is in the ascendancy. Why (and how) this is the case is much more fully explored in my book *'Nothing to do with Islam? - Investigating the West's Most Dangerous Blind Spot'*. Let me just say, in the present context, that I believe that the world will be a much safer place if belief in Islam is fundamentally undermined in the minds of those who now affirm the *Shahada* ('There is no God but God and Muhammad is the Messenger of God').

I have written an entire book on the kinds of questions Muslims will have to answer if they want to hold on to their belief in Islam (*Questioning Islam - Tough Questions and Honest Answers about the Muslim Religion*) and am convinced that some of the most effective of these questions can be found in the realm of history. This is because Muslim believers are able to claim that some the finer points of Islamic theology must simply be taken on faith and can, therefore, not be settled through questioning and debate.

History, however, provides us with an arena where the claims made by Muslim scholars and the Islamic tradition more broadly can be tested. We can, therefore, say that history represents the Achilles Heel of Islam as it is obviously deeply vulnerable in this area. This is because the traditional and commonly accepted account of Islamic origins cannot even begin to survive critical enquiry.

By focusing on history, critics of Islam can also go some way to getting beyond the emotive language that criticism of Islam is routinely greeted with. Those questioning Islam are often accused of being 'bigots' or 'haters' simply for querying certain aspects of Islamic theology or practice. These charges are nonsensical to begin with, but the belief that those who question Islam must 'hate' Muslims are so deeply ingrained that an indirect approach may sometimes be required. Focusing on history represents exactly such an indirect approach as it brings us into the realm of names, dates, people and places. In short, things that can be approached in a more objective and less emotive manner. By this I am not saying that those who question Muslim history should not prepare themselves for bitter denunciations and even threats of violence (see above). What I am suggesting is that questions about history will have a better chance of 'slipping through the defenses' given how seemingly non-theological they are.

I would, considering the above, like to suggest that historical questioning should be at the very heart of all efforts to undermine belief in Islam in our societies. This leaves the question: exactly how vulnerable would Islam be to the disproving of its classical historical certainties?

9.5. Conclusion: What if the 'Full Light of History' is a Mirage?

We have, in a sense, come full circle. I started this book with a discussion of the importance of history to orthodox Islam. I then proceeded over the subsequent chapters to show how the traditional account of Islamic origins simply cannot survive historical scrutiny. Some readers may respond to this question by asking: Does it really matter? Is there not some kernel of truth at the heart of Islam that may be salvaged even if it is not possible to confirm every aspect of its history?

The best answer to this question is perhaps given by Muslim believers themselves. So much of their self-understanding, not to mention practices and beliefs, are shaped by the generally accepted version of Islamic history. If it were not for the traditions and biographies associated with Muhammad, Muslims would not have the *Shahada* (confession of faith) or the five daily prayers. They would, furthermore, not know how to go on pilgrimage, how to keep the Ramadan fast or how to give alms. In short, something as foundational and basic as the so-called 'Five Pillars of Islam' rests firmly, not on the Qur'an, but on the historical tradition.

An Islam, therefore, that ignores history and accepts only the Qur'an will be a severely truncated and unrecognizable version of the faith. Such a reliance on the Qur'an also conveniently ignores the many questions that can be asked about the way the Qur'an came into being. It simply cannot be viewed as the pristine product of a single inspired mind (either human or divine) but is rather the result of the laborious process of forming an authoritative Arab religious tradition out of many different strands.

The stark reality is that the Muslim masses of the world are living under a system that is holding them captive through claims based on nothing more than pseudo-history. Many thousands are, in fact, more than willing to suffer and die for this historical mirage (or to make others suffer for it). Those of us who care about truth and the future of humanity should do everything in our power to ensure that this damaging and false narrative is challenged at every possible opportunity.

Some may suggest that doing this is unnecessary and hurtful, and that Muslim believers should be left alone to enjoy their comforting certainties. To which we can only respond: why leave unchallenged a set of ideas that can conclusively be demonstrated as leading to ways of life, beliefs and attitudes that are fundamentally at odds with human rights, compassion for the rest of humanity and scientific progress? When you add the fact that these 'certainties' lock 21ˢᵗ century people into living their lives in line with a fictitious tradition invented to serve to desires of power hungry 8ᵗʰ and 9ᵗʰ century Arab leaders, the case for relentlessly challenging the tradition becomes overwhelming. Why would it be kind and comforting to allow people to live under this delusion?

Muslims proudly claim that Islam was born in the '*Full Light of History*'. However, when we do, in fact, shine the light of history on Islamic origins all that we find is a gaping black hole. Especially when it comes to finding hard historical evidence to back up the version of history taught in mosques across the globe. This book is offered with the sincere hope that Muslim people around the world will be willing to courageously gaze into this hole and that they will follow the evidence wherever it may lead. *Post tenebras spero lucem.*[883]

More from
Peter Townsend

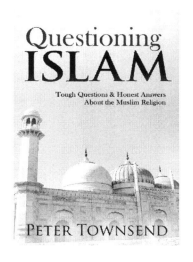

"Questioning Islam – Tough Questions and Honest Answers about the Muslim Religion"

A critical examination of the truth-claims of Islam.

www.qi-book.com

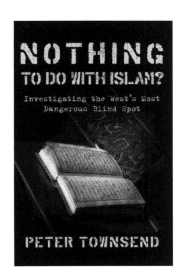

"Nothing to do with Islam? – Investigating the West's Most Dangerous Blind Sport"

An analysis of the link between Islamic teaching and violence.

www.ntdwi.com

Bibliography

A'Zami, Muhammad Mustafa. *Studies in Hadith Methodology and Literature*. Kuala Lumpur: Islamic Book Trust, 2010.

Abdel Haleem, M. A., and ʿĀdil ʿUmar Sharīf. *Criminal Justice in Islam: Judicial Procedure in the Sharīʿa*. London; New York; New York: I.B. Tauris ; Distributed by Palgrave Macmillan in the United States and Canada, 2018.

Adamec, L.W. *Historical Dictionary of Islam*. Rowman & Littlefield Publishers, 2016.

Adel, G.H., M.J. Elmi, and H. Taromi-Rad. *Hadith: An Entry from Encyclopaedia of the World of Islam*. Unknown Publisher, 2012.

Adil, H.A. *Muhammad the Messenger of Islam: His Life & Prophecy*. BookBaby, 2012.

Aḥituv, Shmuel. *The Jewish People: An Illustrated History*. London: Continuum, 2006.

Ahmad, Mahdi Rizqallah, and Syed Iqbal Zaheer. *A Biography of the Prophet of Islam: In the Light of the Original Sources*. 2005.

Akhter, S. *Faith & Philosophy of Islam*. Kalpaz Publications, 2009.

Ali, A. *Islamic Dynasties of the Arab East: State and Civilization During the Later Medieval Times*. M D Publications, 1996.

Allen, R.M.A., and R. Allen. *The Arabic Literary Heritage: The Development of Its Genres and Criticism*. Cambridge University Press, 2005.

Altikulaç, Tayyar, Ekmeleddin Ihsanoglu, and Salih Sadawi. *Al-Mushaf Al-Sharif Attributed to Uthman Bin Affan (the Copy at the Topkapi Palace Museum)*. Istanbul: Organisation of the Islamic Conference/Research Centre for Islamic History, Art and Culture, 2007.

Ammianus, Marcellinus, and Charles Duke Yonge. *The Roman History of Ammianus Marcellinus, During the Reigns of the Emperors Constantius, Julian, Jovianus, Valentian, and Valens*. London: Bell, 1911.

Anderson, Mark Robert. *The Qur'an in Context: A Christian Exploration.* Downers Grove, Illinois: IVP Academic, 2016.

Anklesaria, Behramgore Tehmurasp. *Ethics of Old Iran.* Ahmedabad: Meherbanoo Behramgore Anklesaria Publication Trust, 1973.

Anonymous. *The Arabic Gospel of the Infancy of the Saviour.* Library of Alexandria.

Armstrong, Karen. *Muhammad: A Biography of the Prophet.* London: Phoenix, 2009.

Asheri, David, Alan B. Lloyd, Aldo Corcella, Oswyn Murray, and Alfonso Moreno. *A Commentary on Herodotus Books I-IV.* Oxford: Oxford University Press, 2011.

Athyal, J.M. *Religion in Southeast Asia: An Encyclopedia of Faiths and Cultures: An Encyclopedia of Faiths and Cultures.* ABC-CLIO, 2015.

Aydın, H. *The Sacred Trusts: Pavilion of the Sacred Relics, Topkapı Palace Museum, Istanbul.* Tughra Books, 2011.

Ayoun, Dalila. *French Applied Linguistics.* Amsterdam: John Benjamins, 2007.

Azami, M.M., and A.T. Publications. *Studies in Hadith Methodology and Literature.* Islamic Teaching Center, 1978.

Bacharach, J.L. *Islamic History through Coins: An Analysis and Catalogue of Tenth-Century Ikhshidid Coinage.* American University in Cairo Press, 2006.

Balfour, A. *Solomon's Temple: Myth, Conflict, and Faith.* Wiley, 2015.

Ball, W. *Rome in the East: The Transformation of an Empire.* Taylor & Francis, 2016.

Bang, P.F., and W. Scheidel. *The Oxford Handbook of the State in the Ancient near East and Mediterranean.* OUP USA, 2013.

Barakat, Halim. *The Arab World: Society, Culture, and State.* Berkeley, Calif.: University of California Press, 2007.

Barker, John W. *Justinian and the Later Roman Empire.* Madison; London: University of Wisconsin Press, 1977.

Bashier, Zakaria, and Foundation Islamic. *"War and Peace in the Life of the Prophet Muhammad ".* (2006).

Bearman, P. J. *The Encyclopedia of Islam Volumes 1-6* Leiden: Brill, 1996.

Beaumont, Mark Ivor. "Early Christian Interpretation of the Qur'an." *Transformation* 22, no. 4 (2005): 195-203.

Beeston, A. F. L. "The Arabian Aromatics Trade in Antiquity." *Proceedings of the Seminar for Arabian Studies* (2005): 53-64.

Ben-Ari, Shosh. "The Stories About Abraham in Islam. A Geographical Approach." *Arabica* 54, no. 4 (2007): 526-53.

Ben-Hûrqânôs, E. *Pirke De Rabbi Eliezer: A Critical Ed. Codex C.M. Horowitz; Includes Textual Variants from 15 Manuscripts, Notes, Commentaries and Paralells from Rabbinic Literature.* Makor Publ., 1972.

Ben-Sasson, H. H., and A. Malamat. *A History of the Jewish People.* Cambridge, Mass.: Harvard Univ. Press, 2002.

Bennett, C. *In Search of Muhammad.* Bloomsbury Academic, 1998.

Bennison, Amira K. *The Great Caliphs: The Golden Age of the 'Abbasid Empire.* New Haven: Yale University, 2014.

Berg, H. *The Development of Exegesis in Early Islam: The Authenticity of Muslim Literature from the Formative Period.* Taylor & Francis, 2013.

Berger, Pamela C. *"The Crescent on the Temple the Dome of the Rock as Image of the Ancient Jewish Sanctuary."* (2012).

Berkey, J.P. *The Formation of Islam: Religion and Society in the near East, 600-1800.* Cambridge University Press, 2003.

Berkey, Jonathan. *The Formation of Islam: Religion and Society in the near East, 600-1800.* Cambridge: Cambridge University Press, 2012.

Betts, Robert Brenton. "The Sunni-Shi'a Divide: Islam's Internal Divisions and Their Global Consequences." (2013).

Biggar, Nigel, Jamie S. Scott, and William Schweiker. "Cities of Gods: Faith, Politics, and Pluralism in Judaism, Christianity, and Islam." (1986).

Binns, John. *An Introduction to the Christian Orthodox Churches.* Cambridge, U.K.: Cambridge University Press, 2005.

"Birmingham Qur'an Manuscript Dated among the Oldest in the World." University of Birmingham https://www.birmingham.ac.uk/news/latest/2015/07/quran-manuscript-22-07-15.aspx.

Bitton-Ashkelony, B., D. Krueger, and P.R.S.D. Krueger. *Prayer and Worship in Eastern Christianities, 5th to 11th Centuries.* Taylor & Francis, 2016.

Block, C. *The Qur'an in Christian-Muslim Dialogue: Historical and Modern Interpretations.* Taylor & Francis, 2013.

Bonner, M. *Arab-Byzantine Relations in Early Islamic Times.* Taylor & Francis, 2017.

———. *Jihad in Islamic History: Doctrines and Practice.* Princeton University Press, 2008.

Boraz, Edward S. *Understanding the Talmud: A Modern Reader's Guide for Study.* Northvale, New Jersey: Aronson, 1996.

Bosworth, C.E. *Historic Cities of the Islamic World.* Brill, 2007.

Böwering, Gerhard, Patricia Crone, and Mahan Mirza. *The Princeton Encyclopedia of Islamic Political Thought.* Princeton, N.J.: Princeton University Press, 2013.

Bowersock, G.W. *Roman Arabia.* Harvard University Press, 1994.

Bowersock, G.W., P.R.L. Brown, P. Brown, and O. Grabar. *Late Antiquity: A Guide to the Postclassical World.* Belknap Press of Harvard University Press, 1999.

Brock, Sebastian P., and Susan Ashbrook Harvey. *Holy Women of the Syrian Orient*; London: University of California Press, 1998.

Brockopp, J.E. *The Cambridge Companion to Muhammad.* Cambridge University Press, 2010.

Brockopp, J.E., J. Neusner, and T. Sonn. *Judaism and Islam in Practice: A Sourcebook.* Taylor & Francis, 2005.

Brown, D.W. *A New Introduction to Islam.* Wiley, 2011.

Brown, K., and S. Ogilvie. *Concise Encyclopedia of Languages of the World.* Elsevier Science, 2010.

Brown, Laurence *The Eclipse of Christianity in Asia, by L.E. Brown.* Cambridge, 1933.

Brubaker, Daniel "Intentional Changes in Qur'an Manuscripts." Rice University, 2014.

Bukharin, M. D. "Towards the Earliest History of Kinda." *Arabian Archaeology and Epigraphy* 20, no. 1 (2009): 64-80.

Bulliet, Richard W. *The Camel and the Wheel.* New York: ACLS History E-Book Project, 2005.

Butcher, K. *Roman Syria and the near East.* J. Paul Getty Museum, 2003.

Cakmak, Cenap. *Islam. A Worldwide Encyclopedia. 4 Vols.* Santa Barbara: ABC-CLIO, Inc, 2015.

Calder, Norman, Jawid Ahmad Mojaddedi, and Andrew Rippin. *Classical Islam: A Sourcebook of Religious Literature.* London; New York: Routledge, Taylor & Francis Group, 2013.

Campo, J.E. *Encyclopedia of Islam.* Facts On File, 2009.

Cassini, C. *Islam: Claims and Counterclaims.* iUniverse, 2001.

Chitnis, K.N. *Research Methodology in History.* Atlantic Publishers and Distributors, 1990.

Choksy, Jamsheed K. *Evil, Good and Gender Facets of the Feminine in Zoroastrian Religious History*. New York: Lang, 2009.

Chugg, Andrew Michael. *The Lost Tomb of Alexander the Great*. London: Periplus, 2005.

Cline, Rangar H. *Ancient Angels: Conceptualizing Angeloi in the Roman Empire*. Leiden: Brill, 2011.

Codrington, S. *Planet Geography*. Solid Star Press, 2005.

Coghill, E. *The Rise and Fall of Ergativity in Aramaic: Cycles of Alignment Change*. OUP Oxford, 2016.

Cohen, A. *The Babylonian Talmud: Tractate Berakot*. Cambridge, U.K.; New York: Cambridge University Press, 2013.

Cohn-Sherbok, Dan. *Judaism: History, Belief and Practice*. 2017.

Colby, Frederick. *Narrating Muhammad's Night Journey Tracing the Development of the Ibn 'Abbas Ascension Discourse*. State Univ of New York Press, 2009.

Constable, Anthony R., and William Facey. *The Principles of Arab Navigation*. London: Arabian Publishing, 2013.

Constantelos, Demetrios J. "The Moslem Conquests of the near East as Revealed in the Greek Sources of the Seventh and the Eighth Centuries." *Byzantion* 42, no. 2 (1972): 325-57.

Cornell, V.J. *Voices of Islam: Voices of Tradition*. Praeger Publishers, 2007.

Cragg, K. *The Arab Christian: A History in the Middle East*. Westminster/John Knox Press, 1991.

Crawford, Peter. "*The War of the Three Gods: Romans, Persians, and the Rise of Islam*." (2014).

Crone, P., and M. Hinds. *God's Caliph: Religious Authority in the First Centuries of Islam*. Cambridge University Press, 2003.

Crone, P., and H. Siurua. *The Qur'ānic Pagans and Related Matters: Collected Studies in Three Volumes*. Brill, 2016.

Crone, Patricia. "The First-Century Concept of *Hijra*." *Arabica* 41, no. 3 (1994): 352-87.

———. *Meccan Trade and the Rise of Islam*. Oxford: Basil Blackwell, 1987.

———. "The Religion of the Quranic Pagans: God and the Lesser Deities." *Arabica* 57, no. 2/3 (2010): 151-200.

Crone, Patricia, and M. A. Cook. *Hagarism: The Making of the Islamic World* Cambridge: Cambridge University Press, 1976.

Crone, Patricia, and Michael Allan Cook. *Hagarism: The Making of the Islamic World*. Cambridge: Cambridge University Press, 1980.

Culpeper, J. *History of English*. Routledge, 2005.

D, C.F.P., and A.H. Walker. *Muhammad in History, Thought, and Culture: An Encyclopedia of the Prophet of God*. ABC-CLIO, 2014.

Dalley, S. *The Legacy of Mesopotamia*. Oxford University Press, 1998.

Daryaee, T. *Sasanian Persia: The Rise and Fall of an Empire*. I.B.Tauris, 2014.

Daryaee, Touraj. "The Persian Gulf Trade in Late Antiquity." *Journal of World History* 14, no. 1 (2003): 1-16.

DeClaisse-Walford, Nancy L., Rolf A. Jacobson, and Beth LaNeel Tanner. "The Book of Psalms." (2015).

Deen, S.M. *Science under Islam: Rise, Decline and Revival*. Lulu.com, 2007.

Dhalla, Maneckji Nusservanji. *Zoroastrian Civilization: From the Earliest Times to the Downfall of the Last Zoroastrian Empire 651 A.D.* 2015.

Dignas, Beate, and Engelbert Winter. *Rome and Persia in Late Antiquity: Neighbours and Rivals*. Cambridge: Cambridge University Press, 2012.

Diodorus, and C. H. Oldfather. *Diodorus of Sicily,* Cambridge, Mass.: Harvard University Press, 1935.

Donner, Fred McGraw. "The Expansion of the Early Islamic State." (2016).

———. *Muhammad and the Believers: At the Origins of Islam*. Cambridge, Mass.: The Belknap Press of Harvard University Press, 2010.

———. *Muhammad and the Believers: At the Origins of Islam*. Cambridge, Mass.: Belknap Press of Harvard University Press, 2012.

Dumper, M., and B.E. Stanley. *Cities of the Middle East and North Africa: A Historical Encyclopedia*. ABC-CLIO, 2007.

Dyrness, W.A., V.M. Kärkkäinen, J.F. Martinez, and S. Chan. *Global Dictionary of Theology: A Resource for the Worldwide Church*. InterVarsity Press, 2009.

Edens, Christopher, and Garth Bawden. "History of Teimah and Hejazi Trade During the First Millennium Bc." *Journal of the Economic and Social History of the Orient* 32, no. 1 (1989): 48-103.

Effarah, J. *What Are the Sacred Roots of Islam?: And the Planned Modern Islamic Society*. AuthorHouse, 2016.

Egenes, T. *Introduction to Sanskrit*. Motilal Banarsidass Publishers, 1996.

Egger, V.O. *A History of the Muslim World to 1750: The Making of a Civilization*. Taylor & Francis, 2017.

El-Badawi, E. *The Qur'an and the Aramaic Gospel Traditions.* Taylor & Francis, 2013.

El-Hibri, T. *Parable and Politics in Early Islamic History: The Rashidun Caliphs.* Columbia University Press, 2010.

El-Zein, A. *Islam, Arabs, and Intelligent World of the Jinn.* Syracuse University Press, 2009.

Elm, S. `Virgins of God': The Making of Asceticism in Late Antiquity: The Making of Asceticism in Late Antiquity.* Clarendon Press, 1994.

Elton, H. *Frontiers of the Roman Empire.* Taylor & Francis, 2013.

Emon, Anver M. *Religious Pluralism in Islamic Law: Dhimmīs and Others in the Empire of Law.* Oxford: Oxford University Press, 2012.

Encyclopedia of World Religions. Encyclopaedia Britannica, Incorporated, 2008.

Esposito, John L. *Islam: The Straight Path.* 2016.

———. *What Everyone Needs to Know About Islam.* 2011.

Fadl, K.A.E. *Rebellion and Violence in Islamic Law.* Cambridge University Press, 2006.

Farooq, M.O. *Toward Our Reformation: From Legalism to Value-Oriented Islamic Law and Jurisprudence.* International Institute of Islamic Thought, 2013.

Farquhar, M. *Circuits of Faith: Migration, Education, and the Wahhabi Mission.* Stanford University Press, 2016.

Fattah, H.M., and F. Caso. *A Brief History of Iraq.* Facts On File, 2009.

Faulkner, N. *Apocalypse: The Great Jewish Revolt against Rome Ad 66-73.* Amberley Publishing, 2011.

Ferguson, E., M.P. McHugh, F.W. Norris, and D. Scholer. *Encyclopedia of Early Christianity.* Taylor and Francis, 1992.

Ferguson, Yale H., and Richard W. Mansbach. *A World of Polities: Essays on Global Politics.* London: Routledge, 2008.

Firestone, R. *Journeys in Holy Lands: The Evolution of the Abraham-Ishmael Legends in Islamic Exegesis.* State University of New York Press, 1990.

Fishbein, M. *History of Al-Tabari Vol. 21, The: The Victory of the Marwanids A.D. 685-693/A.H. 66-73.* State University of New York Press, 2015.

Flood, F.B., and G. Necipoglu. *A Companion to Islamic Art and Architecture.* Wiley, 2017.

Fonrobert, C.E., and M.S. Jaffee. *The Cambridge Companion to the Talmud and Rabbinic Literature.* Cambridge University Press, 2007.

Forlong, J.G.R. *Encyclopedia of Religions.* Cosimo, Incorporated, 2008.

Forsyth, J.H. *The Byzantine-Arab Chronicle (938-1034) of Yaḥyā B. Saʿīd Al-Anṭākī.* University Microfilms, 1977.

Foss, Clive. *Arab-Byzantine Coins: An Introduction, with a Catalogue of the Dumbarton Oaks Collection.* Washington, DC: Harvard Univ. Press, 2008.

Frahm, Eckart. *A Companion to Assyria.* 2017.

Gabriel, Richard A. *"Muhammad: Islam's First Great General."* (2007).

Geller, Markham J. *"The Archaeology and Material Culture of the Babylonian Talmud."* (2015).

Ghareeb, E.A., and B. Dougherty. *Historical Dictionary of Iraq.* Scarecrow Press, 2004.

Gibbon, E., and H.H. Milman. *The History of the Decline and Fall of the Roman Empire.* Harper & brothers, 1844.

Gibson, Dan. *Qur'anic Geography.* Saskatoon: Independent Scholars Press, 2011.

Gil, Moshe. *Jews in Islamic Countries in the Middle Ages.* Leiden Brill, 2011.

Gilchrist, John. *The Qur'an: The Scripture of Islam.* Claremont, South Africa: Life Challenge Africa, 2003.

Glasse, Cyril. *The New Encyclopedia of Islam.* 2013.

Gonen, R. *Contested Holiness: Jewish, Muslim, and Christian Perspectives on the Temple Mount in Jerusalem.* KTAV Publishing House, 2003.

Goodman, Martin. *The Roman World 44 Bc-Ad 180.* Florence: Taylor and Francis, 2013.

Grabar, O. *Jerusalem.* Ashgate/Variorum, 2005.

Graf, David F. *Rome and the Arabian Frontier from the Nabataeans to the Saracens.* Aldershot: Ashgate, 1998.

Grant, Michael. *"From Rome to Byzantium: The Fifth Century AD."* (2015).

Greatrex, G., and S.N.C. Lieu. *The Roman Eastern Frontier and the Persian Wars Ad 363-628.* Routledge, 2007.

Gregory, Timothy E. *"A History of Byzantium."* (2011).

Grenz, S.J. *Theology for the Community of God.* Eerdmans Publishing Company, 2000.

Griffith, S.H. *The Church in the Shadow of the Mosque: Christians and Muslims in the World of Islam.* Princeton University Press, 2012.

Grishaver, J.L. *Make a Midrash out of Me: From Chaos to Egypt.* Tora Aura Productions, 2004.

Groom, Nigel. "Eastern Arabia in Ptolemy's Map." *Proceedings of the Seminar for Arabian Studies* 16 (1986): 65-75.

Gruber, Christiane. *The Image of the Prophet between Ideal and Ideology: A Scholarly Investigation.* Berlin: De Gruyter, 2014.

Grypeou, E., M. Swanson, and D.R. Thomas. *The Encounter of Eastern Christianity with Early Islam.* Brill, 2006.

Gu, S. *A Cultural History of the Arabic Language.* McFarland, Incorporated, Publishers, 2013.

Hadromi-Allouche, Zohar. "Review of El-Hibri, Tayeb, Parable and Politics in Early Islamic History: The Rashidun Caliphs." *H-Net Reviews* (2013).

Halivni, David, and Jeffrey L. Rubenstein. *The Formation of the Babylonian Talmud.* 2013.

Hall, J.M. *Artifact and Artifice: Classical Archaeology and the Ancient Historian.* University of Chicago Press, 2014.

Hall, S.G. *Doctrine and Practice in the Early Church.* W.B. Eerdmans, 1992.

Hambly, Gavin. "The Cambridge History of Iran. Vol. 7" (2008).

Hamid, E.A. *The Qur'an and Politics: A Study of the Origins of Political Thought in the Makkan Qur'an.* International Institute of Islamic Thought, 2004.

Hann, G., K. Dabrowska, and T.T. Greaves. *Iraq: The Ancient Sites and Iraqi Kurdistan.* Bradt Travel Guides, 2015.

HAQ, M.I.U.L. *Companion of Hajj.* Xlibris, 2014.

Harman, Allan M. *Psalms.* Fearn, Ross-shire: Mentor, 2011.

Harris, J. *Constantinople: Capital of Byzantium.* Bloomsbury Publishing, 2017.

Harrison, William H. *In Praise of Mixed Religion: The Syncretism Solution in a Multifaith World.* 2014.

Hasan, A.G. *American Muslims: The New Generation Second Edition.* Bloomsbury Academic, 2002.

Hattstein, M., and P. Delius. *Islam: Art and Architecture.* Könemann, 2000.

Hawting, G. R. *The Idea of Idolatry and the Emergence of Islam: From Polemic to History.* Cambridge Studies in Islamic Civilization. Cambridge: Cambridge University Press, 1999.

Hawting, G.R. *The First Dynasty of Islam: The Umayyad Caliphate Ad 661-750.* Taylor & Francis, 2002.

Haykal, Muhammad Husayn, and Ismail Ragi A. Al Faruqi. *The Life of Muhammad*. New York: The Other Press, 1994.

Haylamaz, R. *Aisha: The Wife, the Companion, the Scholar*. Tughra Books, 2013.

Henderson, D.E., and F. Kirkpatrick. *Constantine and the Council of Nicaea: Defining Orthodoxy and Heresy in Christianity, 325 CE*. Reacting Consortium Press, 2016.

Hitti, P.K. *History of the Arabs*. Palgrave Macmillan, 2002.

Hoffman, Joseph. "Revisiting the Birmingham Qur'an Debacle "https://rjosephhoffmann.wordpress.com/2015/07/26/update-on-the-birmingham-quran-debacle/.

Hoffman, Jospeh. "The BBC Birmingham Qur'an Facts Fiasco "https://rjosephhoffmann.wordpress.com/2015/07/23/the-bbc-birmingham-quran-facts-fiasco/.

Holtzclaw, R. Fulton. *The Saints Go Marching In: A One Volume Hagiography of Africans, or Descendants of Africans, Who Have Been Canonized by the Church, Including Three of the Early Popes*. Shaker Heights, OH: Keeble Press, 1980.

Hovannisian, Richard G., and Georges Sabagh. "The Persian Presence in the Islamic World." Cambridge (United Kingdom), 1998.

Hoyland, R.G. *In God's Path: The Arab Conquests and the Creation of an Islamic Empire*. Oxford University Press, 2015.

Hoyland, Robert G. *Arabia and the Arabs: From the Bronze Age to the Coming of Islam*. London: Routledge, 2010.

———. "Arabia and the Arabs: From the Bronze Age to the Coming of Islam." (2001).

———. *In God's Path: The Arab Conquests and the Creation of an Islamic Empire*. Ancient Warfare and Civilization. Oxford ; New York: Oxford University Press, 2015.

———. *Muslims and Others in Early Islamic Society*. Aldershot, Hants; Burlington, VT: Ashgate, 2004.

———. *Seeing Islam as Others Saw It: A Survey and Evaluation of Christian, Jewish, and Zoroastrian Writings on Early Islam*. Princeton, N.J.: Darwin Press, 2007.

Hudson, Winthrop S. *The Story of the Christian Church*. New York: Harper, 1958.

Post, Huffington. "Birmingham Koran Carbon Dating Reveals Book Is Likely Older Than Prophet Muhammad." http://www.huffingtonpost.co.uk/2015/09/01/birmingham-koran-carbon-test_n_8071696.html.

Huff, Wesley. "The Birmingham Quran Folios and a Brief Synopsis of Its Impact on Islam." https://www.academia.edu/22160060/The_Birmingham_Quran_Folios_and_a_Brief_Synopsis_of_its_Impact_on_Islam.

Hughes, A.W. *Muslim Identities: An Introduction to Islam.* Columbia University Press, 2013.

Hughes, Thomas Patrick. *A Dictionary of Islam.* London: W. H. Allen, 1885.

Humphreys, R.S. *Mu'awiya Ibn Abi Sufyan: The Savior of the Caliphate.* Oneworld Publications, 2012.

Hybel, A.R. *Ideology in World Politics.* Taylor & Francis, 2013.

Ibn Hishām, 'Abd al-Malik, Muḥammad Ibn Isḥāq, and Alfred Guillaume. *The Life of Muhammad: A Translation of Ishaq's Sirat Rasul Allaah.* Karachi; New York: Oxford University Press, 1997.

Ibn, Warraq. *Christmas in the Koran: Luxenberg, Syriac, and the near Eastern and Judeo-Christian Background of Islam.* Amherst, New York: Prometheus Books, 2014.

———. *Why I Am Not a Muslim.* Amherst, N.Y.: Prometheus Books, 1995.

Independent, The. "*Channel 4 Cancels Controversial Screening of Islam: The Untold Story Documentary after Presenter Tom Holland Is Threatened.*" (2012).

Insoll, T. *The Oxford Handbook of the Archaeology of Ritual and Religion.* OUP Oxford, 2011.

Institute, Islamic Research, and Central Institute of Islamic Research. *Islamic Studies.* Islamic Research Institute, 1998.

Irvin, D.T., and S. Sunquist. *History of the World Christian Movement: Volume 1: Earliest Christianity to 1453.* Bloomsbury Academic, 2002.

Islam, M. *Decline of Muslim States and Societies: The Real Root Causes and What Can Be Done Next.* Xlibris US, 2008.

Israeli, R. *Muslim Anti-Semitism in Christian Europe: Elemental and Residual Anti-Semitism.* Taylor & Francis, 2017.

Jaffer, Abbas, and Masuma Jaffer. *An Introduction to Qur'anic Sciences.* London: ICAS Press, 2009.

Jansen, Johannes. "The Gospel According to Ibn Ishāq (D. 767), Johannes J.G. Jansen, January 2007." https://badmanna.wordpress.com/2015/05/11/the-gospel-according-to-ibn-ishaq-d-767-johannes-j-g-jansen-january-2007/.

January, B. *The Arab Conquests of the Middle East (Revised Edition).* Lerner Publishing Group, 2013.

Jeffery, A., and I. Mendelsohn. "The Orthography of the Samarqand Quran Codex." *Journal of the American Oriental Society* 62, no. 3 (1942): 175-95.

Jerusalem Studies in Arabic and Islam Volumes 22 and 23. Jerusalem: Hebrew University, 1997.

Johnson, S.F. *The Oxford Handbook of Late Antiquity.* Oxford University Press, 2015.

Johnston, W.M. *Encyclopedia of Monasticism.* Taylor & Francis, 2013.

Jöns, Heike, Peter Meusburger, and Michael Heffernan. "Mobilities of Knowledge." (2017).

Joukowsky, Martha Sharp. "The Petra Great Temple: A Nabataean Architectural Miracle." *Near Eastern Archaeology* 65, no. 4 (2002): 235-48.

Judd, S. *Religious Scholars and the Umayyads: Piety-Minded Supporters of the Marwanid Caliphate.* Taylor & Francis, 2013.

Juergensmeyer, Mark, and Wade Clark Roof. *Encyclopedia of Global Religion.* London: SAGE, 2011.

Kadri, S. *Heaven on Earth: A Journey through Shari'a Law.* Random House, 2013.

Kaegi, W.E. *Muslim Expansion and Byzantine Collapse in North Africa.* Cambridge University Press, 2010.

Kaegi, W.E., and W.E. Kaegi. *Byzantium and the Early Islamic Conquests.* Cambridge University Press, 1995.

Kaplony, Andreas. *The Haram of Jerusalem 324-1099: Temple, Friday Mosque, Area of Spiritual Power.* Stuttgart: Steiner, 2002.

Kathir, I. *Biographies of the Rightly-Guided Caliphs.* Lulu.com, 2016.

Katz, Ethan, Lisa Moses Leff, and Maud Mandel. "Colonialism and the Jews." (2017).

Keaney, Heather N. *Medieval Islamic Historiography: Remembering Rebellion.* London: Routledge, 2015.

Kelly, J.F. *History and Heresy: How Historical Forces Can Create Doctrinal Conflicts.* Liturgical Press, 2012.

Kelly, Joseph F. *The Ecumenical Councils of the Catholic Church: A History.* Collegeville, Minn: Liturgical Press, 2009.

Kennedy, Hugh. "Arabia According to Ptolemy (Circa 150 AD)." In *Historical Atlas of Islam.* Leiden: Brill, 2011.

Kerrigan, Heather. *Historic Documents of 2015.* 2016.

Khadduri, M., and H.J. Liebesny. *Origin and Development of Islamic Law.* Lawbook Exchange, 2010.

Khalek, N. *Damascus after the Muslim Conquest: Text and Image in Early Islam.* Oxford University Press, 2011.

Khalidi, Tarif. *Images of Muhammad: Narratives of the Prophet in Islam across the Centuries.* New York, NY [etc.]: Doubleday, 2009.

Kheirallah, G. *Islam and the Arabian Prophet.* New York: Islamic Pub. Co., 1938.

King, D.A. *World Maps for Finding the Direction and Distance of Mecca: Examples of Innovation and Tradition in Islamic Science.* Al-Furqān Islamic Heritage Foundation, 1999.

Kister, M. J. "Al Hira: Some Notes on Its Relations with Arabia." *Arabica* 15, no. 2 (1968): 143-69.

———. "Some Reports Concerning Mecca from Jahiliyya to Islam." *Journal of the Economic and Social History of the Orient* 15, no. 1/2 (1972): 61-93.

Klorman, Bat-Zion Eraqi. *Traditional Society in Transition: The Yemeni Jewish Experience.* 2014.

Knysh, A. *Islam in Historical Perspective.* Taylor & Francis, 2016.

Kragh, H. *An Introduction to the Historiography of Science.* Cambridge University Press, 1987.

Kuiper, Kathleen. *Mesopotamia: The World's Earliest Civilization.* New York, NY: Britannica Educational Pub. in association with Rosen Educational Services, 2011.

Lambert, W. G. "Nabonidus in Arabia." *Proceedings of the Seminar for Arabian Studies* 2 (1972): 53-64.

Langer, William L., and Peter N. Stearns. *The Encyclopedia of World History: Ancient, Medieval, and Modern Chronologically Arranged.* 6th ed. Cambridge: James Clarke, 2001.

Lapidus, I.M. *A History of Islamic Societies.* Cambridge University Press, 2014.

Lazarus-Yafeh, H. *Some Religious Aspects of Islam: A Collection of Articles.* Brill, 1981.

Leaman, O. *The Qur'an: An Encyclopedia.* Routledge, 2006.

Leaman, Oliver. *Routledge Encyclopedia of the Qur'an.* London: Routledge, 2005.

Lecker, Michael. "The Conversion of Ḥimyar to Judaism and the Jewish Banū Hadl of Medina." *Die Welt des Orients* 26 (1995): 129-36.

———. "Judaism among Kinda and the Ridda of Kinda." *Journal of the American Oriental Society* 115, no. 4 (1995): 635-50.

Leopold, A.M., and J.S. Jensen. *Syncretism in Religion: A Reader.* Taylor & Francis, 2016.

Levine, Louis D. "Sennacherib's Southern Front: 704-689 B.C." *Journal of Cuneiform Studies* 34, no. 1/2 (1982): 28-58.

Lewis, B. *The Middle East: A Brief History of the Last 2,000 Years.* Scribner, 1995.

Lewis, B.E., and B.E. Churchill. *Islam: The Religion and the People.* Pearson Education, 2008.

Levy, C.D. *The Arian Christian Doctrines: The Origins of Christianity.* CreateSpace Independent Publishing Platform, 2010.

Liebeschuetz, J.H.W.F. *East and West in Late Antiquity: Invasion, Settlement, Ethnogenesis and Conflicts of Religion.* Brill, 2015.

Lindsay, J.E. *Daily Life in the Medieval Islamic World.* Greenwood Press, 2005.

Lindsay, James E. *Daily Life in the Medieval Islamic World.* Indianapolis, Ind.: Hackett, 2008.

Lings, Martin. "Muhammad - His Life Based on the Earliest Sources." (2017).

Litvak, Meir, and Ofra Bengio. "*The Sunna and Shi'a in History Division and Ecumenism in the Muslim Middle East.*" (2014).

Lodahl, M. *Claiming Abraham: Reading the Bible and the Qur'an Side by Side.* Baker Publishing Group, 2010.

Loreto, Romolo. "Recent Studies in Pre-Islamic Yemen. An Overview." *Rassegna di Studi Etiopici* 4 (2012): 239-66.

Louth, A., and A. Casiday. *Byzantine Orthodoxies: Papers from the Thirty-Sixth Spring Symposium of Byzantine Studies, University of Durham, 23-25 March 2002.* Ashgate Variorum, 2006.

Luxenberg, Christoph. *The Syro-Aramaic Reading of the Koran: A Contribution to the Decoding of the Language of the Koran.* Berlin: H. Schiler, 2007.

———*The Syro-Aramaic Reading of the Koran: A Contribution to the Decoding of the Language of the Koran.* Amherst: Prometheus, 2009.

Mail, Birmingham. "Worldwide Media Frenzy as 'Oldest Koran' Found Lying Forgotten at University of Birmingham." https://www.birminghammail.co.uk/news/midlands-news/worldwide-media-frenzy-oldest-koran-9710028.

Malamat, Abraham, and Haim Hillel Ben-Sasson. *A History of the Jewish People.* Cambridge, Mass.: Harvard University Press, 2002.

Maqdisi, A.I. *Short Biographies of the Prophet and His Ten Companions Who Were Given the Tidings of Paradise.* Darussalam, 2004.

Maraqten, Mohammed. "Newly Discovered Sabaic Inscriptions from Mahram Bilqis near Marib." *Proceedings of the Seminar for Arabian Studies* 32 (2002): 209-16.

Marjanen, Antti, Petri Luomanen *"A Companion to Second-Century Christian "Heretics"."* (2008).

Markoe, G. *Petra Rediscovered: Lost City of the Nabataeans.* Harry N. Abrams, 2003.

Marsden, P. *The Taliban: War, Religion and the New Order in Afghanistan.* Zed Books, 1998.

Marshall Cavendish, Reference. *Islamic Beliefs, Practices, and Cultures.* Tarrytown, N.Y.: Marshall Cavendish Reference, 2011.

Marsham, A. *Rituals of Islamic Monarchy: Accession and Succession in the First Muslim Empire.* Edinburgh University Press, 2009.

Martin, Richard C. *Encyclopedia of Islam and the Muslim World. Vol. 1 Vol. 1.* New York [u.a.: Macmillan Reference USA, Thomson Gale, 2004.

Materials for the History of the Text of the Quran; the Old Codices. Brill Archive.

Maulana, M. *Encyclopaedia of Quranic Studies.* Anmol Publications Pvt. Ltd, 2006.

Mavani, H. *Religious Authority and Political Thought in Twelver Shi'ism: From Ali to Post-Khomeini.* Taylor & Francis, 2013.

Mayer, W., and B. Neil. *Religious Conflict from Early Christianity to the Rise of Islam.* De Gruyter, 2013.

Mayer, Wendy, Bronwen Neil, Gruyter Walter de, and K. G. Co. *Religious Conflict from Early Christianity to the Rise of Islam.* 2016.

McAuliffe, J.D. *The Cambridge Companion to the Qur'ān.* Cambridge University Press, 2006.

McGrath, A.E. *Christian Theology: An Introduction.* Wiley, 2011.

McKim, Donald K. *The Cambridge Companion to Martin Luther.* Cambridge [etc.]: Cambridge University Press, 2009.

McLachlan, Sean. *Byzantium: An Illustrated History.* New York: Hippocrene Books, 2005.

McLaughlin, D. *Yemen.* Bradt Travel Guides, 2008.

Melchert, C. *The Formation of the Sunni Schools of Law: 9th-10th Centuries C.E.* Brill, 1997.

Melton, J.G. *The Encyclopedia of Religious Phenomena.* Visible Ink Press, 2007.

Meri, J.W. *Medieval Islamic Civilization: An Encyclopedia*. Taylor & Francis, 2005.

———. *Medieval Islamic Civilization: An Encyclopedia*. Routledge.

Merril, John Ernest. "Of the Tractate of John of Damascus on Islam." *The Muslim World* XLI (1951).

Mikaberidze, A. *Conflict and Conquest in the Islamic World: A Historical Encyclopedia*. ABC-CLIO, 2011.

———. *Conflict and Conquest in the Islamic World: A Historical Encyclopedia [2 Volumes]: A Historical Encyclopedia*. ABC-CLIO, 2011.

Millar, F. *The Roman near East, 31 B.C.-A.D. 337*. Harvard University Press, 1993.

Miller, F.P., A.F. Vandome, and J. McBrewster. *Dating the Bible: Higher Criticism, Textual Criticism, Biblical Manuscript, Torah, Documentary Hypothesis, the Bible and History, Synoptic Problem, Markan Priority*. Alphascript Publishing, 2010.

Mingana, Alphonse. "Syriac Influence on the Style of the Kur'an." *The John Rylands Bulletin* 11 (1927).

Mitchell, J.R., and H.B. Mitchell. *Annual Editions: World History, Volume I, 8/E*. McGraw-Hill, 2004.

Morgan, D. *Essential Islam: A Comprehensive Guide to Belief and Practice*. Praeger/ABC-CLIO, 2010.

Morrow, J.A. *Islamic Images and Ideas: Essays on Sacred Symbolism*. McFarland, Incorporated, Publishers, 2013.

Moshay, G. J. O. *Anatomy of the Qur'an*. Ontario, Calif.: Chick Publications, 2007.

Motzki, Harald. *The Biography of Muhammad: The Issue of the Sources*. Boston, MA: Brill, 2000.

Muḥ̃ammad, and John A. Morrow. *Six Covenants of the Prophet Muhammad with the Christians of His Time: The Primary Documents*. 2015.

Munro-Hay, Stuart. "Aksumite Overseas Interests." *Northeast African Studies* 13, no. 2/3 (1991): 127-40.

"The Mushaf Al-Madina and the King Fahd Holy Qur'an Printing Complex." *Journal of Qur'anic Studies* 1, no. 1 (1999): 155-58.

Nasser, S. *The Transmission of the Variant Readings of the Qur'an*. Brill, 2012.

National Association for the Promotion of Studies in Religions, Education, Languages, and General Studies. *The Authenticity and Literary Styles of Surah Al-Walayah and Surah Al-Nurayn*. Jilat Publishing Company, 2007.

Neuwirth, Angelika, Nicolai Sinai, and Michael Marx. *The Qur'an in Context: Historical and Literary Investigations into the Qur'anic Milieu.* Leiden; Boston, Mass.: Brill, 2011.

Nevo, Yehuda. "Towards a Pre-History of Islam." *Jerusalem Studies in Arabic and Islam* 17 (1994).

Nevo, Yehuda D., and Judith Koren. "The Origins of the Muslim Descriptions of the Meccan Sanctuary." *Journal of Near Eastern Studies* 49, no. 1 (1990): 23-44.

Nevo, Yehuda D., Judith Koren, and Cultures Negev Archaeological Project for the Study of Ancient Arab Desert. *Crossroads to Islam: The Origins of the Arab Religion and the Arab State.* Amherst, NY: Prometheus Books, 2003.

Nicolle, David. *"The Great Islamic Conquests AD 632-750."* (2014).

Nigosian, S. A. *"Islam Its History, Teaching, and Practices."* Bloomington: Indiana University Press, 2004.

Nigosian, S.A., and S.A. Nigosian. *The Zoroastrian Faith: Tradition and Modern Research.* McGill-Queen's University Press, 1993.

O'Connell, M., and E.R. Dursteler. *The Mediterranean World: From the Fall of Rome to the Rise of Napoleon.* Johns Hopkins University Press, 2016.

O'Kane, B. *New Perspectives on Islamic Architecture.* American University In Cairo Press, 2009.

O'Leary, De Lacy. *Arabia before Muhammad.* [Place of publication not identified]: Routledge, 2013.

Ohlig, Karl-Heinz, and Gerd- R. Puin. *The Hidden Origins of Islam: New Research into Its Early History.* Amherst, N.Y.: Prometheus Books, 2010.

Olson, R.E. *The Story of Christian Theology: Twenty Centuries of Tradition & Reform.* InterVarsity Press, 1999.

Origins, Ancient. "Archaeologists Discover That Earliest Known Arabic Writing Was Penned by a Christian | Ancient Origins." (2016).

Packer, George "The Moderate Martyr." (2006).

Pagolu, Augustine. *The Religion of the Patriarchs.* Sheffield, England: Sheffield Academic Press, 1998.

Panaino, Antonio. *The Lists of Names of Ahura Mazda (Yast I) and Vayu (Yast X).* Roma: Istituto italiano per l'Africa e l'Oriente, 2002.

Parry, K. *The Blackwell Companion to Eastern Christianity.* Wiley, 2010.

Peña, I. *The Christian Art of Byzantine Syria.* Garnet Publishing, 1997.

Penn, M.P. *When Christians First Met Muslims: A Sourcebook of the Earliest Syriac Writings on Islam.* University of California Press, 2015.

Peters, F. E. *The Hajj: The Muslim Pilgrimage to Mecca and the Holy Places.* Delhi: Oxford UP, 1996.

Peters, F.E. *Mecca: A Literary History of the Muslim Holy Land.* Princeton University Press, 2017.

Petersen, A. *Dictionary of Islamic Architecture.* Taylor & Francis, 2002.

Philipp, T., and U. Haarmann. *The Mamluks in Egyptian Politics and Society.* Cambridge University Press, 1998.

Phillips, W. *Brothers Kept Apart: Examining the Christian and Islamic Barriers That Have Divided Christians and Muslims for over 1,300 Years.* iUniverse, 2009.

Pickard, J. *Behind the Myths: The Foundations of Judaism, Christianity and Islam.* AuthorHouse UK, 2013.

Pliny, the Elder, John Bostock, and H. T. Riley. *The Natural History of Pliny.* [S.l.]: Bohn, 1855.

Pollard, Nigel. *Soldiers, Cities, and Civilians in Roman Syria.* Ann Arbor: University of Michigan Press, 2003.

Popenoe, Paul, and Henry Field. *The Date Palm.* Coconut Grove, Fla.: Field Research Projects, 1973.

Potter, D.S. *A Companion to the Roman Empire.* Wiley, 2009.

Potts, D.T., R. Boucharlat, and M. Drieux. *The Pre-Islamic Coinage of Eastern Arabia.* Carsten Niebuhr Institute of Ancient Near Eastern Studies, University of Copenhagen, 1991.

Powell, L., and P. Dennis. *The Bar Kokhba War AD 132–135: The Last Jewish Revolt against Imperial Rome.* Bloomsbury Publishing, 2017.

Powers, David Stephan. *Muhammad Is Not the Father of Any of Your Men: The Making of the Last Prophet.* Philadelphia, Pa.; University of Pennsylvania Press ; Oxford Creative Marketing [distributor], 2011.

Prawdin, M. *The Mongol Empire: Its Rise and Legacy.* Taylor & Francis, 2017.

Price, R., and M. Gaddis. *The Acts of the Council of Chalcedon.* Liverpool University Press, 2005.

Procopius, and Henry Bronson Dewing. *History of the Wars. Bk. 1-2* Cambridge; London: Harvard University Press, 2006.

Qutaybah, A.A.M.I., J. Montgomery, P. Webb, S.B. Savant, and M. Cooperson. *The Excellence of the Arabs.* NYU Press, 2017.

Rashed, R. *Encyclopedia of the History of Arabic Science*. Taylor & Francis, 2002.

Ratliff, B., H.C. Evans, and Metropolitan Museum of Art. *Byzantium and Islam: Age of Transition, 7th-9th Century*. Metropolitan Museum of Art, 2012.

Reference, Marshall Cavendish. *Illustrated Dictionary of the Muslim World*. Marshall Cavendish Reference, 2011.

Renard, J. *Friends of God: Islamic Images of Piety, Commitment, and Servanthood*. University of California Press, 2008.

Retso, J. *The Arabs in Antiquity: Their History from the Assyrians to the Umayyads*. Taylor & Francis, 2013.

Reynolds, G.S. *New Perspectives on the Qur'an: The Qur'an in Its Historical Context 2*. Taylor & Francis, 2012.

———. *The Qur'an and Its Biblical Subtext*. Taylor & Francis, 2010.

Reynolds, Gabriel Said. *The Emergence of Islam: Classical Traditions in Contemporary Perspective*. Minneapolis: Fortress Press, 2012.

———. *The Qur'an in Its Historical Context*. Routledge Studies in the QurⱭāN. London ; New York: Routledge, 2008.

Richman, P. *Many Ramayanas: The Diversity of a Narrative Tradition in South Asia*. University of California Press, 1991.

Rippin, A. *The Blackwell Companion to the Qur'an*. Wiley, 2008.

———. "The Function of 'Asbāb Al-Nuzūl' in Qur'ānic Exegesis." *Bulletin of the School of Oriental and African Studies, University of London* 51, no. 1 (1988): 1-20.

Rippin, A., and J. Mojaddedi. *The Wiley Blackwell Companion to the Qur'an*. Wiley, 2017.

Rippin, Andrew. *Muslims: Their Religious Beliefs and Practices*. Routledge, 2001.

Roberts, A. *The Ante-Nicene Fathers: The Writings of the Fathers Down to A. D. 325, Volume Viii Fathers of the Third and Fourth Century - the Twelve Patriarchs, Ex*. Cosimo Classics, 2007.

Robin, Christian Julien. "Arabia and Ethiopia." In *The Oxford Handbook of Late Antiquity*, edited by Scott Fitzgerald Johnson. Oxford: Oxford University Press, 2012.

Robinson, C. *Abd Al-Malik*. Oneworld Publications, 2012.

Robinson, Chase F. *Islamic Historiography*. Cambridge; New York: Cambridge University Press, 2011.

Robinson, F. *The Cambridge Illustrated History of the Islamic World*. Cambridge University Press, 1996.

Rodgers, K. *The Byzantine Empire: A Society That Shaped the World*. Teacher Created Materials, 2012.

Rodinson, Maxime. *Muhammad: Prophet of Islam*. London: Tauris Parke, 2002.

Rogerson, Barnaby. *The Heirs of Muhammad: Islam's First Century and the Origins of the Sunni-Shia Split*. Woodstock, NY: Overlook, 2008.

Ross, Martha, and R. R. Bowker Company. *Rulers and Governments of the World. Vol. 1*, London; New York: Bowker, 1980.

Roth, Norman. "*Medieval Jewish Civilization: An Encyclopedia*." (2016).

Roth, Norman, and Press Greenwood. *Daily Life of the Jews in the Middle Ages*. Westport, Connecticut; London: Greenwood Press, 2005.

Ruthven, M., and A. Nanji. *Historical Atlas of Islam*. Harvard University Press, 2004.

Saeed, Abdullah. "*Interpreting the Quran, Towards a Contemporary Approach*." (2006).

Saghy, M., and E.M. Schoolman. *Pagans and Christians in the Late Roman Empire: New Evidence, New Approaches (4th-8th Centuries)*. Central European University Press, 2018.

Sahas, D.J. *John of Damascus on Islam: The "Heresy of the Ishmaelites."*. Brill, 1972.

Salamon, Hagar. "*The Hyena People: Ethiopian Jews in Christian Ethiopia*." (1999).

Salaymeh, L. *The Beginnings of Islamic Law: Late Antique Islamicate Legal Traditions*. Cambridge University Press, 2016.

Sanders, F., K.D. Issler, and G.L. Bray. *Jesus in Trinitarian Perspective: An Introductory Christology*. B & H Academic, 2007.

Sartre, M. *The Middle East under Rome*. Belknap Press of Harvard University Press, 2005.

Sawma, G. *The Qur'an, Misinterpreted, Mistranslated, and Misread: The Aramaic Language of the Qur'an*. Adibooks.com, 2006.

Schadler, P. *John of Damascus and Islam: Christian Heresiology and the Intellectual Background to Earliest Christian-Muslim Relations*. Brill, 2017.

Schaff, P. *Nicene and Post-Nicene Fathers: First Series, Volume Iii St. Augustine: On the Holy Trinity, Doctrinal Treatises, Moral Treatises*. Cosimo Classics, 2007.

Schimmel, Annemarie. *Islam: An Introduction*. Albany: State University of New York Press, 1992.

Schoff, W. H. "The Periplus of the Erythraean Sea: Travel and Trade in the Indian Ocean by a Merchant of the First Century." http://sourcebooks.fordham.edu/halsall/ancient/periplus.asp.

Schomp, V. *The Ancient Persians*. Marshall Cavendish Corporation, 2009.

Schumann, Olaf H. *"Jesus the Messiah in Muslim Thought."* (2002).

Scott, E. *A Guide to the Phantom Dark Age*. Algora Publishing, 2014.

Sfar, Mondher. *In Search of the Original Koran: The True Story of the Revealed Text*. Amherst, NY: Prometheus Books, 2008.

Shahîd, I. *Byzantium and the Arabs in the Fifth Century*. Dumbarton Oaks Research Library and Collection, 1989.

Shamsi, F. A. "The Meaning of Nasi': An Interpretation of Verse 9:37." *Islamic Studies* 26, no. 2 (1987): 143-64.

Sharma, T.R. *Historiography: A History of Historical Writing*. Concept Publishing, 2005.

Shillington, K. *Encyclopedia of African History* Taylor & Francis, 2013.

Sicker, M. *The Pre-Islamic Middle East*. Praeger, 2000.

Singh, D.E. *Jesus and the Cross: Reflections of Christians from Islamic Contexts*. Regnum, 2008.

Skelly, Joseph Morrison. *Political Islam from Muhammad to Ahmadinejad: Defenders, Detractors, and Definitions*. Santa Barbara, Calif.: Praeger Security International, 2010.

Small, K.E. *Textual Criticism and Qur'an Manuscripts*. Lexington Books, 2011.

Smith, Sidney. "Events in Arabia in the 6th Century A. D." *Bulletin of the School of Oriental and African Studies, University of London* 16, no. 3 (1954): 425-68.

Snell, D.C. *Life in the Ancient near East, 3100-332 B.C.E.* Yale University Press, 1997.

Snodgrass, Mary Ellen. *Encyclopedia of World Scriptures*. Jefferson, NC: McFarland, 2011.

Somervill, Barbara A. "Empires of Ancient Mesopotamia." (2010).

Spalding, R., and C. Parker. *Historiography: An Introduction*. Manchester University Press, 2013.

St. J. B. Philby, H., and A. S. Tritton. "Najran Inscriptions." *Journal of the Royal Asiatic Society of Great Britain and Ireland*, no. 2 (1944): 119-29.

Stathakopoulos, D. *A Short History of the Byzantine Empire*. I. B. Tauris, 2014.

Stetkevych, Jaroslav. *Muhammad and the Golden Bough: Reconstructing Arab Myth*. Bloomington: Indiana UP, 1996.

Stora, Benjamin, and Abdelwahab Meddeb. *"A History of Jewish-Muslim Relations: From the Origins to the Present Day."* (2014).

Strabo. *The Geography of Strabo*. London: William Heinemann Ltd., 1932.

Stunkel, K.R. *Fifty Key Works of History and Historiography*. Taylor & Francis, 2012.

Subḥānī, J., and R. Shah-Kazemi. *The Doctrines of Shi'ism: A Compendium of Imami Beliefs and Practices*. I. B. Tauris, 2001.

Suleman, Fahmida. *Word of God, Art of Man: The Qur'an and Its Creative Expressions: Selected Proceedings from the International Colloquium, London, 18-21 October 2003*. Oxford: Oxford University Press in association with the Institute of Ismaili Studies, 2010.

Sundiata, A. *Look Behind the Facade*. Xulon Press, Incorporated, 2006.

Syed, M.H., S.S. Akhtar, and B.D. Usmani. *Concise History of Islam*. Vij Books India Private Limited, 2011.

Tabari, Muhammad , and Michael Fishbein. *The History of Al-Tabari*. Albany, NY: State Univ. of New York Pr., 1990.

Tacitus, Cornelius, Alfred John Church, and William Jackson Brodribb. *The Annals of Imperial Rome*. 2007.

Tadmor, Hayim. "The Campaigns of Sargon Ii of Assur: A Chronological-Historical Study (Conclusion)." *Journal of Cuneiform Studies* 12, no. 3 (1958): 77-100.

Taqi, A.M.M.B.M., and J.L. Merrick. *The Life and Religion of Mohammed, as Contained in the Sheeâh Traditions of the Hyât-Ul-Kuloob. Translated from the Persian by J. L. Merrick*. Phillips, 1850.

Tate, Marvin E. *Psalms 51-100* Grand Rapids, Michigan: Zondervan, 2015.

Taylor, Jane. *Petra and the Lost Kingdom of the Nabataeans*. London: I.B. Tauris, 2012.

Teshale, Tibebu. *The Making of Modern Ethiopia: 1896-1974*. Lawrenceville, NJ: Red Sea Press, 1995.

Teske, R.J., and J.E. Rotelle. *Arianism and Other Heresies*. New City Press, 1995.

Tessmann, Anna. *"The Wiley-Blackwell Companion to Zoroastrianism."* (2015).

Thomas, D.R. *The Bible in Arab Christianity*. Brill, 2007.

Thomas, David, Barbara Roggema, and Juan Pedro Monferrer Sala. *Christian-Muslim Relations. A Bibliographical History: 600-900 1 1*. Leiden; Boston: Brill, 2009.

Thomson, R., and J. Howard-Johnston. *Armenian History Attributed to Sebeos*. Liverpool University Press, 1999.

Tillier, Mathieu. *Journal of Qur'anic Studies* 13, no. 2 (2011): 109-15.

Tindel, Raymond D. "Zafar: Archaeology in the Land of Frankincense and Myrrh." *Archaeology* 37, no. 2 (1984): 40-45.

Tisdall, William St Clair. *Noble Eightfold Path*. London Nabu Press, 2010.

Tolan, J.V. *Saracens: Islam in the Medieval European Imagination*. Columbia University Press, 2002.

Tottoli, R. *Biblical Prophets in the Qur'an and Muslim Literature*. Taylor & Francis, 2013.

Trimingham, J. Spencer. *Islam in Ethiopia*. London, New York,: Oxford University Press, 1952.

Turner, Bryan S. *The New Blackwell Companion to the Sociology of Religion*. Wiley-Blackwell, 2016.

Van Bladel, Kevin Thomas. *From Sasanian Mandaeans to Sabians of the Marshes*. 2017.

van der Horst, P.W. *Studies in Ancient Judaism and Early Christianity*. Brill, 2014.

van Donzel, E.J., and A. Schmidt. *Gog and Magog in Early Eastern Christian and Islamic Sources: Sallam's Quest for Alexander's Wall*. Brill, 2010.

Van Gorder, A. Christian. *No God but God: A Path to Muslim-Christian Dialogue on God's Nature*. New York; Edinburgh: Orbis ; Alban, 2003.

Van Voorst, R. *Jesus Outside the New Testament: An Introduction to the Ancient Evidence*. Eerdmans Publishing Company, 2000.

Vaux, W.S.W. *Persia from the Earliest Period to the Arab Conquest*. BiblioBazaar, 2008.

Von Denffer, A. *Ulum Al Qur'an: An Introduction to the Sciences of the Qur'an (Koran)*. Kube Publishing Limited, 2015.

Watson, Richard. *Biblical and Theological Dictionary*. FORGOTTEN BOOKS, 2017.

Watt, W. Montgomery. *Muhammad at Mecca*. Karachi: Oxford University Press, 1979, 1953.

271

Watt, William Montgomery. *Muhammad: Prophet and Statesman.* London: Oxford Univ. Press, 1990.

Weiss, B.G. *The Spirit of Islamic Law.* University of Georgia Press, 1998.

Wheeler, B.M. *Moses in the Quran and Islamic Exegesis.* RoutledgeCurzon, 2002.

———. *Prophets in the Quran: An Introduction to the Quran and Muslim Exegesis.* Bloomsbury Academic, 2002.

White, James R. *What Every Christian Needs to Know About the Qur'an.* Minneapolis, Minnesota: Bethany House, 2013.

Wild, S. *Self-Referentiality in the Qur'ān.* Isd, 2006.

Williams, A. *The Zoroastrian Myth of Migration from Iran and Settlement in the Indian Diaspora: Text, Translation and Analysis of the 16ᵗʰ Century Qesse-Ye Sanjān 'the Story of Sanjan'.* Brill, 2009.

Williams, R. *Muhammad and the Supernatural: Medieval Arab Views.* Taylor & Francis, 2013.

Yamada, Shigeo. "Peter Hulin's Hand Copies of Shalmaneser III's Inscriptions." *Iraq* 62 (2000): 65-87.

Ye'or, B., and M. Kochan. *Islam and Dhimmitude: Where Civilizations Collide.* Fairleigh Dickinson University Press, 2002.

Yoffee, Norman. *The Cambridge World History Volume 3,* Cambridge: Cambridge University Press, 2015.

York, M. *Pagan Ethics: Paganism as a World Religion.* Springer International Publishing, 2015.

Young, G.K. *Rome's Eastern Trade: International Commerce and Imperial Policy 31 BC - AD 305.* Taylor & Francis, 2003.

Zahran, Yasmine. *The Lakhmids of Hira: Sons of the Water of Heaven.* Gilgamesh Publishing, 2014.

Endnotes

Introduction

[1] Quoted in: S.F. Johnson, *The Oxford Handbook of Late Antiquity* (Oxford University Press, 2015). 1078

[2] For example, the so-called 'Higher Criticism' that focused on the historical reliability of the key texts of Christianity. See, for example: F.P. Miller, A.F. Vandome, and J. McBrewster, *Dating the Bible: Higher Criticism, Textual Criticism, Biblical Manuscript, Torah, Documentary Hypothesis, the Bible and History, Synoptic Problem, Markan Priority* (Alphascript Publishing, 2010).

[3] The most distinctive doctrine of this movement was their denial that the Qur'an is eternal. They, instead, insisted that Allah must have created it at some point after creation. The execution of many of the leading lights of this movement has served as a salutary warning to any Muslim scholar tempted to step beyond accepted orthodoxy ever since.

[4] See: S.M. Deen, *Science under Islam: Rise, Decline and Revival* (Lulu.com, 2007). 58

[5] For more about the circumstances that led to Taha's execution, see: George Packer, "The Moderate Martyr," (2006).

[6] An excellent representative sample of the ideas of some of these scholars can be found in: Karl-Heinz Ohlig and Gerd- R. Puin, *The Hidden Origins of Islam: New Research into Its Early History* (Amherst, N.Y.: Prometheus Books, 2010).

[7] In case some younger readers find this reference obscure. I am, of course, referring to Brown's 'The Da Vinci Code' in which a radically revisionist version of the early history of Christianity was presented in the form of a novel.

A Brief Geographical Introduction

[8] For an overview of this period, see: G.W. Bowersock et al., *Late Antiquity: A Guide to the Postclassical World* (Belknap Press of Harvard University Press, 1999).

[9] See: J. Harris, *Constantinople: Capital of Byzantium* (Bloomsbury Publishing, 2017). 27 ff.

[10] For an overview of the phase of Roman history, see: K. Rodgers, *The Byzantine Empire: A Society That Shaped the World* (Teacher Created Materials, 2012).

[11] K. Butcher, *Roman Syria and the near East* (J. Paul Getty Museum, 2003).

[12] D.S. Potter, *A Companion to the Roman Empire* (Wiley, 2009). 565

[13] N. Faulkner, *Apocalypse: The Great Jewish Revolt against Rome Ad 66-73* (Amberley Publishing, 2011).

[14] L. Powell and P. Dennis, *The Bar Kokhba War Ad 132–135: The Last Jewish Revolt against Imperial Rome* (Bloomsbury Publishing, 2017).

[15] F. Millar, *The Roman near East, 31 B.C.-A.D. 337* (Harvard University Press, 1993). 374

[16] S. Elm, *'Virgins of God': The Making of Asceticism in Late Antiquity : The Making of Asceticism in Late Antiquity* (Clarendon Press, 1994). 273

[17] For a full discussion of the history of 'Roman Arabia', see: G.W. Bowersock, *Roman Arabia* (Harvard University Press, 1994).

[18] W. Ball, *Rome in the East: The Transformation of an Empire* (Taylor & Francis, 2016). 110

[19] See: Y. Zahran and P.R. Hoyland, *The Lakhmids of Hira: Sons of the Water of Heaven* (Gilgamesh Publishing, 2014).

[20] M. Ruthven and A. Nanji, *Historical Atlas of Islam* (Harvard University Press, 2004). 50

[21] Ibid. 30

[22] D. McLaughlin, *Yemen* (Bradt Travel Guides, 2008). 7

[23] For a history of the Sassanian Empire, see: T. Daryaee, *Sasanian Persia: The Rise and Fall of an Empire* (I.B.Tauris, 2014).

[24] This idea is, of course, a major theme in George Orwell's dystopian novel '1984'.

Chapter 1 – What is the Basis for Traditional Beliefs About the Early Years of Islam

[25] 'There has certainly been for you in the Messenger of Allah an excellent pattern for anyone whose hope is in Allah and the Last Day and [who] remembers Allah often.' Qur'an 33:21, Sahih Internation. Available in Arabic and several English traditions at: www.quran.com/33/21

[26] H. Mavani, *Religious Authority and Political Thought in Twelver Shi'ism: From Ali to Post-Khomeini* (Taylor & Francis, 2013). 97

[27] T. El-Hibri, *Parable and Politics in Early Islamic History: The Rashidun Caliphs* (Columbia University Press, 2010). 349

[28] B.E. Lewis and B.E. Churchill, *Islam: The Religion and the People* (Pearson Education, 2008).

[29] For an example of how Muslim scholars attempt to sort the 'wheat from the chaff' when it comes to the reliability of narrators, see: M.M. Azami and A.T. Publications, *Studies in Hadith Methodology and Literature* (Islamic Teaching Center, 1978). 64 ff.

[30] For an accessible introduction to the science of historiography, see: R. Spalding and C. Parker, *Historiography: An Introduction* (Manchester University Press, 2013).

31 For an overview of the use of sources for the reconstruction of ancient history, see: ibid. 47-92

32 K.N. Chitnis, *Research Methodology in History* (Atlantic Publishers and Distributors, 1990). 4-29

33 For some of the challenges associated with using artifacts in the process of writing history, see: J.M. Hall, *Artifact and Artifice: Classical Archaeology and the Ancient Historian* (University of Chicago Press, 2014).

34 P. Marsden, *The Taliban: War, Religion and the New Order in Afghanistan* (Zed Books, 1998). 16

35 J.G. Melton, *The Encyclopedia of Religious Phenomena* (Visible Ink Press, 2007). 337

36 H. Kragh, *An Introduction to the Historiography of Science* (Cambridge University Press, 1987). 121

37 For an overview of the use of oral history in modern historiography, see: T.R. Sharma, *Historiography: A History of Historical Writing* (Concept Publishing, 2005). 154-159

38 T. Egenes, *Introduction to Sanskrit* (Motilal Banarsidass Publishers, 1996). 46

39 See, for example: P. Richman, *Many Ramayanas: The Diversity of a Narrative Tradition in South Asia* (University of California Press, 1991).

40 For example: 'Abd al-Malik Ibn Hishām, Muḥammad Ibn Isḥāq, and Alfred Guillaume, *The Life of Muhammad: A Translation of Ishaq's Sirat Rasul Allaah* (Karachi; New York: Oxford University Press, 1997).

41 John L. Esposito, *What Everyone Needs to Know About Islam* (2011).

42 Karen Armstrong, *Muhammad: A Biography of the Prophet* (London: Phoenix, 2009).

43 "And it is He who withheld their hands from you and your hands from them within [the area of] Makkah after He caused you to overcome them. And ever is Allah, of what you do, Seeing." Qur'an 48:24, Saheeh International. The Quran: English Meanings and Notes. Al-Muntada Al-Islami. Available online in the original Arabic and several English translations at: www.quran.com/48/24

44 "Muhammad is not the father of [any] one of your men, but [he is] the Messenger of Allah and seal [i.e., last] of the prophets. And ever is Allah, of all things, Knowing." Qur'an 33:40, Saheeh International. The Quran: English Meanings and Notes. Al-Muntada Al-Islami. Available online in the original Arabic and several English translations at: www.quran.com/33/40

45 "And those who believe and do righteous deeds and believe in what has been sent down upon Muhammad – and it is the truth from their Lord – He will remove from them their misdeeds and amend their condition." Qur'an 47:2: Saheeh International. The Quran: English Meanings and Notes. Al-Muntada Al-Islami. Available online in the original Arabic and several English translations at: www.quran.com/47/2

[46] "Muhammad is the Messenger of Allah; and those with him are forceful against the disbelievers, merciful among themselves." Qur'an 48:29: Saheeh International. The Quran: English Meanings and Notes. Al-Muntada Al-Islami. Available online in the original Arabic and several English translations at: www.quran.com/48:29

[47] These references will be discussed in detail in Section 4.2.

[48] For a much more detailed discussion of the lack of geographical references in the Qur'an see: Dan Gibson, *Qur'anic Geography* (Saskatoon: Independent Scholars Press, 2011). 9

[49] For a discussion of the nature of the 'Occasions of Revelation' literature and the way this is used in Qur'anic exegesis, see: A. Rippin, "The Function of 'Asbāb Al-Nuzūl' in Qur'ānic Exegesis," *Bulletin of the School of Oriental and African Studies, University of London* 51, no. 1 (1988).

[50] S. Gu, *A Cultural History of the Arabic Language* (McFarland, Incorporated, Publishers, 2013). 124

[51] B.G. Weiss, *The Spirit of Islamic Law* (University of Georgia Press, 1998). 13

[52] Ibid. 13

[53] M.O. Farooq, *Toward Our Reformation: From Legalism to Value-Oriented Islamic Law and Jurisprudence* (International Institute of Islamic Thought, 2013). 103

[54] Marshall Cavendish Reference, *Illustrated Dictionary of the Muslim World* (Marshall Cavendish Reference, 2011). 106

[55] J. Subhānī and R. Shah-Kazemi, *The Doctrines of Shi'ism: A Compendium of Imami Beliefs and Practices* (I. B. Tauris, 2001). 181

[56] O. Leaman, *The Qur'an: An Encyclopedia* (Routledge, 2006). 41

[57] M.I.U.L. HAQ, *Companion of Hajj* (Xlibris, 2014). 24

[58] J.E. Brockopp, J. Neusner, and T. Sonn, *Judaism and Islam in Practice: A Sourcebook* (Taylor & Francis, 2005). 4

[59] S. Akhter, *Faith & Philosophy of Islam* (Kalpaz Publications, 2009). 155

[60] Weiss, *The Spirit of Islamic Law.* 13

[61] L.W. Adamec, *Historical Dictionary of Islam* (Rowman & Littlefield Publishers, 2016). 154

[62] A. Rippin, *The Blackwell Companion to the Qur'an* (Wiley, 2008). 168 ff.

[63] H. Berg, *The Development of Exegesis in Early Islam: The Authenticity of Muslim Literature from the Formative Period* (Taylor & Francis, 2013).

[64] Nigel Biggar, Jamie S. Scott, and William Schweiker, "Cities of Gods: Faith, Politics, and Pluralism in Judaism, Christianity, and Islam," (1986). 163

[65] "The Prophet performed ablution by washing the body parts only once." Sahih Bukhari Volume 1 Book 4 *Hadith* 159. Available online at: https://sunnah.com/bukhari/4

[66] "The Prophet performed ablution by washing the body parts twice." Sahih Bukhari Volume 1 Book 4 *Hadith* 160. Available online at: https://sunnah.com/bukhari/4

67   Sahih Bukhari Volume 1 Book 4 *Hadith* 161. Available online at: https://sunnah.com/bukhari/4

68   C. Bennett, *In Search of Muhammad* (Bloomsbury Academic, 1998). 45 ff.

69   "And those who disbelieved say, "Why has a sign not been sent down to him from his Lord?" You are only a warner, and for every people is a guide." Qur'an 13:7 Saheeh International. The Quran: English Meanings and Notes. Al-Muntada Al-Islami. Available in the original Arabic and in several English translations, at: www.quran.com/13/7

70   C.F.P. D and A.H. Walker, *Muhammad in History, Thought, and Culture: An Encyclopedia of the Prophet of God* (ABC-CLIO, 2014). 284

71   A.A.M.I. Qutaybah et al., *The Excellence of the Arabs* (NYU Press, 2017). 237

72   A. Jaffer and M. Jaffer, *Quranic Sciences* (Islamic College for Advanced Studies Publications, 2009). 117

73   "Then is it other than Allah I should seek as judge while it is He who has revealed to you the Book [i.e., the Qur'an] explained in detail?" And those to whom We [previously] gave the Scripture know that it is sent down from your Lord in truth, so never be among the doubters." Qur'an 6:114. Saheeh International. The Quran: English Meanings and Notes. Al-Muntada Al-Islami. Available in the original Arabic and several English translations at: www.quran.com/6/114

74   "And there is no creature on [or within] the earth or bird that flies with its wings except [that they are] communities like you. We have not neglected in the Register a thing. Then unto their Lord they will be gathered." Qur'an 6:38. Saheeh International. The Quran: English Meanings and Notes. Al-Muntada Al-Islami. Available in the original Arabic and several English translations at: www.quran.com/6/38

75   The definitive English translation of the 'Sira' is that Alfred Guillaume: Ibn Hishām, Ibn Isḥāq, and Guillaume, *The Life of Muhammad: A Translation of Ishaq's Sirat Rasul Allaah*.

76   Chase F. Robinson, *Islamic Historiography* (Cambridge; New York: Cambridge University Press, 2011). 65

77   Ibn Hishām, Ibn Isḥāq, and Guillaume, *The Life of Muhammad: A Translation of Ishaq's Sirat Rasul Allaah.*, 961.

78   D and Walker, *Muhammad in History, Thought, and Culture: An Encyclopedia of the Prophet of God [2 Volumes]*. 572

79   A.I.A.H.A.G.A. Maqdisi, *Short Biographies of the Prophet and His Ten Companions Who Were Given the Tidings of Paradise* (Darussalam, 2004). 73

80   Bennett, *In Search of Muhammad*. 68

81   "And those who disbelieved say, "Why has a sign not been sent down to him from his Lord?" You are only a warner, and for every people is a guide." Qur'an 13:7. Saheeh International. The Quran: English Meanings and Notes. Al-Muntada Al-Islami. Available in the original Arabic and several English translations at: www.quran.com/13/7

82 J.E. Brockopp, *The Cambridge Companion to Muhammad* (Cambridge University Press, 2010). 50

83 J. Renard, *Friends of God: Islamic Images of Piety, Commitment, and Servanthood* (University of California Press, 2008). 97

84 A.M.M.B.M. Taqi and J.L. Merrick, *The Life and Religion of Mohammed, as Contained in the Sheeâh Traditions of the Hyât-Ul-Kuloob. Translated from the Persian by J. L. Merrick* (Phillips, 1850). 118

85 R. Williams, *Muhammad and the Supernatural: Medieval Arab Views* (Taylor & Francis, 2013). 86

86 A.W. Hughes, *Muslim Identities: An Introduction to Islam* (Columbia University Press, 2013). 44

87 Islamic Research Institute and Central Institute of Islamic Research, *Islamic Studies* (Islamic Research Institute, 1998). 365

88 The leap month is, in fact, expressly forbidden in the Qur'an (9:36-37)

89 Johannes Jansen, "The Gospel According to Ibn Ishāq (D. 767), Johannes J.G. Jansen, January 2007," https://badmanna.wordpress.com/2015/05/11/the-gospel-according-to-ibn-ishaq-d-767-johannes-j-g-jansen-january-2007/.

90 H.A. Adil, *Muhammad the Messenger of Islam: His Life & Prophecy* (BookBaby, 2012). Rabbi al Awwal

91 Muhammad Tabari and Michael Fishbein, *The History of Al-Tabari* (Albany, NY: State Univ. of New York Pr., 1990).

92 K.R. Stunkel, *Fifty Key Works of History and Historiography* (Taylor & Francis, 2012). 43

93 J.W. Meri, *Medieval Islamic Civilization: An Encyclopedia* (Routledge). 792

94 Heather N. Keaney, *Medieval Islamic Historiography: Remembering Rebellion* (London: Routledge, 2015).

95 Robinson, *Islamic Historiography*. 26

96 For an example of an introductory work on Islam that simply repeats standard Islamic history, see: John L. Esposito, *Islam: The Straight Path* (2016).

97 E. Gibbon and H.H. Milman, *The History of the Decline and Fall of the Roman Empire* (Harper & brothers, 1844). 389

98 For example 'Cristoph Luxenberg': Christoph Luxenberg, *Syro-Aramaic Reading of the Koran: A Contribution to the Decoding of the Language of the Koran* (Amherst: Prometheus, 2009).; and 'Ibn Warraq': Warraq Ibn, *Why I Am Not a Muslim* (Amherst, N.Y.: Prometheus Books, 1995).

99 M. Farquhar, *Circuits of Faith: Migration, Education, and the Wahhabi Mission* (Stanford University Press, 2016). 67-86

100 Jaroslav Stetkevych, *Muhammad and the Golden Bough: Reconstructing Arab Myth* (Bloomington: Indiana UP, 1996). 5-6

101 See: Robert G. Hoyland, "Arabia and the Arabs: From the Bronze Age to the Coming of Islam," (2001).

102 A good example of such a trade description was penned by a 1st century trader dubbed the 'Periplus of the Erythean Sea'. His description gives a

highly-detailed account of trading opportunities in and beyond the Arabian Peninsula. See: W. H. Schoff, *"The Periplus of the Erythraean Sea: Travel and Trade in the Indian Ocean by a Merchant of the First Century,"* http://sourcebooks.fordham.edu/halsall/ancient/periplus.asp.

103 The contribution of these figures to our understanding of Arabia will be discussed in much more detail later in this book.

104 See, for example: M.P. Penn, *When Christians First Met Muslims: A Sourcebook of the Earliest Syriac Writings on Islam* (University of California Press, 2015).

Chapter 2 - The Incredible Vanishing City: Mecca and Pre-Islamic Arabia

105 "And thus We have revealed to you an Arabic Qur'an that you may warn the Mother of Cities [i.e., Makkah] and those around it and warn of the Day of Assembly, about which there is no doubt. A party will be in Paradise and a party in the Blaze. Qu'ran 42:7. Saheeh International. The Quran: English Meanings and Notes. Al-Muntada Al-Islami. Available in the original Arabic and several English translations at www.quran.com/42/7 Please note that the reference to 'Makkah' in this translation does not appear in the original text but have been inserted by the translators on the basis of the commonly accepted Muslim belief that this text refers to Mecca. This should, however, not simply be taken as read, as will become clear later in this book.

106 "And [mention] when Abraham was raising the foundations of the House and [with him] Ishmael, [saying], "Our Lord, accept [this] from us. Indeed, You are the Hearing, the Knowing." Qur'an 2:127. Saheeh International. The Quran: English Meanings and Notes. Al-Muntada Al-Islami. Available in the original Arabic and several English translations at www.quran.com/2/127

107 It is very significant, in terms of later discussions that Ibn Hisham identifies Syria as one of the places of origin of Meccan paganism. It is worth quoting the relevant passage in full: "A certain learned person told me that Amr bin Luhayy went from Mecca to Syria on a certain matter, and when he reached Moab...he saw the people worshipping idols, and asked what they were. They replied that they were idols which they were worshipping, and when they prayed for rain they got it and when they asked for help they received it. He asked them to spare him an idol to take away to the land of the Arabs and they gave him one called Hubal. So he took it to Mecca and set it up and ordered the people to serve it and to venerate it." Ibn Hishām, Ibn Ishāq, and Guillaume, *The Life of Muhammad: A Translation of Ishaq's Sirat Rasul Allaah.*, 701.

108 Ibid., 54-61.

109 This claim which, as we shall see, borders on the fanciful is even repeated in very respected Western histories of Islam. See, for example: W. Montgom-

ery Watt, *Muhammad at Mecca* (Karachi: Oxford University Press, 1979, 1953).

110 Even Muhahmmad himself supposedly participated in this trade according to Ibn Ishaq's biography: "Khadija was a merchant woman of dignity and wealth. She used to hire men to carry merchandise outside the country on a profit-sharing basis, for *Quraysh* were a people given to commerce. Now when she heard about the prophet's truthfulness, trustworthiness, and honourable character, she sent for him and proposed that he should take her goods to Syria and trade with them, while she would pay him more than she paid others. He was to take a lad of hers called Maysara. The apostle of God accepted the proposal, and the two set forth until they came to Syria." Ibn Hishām, Ibn Isḥāq, and Guillaume, *The Life of Muhammad: A Translation of Ishaq's Sirat Rasul Allaah.*, 82.

111 Ibid., 69.

112 Ibid., 54-61.

113 "The foolish among the people will say, "What has turned them away from their *qiblah*, which they used to face?" Say, "To Allah belongs the east and the west. He guides whom He wills to a straight path." And thus We have made you a median [i.e, just] community that you will be witnesses over the people and the Messenger will be a witness over you. And We did not make the *qiblah* which you used to face except that We might make evident who would follow the Messenger from who would turn back on his heels. And indeed, it is difficult except for those whom Allah has guided. And never would Allah have caused you to lose your faith [i.e, your previous prayers]. Indeed Allah is, to the people, Kind and Merciful." Qur'an 2:142-143. Saheeh International. The Quran: English Meanings and Notes. Al-Muntada Al-Islami.. These verses are viewed as the classical justification for the fact that Muslims orient their prayers towards Mecca (instead of continuing with and earlier orientation towards Jerusalem). There is, however, as we shall see significant problems with this interpretation.

114 See for example, Sahih Muslim Book 1 *Hadith* 21: "It is narrated on the authority of 'Abdullah son of 'Umar that the Messenger of Allah said: (The superstructure of) al-Islam is raised on five (pillars), testifying (the fact) that there is no god but Allah, that Muhammad is His bondsman and messenger, and the establishment of prayer, payment of Zakat, Pilgrimage to the House (Ka'ba) and the fast of Ramadan." Available online at: https://sunnah.com/muslim/1/21

115 H. St. J. B. Philby and A. S. Tritton, "Najran Inscriptions," *Journal of the Royal Asiatic Society of Great Britain and Ireland*, no. 2 (1944).

116 Strabo, *The Geography of Strabo* (London: William Heinemann Ltd., 1932). Book XVI, Chapter 4, pages 22–24

117 The Elder Pliny, John Bostock, and H. T. Riley, *The Natural History of Pliny* ([S.l.]: Bohn, 1855). Book VI, Chapter 1

[118] Nigel Groom, "Eastern Arabia in Ptolemy's Map," *Proceedings of the Seminar for Arabian Studies* 16 (1986).

[119] See: A. F. L. Beeston, "The Arabian Aromatics Trade in Antiquity," ibid. (2005).

[120] See: Christian Julien Robin, "Arabia and Ethiopia," in *The Oxford Handbook of Late Antiquity*, ed. Scott Fitzgerald Johnson (Oxford: Oxford University Press, 2012). page 282

[121] See: J. Spencer Trimingham, *Islam in Ethiopia* (London, New York,: Oxford University Press, 1952). 40

[122] For a primary source based description of the events associated with the death of the Najran martyrs, see: Sebastian P. Brock and Susan Ashbrook Harvey, *Holy Women of the Syrian Orient*, Updated ed. with a new preface. ed. (Berkeley ; London: University of California Press, 1998).,117.

[123] Some Muslim scholars teach that the so-called 'companions of the trench' referred to in this passage are the slaughtered Christians of Najran.

[124] See: R. Fulton Holtzclaw, *The Saints Go Marching In: A One Volume Hagiography of Africans, or Descendants of Africans, Who Have Been Canonized by the Church, Including Three of the Early Popes* (Shaker Heights, OH: Keeble Press, 1980).

[125] See: Patricia Crone and M. A. Cook, *Hagarism: The Making of the Islamic World, Patricia Crone, Michael Cook* (Cambridge: Cambridge University Press, 1976). 22.

[126] For an overview of the historical data relating to the pre-Islamic existence of Ta'if, see: Michael Dumper and Bruce E. Stanley, *Cities of the Middle East and North Africa: A Historical Encyclopedia* (Santa Barbara, Calif.: ABC-CLIO, 2007)., 242.

[127] Crone and Cook, *Hagarism: The Making of the Islamic World, Patricia Crone, Michael Cook.* 22

[128] Gibson, *Qur'anic Geography.*, 224.

[129] We have nothing more than names, added to 'Pope Lists' in later centuries, for many of the earliest popes. These figures are featured nowhere but on these lists (i.e. they are absent from the primary source record) so in this sense the idea of an unbroken line of succession from the first pope must be viewed as a matter of belief that cannot be substantiated from the historical record.

[130] Robert G. Hoyland, *Arabia and the Arabs: From the Bronze Age to the Coming of Islam* (London: Routledge, 2010). 51.

[131] In his work 'Qur'anic Geography' makes a very striking and persuasive case that the Thamud of Islamic tradition is none other than the people of the Nabatean Kingdom. This would, of course, place them firmly in northern Arabia instead of the Hejaz. See: Gibson, *Qur'anic Geography.* 131-186.

[132] William L. Langer and Peter N. Stearns, *The Encyclopedia of World History: Ancient, Medieval, and Modern Chronologically Arranged*, 6th ed. / Peter Stearns, general editor. ed. (Cambridge: James Clarke, 2001). 41.

[133] It is, for example, mentioned no less than 13 times in the Hebrew Bible, with the first reference occurring in Genesis 25:13.

[134] For an excellent overview of Nabatean history, and especially the relations of this ancient kingdom with the Roman Empire, see: David F. Graf, *Rome and the Arabian Frontier from the Nabataeans to the Saracens* (Aldershot: Ashgate, 1998).

[135] See: Martha Ross and R. R. Bowker Company, *Rulers and Governments of the World. Vol. 1, Vol. 1* (London; New York: Bowker, 1980).

[136] For a fuller discussion of the extent of Nabatean trading activities see: Gibson, *Qur'anic Geography.*, 154-157.

[137] For a detailed discussion of the history of the Kingdom of Kinda, see: M. D. Bukharin, "Towards the Earliest History of Kinda," *Arabian Archaeology and Epigraphy* 20, no. 1 (2009).

[138] For a discussion of Himyarite Judaism, see: Michael Lecker, "The Conversion of Ḥimyar to Judaism and the Jewish Banū Hadl of Medina," *Die Welt des Orients* 26 (1995).

[139] A good overview of the available material can be found in: Romolo Loreto, "Recent Studies in Pre-Islamic Yemen. An Overview," *Rassegna di Studi Etiopici* 4 (2012).

[140] For an example of just how rich the Himyarite archaeological record can be, see: Raymond D. Tindel, "Zafar: Archaeology in the Land of Frankincense and Myrrh," *Archaeology* 37, no. 2 (1984).

[141] The Kingdom of Aksum was roughly contemporary with the rise of Islam. It traded extensively with cities and regions across Arabia. Yet, no mention is ever made of Mecca in any Aksumite document. See: Stuart Munro-Hay, "Aksumite Overseas Interests," *Northeast African Studies* 13, no. 2/3 (1991).

[142] For a detailed discussion of time Nabonidus spent in Arabia, see: W. G. Lambert, "Nabonidus in Arabia," *Proceedings of the Seminar for Arabian Studies* 2 (1972).

[143] Shigeo Yamada, "Peter Hulin's Hand Copies of Shalmaneser III's Inscriptions," *Iraq* 62 (2000).

[144] Hayim Tadmor, "The Campaigns of Sargon II of Assur: A Chronological-Historical Study (Conclusion)," *Journal of Cuneiform Studies* 12, no. 3 (1958).

[145] Louis D. Levine, "Sennacherib's Southern Front: 704-689 B.C," ibid.34, no. 1/2 (1982).

[146] Eckart Frahm, *A Companion to Assyria* (2017)., 307.

[147] For a full description of the important role that Hira played in Sassanian 'Arabia Policy', see: M. J. Kister, "Al Hira: Some Notes on Its Relations with Arabia," *Arabica* 15, no. 2 (1968).

[148] For a comprehensive discussion of pre-Islamic Persian-Arabian trade, in which any mention of Mecca as a trading partner is glaringly absent, see: Touraj Daryaee, "The Persian Gulf Trade in Late Antiquity ," *Journal of World History* 14, no. 1 (2003).

149 We are so used to thinking of Alexander the Great as a 'Greek' that the fact of his origins as a Macedonian prince (albeit deeply influenced by the Greek language and culture) is sometimes obscured. The term Hellenistic Empire is a good compromise description of what Alexander achieved as it places, in the minds of some historians at least, the emphasis on Greek cultural and linguistic influence. Besides, 'Macedonian Empire' does not quite have the same ring to it.

150 For a summary of the discussion of Arabia in Herodotus see: David Asheri et al., *A Commentary on Herodotus Books I-IV* (Oxford: Oxford University Press, 2011).,

151 Some have attempted to prove that a reference to an Arabian temple in the writings of Diodorus is, in fact, a reference to the Ka'aba. This temple is, however, discussed in a section dealing with north-western Arabia. See: Diodorus and C. H. Oldfather, *Diodorus of Sicily. 2, 2* (London; Cambridge, Mass.: Heinemann ; Harvard University Press)., 216-217

152 Sidney Smith, "Events in Arabia in the 6th Century A. D," *Bulletin of the School of Oriental and African Studies, University of London* 16, no. 3 (1954)., 431

153 G. Kheirallah, *Islam and the Arabian Prophet* (New York: Islamic Pub. Co., 1938). 10

154 Some Muslim historians do try to claim that an obscure reference in Pliny's writings refer to Mecca. This claim will be discussed in more detail in Section 2.3.5.

155 Marcellinus Ammianus and Charles Duke Yonge, *The Roman History of Ammianus Marcellinus, During the Reigns of the Emperors Constantius, Julian, Jovianus, Valentian, and Valens* (London: Bell, 1911)., 11-12.

156 Procopius and Henry Bronson Dewing, *History of the Wars. Bk. 1-2* (Cambridge; London: Harvard University Press, 2006)., 179-195.

157 Patricia Crone, *Meccan Trade and the Rise of Islam* (Oxford: Basil Blackwell, 1987). 7

158 Ibid. 105

159 Richard W. Bulliet, *The Camel and the Wheel* (New York: ACLS History E-Book Project, 2005). 105

160 See, for example: Beeston, "The Arabian Aromatics Trade in Antiquity."

161 See, for example: Schoff, "The Periplus of the Erythraean Sea: Travel and Trade in the Indian Ocean by a Merchant of the First Century".

162 It is possible to trace trade relations down to the level of local centres and regions. It is, therefore, not unreasonable to expect references to Meccan traders to appear in our sources. See, for example: Christopher Edens and Garth Bawden, "History of Teimah and Hejazi Trade During the First Millennium BC," *Journal of the Economic and Social History of the Orient* 32, no. 1 (1989).

163 "And thus We have revealed to you an Arabic Qur'an that you may warn the Mother of Cities [i.e, Makkah] and those around it and warn of the Day of

Assembly, about which there is no doubt. A party will be in Paradise and a party in the Blaze. Qu'ran 42:7. Saheeh International. The Quran: English Meanings and Notes. Al-Muntada Al-Islami. Available in the original Arabic and several English translations at www.quran.com/42/7 Please note that the reference to 'Makkah' in this translation does not appear in the original text but have been inserted by the translators on the basis of commonly accepted Muslim belief that this text refers to Mecca. This should, however, not simply be taken as read, as will become clear later in this book.

164 "And [mention] when Abraham was raising the foundations of the House and [with him] Ishmael, [saying], "Our Lord, accept [this] from us. Indeed, You are the Hearing, the Knowing." Qur'an 2:127. Saheeh International. The Quran: English Meanings and Notes. Al-Muntada Al-Islami. Available in the original Arabic and several English translations at www.quran.com/2/127

165 Rangar H. Cline, *Ancient Angels: Conceptualizing Angeloi in the Roman Empire* (Leiden: Brill, 2011)., 116.

166 See: Mohammed Maraqten, "Newly Discovered Sabaic Inscriptions from Mahram Bilqis near Marib," *Proceedings of the Seminar for Arabian Studies* 32 (2002).

167 Martha Sharp Joukowsky, "The Petra Great Temple: A Nabataean Architectural Miracle," *Near Eastern Archaeology* 65, no. 4 (2002).

168 For a critical examination of the ways in which the Qur'an interacts with pre-Islamic pagan traditions, see: Patricia Crone, "The Religion of the Quranic Pagans: God and the Lesser Deities," *Arabica* 57, no. 2/3 (2010).

169 See: F. A. Shamsi, "The Meaning of Nasi': An Interpretation of Verse 9:37," *Islamic Studies* 26, no. 2 (1987).

170 Annemarie Schimmel, *Islam: An Introduction* (Albany: State University of New York Press, 1992)., 7

171 M. J. Kister, "Some Reports Concerning Mecca from Jahiliyya to Islam," *Journal of the Economic and Social History of the Orient* 15, no. 1/2 (1972).

172 For a full discussion of the 'Abraham Stories' in Islam, see: Shosh Ben-Ari, "The Stories About Abraham in Islam. A Geographical Approach," *Arabica* 54, no. 4 (2007).

173 Gibbon and Milman, *The History of the Decline and Fall of the Roman Empire*. 389

174 See, for example: Hugh Kennedy, "Arabia According to Ptolemy (Circa 150 Ad)," in *Historical Atlas of Islam* (Leiden: Brill, 2011).

175 Crone, *Meccan Trade and the Rise of Islam*., 134-135.

176 In fact, some modern Qur'an translations even go so far as to the replace the word Bakka with Mecca.

177 Qur'an 3:96-97. Saheeh International. The Quran: English Meanings and Notes. Al-Muntada Al-Islami. Available in the original Arabic and several English translations at www.quran.com/3/96

178 Marvin E. Tate, *Psalms 51-100* (Grand Rapids, Michigan: Zondervan, 2015). 356

179 Nancy L. DeClaisse-Walford, Rolf A. Jacobson, and Beth LaNeel Tanner, "The Book of Psalms," (2015). 652

180 Allan M. Harman, *Psalms* (Fearn, Ross-shire: Mentor, 2011). 631

181 Tate, *Psalms 51-100* 363

Chapter 3 - Setting the Scene: The Arabian Peninsula at the Dawn of Islam

182 Stetkevych, *Muhammad and the Golden Bough: Reconstructing Arab Myth.* 5-6

183 For an excellent discussion of pre-Islamic Arabian paganism, see: Hoyland, "Arabia and the Arabs: From the Bronze Age to the Coming of Islam." 139-166

184 Ibid. 161

185 "Indeed, the number of months with Allah is twelve [lunar] months in the register of Allah [from] the day He created the heavens and the earth; of these, four are sacred. That is the correct religion, so do not wrong yourselves during them. And fight against the disbelievers collectively as they fight against you collectively. And know that Allah is with the righteous [who fear Him]." The Quran: English Meanings and Notes. Al-Muntada Al-Islami. Available in the original Arabic and several English translations at www.quran.com/9/36

186 Hoyland, "Arabia and the Arabs: From the Bronze Age to the Coming of Islam." 161

187 It is interesting, in light of this, to note that the Qur'an is actually much more ambivalent about alcohol than the current strict Islamic prohibition would suggest. Its counsels range from calling alcohol a gift from God (Qur'an 16:67), to stating that you should not pray while drunk (Qur'an 4:43) and eventually to strict prohibition (Qur'an 5:90).

188 Ibn-Ishaq relates a story which has far reaching implications as far as the inspiration of the Qur'an is concerned. According to Ibn-Ishaq, Muhammad narrated the following statement to be added to Qur'an 53:19-20: "Have you thought of al-Lat and al-'Uzza and Manat the third, the other. These are the high-flying cranes; verily their intercession is accepted with approval." The names referred to here (al-Lat, al-'Uzza and Manat) belong to pre-Islamic goddesses who were greatly revered by the people of Mecca (most of whom were at first strongly opposed to Muhammad's message of only one God). They welcomed this revelation with great joy since it seemed to grant a role to their beloved goddesses within Islam. Muhammad's followers on the other hand were not too excited about this. They had sacrificed many things for the sake of monotheism and could not understand why this was now being left behind. Facing a revolt, Muhammad had to backtrack. He came up with an ingenious solution by claiming that the last line was in fact revealed by Satan and should therefore be removed from the Qur'an (hence the term 'Satanic Verses').

189 Ibn Warraq, *Why I Am Not a Muslim*. 46

190 Jane Taylor, *Petra and the Lost Kingdom of the Nabataeans* (London: I.B. Tauris, 2012). 105

191 Augustine Pagolu, *The Religion of the Patriarchs* (Sheffield, England: Sheffield Academic Press, 1998). 59

192 P. J. Bearman, *The Encyclopedia of Islam Volumes 1-6* (Leiden: Brill, 1996). 562.

193 For a book-length discussion of the kind of idolatry in view in the Qur'an, see: G. R. Hawting, *The Idea of Idolatry and the Emergence of Islam: From Polemic to History*, Cambridge Studies in Islamic Civilization (Cambridge, UK ; New York, NY, USA: Cambridge University Press, 1999).

194 "Indeed, those who do not believe in the Hereafter name the angels female names" (Qur'an 53:27) The Quran: English Meanings and Notes. Al-Muntada Al-Islami. Available in the original Arabic and several English translations at www.quran.com/53/27

195 "And [commanded], 'Direct your face toward the religion, inclining to truth, and never be of those who associate others with Allah" (Qur'an 10:26) The Quran: English Meanings and Notes. Al-Muntada Al-Islami. Available in the original Arabic and several English translations at www.quran.com/10/26

196 "And most of them believe not in Allah except while they associate others with Him." (Qur'an 12:106) The Quran: English Meanings and Notes. Al-Muntada Al-Islami. Available in the original Arabic and several English translations at www.quran.com/12/106

197 Indeed the references to idolatrous practices in the Qur'an are almost exclusively made in the in the context of the retelling of Biblical stories dealing with the idolatry. See, for example, Qur'an 6:74-82.

198 "And indeed, Lot was among the messengers. [So mention] when We saved him and his family, all, Except his wife among those who remained [with the evildoers]. Then We destroyed the others. And indeed, you pass by them in the morning And at night. Then will you not use reason?" (Qur'an 37:133-138) The Quran: English Meanings and Notes. Al-Muntada Al-Islami. Available in the original Arabic and several English translations at www.quran.com/37

199 "And it is He who sends down rain from the sky, and We produce thereby the growth of all things. We produce from it greenery from which We produce grains arranged in layers. And from the palm trees - of its emerging fruit are clusters hanging low. And [We produce] gardens of grapevines and olives and pomegranates, similar yet varied. Look at [each of] its fruit when it yields and [at] its ripening. Indeed in that are signs for a people who believe." (Qur'an 6:99) The Quran: English Meanings and Notes. Al-Muntada Al-Islami. Available in the original Arabic and several English translations at www.quran.com/6/99

200 "And I will mislead them, and I will arouse in them [sinful] desires, and I will command them so they will slit the ears of cattle, and I will command them so they will change the creation of Allah ." And whoever takes Satan as an ally instead of Allah has certainly sustained a clear loss." (Qur'an 4:119) The Quran: English Meanings and Notes. Al-Muntada Al-Islami. Available in the original Arabic and several English translations at www.quran.com/4/119

201 Then We gave Moses the Scripture, making complete [Our favor] upon the one who did good and as a detailed explanation of all things and as guidance and mercy that perhaps in [the matter of] the meeting with their Lord they would believe. And this [Qur'an] is a Book We have revealed [which is] blessed, so follow it and fear Allah that you may receive mercy. Lest ye should say: "The Book was sent down to two Peoples before us, and for our part, we remained unacquainted with all that they learned by assiduous study:" (Qur'an 6:154-156) The Quran: English Meanings and Notes. Al-Muntada Al-Islami. Available in the original Arabic and several English translations at www.quran.com/6

202 Ibn Hishām, Ibn Isḥāq, and Guillaume, *The Life of Muhammad: A Translation of Ishaq's Sirat Rasul Allaah.* 240

203 Ibid. 241

204 See, for example: Michael Lecker, "Judaism among Kinda and the Ridda of Kinda," *Journal of the American Oriental Society* 115, no. 4 (1995).

205 H. H. Ben-Sasson and A. Malamat, *A History of the Jewish People* (Cambridge, Mass.: Harvard Univ. Press, 2002). 358

206 Shmuel Aḥituv, *The Jewish People: An Illustrated History* (London: Continuum, 2006). 131

207 Bat-Zion Eraqi Klorman, *Traditional Society in Transition: The Yemeni Jewish Experience* (2014). 113

208 Tibebu Teshale, *The Making of Modern Ethiopia: 1896-1974* (Lawrenceville, NJ: Red Sea Press, 1995). 11

209 For a fuller discussion of Ethiopian Judaism, see: Hagar Salamon, "The Hyena People: Ethiopian Jews in Christian Ethiopia," (1999).

210 David Thomas, Barbara Roggema, and Juan Pedro Monferrer Sala, *Christian-Muslim Relations. A Bibliographical History: 600-900 1 1* (Leiden; Boston: Brill, 2009). 69

211 Christiane Gruber, *The Image of the Prophet between Ideal and Ideology: A Scholarly Investigation* (Berlin: De Gruyter, 2014). 20

212 William Montgomery Watt, *Muhammad: Prophet and Statesman* (London [u.a.]: Oxford Univ. Press, 1990). 1-2

213 S. A. Nigosian, "Islam Its History, Teaching, and Practices," (Bloomington: Indiana University Press, 2004). 8

214 Ancient Origins, "Archaeologists Discover That Earliest Known Arabic Writing Was Penned by a Christian | Ancient Origins," (2016).

215 "They have certainly disbelieved who say that Allah is Christ, the son of Mary. Say, "Then who could prevent Allah at all if He had intended to destroy Christ, the son of Mary, or his mother or everyone on the earth?" And to Allah belongs the dominion of the heavens and the earth and whatever is between them. He creates what He wills, and Allah is over all things competent." The Quran: English Meanings and Notes. Al-Muntada Al-Islami. Available in the original Arabic and several English translations at www.quran.com/5/17

216 "O People of the Scripture, do not commit excess in your religion or say about Allah except the truth. The Messiah, Jesus, the son of Mary, was but a messenger of Allah and His word which He directed to Mary and a soul [created at a command] from Him. So believe in Allah and His messengers. And do not say, "Three"; desist - it is better for you. Indeed, Allah is but one God. Exalted is He above having a son. To Him belongs whatever is in the heavens and whatever is on the earth. And sufficient is Allah as Disposer of affairs." (Qur'an 4:171) The Quran: English Meanings and Notes. Al-Muntada Al-Islami. Available in the original Arabic and several English translations at www.quran.com/4/171

217 "And [for] their saying, "Indeed, we have killed the Messiah, Jesus, the son of Mary, the messenger of Allah." And they did not kill him, nor did they crucify him; but [another] was made to resemble him to them. And indeed, those who differ over it are in doubt about it. They have no knowledge of it except the following of assumption. And they did not kill him, for certain." (Qur'an 4:157) The Quran: English Meanings and Notes. Al-Muntada Al-Islami. Available in the original Arabic and several English translations at www.quran.com/4/157

218 James R. White, *What Every Christian Needs to Know About the Qur'an* (Minneapolis, Minnesota: Bethany House, 2013). 236-238

219 See for example: "And [beware the Day] when Allah will say, "O Jesus, Son of Mary, did you say to the people, 'Take me and my mother as deities besides Allah ?'" He will say, "Exalted are You! It was not for me to say that to which I have no right. If I had said it, You would have known it. You know what is within myself, and I do not know what is within Yourself. Indeed, it is You who is Knower of the unseen." (Qur'an 5:116) The Quran: English Meanings and Notes. Al-Muntada Al-Islami. Available in the original Arabic and several English translations at www.quran.com/5/116

220 White, *What Every Christian Needs to Know About the Qur'an*. 99-100

221 Mark Robert Anderson, *The Qur'an in Context: A Christian Exploration* (Downers Grove, Illinois: IVP Academic, 2016). 258

222 There is, of course, a modern day 'Church of the Nazarene' but it adopted this name only in the first decade of the 20th century.

223 Richard Watson, *Biblical and Theological Dictionary*; Forgotten Books, 2017. 321

224 Antti Marjanen, Petri Luomanen "A Companion to Second-Century Christian "Heretics"," (2008). 258

225 Christology is the branch of the Christian theology that deals with the person and nature of Jesus Christ.

226 Joseph F. Kelly, *The Ecumenical Councils of the Catholic Church: A History* (Collegeville, Minn: Liturgical Press, 2009). 21-27

227 Ibid. 40-47

228 John Binns, *An Introduction to the Christian Orthodox Churches* (Cambridge, U.K.: Cambridge University Press, 2005). 6-8

229 Jonathan Berkey, *The Formation of Islam: Religion and Society in the near East, 600-1800* (Cambridge: Cambridge University Press, 2012). 40

230 Gerhard Böwering, Patricia Crone, and Mahan Mirza, *The Princeton Encyclopedia of Islamic Political Thought* (Princeton, N.J.: Princeton University Press, 2013). 269

231 Hoyland, "Arabia and the Arabs: From the Bronze Age to the Coming of Islam." 161

232 Halim Barakat, *The Arab World: Society, Culture, and State* (Berkeley, Calif.: University of California Press, 2007). 68

233 Joseph Morrison Skelly, *Political Islam from Muhammad to Ahmadinejad: Defenders, Detractors, and Definitions* (Santa Barbara, Calif.: Praeger Security International, 2010). 19

234 Ibid. 19

235 Yale H. Ferguson and Richard W. Mansbach, *A World of Polities: Essays on Global Politics* (London: Routledge, 2008). 148

236 Timothy E. Gregory, "A History of Byzantium," (2011). 63

237 Michael Grant, "From Rome to Byzantium: The Fifth Century Ad," (2015). 14

238 The Pope's official title is 'The Bishop of Rome'.

239 Gregory, "A History of Byzantium." 389-400

240 Sean McLachlan, *Byzantium: An Illustrated History* (New York: Hippocrene Books, 2005). 18

241 For an excellent overview of the historical data relating Roman Syria, see: Nigel Pollard, *Soldiers, Cities, and Civilians in Roman Syria* (Ann Arbor: University of Michigan Press, 2003).

242 F. E. Peters, *Mecca: A Literary History of the Muslim Holy Land* PRINCETON UNIV PRESS, 2017). 133

243 Peter Crawford, "The War of the Three Gods: Romans, Persians, and the Rise of Islam," (2014). 180

244 Warwick Ball, *Rome in the East: The Transformation of an Empire* Routledge, 2016). 17

245 Kathleen Kuiper, *Mesopotamia: The World's Earliest Civilization* (New York, NY: Britannica Educational Pub. in association with Rosen Educational Services, 2011). 130

246 Geoffrey Greatrex and Samuel N. C. Lieu, *The Roman Eastern Frontier and the Persian Wars Ad 363-628 Part II, Ad 363-630: A Narrative Sourcebook* (2002).. 104

247 For a discussion of the Roman-Persian wars and their impact on the rise of Islam, see: Crawford, "The War of the Three Gods: Romans, Persians, and the Rise of Islam."

248 G. W. Bowersock, *Roman Arabia* (Cambridge, Mass.: Harvard University Press, 1998). 146

249 Crawford, "The War of the Three Gods: Romans, Persians, and the Rise of Islam." 29

250 G. W. Bowersock, Peter Brown, and Oleg Grabar, "Late Antiquity : A Guide to the Postclassical World," (2012). 468

251 G. Kheirallah, *Islam and the Arabian Prophet* (New York: Islamic Pub. Co., 1938). 10

252 Qur'an 30:2-4.

253 Ball, *Rome in the East: The Transformation of an Empire.* 104

254 Luxenberg, *Syro-Aramaic Reading of the Koran: A Contribution to the Decoding of the Language of the Koran.* 237

255 Beate Dignas and Engelbert Winter, *Rome and Persia in Late Antiquity : Neighbours and Rivals* (Cambridge: Cambridge University Press, 2012). 238

256 John W. Barker, *Justinian and the Later Roman Empire* (Madison; London: University of Wisconsin Press, 1977). 123

257 Yasmine Zahran, *The Lakhmids of Hira: Sons of the Water of Heaven* (Gilgamesh Publishing, 2014). 61

258 Richard G. Hovannisian and Georges Sabagh, "The Persian Presence in the Islamic World" (Cambridge (United Kingdom), 1998). 47

259 For a comprehensive discussion of this issue, see: Kevin Thomas Van Bladel, *From Sasanian Mandaeans to Sabians of the Marshes* (2017).

260 Cyril Glasse, *The New Encyclopedia of Islam* (2013). 494

Chapter 4 - Where did Islam Originate? Examining the Islamic Sources

261 Cornelius Tacitus, Alfred John Church, and William Jackson Brodribb, *The Annals of Imperial Rome* (2007).

262 Crone and Cook, *Hagarism: The Making of the Islamic World, Patricia Crone, Michael Cook.* 22

263 See for example Qur'an 16:103: "And We certainly know that they say, "It is only a human being who teaches the Prophet." The tongue of the one they refer to is foreign, and this Qur'an is [in] a clear Arabic language." The Quran: English Meanings and Notes. Al-Muntada Al-Islami. Available in the original Arabic and several English translations at www.quran.com/16/103

264 Perhaps one of the most famous historical examples of this was when the Italian humanist Lorenzo Valla showed that the so-called 'Donation of

Constantine' (a key plank of papal authority) could not have been written at the time of Constantine the Great but was, instead, a much later medieval forgery.

265 Donald K. McKim, *The Cambridge Companion to Martin Luther* (Cambridge: Cambridge University Press, 2009). 71

266 Dalila Ayoun, *French Applied Linguistics* (Amsterdam: John Benjamins, 2007). 29

267 G. J. O. Moshay, *Anatomy of the Qur'an* (Ontario, Calif.: Chick Publications, 2007). 74

268 For a classical, and full, analysis, of the influence of the Syriac language on the Qur'an, see: Alphonse Mingana, "Syriac Influence on the Style of the Kur'an," *The John Rylands Bulletin* 11 (1927).

269 For a description and profile of the Syriac language, see: Keith Brown and Sarah Ogilvie, "Concise Encyclopedia of Languages of the World," (2010).

270 This startling discovery is the based on ground breaking research into the linguistic background of the Qur'an by Cristoph Luxenberg. See: Christoph Luxenberg, *The Syro-Aramaic Reading of the Koran: A Contribution to the Decoding of the Language of the Koran* (Berlin: H. Schiler, 2007).

271 Ibid.

272 Sawma, *The Qur'an, Misinterpreted, Mistranslated, and Misread: The Aramaic Language of the Qur'an.* 84

273 Ibn Warraq, *Christmas in the Koran: Luxenberg, Syriac, and the near Eastern and Judeo-Christian Background of Islam* (Amherst, New York: Prometheus Books, 2014).

274 Emran Iqbal El-Badawi, *The Qur'an and the Aramaic Gospel Traditions* (2016). 29

275 Martin Goodman, *The Roman World 44 BC - AD 180* (Florence: Taylor and Francis, 2013). 274

276 Gibson, *Qur'anic Geography.* 9

277 Ibid. 9

278 Qur'an 48:24 The Quran: English Meanings and Notes. Al-Muntada Al-Islami. Available in the original Arabic and several English translations at www.quran.com/48/24

279 Qur'an 3:96. The Quran: English Meanings and Notes. Al-Muntada Al-Islami. Available in the original Arabic and several English translations at www.quran.com/3/96

280 This is, for example, how it is rendered in the Saudi-sponsored Saheeh International translation. See: www.quran.com/3/96

281 Peters, *Mecca: A Literary History of the Muslim Holy Land.* Footnote 3, Chapter 1 – A Speculative History of Mecca

282 See, for example: Patricia Crone and Michael Allan Cook, *Hagarism: The Making of the Islamic World* (Cambridge: Cambridge University Press, 1980). 22

283 "And [commanded], 'Direct your face toward the religion, inclining to truth, and never be of those who associate others with Allah" (Qur'an 10:26) Quran: English Meanings and Notes. Al-Muntada Al-Islami. Available in the original Arabic and several English translations at www. quran.com/10/26

284 "And most of them believe not in Allah except while they associate others with Him." (Qur'an 12:106) The Quran: English Meanings and Notes. Al-Muntada Al-Islami. Available in the original Arabic and several English translations at www.quran.com/12/106

285 "And I will mislead them, and I will arouse in them [sinful] desires, and I will command them so they will slit the ears of cattle, and I will command them so they will change the creation of Allah ." And whoever takes Satan as an ally instead of Allah has certainly sustained a clear loss." (Qur'an 4:119) The Quran: English Meanings and Notes. Al-Muntada Al-Islami. Available in the original Arabic and several English translations at www. quran.com/4/119

286 "And it is He who sends down rain from the sky, and We produce thereby the growth of all things. We produce from it greenery from which We produce grains arranged in layers. And from the palm trees - of its emerging fruit are clusters hanging low. And [We produce] gardens of grapevines and olives and pomegranates, similar yet varied. Look at [each of] its fruit when it yields and [at] its ripening. Indeed in that are signs for a people who believe." (Qur'an 6:99) The Quran: English Meanings and Notes. Al-Muntada Al-Islami. Available in the original Arabic and several English translations at www.quran.com/6/99

287 Gibson, Qur'anic Geography. 233

288 "And indeed, Lot was among the messengers. [So mention] when We saved him and his family, all, Except his wife among those who remained [with the evildoers]. Then We destroyed the others. And indeed, you pass by them in the morning And at night. Then will you not use reason?" (Qur'an 37:133-138) The Quran: English Meanings and Notes. Al-Muntada Al-Islami. Available in the original Arabic and several English translations at www.quran.com/37

289 Qur'an 2:158. The Quran: English Meanings and Notes. Al-Muntada Al-Islami. Available in the original Arabic and several English translations at www.quran.com/2/158

290 These two 'mountains' play a central part in the Hajj as pilgrims are required to walk between them several times as part of the prescribed rituals. See: F. E. Peters, The Hajj: The Muslim Pilgrimage to Mecca and the Holy Places (Delhi: Oxford UP, 1996). 131

291 Tabari and Fishbein, The History of Al-Tabari.

292 "While they were in this state Abu- Jandal bin Suhail bin 'Amr **came from the valley of Mecca** staggering with his fetters and fell down amongst the

Muslims.' Sahih al-Bukhari Vol. 3, Book 50, *Hadith* 891 (Available online at: https://sunnah.com/bukhari/54/19) «O Abraham! Where are you going, **leaving us in this valley** where there is no person whose company we may enjoy, nor is there anything (to enjoy)?" Sahih Bukhari Vol. 4, Book 55, *Hadith* 583 (Available online at: https://sunnah.com/bukhari/60/43).

293 'When the Prophet performed the Tawaf of the Ka`ba, he did Ramal during the first three rounds and in the last four rounds he used to walk and while doing Tawaf between Safa and Marwa, **he used to run in the midst of the rain water passage**.' Sahih Bukhari Vol. 2, Book 26, *Hadith* 685 (Available online at: https://sunnah.com/bukhari/25/102)

294 Ibn Hishām, Ibn Ishāq, and Guillaume, *The Life of Muhammad: A Translation of Ishaq's Sirat Rasul Allaah*. 25

295 Sahih Bukhari Vol. 4, Book 55, *Hadith* 583. Available online at: https://sunnah.com/bukhari/60/43

296 Sahih Bukhari Vol. 4, Book 55, *Hadith* 583. Available online at: https://sunnah.com/bukhari/60/43

297 "'Amr set up an image on al-Safa called Nahlik Mujawid al-Rih and one on al-Marwa called Mut'im al-Tayr." Ibn Hishām, Ibn Ishāq, and Guillaume, The Life of Muhammad: A Translation of Ishaq's Sirat Rasul Allaah. 30

298 "When the Verse: 'And warn your tribe of near kindred.' (26.214) was revealed. Allah's Messenger went out, and when he had ascended As-Safa mountain, he shouted, "O Sabahah!" The people said, "Who is that?" "Then they gathered around him, whereupon he said, "Do you see? If I inform you that cavalrymen are proceeding up the side of this mountain, will you believe me?" They said, "We have never heard you telling a lie." Sahih Bukhari Vol. 6, Book 60, *Hadith* 495 (Available online at: https://sunnah.com/urn/46500)

299 Peters, *The Hajj: The Muslim Pilgrimage to Mecca and the Holy Places*. 131

300 Sahih al-Bukhari Vol. 2, Book 26, *Hadith* 647. Available online at: https://sunnah.com/bukhari/25/63

301 Ibn Hishām, Ibn Ishāq, and Guillaume, *The Life of Muhammad: A Translation of Ishaq's Sirat Rasul Allaah*. 226

302 Sahih al-Bukhari Vol. 2, Book 26, *Hadith* 646. Available online at: https://sunnah.com/bukhari/25/62

303 Al-Tabari recounts a story of how Muhammad's father had to wash the soil from his body (after working in his fields) before having sexual relations with his wife. Volume IV, 6

304 "When they came to Mecca they saw a town blessed with **water and trees** and delighted with it, they settled there." Ibn Hishām, Ibn Ishāq, and Guillaume, *The Life of Muhammad: A Translation of Ishaq's Sirat Rasul Allaah*. 46

305 Sahih al-Bukhari Vol. 4, Book 52, *Hadith* 281. Available online at: https://sunnah.com/bukhari/56/251

306 Ibn Hishām, Ibn Isḥāq, and Guillaume, *The Life of Muhammad: A Translation of Ishaq's Sirat Rasul Allaah.* 53

307 Gibson, *Qur'anic Geography*.233

308 An example: Al-Tabari relates a story where word is sent about the death of the Caliph from the Damascus to the holy city. The new Caliph lived for only 40 days after his accession yet news about events (and a slow moving, fully mobilized army on the return leg) traveled between Damascus and the holy city during this very short period. This would have been utterly impossible if the holy city was indeed located at the location of the modern city of Mecca.

309 Tabari and Fishbein, *The History of Al-Tabari.* Volume 8, 7

310 Gibson, *Qur'anic Geography.* 312

311 Sahih Muslim Book 19, *Hadith* 4340. Available online at: https://sunnah.com/muslim/32

312 Dumper and Stanley, *Cities of the Middle East and North Africa: A Historical Encyclopedia.* 120

313 This is true for the reign of the so-called 'Rightly Guided Caliphs' (632-661 CE) and the Umayyad Dynasty (661-750 CE)

314 Amira K. Bennison, *The Great Caliphs: The Golden Age of the 'Abbasid Empire* (New Haven: Yale University, 2014). 10

315 James E. Lindsay, *Daily Life in the Medieval Islamic World* (Indianapolis, Ind.: Hackett, 2008). 17

316 Barbara A. Somervill, "Empires of Ancient Mesopotamia," (2010). 126

317 Mark Juergensmeyer and Wade Clark Roof, *Encyclopedia of Global Religion* (London: SAGE, 2011). 1408

318 William H. Harrison, *In Praise of Mixed Religion: The Syncretism Solution in a Multifaith World* (2014). Chapter 1, Syncretism Happens

319 Maneckji Nusservanji Dhalla, *Zoroastrian Civilization: From the Earliest Times to the Downfall of the Last Zoroastrian Empire 651 A.D.;* Forgotten Books, 2015). 276

320 Anna Tessmann, "The Wiley-Blackwell Companion to Zoroastrianism," (2015). 285

321 "Lo! Those who disbelieve after their (profession of) belief, and afterward grow violent in disbelief: their repentance will not be accepted. And such are those who are astray. Lo! Those who disbelieve, and die in disbelief, the (whole) earth full of gold would not be accepted from such a one if it were offered as a ransom (for his soul). Theirs will be a painful doom and they will have no helpers." (Qur'an 3:90-91) The Quran: English Meanings and Notes. Al-Muntada Al-Islami. Available in the original Arabic and several English translations at www.quran.com/3

322 Sahih Bukhari Vol. 4, Book 52, *Hadith* 260. Available online: https://sunnah.com/bukhari/56/226

323 Hovannisian and Sabagh, "The Persian Presence in the Islamic World." 36

324 "Whenever the Prophet got up at night, he used to clean his mouth with Siwak." (Sahih Bukhari Volume 1, Book 4, *Hadith* 246). Available online at: https://sunnah.com/bukhari/4/112

325 Qu'ran 24:31. The Quran: English Meanings and Notes. Al-Muntada Al-Islami. Available in the original Arabic and several English translations at www.quran.com/24/31

326 Qu'ran 33:21. The Quran: English Meanings and Notes. Al-Muntada Al-Islami. Available in the original Arabic and several English translations at www.quran.com/33/21

327 Gavin Hambly, "The Cambridge History of Iran. Vol. 7, Vol. 7," (2008). 955

328 "Riders would pass us when we accompanied the Messenger of Allah while we were in the sacred state (wearing ihram). When they came by us, one of us would let down her outer garment from her head over her face, and when they had passed on, we would uncover our faces." Sunan Abi Dawud, Book 10, *Hadith* 1829. Available online at: https://sunnah.com/abudawud/11/113

329 A. Cohen, *The Babylonian Talmud: Tractate Berakot* (Cambridge, U.K.; New York: Cambridge University Press, 2013). xxiv

330 Edward S. Boraz, *Understanding the Talmud: A Modern Reader's Guide for Study* (Northvale, New Jersey: Aronson, 1996). 44

331 Markham J. Geller, "The Archaeology and Material Culture of the Babylonian Talmud," (2015). 21

332 Abraham Malamat and Haim Hillel Ben-Sasson, *A History of the Jewish People* (Cambridge, Mass.: Harvard University Press, 2002). 378

333 For an example of the debates about sources to be used in compiling the Mishnah, see: Dayid Halivni and Jeffrey L. Rubenstein, *The Formation of the Babylonian Talmud* (2013). 115

334 Malamat and Ben-Sasson, *A History of the Jewish People.* 379

335 Dan Cohn-Sherbok, *Judaism: History, Belief and Practice* (2017). 135

336 Moshe Gil, *Jews in Islamic Countries in the Middle Ages* (Leiden Brill, 2011). 404

337 Norman Roth, "Medieval Jewish Civilization: An Encyclopedia," (2016). 372

338 For a comparison between the 'Mishnah' and the *hadiths*, see: Benjamin Stora and Abdelwahab Meddeb, "A History of Jewish-Muslim Relations: From the Origins to the Present Day," (2014). 685

339 Ethan Katz, Lisa Moses Leff, and Maud Mandel, "Colonialism and the Jews," (2017). 66

340 Sahih Bukhari Book 65 *Hadith* 4556. Available online at: https://sunnah.com/urn/42340

341 Anver M. Emon, *Religious Pluralism in Islamic Law: Dhimmis and Others in the Empire of Law* (Oxford: Oxford University Press, 2012). 150

342 ʿUmar said, "I am afraid that after a long time has passed, people may say, "We do not find the Verses of the Rajam (stoning to death) in the Holy Book," and

consequently they may go astray by leaving an obligation that Allah has revealed. Lo! I confirm that the penalty of Rajam be inflicted on him who commits illegal sexual intercourse, if he is already married and the crime is proved by witnesses or pregnancy or confession." Sufyan added, "I have memorized this narration in this way." `Umar added, "Surely Allah's Messenger carried out the penalty of Rajam, and so did we after him." (Sahih Bukhari Volume 8, Book 82, *Hadith* 816). Available online at: https://sunnah.com/bukhari/86/56

Chapter 5 - Finding Muhammad behind the Shadows

343 Yehuda Nevo, "Towards a Pre-History of Islam," *Jerusalem Studies in Arabic and Islam* 17 (1994). 109-110

344 Oliver Leaman, *Routledge Encyclopedia of the Qur'an* (London: Routledge, 2005). AQIDA

345 "Whenever the Prophet got up at night, he used to clean his mouth with Siwak." (Sahih Bukhari Volume 1, Book 4, *Hadith* 246). Available online at: https://sunnah.com/bukhari/4/112

346 Qu'ran 3:144. The Quran: English Meanings and Notes. Al-Muntada Al-Islami. Available in the original Arabic and several English translations at www.quran.com/3/144

347 Qu'ran 33:40. The Quran: English Meanings and Notes. Al-Muntada Al-Islami. Available in the original Arabic and several English translations at www.quran.com/33/40

348 Qur'an 47:2. The Quran: English Meanings and Notes. Al-Muntada Al-Islami. Available in the original Arabic and several English translations at www.quran.com/47/2

349 Qur'an 48:29. The Quran: English Meanings and Notes. Al-Muntada Al-Islami. Available in the original Arabic and several English translations at www.quran.com/48/29

350 Qur'an 61:6. The Quran: English Meanings and Notes. Al-Muntada Al-Islami. Available in the original Arabic and several English translations at www.quran.com/61/6

351 Qur'an 68:15. The Quran: English Meanings and Notes. Al-Muntada Al-Islami. Available in the original Arabic and several English translations at www.quran.com/68/15

352 They say: "Why are not Signs sent down to him from his Lord?" Say: "The signs are indeed with Allah: and I am indeed a clear Warner. And is it not enough for them that we have sent down to thee the Book which is rehearsed to them? Verily, in it is Mercy and a Reminder to those who believe." (Qur'an 29:50-51) The Quran: English Meanings and Notes. Al-Muntada Al-Islami. Available in the original Arabic and several English translations at www.quran.com/29/50

353 Maxime Rodinson, *Muhammad: Prophet of Islam* (London: Tauris Parke, 2002). 212

354 This is done in the so-called 'Occasions of Revelation' literature. See: Abbas Jaffer and Masuma Jaffer, *An Introduction to Qur'anic Sciences* (London: ICAS Press, 2009). 64

355 And if you fear that you will not deal justly with the orphan girls, then marry those that please you of [other] women, two or three or four. But if you fear that you will not be just, then [marry only] one or those your right hand possesses. That is more suitable that you may not incline [to injustice]. (Qur'an 4:3) The Quran: English Meanings and Notes. Al-Muntada Al-Islami. Available in the original Arabic and several English translations at www.quran.com/4/3

356 O Prophet, indeed We have made lawful to you your wives to whom you have given their due compensation and those your right hand possesses from what Allah has returned to you [of captives] and the daughters of your paternal uncles and the daughters of your paternal aunts and the daughters of your maternal uncles and the daughters of your maternal aunts who emigrated with you and a believing woman if she gives herself to the Prophet [and] if the Prophet wishes to marry her, [this is] only for you, excluding the [other] believers. (Qur'an 33:50) The Quran: English Meanings and Notes. Al-Muntada Al-Islami. Available in the original Arabic and several English translations at www.quran.com/33/50

357 You, [O Muhammad], may put aside whom you will of them or take to yourself whom you will. And any that you desire of those [wives] from whom you had [temporarily] separated - there is no blame upon you [in returning her]. That is more suitable that they should be content and not grieve and that they should be satisfied with what you have given them - all of them. And Allah knows what is in your hearts. And ever is Allah Knowing and Forbearing. The Quran: English Meanings and Notes. Al-Muntada Al-Islami. Available in the original Arabic and several English translations at www.quran.com/33/51

358 And [remember, O Muhammad], when you said to the one on whom Allah bestowed favor and you bestowed favor, "Keep your wife and fear Allah," while you concealed within yourself that which Allah is to disclose. And you feared the people, while Allah has more right that you fear Him. So when Zayd had no longer any need for her, We married her to you in order that there not be upon the believers any discomfort concerning the wives of their adopted sons when they no longer have need of them. And ever is the command of Allah accomplished. (Qur'an 33:37) The Quran: English Meanings and Notes. Al-Muntada Al-Islami. Available in the original Arabic and several English translations at www.quran.com/33/37

359 Qur'an 66:1-16. The Quran: English Meanings and Notes. Al-Muntada Al-Islami. Available in the original Arabic and several English translations at www.quran.com/6

360 Sahih Bukhari Vol. 6, Book 61, *Hadith* 512. Available online at: https://sunnah.com/bukhari/66

361 The believers are only those who believe in Allah and His Messenger and, when they are [meeting] with him for a matter of common interest, do not depart until they have asked his permission. Indeed, those who ask your permission, [O Muhammad] - those are the ones who believe in Allah and His Messenger. So when they ask your permission for something of their affairs, then give permission to whom you will among them and ask forgiveness for them of Allah. Indeed, Allah is Forgiving and Merciful. (Qur'an 24:62) The Quran: English Meanings and Notes. Al-Muntada Al-Islami. Available in the original Arabic and several English translations at www.quran.com/24/62

362 Sahih Bukhari Vol. 6, Book 60, *Hadith* 311. Available online at: https://sunnah.com/urn/44660

363 Muhammad Mustafa A'Zami, *Studies in Hadith Methodology and Literature* (Kuala Lumpur: Islamic Book Trust, 2010). 39

364 Ibn Hishām, Ibn Isḥāq, and Guillaume, *The Life of Muhammad: A Translation of Ishaq's Sirat Rasul Allaah*. 522

365 Nigosian, "Islam Its History, Teaching, and Practices." 8

366 Sahih Bukhari Volume 1 Book 1 *Hadith* 3. Available online at: https://sunnah.com/bukhari/1

367 Sahih Bukhari Volume 7, Book 69, *Hadith* 543. Available online at: https://sunnah.com/bukhari/74/65

368 Sahih Bukhari Volume 4, Book 56, *Hadith* 779. Available online at: https://sunnah.com/bukhari/61/88

369 Ibn Hishām, Ibn Isḥāq, and Guillaume, *The Life of Muhammad: A Translation of Ishaq's Sirat Rasul Allaah*. 241

370 Gabriel Said Reynolds, *The Qur'an in Its Historical Context*, Routledge Studies in the Qur'āN (London ; New York: Routledge, 2008). 166

371 See, for example, the following very strange test that supposedly 'proves' that Muhammad is a prophet. Sahih Bukhari Volume 4 Book 55 *Hadith* 546: "When 'Abdullah bin Salam heard the arrival of the Prophet at Medina, he came to him and said, "I am going to ask you about three things which nobody knows except a prophet: What is the first portent of the Hour? What will be the first meal taken by the people of Paradise? Why does a child resemble its father, and why does it resemble its maternal uncle?" Allah's Apostle said, "Gabriel has just now told me of their answers." 'Abdullah said, "He (i.e. Gabriel), from amongst all the angels, is the enemy of the Jews." Allah's Apostle said, "The first portent of the Hour will be a fire that will bring together the people from the east to the west; the first meal of the people of Paradise will be Extra-lobe (caudate lobe) of fish-liver. As for the resemblance of the child to its parents: If a man has sexual intercourse with his wife and gets discharge first, the child will resemble the father, and if the woman gets discharge first, the child will resemble her. Available online at: https://sunnah.com/urn/31100

372 God warns Muhammad in the Qur'an that his aorta will be cut off if he utters a prophecy not given to him from above (Qur'an Qur'an 69:44-46). In Sahih Bukhari Volume 5, Book 59, *Hadith* 713 his death is described as follows: The Prophet in his ailment in which he died, used to say, "O Aishah! I still feel the pain caused by the food I ate at Khaibar, and at this time, I feel as if my aorta is being cut from that poison. Available online at: https://sunnah.com/bukhari/64/450

373 They say: "Why are not Signs sent down to him from his Lord?" Say: "The signs are indeed with Allah: and I am indeed a clear Warner. And is it not enough for them that we have sent down to thee the Book which is rehearsed to them? Verily, in it is Mercy and a Reminder to those who believe." (Qur'an 29:50-51) The Holy Qur'an, The Quran: English Meanings and Notes. Al-Muntada Al-Islami. Available in the original Arabic and several English translations at www.quran.com/29/50

374 Martin Lings, "Muhammad - His Life Based on the Earliest Sources," (2017). 22

375 Theirs was apparently a strong bond. So much so that one of Muhammad's later wives, Aisha, repeatedly expressed jealousy towards the (deceased) Khadija. See, for example, Sahih Bukhari Volume 5, Book 58, *Hadith* 166. Available online at: https://sunnah.com/bukhari/63/44

376 See, for example, Sahih Bukhari Volume 1, Book 1, *Hadith* 3. Available online at: https://sunnah.com/bukhari/1

377 Clinton Bennett, "In Search of Muhammad," (1999). 251

378 Sahih Bukhari Volume 4, Book 58, *Hadith* 234. Available online at: https://sunnah.com/bukhari/63/120

379 Sahih Bukhari Volume 7, Book 62, *Hadith* 65. Available online at: https://sunnah.com/bukhari/67/70

380 For an analysis of this story and its importance, see: Angelika Neuwirth, Nicolai Sinai, and Michael Marx, *The Qur'an in Context: Historical and Literary Investigations into the Qur'anic Milieu* (Leiden; Boston, Mass.: Brill, 2011). 576

381 David Stephan Powers, *Muhammad Is Not the Father of Any of Your Men: The Making of the Last Prophet* (Philadelphia, Pa.; Oxford: University of Pennsylvania Press ; Oxford Creative Marketing [distributor], 2011). 28

382 Thomas Patrick Hughes, *A Dictionary of Islam* (London: W. H. Allen, 1885). Zaid, 698

383 Bryan S. Turner, *The New Blackwell Companion to the Sociology of Religion* (Wiley-Blackwell, 2016). 366

384 Powers, *Muhammad Is Not the Father of Any of Your Men: The Making of the Last Prophet*. 8

385 See, for example: "Narrated Qatada: Anas bin Malik said, "The Prophet used to visit all his wives in a round, during the day and night and they were eleven in number." I asked Anas, "Had the Prophet the strength for

it?" Anas replied, "We used to say that the Prophet was given the strength of thirty (men)." Sahih Bukhari Vol. 1, Book 5, *Hadith* 268. Available online at: https://sunnah.com/bukhari/5/21

386 Muhammad Husayn Haykal and Ismail Ragi A. Al Faruqi, *The Life of Muhammad* (New York: The Other Press, 1994). 76-77

387 Qur'an 33:40. The Holy Qur'an, The Quran: English Meanings and Notes. Al-Muntada Al-Islami. Available in the original Arabic and several English translations at www.quran.com/33/40

388 For a fuller discussion of the way in which the historical record was manipulated in order to shut people out from any claim to succession, see: Powers, *Muhammad Is Not the Father of Any of Your Men: The Making of the Last Prophet.*

389 Robert Brenton Betts, "The Sunni-Shi'a Divide: Islam's Internal Divisions and Their Global Consequences," (2013).Note> 17

390 Richard A. Gabriel, "Muhammad: Islam's First Great General," (2007). xix

391 David Nicolle, "The Great Islamic Conquests Ad 632-750," (2014). 23

392 Gabriel, "Muhammad: Islam's First Great General." xix

393 See, for example: Zakaria Bashier and Foundation Islamic, "War and Peace in the Life of the Prophet Muhammad" (2006). 218

394 "[Muhammad] said, "Woe to you, Abu Sufyan, isn't it time that you recognize that I am Allah's apostle?" He (Abu Sufyan) answered, "As to that I still have some doubt." I (the narrator) said to him, "Submit and testify that there is no god but Allah and that Muhammad is the apostle of Allah before you lose your head," so he did so." Ibn Hishām, Ibn Isḥāq, and Guillaume, *The Life of Muhammad: A Translation of Ishaq's Sirat Rasul Allaah.* 814

395 Sahih Bukhari Volume 1 Book 8 *Hadith* 367. Available at: http://sunnah.com/bukhari/8

396 Sunan Abu Dawud Book 38 *Hadith* 4390. Available at: http://sunnah.com/abudawud/40/54.

397 Ibn Hishām, Ibn Isḥāq, and Guillaume, *The Life of Muhammad: A Translation of Ishaq's Sirat Rasul Allaah.* 675-676.

398 Mahdi Rizqallah Ahmad and Syed Iqbal Zaheer, *A Biography of the Prophet of Islam: In the Light of the Original Sources* (2005). 433

399 Ibn Hishām, Ibn Isḥāq, and Guillaume, *The Life of Muhammad: A Translation of Ishaq's Sirat Rasul Allaah.* 144-145

400 Ibid. 509

401 "O you who have believed, when the believing women come to you as emigrants, examine them. Allah is most knowing as to their faith. And if you know them to be believers, then do not return them to the disbelievers; they are not lawful [wives] for them, nor are they lawful [husbands] for them. But give the disbelievers what they have spent. And there is no blame upon you if you marry them when you have given them their due compen-

sation. And hold not to marriage bonds with disbelieving women, but ask for what you have spent and let them ask for what they have spent. That is the judgment of Allah ; He judges between you. And Allah is Knowing and Wise." (Qur'an 60:10) The Holy Qur'an, The Quran: English Meanings and Notes. Al-Muntada Al-Islami. Available in the original Arabic and several English translations at www.quran.com/60/10

402 Sahih Bukhari Volume 3 Book 34 *Hadith* 432: "O Allah's Apostle! We get female captives as our share of booty, and we are interested in their prices, what is your opinion about coitus interruptus?" The Prophet said, "Do you really do that? It is better for you not to do it. No soul that which Allah has destined to exist, but will surely come into existence." Available at: http://sunnah.com/bukhari/34/176

403 Sahih Bukhari Book 1 Volume 2 *Hadith* 26. Available at: http://www.usc.edu/org/cmje/religious-texts/*hadith*/bukhari/002-sbt.php

404 Sahih Bukhari Volume 4 Book 52 *Hadith* 260. Available at: http://sunnah.com/bukhari/56/226.

405 Sahih Bukhari Volume 4 Book 52 *Hadith* 271. Available at: http://www.usc.edu/org/cmje/religious-texts/*hadith*/bukhari/052-sbt.php

406 Available at: www.ntdwi.com

407 Ahmad and Zaheer, *A Biography of the Prophet of Islam: In the Light of the Original Sources.* 410

408 Gabriel, "Muhammad: Islam's First Great General." 86

409 Ibn Hishām, Ibn Isḥāq, and Guillaume, *The Life of Muhammad: A Translation of Ishaq's Sirat Rasul Allaah.* 281-288

410 See, example: Reference Marshall Cavendish, *Islamic Beliefs, Practices, and Cultures* (Tarrytown, N.Y.: Marshall Cavendish Reference, 2011). 194

411 This is commonly known as Muhammad's 'Night Journey'. For a full discussion of this tradition, see: Frederick Colby, *Narrating Muhammad's Night Journey Tracing the Development of the Ibn 'Abbas Ascension Discourse* (State Univ of New York Pr, 2009) As we shall see later on, the visit is not acutally included in the inscriptions on the building.

412 Andreas Kaplony, *The Haram of Jerusalem 324-1099: Temple, Friday Mosque, Area of Spiritual Power* (Stuttgart: Steiner, 2002). 64

413 For a discussion of the importance of Jerusalem as a pilgrimage destination for Christians in the Eastern Roman Empire, see: Norman Yoffee, *The Cambridge World History Volume 3,* (Cambridge: Cambridge University Press, 2015). 431

414 Exalted is He who took His Servant by night from al-Masjid al-Haram to al-Masjid al- Aqsa, whose surroundings We have blessed, to show him of Our signs. Indeed, He is the Hearing, the Seeing. (Qur'an 17:1) The Holy Qur'an, The Quran: English Meanings and Notes. Al-Muntada Al-Islami. Available in the original Arabic and several English translations at www.quran.com/17/1

415 "Umm, Abu Talib's daughter, said: 'The Apostle went on no journey except while he was in my house. *He slept in my home that night after he prayed the final night prayer. A little before dawn he woke us, saying, 'O Umm, I went to Jerusalem.' He got up to go out and I grabbed hold of his robe and laid bare his belly.* I pleaded, 'O Muhammad, don't tell the people about this for they will know you are lying and will mock you.' *He said, 'By Allah, I will tell them.' I told a Negress slave of mine, 'Follow him and listen.'* "Ibn Hishām, Ibn Isḥāq, and Guillaume, *The Life of Muhammad: A Translation of Ishaq's Sirat Rasul Allaah.* 184

416 Norman Calder, Jawid Ahmad Mojaddedi, and Andrew Rippin, *Classical Islam: A Sourcebook of Religious Literature* (London; New York: Routledge, Taylor & Francis Group, 2013). 19

417 It is, in fact, often evoked whenever there is conflict between Muslims and Jewish people. For some within the Muslim community events like these represent some kind of perverted 'ideal' when it comes to Muslim treatment of Jews. As the Jerusalem Post states: "In Islamic tradition, the chant "Khaybar Khaybar, ya yahud, Jaish Muhammad, sa yahud," which means, "Jews, remember Khaybar, the army of Muhammad is returning," is used as a battle cry when attacking Jews or Israelis." See: http://m.jpost.com/Middle-East/Ramadan-Series-Khaybar-re-enforces-anti-Semitic-stereotypes-319568

418 See, for example, Sunan Abu Dawud Book 38 *Hadith* 4390. Available at: http://sunnah.com/abudawud/40/54.

419 For a discussion of the charge that these events, as presented in the traditions, amounted to genocide, see: M. A. Abdel Haleem and 'Ādil 'Umar Sharīf, *Criminal Justice in Islam: Judicial Procedure in the Sharī'a* (London; New York; New York: I.B. Tauris ; Distributed by Palgrave Macmillan in the United States and Canada, 2018). 138

420 For a discussion of the Jewish presence, as well as their response to persecution, see: De Lacy O'Leary, *Arabia before Muhammad* (Routledge, 2013). 173

421 The Jewish community of Arabia was by no means isolated from Jews in the rest of the world. See, for example: Norman Roth and Press Greenwood, *Daily Life of the Jews in the Middle Ages* (Westport, Connecticut; London: Greenwood Press, 2005). ix

422 For a detailed discussion of the 'Constitution of Medina' including its dating, see: ibid. 57

423 This fact is very significant as far as the content of the document is concerned. Some scholars believe that the first stage of the development of Islam was an attempt at a synthesis between proto-Muslim and Jewish identities at places like Medina. See, for example: Fred McGraw Donner, *Muhammad and the Believers: At the Origins of Islam* (Cambridge, Mass.: Belknap Press of Harvard University Press, 2012).

424 Roth and Greenwood, *Daily Life of the Jews in the Middle Ages.* 57

425 For an analysis of this sermon and its implications for the development of the Islamic community, see: Cenap Cakmak, *Islam. A Worldwide Encyclopedia. 4 Vols* (Santa Barbara: ABC-CLIO, Inc, 2015). 163

426 For the full text of this document, see: Muḥammad and John A. Morrow, *Six Covenants of the Prophet Muhammad with the Christians of His Time: The Primary Documents*. Please note that although these 'covenants' are called 'Primary Sources' by the authors they are clearly nothing of the sort in the sense which this term is normally understood by historians since there is no way that it can be definitively proved that they date from the time of Muhammad.

427 For a description of the conquest of Sinai by the Muslim forces, see: Laurence Brown, *The Eclipse of Christianity in Asia, by L.E. Brown* (Cambridge, 1933). 38. What is rather interesting in this account is that it contains a description of what can only be described as a forced conversion. If there was indeed a 'covenant' between Muhammad and the people of Sinai this would have been a clear violation of it.

428 Perhaps the most famous forgery of this kind is the so-called 'Donation of Constantine' which supposedly confirmed the rights of the popes to be the temporal rulers of central Italy. It was definitively proved to be a forgery by the brilliant Renaissance humanist, Lorenzo Valla.

429 For a concise overview of available sources for reconstructing the life of Muhammad, see: P.K. Hitti, *History of the Arabs* (Palgrave Macmillan, 2002). 212

430 A full account of possible Syriac references to Muhammad can be found in: Penn, *When Christians First Met Muslims: A Sourcebook of the Earliest Syriac Writings on Islam*.

431 In doing this both Syriac and Byzantine sources more broadly should be included. This is what I propose to do in the rest of this chapter and in the chapter dealing with the Arab conquests.

432 For a description of the contents of the inscriptions on the Dome of the Rock, see: R. Gonen, *Contested Holiness: Jewish, Muslim, and Christian Perspectives on the Temple Mount in Jerusalem* (KTAV Publishing House, 2003). 87ff

433 Reference, *Illustrated Dictionary of the Muslim World*. 38

434 For a comprehensive discussion of the Arab conquests, including a discussion of why it would be simplistic to refer to these events as 'Muslim Conquests', see: R.G. Hoyland, *In God's Path: The Arab Conquests and the Creation of an Islamic Empire* (Oxford University Press, 2015).

435 An overview of how, for example, the conquests were experienced by Greek-speaking authors can be found here: Demetrios J. Constantelos, "The Moslem Conquests of the near East as Revealed in the Greek Sources of the Seventh and the Eighth Centuries," *Byzantion* 42, no. 2 (1972). 325-357

436 While there was some awareness of religious motives, the most obvious religious fact (to modern Muslims at least) namely that they were acting in the name of God's final prophet, is absent: S.H. Griffith, *The Church in the Shadow of the Mosque: Christians and Muslims in the World of Islam* (Princeton University Press, 2012); ibid. 24-25

437 For an overview of Byzantine mentions and discussion of Muhammad, see: D and Walker, *Muhammad in History, Thought, and Culture: An Encyclopedia of the Prophet of God.* 79-81

438 For a book length discussion of Syriac sources dealing with the early Arab conquests, see: Penn, *When Christians First Met Muslims: A Sourcebook of the Earliest Syriac Writings on Islam.*

439 There is considerable debate about which of the Syriac documents contains the first non-Muslim reference to Muhammad. The one which is possibly the oldest is the Chronicle of Thomas the Presbyter which refers to a battle between the Romans and the 'Arabs of Muhammad'. It is however not altogether certain that this text was preserved intact and the reference to Muhammad may have been added later: See: ibid. 25-27

440 W.E. Kaegi, *Muslim Expansion and Byzantine Collapse in North Africa* (Cambridge University Press, 2010). 36

441 W. Mayer and B. Neil, *Religious Conflict from Early Christianity to the Rise of Islam* (De Gruyter, 2013). 232

442 R. Thomson and J. Howard-Johnston, *Armenian History Attributed to Sebeos* (Liverpool University Press, 1999).

443 Harald Motzki, *The Biography of Muhammad: The Issue of the Sources* (Boston, MA: Brill, 2000). 278

444 F.M. Donner, *Muhammad and the Believers* (Harvard University Press, 2012). 114

445 P. Schadler, *John of Damascus and Islam: Christian Heresiology and the Intellectual Background to Earliest Christian-Muslim Relations* (Brill, 2017). 6

Chapter 6 - The Qur'an: Proof of Islam's Origin Narrative?
446 D.W. Brown, *A New Introduction to Islam* (Wiley, 2011). 72

447 Ibid. 35

448 *Materials for the History of the Text of the Quran; the Old Codices,* (Brill Archive). 44

449 It is worth quoting the *hadith* in which Zaid was given his instructions in full: "Abu Bakr sent for me owing to the large number of casualties in the battle of Al-Yamama, while 'Umar was sitting with him. Abu Bakr said (to me), 'Umar has come to me and said, 'A great number of Qaris of the Holy Qur'an were killed on the day of the battle of Al-Yamama, and I am afraid that the casualties among the Qaris of the Qur'an may increase on other battle-fields whereby a large part of the Qur'an may be lost. Therefore I consider it advisable that you (Abu Bakr) should have the Qur'an collected.'

I said, 'How dare I do something which Allah's Messenger did not do?' 'Umar said, By Allah, it is something beneficial.' 'Umar kept on pressing me for that till Allah opened my chest for that for which He had opened the chest of 'Umar and I had in that matter, the same opinion as 'Umar had." Abu Bakr then said to me (Zaid), "You are a wise young man and we do not have any suspicion about you, and you used to write the Divine Inspiration for Allah's Messenger. So you should search for the fragmentary scripts of the Qur'an and collect it (in one Book)." Zaid further said: By Allah, if Abu Bakr had ordered me to shift a mountain among the mountains from one place to another it would not have been heavier for me than this ordering me to collect the Qur'an. Then I said (to 'Umar and Abu Bakr), "How can you do something which Allah's Messenger did not do?" Abu Bakr said, "By Allah, it is something beneficial." Zaid added: So he (Abu Bakr) kept on pressing me for that until Allah opened my chest for that for which He had opened the chests of Abu Bakr and 'Umar, and I had in that matter, the same opinion as theirs. So I started compiling the Qur'an by collecting it from the leafless stalks of the date-palm tree and from the pieces of leather and hides and from the stones, and from the chests of men (who had memorized the Qur'an). I found the last verses of Sirat-at-Tauba: ("Verily there has come unto you an Apostle (Muhammad) from amongst yourselves--' (9.128-129)) from Khuza'ima or Abi Khuza'ima and I added to it the rest of the Sura. The manuscripts of the Qur'an remained with Abu Bakr till Allah took him unto Him. Then it remained with 'Umar till Allah took him unto Him, and then with Hafsa bint 'Umar. Sahih Bukhari Volume 9 Book 89 *Hadith* 301. Available online at: https://sunnah.com/bukhari/93/53

450 Sahih Bukhari Volume 6 Book 61 *Hadith* 510. Available online at: https://sunnah.com/bukhari/66/9

451 Sahih Bukhari Volume 6 Book 61 *Hadith* 510. Available online at: https://sunnah.com/bukhari/66/10

452 For example: "The verse of stoning and of suckling an adult ten times were revealed, and they were (written) **on a paper** and kept under my bed. When the Messenger of Allah expired and we were preoccupied with his death, a goat entered and ate away **the paper**." Sunan Ibn Majah Volume 3 Book *Hadith* 1944. Available online at: https://sunnah.com/urn/1262630

453 Heike Jöns, Peter Meusburger, and Michael Heffernan, "Mobilities of Knowledge," (2017). 51-66

454 Ibid. 51-66

455 John of Damascus (675-749 CE) discusses the 'writings of Muhammad' but deals with it as a collection of separate writings rather than as a single book. Keep in mind that John lived and worked in Damascus, the Muslim capital of the time, and that he was writing to equip Christians to interact with Muslims. He can, therefore, be assumed to possess a good working knowl-

edge of Muslim faith and practice. All of which would seem to indicate that the text of the Qur'an was not formalised as late as the mid-8th century. For an overview of early non-Muslim interactions with the Qur'an, see: Mark Ivor Beaumont, "Early Christian Interpretation of the Qur'an," *Transformation* 22, no. 4 (2005). 195-203

456 For example: "Allah's Messenger heard a man reciting the Qur'an at night, and said, "May Allah bestow His Mercy on him, as he has reminded me of such-and-such Verses of such-and-such Suras, **which I was caused to forget**." Sahih Bukhari Volume 6 Book 61 *Hadith* 558. Available online at: https://sunnah.com/bukhari/66/62

457 For example: "Zaid ibn Thabit added, "A Verse from Surat Ahzab was missed by me when we copied the Qur'an and I used to hear Allah's Apostle reciting it. So we searched for it and found it with Khuzaima bin Thabit Al-Ansari. (That Verse was): 'Among the Believers are men who have been true in their covenant with Allah.' (33.23)" Sahih Bukhari Volume 6 Book 61 *Hadith* 510. Available online at: https://sunnah.com/bukhari/66/10

458 There are, in fact, two entire chapters added to some Shi'a Qur'ans. It should come as no surprise that these chapters support Shi'a views on the succession to Muhammad.

459 Hughes, *Muslim Identities: An Introduction to Islam.* 74

460 There is clear evidence, even within the accepted Muslim tradition, that there were many people who were uncomfortable with the idea of burning copies of the 'word of God' in this way. Some of this unease even makes it into the *hadiths.* See: G. Sawma, *The Qur'an, Misinterpreted, Mistranslated, and Misread: The Aramaic Language of the Qur'an* (Adibooks.com, 2006). 84

461 C. Cassini, *Islam: Claims and Counterclaims* (iUniverse, 2001). 59

462 G. Bowering et al., *The Princeton Encyclopedia of Islamic Political Thought* (Princeton University Press, 2012). vii

463 For a fuller discussion of the discipline of textual criticism as it applies to the text of the Qur'an, see: K.E. Small, *Textual Criticism and Qur'an Manuscripts* (Lexington Books, 2011).

464 G.S. Reynolds, *New Perspectives on the Qur'an: The Qur'an in Its Historical Context 2* (Taylor & Francis, 2012). Box 4.3

465 Dumper and Stanley, *Cities of the Middle East and North Africa: A Historical Encyclopedia.* 213

466 Gabriel Said Reynolds, *The Emergence of Islam: Classical Traditions in Contemporary Perspective* (Minneapolis: Fortress Press, 2012). 186

467 "The Mushaf Al-Madina and the King Fahd Holy Qur'an Printing Complex," *Journal of Qur'anic Studies* 1, no. 1 (1999).

468 *The Qur'an in Its Historical Context.* 3

469 C. Çakmak, *Islam: A Worldwide Encyclopedia* (ABC-CLIO, 2017). 659

470 For a complete overview of divergent Qur'anic textual traditions, see: Small, *Textual Criticism and Qur'an Manuscripts.* 31-104

[471] S. Nasser, *The Transmission of the Variant Readings of the Qur'an* (Brill, 2012). 149

[472] Ibn Warraq, *Why I Am Not a Muslim*. 110

[473] Education National Association for the Promotion of Studies in Religions, Languages, and General Studies, *The Authenticity and Literary Styles of Surah Al-Walayah and Surah Al-Nurayn* (Jilat Publishing Company, 2007). 283

[474] H. Aydın, *The Sacred Trusts: Pavilion of the Sacred Relics, Topkapı Palace Museum, Istanbul* (Tughra Books, 2011). 91

[475] M. Maulana, *Encyclopaedia of Quranic Studies* (Anmol Publications Pvt. Ltd, 2006). 55

[476] Tayyar Altikulaç, Ekmeleddin Ihsanoglu, and Salih Sadawi, *Al-Mushaf Al-Sharif Attributed to Uthman Bin Affan (the Copy at the Topkapi Palace Museum)* (Istanbul: Organisation of the Islamic Conference/Research Centre for Islamic History, Art and Culture, 2007). 10

[477] Ibid. 23

[478] A. Von Denffer, *Ulum Al Qur'an: An Introduction to the Sciences of the Qur'an (Koran)* (Kube Publishing Limited, 2015). 42-26

[479] Altikulaç, Ihsanoglu, and Sadawi, *Al-Mushaf Al-Sharif Attributed to Uthman Bin Affan (the Copy at the Topkapi Palace Museum)*. 71-72

[480] Mathieu Tillier, *Journal of Qur'anic Studies* 13, no. 2 (2011).

[481] A. Jeffery and I. Mendelsohn, "The Orthography of the Samarqand Quran Codex," *Journal of the American Oriental Society* 62, no. 3 (1942).

[482] Ibn, *Why I Am Not a Muslim*. 109-111

[483] Mondher Sfar, *In Search of the Original Koran: The True Story of the Revealed Text* (Amherst, NY: Prometheus Books, 2008). 95

[484] John Gilchrist, *The Qur'an: The Scripture of Islam* (Claremont, South Africa: Life Challenge Africa, 2003). 115-120

[485] Daniel Brubaker, "Intentional Changes in Qur'an Manuscripts" (Rice University, 2014). 4

[486] See also: Ohlig and Puin, *The Hidden Origins of Islam: New Research into Its Early History*. 311-334

[487] J. Effarah, *What Are the Sacred Roots of Islam?: And the Planned Modern Islamic Society* (AuthorHouse, 2016). 109

[488] Mary Ellen Snodgrass, *Encyclopedia of World Scriptures* (Jefferson, NC: McFarland, 2011). 210

[489] J.R. Mitchell and H.B. Mitchell, *Annual Editions: World History, Volume I, 8/E* (McGraw-Hill, 2004). 99

[490] For a discussion of the impact of the discovery of the Sana'a Qur'an on our understanding of the textual history of the Qur'anic text, see: Jospeh Hoffman, "The Bbc Birmingham Qur'an Facts Fiasco " https://rjosephhoffmann.wordpress.com/2015/07/23/the-bbc-birmingham-quran-facts-fiasco/.

491 Dr Gerd Puin, one of the only Western scholars to have been granted access to the Sana'a Qur'an continued his career as one of the most important revisionist scholars of early Islamic history. See, for example: Ohlig and Puin, *The Hidden Origins of Islam: New Research into Its Early History*.

492 "Birmingham Qur'an Manuscript Dated among the Oldest in the World," University of Birmingham https://www.birmingham.ac.uk/news/latest/2015/07/quran-manuscript-22-07-15.aspx.

493 Birmingham Mail, "Worldwide Media Frenzy as 'Oldest Koran' Found Lying Forgotten at University of Birmingham," https://www.birminghammail.co.uk/news/midlands-news/worldwide-media-frenzy-oldest-koran-9710028.

494 It has not yet been definitively determined whether the Birmingham Folios contain a 'palimpsest' (i.e. a layer of text under the visible one). See: Joseph Hoffman, "Revisiting the Birmingham Qur'an Debacle " https://rjosephhoffmann.wordpress.com/2015/07/26/update-on-the-birmingham-quran-debacle/.

495 Huffington Post, "Birmingham Koran Carbon Dating Reveals Book Is Likely Older Than Prophet Muhammad," http://www.huffingtonpost.co.uk/2015/09/01/birmingham-koran-carbon-test_n_8071696.html.

496 Wesley Huff, "The Birmingham Quran Folios and a Brief Synopsis of Its Impact on Islam," https://www.academia.edu/22160060/The_Birmingham_Quran_Folios_and_a_Brief_Synopsis_of_its_Impact_on_Islam.

497 G.S. Reynolds, *The Qur'an and Its Biblical Subtext* (Taylor & Francis, 2010). 181

498 Hoffman, "The BBC Birmingham Qur'an Facts Fiasco ".

499 Huff, "The Birmingham Quran Folios and a Brief Synopsis of Its Impact on Islam".

500 For a Muslim discussion of Aisha's role as a '*hadith*' scholar', see: R. Haylamaz, *Aisha: The Wife, the Companion, the Scholar* (Tughra Books, 2013).

501 Sunan Ibn Majah Volume 3 Book *Hadith* 1944. Available online at: https://sunnah.com/urn/1262630

502 Sahih Bukhari Volume 8 Book 82 *Hadith* 817. Available online at: https://sunnah.com/bukhari/86/57

503 Sahih Bukhari Volume 8 Book 82 *Hadith* 816. Available online at: https://sunnah.com/bukhari/86/56

504 C. Çakmak, *Islam: A Worldwide Encyclopedia* (ABC-CLIO, 2017).

505 Qu'ran 4:157. The Quran: English Meanings and Notes. Al-Muntada Al-Islami. Available in the original Arabic and several English translations at www.quran.com/4/157

506 Brown, *A New Introduction to Islam*. 124

507 M. Hattstein and P. Delius, *Islam: Art and Architecture* (Könemann, 2000). 64

508 The full text of the inscription on the inner ambulatory reads as follows: "O people of the book do not go beyond the bounds of your religions and not say about God except the truth. Indeed the Messiah Jesus son of Mary was an envoy of God and his word bestowed on her as well as a spirit from Him. So believe in God and in His envoys and say not 'Three'. Desist, it is better for you. For indeed God is one God, glory be to Him that he should have a son. To him belong what is in heaven and what is on earth and it is sufficient for Him to be a guardian. The Messiah does not disdain to be a servant of god. Nor do the angels nearest to Him. Those who disdain to serving him and who are arrogant, he will gather all to himself. Bless you envoy and your servant Jesus Son of Mary and Peace be on Him on the day of birth and on the day of death and the day he is raised up again This is Jesus Son of Mary. It is a word of truth in which they doubt. It is not for God to take a son. Glory be to him when he decrees a thing. He only says 'Be' and it is. Indeed God is my Lord and your Lord, therefore serve Him, this is the straight path." Brown, *A New Introduction to Islam*. 124

509 White, *What Every Christian Needs to Know About the Qur'an*. 141

510 Brown, *A New Introduction to Islam*. 124

511 John Ernest Merril, "Of the Tractate of John of Damascus on Islam," *The Muslim World* XLI (1951). pages 88-89

512 Qur'an 8:31. The Quran: English Meanings and Notes. Al-Muntada Al-Islami. Available in the original Arabic and several English translations at www.quran.com/8/31

513 And among them are those who listen to you, but We have placed over their hearts coverings, lest they understand it, and in their ears deafness. And if they should see every sign, they will not believe in it. Even when they come to you arguing with you, those who disbelieve say, "This is not but legends of the former peoples." Qur'an 6:25. The Quran: English Meanings and Notes. Al-Muntada Al-Islami. Available in the original Arabic and several English translations at www.quran.com/6/25

514 Mingana, "Syriac Influence on the Style of the Kur'an."

515 Ibn Warraq, *Christmas in the Koran: Luxenberg, Syriac, and the near Eastern and Judeo-Christian Background of Islam*. 391-410

516 Luxenberg, *Syro-Aramaic Reading of the Koran: A Contribution to the Decoding of the Language of the Koran*.

517 Ibn Warraq's work 'Christmas in the Qur'an' is a further elaboration on Luxenberg's work and contains an excellent collection of essays testing and essentially proving Luxenberg's theories. See: Ibn Warraq, *Christmas in the Koran: Luxenberg, Syriac, and the near Eastern and Judeo-Christian Background of Islam*.

518 Qur'an 8:21-51. The Quran: English Meanings and Notes. Al-Muntada Al-Islami. Available in the original Arabic and several English translations at www.quran.com/5/21 ff.

519 J.L. Grishaver, *Make a Midrash out of Me: From Chaos to Egypt* (Tora Aura Productions, 2004). 44

520 P.W. van der Horst, *Studies in Ancient Judaism and Early Christianity* (Brill, 2014). 3

521 In order to illustrate just how heavily the Qur'an relies on the Mishnah in telling this story the Jewish text is reproduced below with the corresponding references from the Qur'an in brackets. "And Haran died in front of Terach his father R. Hiyya the grandson of R. Ada of Yafo [said]: Terach was an idolater (Qur'an 21:51). One day he went out somewhere (Qur'an 21:57), and put Avraham in charge of selling [the idols]. When a man would come who wanted to purchase, he would say to him: "How old are you"? [The customer] would answer: "Fifty or sixty years old". [Avraham] would say: "Woe to the man who is sixty years old And desires to worship something one day old." [The customer] would be ashamed and leave. One day a woman came, carrying in her hand a basket of fine flour. She said: "Here, offer it before them." Abraham seized a stick, And smashed all the idols, And placed the stick in the hand of the biggest of them (Qur'an 21:58). When his father came, he said to him: "Who did this to them"? (Qur'an 21:59) [Avraham] said:, "Would I hide anything from my father? a woman came, carrying in her hand a basket of fine flour. She said: "Here, offer it before them." When I offered it, one god said: "I will eat first," And another said, "No, I will eat first." Then the biggest of them rose up and smashed all the others. (Qur'an 21:63) [His father] said:, "Are you making fun of me? Do they know anything?" [Avraham] answered: Shall your ears not hear what your mouth is saying? He took [Avraham] and handed him over to Nimrod. [Nimrod] said to him: "Let us worship the fire". [Avraham said to him: "If so, let us worship the water which extinguishes the fire." [Nimrod] said to him: "Let us worship the water". [Avraham said to him: "If so, let us worship the clouds which bear the water." [Nimrod] said to him: "Let us worship the clouds". [Avraham said to him: "If so, let us worship the wind which scatters the clouds." [Nimrod] said to him: "Let us worship the wind". [Avraham said to him: "If so, let us worship man who withstands the wind." [Nimrod] said to him: "You are speaking nonsense; I only bow to the fire. "I will throw you into it. (Qur'an 21:68) "Let the God to Whom you bow come and save you from it." Haran was there. He said [to himself] Either way; If Avraham is successful, I will say that I am with Avraham; If Nimrod is successful, I will say that I am with Nimrod. Once Avraham went into the furnace and was saved (Qur'an 21:69), They asked [Haran]: "With which one are you [allied]"? He said to them: "I am with Avraham." They took him and threw him into the fire and his bowels were burned out. He came out and died in front of Terach his father. This is the meaning of the verse: And Haran died in front of Terach."

522 Qur'an 5:30-35. The Quran: English Meanings and Notes. Al-Muntada Al-Islami. Available in the original Arabic and several English translations at www.quran.com/5/30 ff.

523 E. Ben-Ḥûrqānôs, *Pirke De Rabbi Eliezer: A Critical Ed. Codex C.M. Horowitz; Includes Textual Variants from 15 Manuscripts, Notes, Commentaries and Paralells from Rabbinic Literature* (Makor Publ., 1972).

524 Qur'an 5:32. The Quran: English Meanings and Notes. Al-Muntada Al-Islami. Available in the original Arabic and several English translations at www.quran.com/5/32

525 A. Rippin and J. Mojaddedi, *The Wiley Blackwell Companion to the Qur'an* (Wiley, 2017). 313

526 Qur'an 27-20-40. The Quran: English Meanings and Notes. Al-Muntada Al-Islami. Available in the original Arabic and several English translations at www.quran.com/27/20 ff.

527 R. Tottoli, *Biblical Prophets in the Qur'an and Muslim Literature* (Taylor & Francis, 2013). 61

528 Qur'an 19:29-31. The Quran: English Meanings and Notes. Al-Muntada Al-Islami. Available in the original Arabic and several English translations at www.quran.com/19/29 ff.

529 Qur'an 3:46. The Quran: English Meanings and Notes. Al-Muntada Al-Islami. Available in the original Arabic and several English translations at www.quran.com/3/46

530 Anonymous, *The Arabic Gospel of the Infancy of the Saviour* (Library of Alexandria).

531 A. Roberts, *The Ante-Nicene Fathers: The Writings of the Fathers Down to A. D. 325, Volume VIII Fathers of the Third and Fourth Century - the Twelve Patriarchs* (Cosimo Classics, 2007). 405

532 Qur'an 3:49. The Quran: English Meanings and Notes. Al-Muntada Al-Islami. Available in the original Arabic and several English translations at www.quran.com/3/49

533 Qur'an 5:110. The Quran: English Meanings and Notes. Al-Muntada Al-Islami. Available in the original Arabic and several English translations at www.quran.com/5/110

534 Anonymous, *The Arabic Gospel of the Infancy of the Saviour.*

535 W. Phillips, *Brothers Kept Apart: Examining the Christian and Islamic Barriers That Have Divided Christians and Muslims for over 1,300 Years* (iUniverse, 2009). 149

536 Leaman, *The Qur'an: An Encyclopedia.* 394

537 Qur'an 19:22-26. The Quran: English Meanings and Notes. Al-Muntada Al-Islami. Available in the original Arabic and several English translations at www.quran.com/19/22 ff.

538 Paul Popenoe and Henry Field, *The Date Palm* (Coconut Grove, Fla.: Field Research Projects, 1973). 14

539 William St Clair Tisdall, *Noble Eightfold Path* (London Nabu Press, 2010). 197
540 Qur'an 18:10-22. The Quran: English Meanings and Notes. Al-Muntada Al-Islami. Available in the original Arabic and several English translations at www.quran.com/18/10 ff.
541 Ibn, *Why I Am Not a Muslim*. 66
542 Qur'an 18:22. The Quran: English Meanings and Notes. Al-Muntada Al-Islami. Available in the original Arabic and several English translations at www.quran.com/18/22
543 B.M. Wheeler, *Moses in the Quran and Islamic Exegesis* (RoutledgeCurzon, 2002). 10-36
544 E.J. van Donzel and A. Schmidt, *Gog and Magog in Early Eastern Christian and Islamic Sources: Sallam's Quest for Alexander's Wall* (Brill, 2010). 58-59
545 Andrew Michael Chugg, *The Lost Tomb of Alexander the Great* (London: Periplus, 2005). 168
546 Antonio Panaino, *The Lists of Names of Ahura Mazda (Yast I) and Vayu (Yast XV)* (Roma: Istituto italiano per l'Africa e l'Oriente, 2002).
547 J.M. Athyal, *Religion in Southeast Asia: An Encyclopedia of Faiths and Cultures: An Encyclopedia of Faiths and Cultures* (ABC-CLIO, 2015). Zoroastrianism
548 The only exception is Chapter 9 (At-Tawba). Some Muslim scholars speculate that this is because this chapter is so focused on warfare against unbelievers, who should not expect mercy from Allah or his followers.
549 A. Sundiata, *Look Behind the Facade* (Xulon Press, Incorporated, 2006). 140
550 It has to be admitted that there is considerable debate about the date of composition of the Dasatir. This should not, however, detract from the fact that the formula at the beginning of the Qur'anic chapters harks back to the more ancient traditions of Zoroastrianism. See, for example, Chapter Four of: A. Williams, *The Zoroastrian Myth of Migration from Iran and Settlement in the Indian Diaspora: Text, Translation and Analysis of the 16th Century Qesse-Ye Sanjān 'the Story of Sanjan'* (Brill, 2009).
551 In the name of Allah, Most Gracious, Most Merciful.
Praise be to Allah, the Cherisher and Sustainer of the worlds;
Most Gracious, Most Merciful;
Master of the Day of Judgment.
Thee do we worship, and Thine aid we seek.
Show us the **straight way**,
The way of those on whom Thou hast bestowed Thy Grace, those whose (portion) is not wrath, and who go not astray.
Qur'an 1:1-7 (Yusuf Ali). The Quran: English Meanings and Notes. Al-Muntada Al-Islami. Available in the original Arabic and several English translations at www.quran.com/1/1 ff.
552 J.A. Morrow, *Islamic Images and Ideas: Essays on Sacred Symbolism* (McFarland, Incorporated, Publishers, 2013). 48

553 Behramgore Tehmurasp Anklesaria, *Ethics of Old Iran* (Ahmedabad: Meherbanoo Behramgore Anklesaria Publication Trust, 1973). 31

554 Qur'an 52:20. The Quran: English Meanings and Notes. Al-Muntada Al-Islami. Available in the original Arabic and several English translations at www.quran.com/52/20

555 Hughes, *Muslim Identities: An Introduction to Islam.* 200

556 Jamsheed K. Choksy, *Evil, Good and Gender Facets of the Feminine in Zoroastrian Religious History* (New York [u.a.: Lang, 2009). 73

557 E.A. Ghareeb and B. Dougherty, *Historical Dictionary of Iraq* (Scarecrow Press, 2004). 81

558 G.R. Hawting, *The First Dynasty of Islam: The Umayyad Caliphate AD 661-750* (Taylor & Francis, 2002). 58

559 M. Dumper and B.E. Stanley, *Cities of the Middle East and North Africa: A Historical Encyclopedia* (ABC-CLIO, 2007). 343

560 Sawma, *The Qur'an, Misinterpreted, Mistranslated, and Misread: The Aramaic Language of the Qur'an.* 84

561 The standardization of the Qur'anic text was obviously thought to be a necessity, for the sake of unity, as the Muslim empire grew. See: S. Wild, *Self-Referentiality in the Qur'ān* (Isd, 2006). 98

562 Sawma, *The Qur'an, Misinterpreted, Mistranslated, and Misread: The Aramaic Language of the Qur'an.* 84

Chapter 7 - The Post-Muhammad Period: Muslim Conquest and Victory?

563 For a very good overview of the conquests that takes non-Islamic sources seriously, see: Robert G. Hoyland, *In God's Path: The Arab Conquests and the Creation of an Islamic Empire*, Ancient Warfare and Civilization (Oxford ; New York: Oxford University Press, 2015).

564 Ibid. 135

565 Penn, *When Christians First Met Muslims: A Sourcebook of the Earliest Syriac Writings on Islam.* 22

566 Crone and Cook, *Hagarism: The Making of the Islamic World.* 259

567 J. Retso, *The Arabs in Antiquity: Their History from the Assyrians to the Umayyads* (Taylor & Francis, 2013). 98

568 Hoyland, *In God's Path: The Arab Conquests and the Creation of an Islamic Empire.* 102

569 Griffith, *The Church in the Shadow of the Mosque: Christians and Muslims in the World of Islam.* 24

570 J.V. Tolan, *Saracens: Islam in the Medieval European Imagination* (Columbia University Press, 2002). 45

571 For an excellent overview of Syriac responses to the Arab conquest, see: Penn, *When Christians First Met Muslims: A Sourcebook of the Earliest Syriac Writings on Islam.*

572 See: W.S.W. Vaux, *Persia from the Earliest Period to the Arab Conquest* (BiblioBazaar, 2008).

573 For an overview of Roman (Byzantine) responses to the Arab conquests, see: W.E. Kaegi, *Byzantium and the Early Islamic Conquests* (Cambridge University Press, 1995).

574 D.R. Thomas, *The Bible in Arab Christianity* (Brill, 2007). 49

575 Wendy Mayer et al., *Religious Conflict from Early Christianity to the Rise of Islam* (2016). 232

576 B. January, *The Arab Conquests of the Middle East (Revised Edition)* (Lerner Publishing Group, 2013). 50

577 Fred McGraw Donner, "The Expansion of the Early Islamic State," (2016). 117

578 See, for example: E. Grypeou, M. Swanson, and D.R. Thomas, *The Encounter of Eastern Christianity with Early Islam* (Brill, 2006). 39

579 Robert G. Hoyland, *Seeing Islam as Others Saw It: A Survey and Evaluation of Christian, Jewish, and Zoroastrian Writings on Early Islam* (Princeton, N.J.: Darwin Press, 2007). 67-73

580 Thomson and Howard-Johnston, *Armenian History Attributed to Sebeos*.

581 Qur'an 5:82. The Quran: English Meanings and Notes. Al-Muntada Al-Islami. Available in the original Arabic and several English translations at www.quran.com/5/82

582 For a full discussion of John of Damascus'; treatment of Islam, see: D.J. Sahas, *John of Damascus on Islam: The "Heresy of the Ishmaelites."* (Brill, 1972).

583 See: Hoyland, *Seeing Islam as Others Saw It: A Survey and Evaluation of Christian, Jewish, and Zoroastrian Writings on Early Islam*. 480

584 Sunni Muslims rely very heavily on the history of Ibn Kathir (1300-1373 CE) for his description of the life and reign of the caliphs. See: I. Kathir, *Biographies of the Rightly-Guided Caliphs* (Lulu.com, 2016).

585 For a modern Muslim discussion of the caliphs, see: El-Hibri, *Parable and Politics in Early Islamic History: The Rashidun Caliphs*.

586 I.M. Lapidus, *A History of Islamic Societies* (Cambridge University Press, 2014). 65

587 A. Balfour, *Solomon's Temple: Myth, Conflict, and Faith* (Wiley, 2015). 146

588 A. Mikaberidze, *Conflict and Conquest in the Islamic World: A Historical Encyclopedia* (ABC-CLIO, 2011). 750

589 Kaegi and Kaegi, *Byzantium and the Early Islamic Conquests*. 245

590 Ghareeb and Dougherty, *Historical Dictionary of Iraq*. 487

591 Hughes, *Muslim Identities: An Introduction to Islam*. 74

592 M.H. Syed, S.S. Akhtar, and B.D. Usmani, *Concise History of Islam* (Vij Books India Private Limited, 2011). 33

593 When these leaders finally enter the historical record, they are presented with a theological rather than an historical purpose in mind. Their stories are often told to legitimize the claims of one of the parties in the developing conflict between Sunni and Shi'a Islam. See: Zohar Hadromi-Allouche, "Review of El-Hibri, Tayeb, Parable and Politics in Early Islamic History: The Rashidun Caliphs," *H-Net Reviews* (2013). 2

594 See: G. Greatrex and S.N.C. Lieu, *The Roman Eastern Frontier and the Persian Wars Ad 363-628* (Routledge, 2007).

595 Ruthven and Nanji, *Historical Atlas of Islam*. 34

596 Donner, *Muhammad and the Believers*. 99

597 See, for example: B. O'Kane, *New Perspectives on Islamic Architecture* (American University In Cairo Press, 2009).

598 D.A. King, *World Maps for Finding the Direction and Distance of Mecca: Examples of Innovation and Tradition in Islamic Science* (Al-Furqān Islamic Heritage Foundation, 1999). 47

599 Qur'an 2:142-145, 149-15-. The Quran: English Meanings and Notes. Al-Muntada Al-Islami. Available in the original Arabic and several English translations at www.quran.com/2

600 J.E. Campo, *Encyclopedia of Islam* (Facts On File, 2009). 569

601 J.W. Meri, *Medieval Islamic Civilization: An Encyclopedia* (Taylor & Francis, 2005).

602 Gibson, *Qur'anic Geography*. 260

603 C.E. Bosworth, *Historic Cities of the Islamic World* (Brill, 2007). 551

604 Gibson, *Qur'anic Geography*. 258

605 G. Hann, K. Dabrowska, and T.T. Greaves, *Iraq: The Ancient Sites and Iraqi Kurdistan* (Bradt Travel Guides, 2015). 280

606 A. Petersen, *Dictionary of Islamic Architecture* (Taylor & Francis, 2002). 44

607 R. Rashed, *Encyclopedia of the History of Arabic Science* (Taylor & Francis, 2002). 55

608 Gibson, *Qur'anic Geography*. 251-274

609 Ibid. 253-254

610 Ibid. 256

611 Ibid. 257

612 Ibid. 270

613 Ibid. 261

614 Ibid. 274

615 Ibid. 257

616 Ibid. 258

617 See, for example, Rashed, *Encyclopedia of the History of Arabic Science*. 55

618 See, for example: Anthony R. Constable and William Facey, *The Principles of Arab Navigation* (London: Arabian Publishing, 2013).

619 Ibid. 135

620 Crone and Cook, *Hagarism: The Making of the Islamic World*, Patricia Crone, Michael Cook. 24, 73

621 We have already noted that this title is derived from the fact that they were migrants (i.e. 'incomers') and that it does not primarily refer to a religious identity.

622 Crone and Cook, *Hagarism: The Making of the Islamic World*, Patricia Crone, Michael Cook. 73

623 See: Yehuda D. Nevo and Judith Koren, "The Origins of the Muslim Descriptions of the Meccan Sanctuary," *Journal of Near Eastern Studies* 49, no. 1 (1990).

624 Gibson, *Qur'anic Geography*. 274

625 The Abassids were Islam's second dynasty and they played a very significant role in the standardizing Islam as we know it today. Their contribution will be discussed in much more detail in Section 9.

626 Gibson, *Qur'anic Geography*. 221-237

627 Qur'an 2:142-145, 149-150 (supposedly revealed in 622 CE) makes it clear that believers are to pray towards the 'sacred mosque' (universally believed to refer to Mecca by Muslim scholars). Thus, according the traditional account the shift towards Mecca as the direction for prayer occurred as early as 10 years before Muhammad's traditional death date (632 CE).

628 Gibson, *Qur'anic Geography*. 251-274

629 S. Kadri, *Heaven on Earth: A Journey through Shari'a Law* (Random House, 2013). 20

630 Robert G. Hoyland, *Muslims and Others in Early Islamic Society* (Aldershot, Hants; Burlington, VT: Ashgate, 2004). 84

631 Yehuda D. Nevo, Judith Koren, and Cultures Negev Archaeological Project for the Study of Ancient Arab Desert, *Crossroads to Islam: The Origins of the Arab Religion and the Arab State* (Amherst, NY: Prometheus Books, 2003). 217

632 For an exhaustive study of the life of Muawiya (drawn mainly from Islamic sources), see: R.S. Humphreys, *Mu'awiya Ibn Abi Sufyan: The Savior of the Caliphate* (Oneworld Publications, 2012).

633 For a history of the Umayyad Caliphate, see: Hawting, *The First Dynasty of Islam: The Umayyad Caliphate Ad 661-750*.

634 The Umayyad Mosque in Damascus is perhaps the greatest surviving monument to Umayyad Power. See: Meri, *Medieval Islamic Civilization: An Encyclopedia*. 845

635 A. Ali, *Islamic Dynasties of the Arab East: State and Civilization During the Later Medieval Times* (M D Publications, 1996). 115

636 A. Marsham, *Rituals of Islamic Monarchy: Accession and Succession in the First Muslim Empire* (Edinburgh University Press, 2009). 85

637 S. Judd, *Religious Scholars and the Umayyads: Piety-Minded Supporters of the Marwanid Caliphate* (Taylor & Francis, 2013). 4

638 Patricia Crone points out, for example, that no role seems to have been accorded to Muhammad during the Sufyanid period and that this changed radically with the coming of the Marwanids. See: P. Crone and M. Hinds, *God's Caliph: Religious Authority in the First Centuries of Islam* (Cambridge University Press, 2003). 25

639 F.B. Flood and G. Necipoglu, *A Companion to Islamic Art and Architecture* (Wiley, 2017). 90

640 Crone and Hinds, *God's Caliph: Religious Authority in the First Centuries of Islam*. 24

641 Ohlig and Puin, *The Hidden Origins of Islam: New Research into Its Early History*. 34-36

642 Ibid. 395

643 Fred McGraw Donner, *Muhammad and the Believers: At the Origins of Islam* (Cambridge, Mass.: The Belknap Press of Harvard University Press, 2010). 99

644 B. Lewis, *The Middle East: A Brief History of the Last 2,000 Years* (Scribner, 1995). 397

645 Crone, *Meccan Trade and the Rise of Islam*. 75

646 For a detailed discussion of the coins and inscriptions associated with the earliest period of Islamic history, see: Ohlig and Puin, *The Hidden Origins of Islam: New Research into Its Early History*. 17 ff.

647 Arabia is a particularly fertile field for numismatic studies as it was home to an ancient tradition of coin minting. See, for example: D.T. Potts, R. Boucharlat, and M. Drieux, *The Pre-Islamic Coinage of Eastern Arabia* (Carsten Niebuhr Institute of Ancient Near Eastern Studies, University of Copenhagen, 1991).

648 Crone and Hinds, *God's Caliph: Religious Authority in the First Centuries of Islam*. 24

649 Nevo, Koren, and Negev Archaeological Project for the Study of Ancient Arab Desert, *Crossroads to Islam: The Origins of the Arab Religion and the Arab State*. 250

650 Clive Foss, *Arab-Byzantine Coins: An Introduction, with a Catalogue of the Dumbarton Oaks Collection* (Washington, DC: Harvard Univ. Press, 2008). 34

651 Bennett, *In Search of Muhammad*.

652 Qur'an 4:157. See Section 6.3.6. for a discussion of this verse and its place in the Qur'an.

653 See: D.E. Singh, *Jesus and the Cross: Reflections of Christians from Islamic Contexts* (Regnum, 2008).

654 For a fuller discussion of this thesis, see: Donner, *Muhammad and the Believers: At the Origins of Islam*.

655 A. Christian Van Gorder, *No God but God: A Path to Muslim-Christian Dialogue on God's Nature* (New York; Edinburgh: Orbis ; Alban, 2003). 170

656 Nevo was a prolific researcher and author. For an excellent summary of his research into the earliest years of Islam, see: Nevo, Koren, and Negev Archaeological Project for the Study of Ancient Arab Desert, *Crossroads to Islam: The Origins of the Arab Religion and the Arab State*.

657 *Jerusalem Studies in Arabic and Islam Volumes 22 and 23*, (Jerusalem: Hebrew University, 1997). 78

658 J.L. Bacharach, *Islamic History through Coins: An Analysis and Catalogue of Tenth-Century Ikhshidid Coinage* (American University in Cairo Press, 2006). 15

659 Andrew Rippin, *Muslims: Their Religious Beliefs and Practices* (Routledge, 2001). 99

660 Nevo, "Towards a Pre-History of Islam." 109

661 Crone and Hinds, *God's Caliph: Religious Authority in the First Centuries of Islam.* 24

662 Meir Litvak and Ofra Bengio, "The Sunna and Shi'a in History Division and Ecumenism in the Muslim Middle East," (2014). 23

663 Damascus in modern-day Syria is still the city most closely associated with the period of Umayyad rule.

664 Litvak and Bengio, "The Sunna and Shi'a in History Division and Ecumenism in the Muslim Middle East." 23

665 J.P. Berkey, *The Formation of Islam: Religion and Society in the near East, 600-1800* (Cambridge University Press, 2003). 76

666 K.A.E. Fadl, *Rebellion and Violence in Islamic Law* (Cambridge University Press, 2006). 68

667 J. Pickard, *Behind the Myths: The Foundations of Judaism, Christianity and Islam* (AuthorHouse UK, 2013). 395

668 *Jerusalem Studies in Arabic and Islam Volumes 22 and 23.*

669 Crone and Hinds, *God's Caliph: Religious Authority in the First Centuries of Islam.* 78

670 Nevo, "Towards a Pre-History of Islam." 110

671 *Jerusalem Studies in Arabic and Islam Volumes 22 and 23.*

672 For a full-length biography of Abd Al-Malik that draws both upon the classical Islamic tradition and wider historical research, see: C. Robinson, *Abd Al-Malik* (Oneworld Publications, 2012).

673 For Al-Tabari's views on the reign of Abd Al-Malik, see: M. Fishbein, *History of Al-Tabari Vol. 21, The Victory of the Marwanids A.D. 685-693/A.H. 66-73* (State University of New York Press, 2015). 155 ff.

674 See: V.O. Egger, *A History of the Muslim World to 1750: The Making of a Civilization* (Taylor & Francis, 2017). 44-53

675 R.M.A. Allen and R. Allen, *The Arabic Literary Heritage: The Development of Its Genres and Criticism* (Cambridge University Press, 2005). 229

676 Meri, *Medieval Islamic Civilization: An Encyclopedia.* 3

677 N. Khalek, *Damascus after the Muslim Conquest: Text and Image in Early Islam* (Oxford University Press, 2011). 55

678 Brown, *A New Introduction to Islam.* 123

679 For a full description of the decorations and inscriptions of the Dome of the Rock, see: Pamela C. Berger, "The Crescent on the Temple the Dome of the Rock as Image of the Ancient Jewish Sanctuary," (2012).

680 O. Grabar, *Jerusalem* (Ashgate/Variorum, 2005). 35

681 Grypeou, Swanson, and Thomas, *The Encounter of Eastern Christianity with Early Islam.* 154

682 Brown, *A New Introduction to Islam.* 124

683 Fahmida Suleman, *Word of God, Art of Man: The Qur'an and Its Creative Expressions: Selected Proceedings from the International Colloquium, London, 18-21 October 2003* (Oxford: Oxford University Press in association with the Institute of Ismaili Studies, 2010). 276

684 Grypeou, Swanson, and Thomas, *The Encounter of Eastern Christianity with Early Islam.* 154

685 B. Ratliff, H.C. Evans, and Metropolitan Museum of Art, *Byzantium and Islam: Age of Transition, 7th-9th Century* (Metropolitan Museum of Art, 2012). 266

686 J.E. Lindsay, *Daily Life in the Medieval Islamic World* (Greenwood Press, 2005). 140

687 Ibid. 140

688 This was done through the inclusion of the verse that would eventually become Qur'an 3:19 as part of the inscriptions: "Indeed, the religion in the sight of Allah is Islam. And those who were given the Scripture did not differ except after knowledge had come to them - out of jealous animosity between themselves. And whoever disbelieves in the verses of Allah, then indeed, Allah is swift in [taking] account." The Quran: English Meanings and Notes. Al-Muntada Al-Islami. Available in the original Arabic and several English translations at www.quran.com/3/19

689 This was done through the inclusion of the verse that would eventually become Qur'an 4:171: "O People of the Scripture, do not commit excess in your religion or say about Allah except the truth. The Messiah, Jesus, the son of Mary, was but a messenger of Allah and His word which He directed to Mary and a soul [created at a command] from Him. So believe in Allah and His messengers. And do not say, "Three"; desist - it is better for you. Indeed, Allah is but one God. Exalted is He above having a son. To Him belongs whatever is in the heavens and whatever is on the earth. And sufficient is Allah as Disposer of affairs." The Quran: English Meanings and Notes. Al-Muntada Al-Islami. Available in the original Arabic and several English translations at www.quran.com/4/171

Chapter 8 - What Happened? Some Tentative Conclusions

690 J.D. McAuliffe, *The Cambridge Companion to the Qur'ān* (Cambridge University Press, 2006). 163 ff.

691 Gonen, *Contested Holiness: Jewish, Muslim, and Christian Perspectives on the Temple Mount in Jerusalem.* 87

692 This is done through the inclusion of the verse that would eventually become Qur'an 3:19 as part of the inscriptions: "Indeed, the religion in the sight of Allah is Islam. And those who were given the Scripture did not differ except after knowledge had come to them - out of jealous animosity between themselves. And whoever disbelieves in the verses of Allah, then indeed, Allah is swift in [taking] account." The Quran: English Meanings

and Notes. Al-Muntada Al-Islami. Available in the original Arabic and several English translations at www.quran.com/3/19

693 Sahas, *John of Damascus on Islam: The "Heresy of the Ishmaelites.".*

694 This occurs in the Byzantine-Arabic Chronicle. J.H. Forsyth, *The Byzantine-Arab Chronicle (938-1034) of Yaḥyā B. Saʿīd Al-Anṭākī* (University Microfilms, 1977).

695 The most famous and earliest biography of Muhammad of which we have a written record is the *Sirat Rasul Allah* (Biography of the Apostle of Allah) by Muhammad ibn Ishaq ibn Yasār (often known simply as Ibn Ishaq) who lived from 704-770 CE.

696 Gibson, *Qur'anic Geography.* 22

697 These are: Sahih Bukhari compiled by Imam Bukhari (died 870 CE); Sahih Muslim compiled by Muslim bin al Hajjaj (died 875 CE); Sunan al-Sughra compiled by Al-Nasa'i (died 915 CE); Sunan Abu Dawood compiled by Abu Dawood (died 888 CE); Jami al-Tirmidhi compiled by Al-Tirmidhi (died 892 CE); Sunan ibn Majah compiled by Ibn Majah (died 887 CE)

698 This was the controversial thesis proposed, and later partially disavowed by Prof Patricia Crone. See: Crone and Cook, *Hagarism: The Making of the Islamic World.*

699 See: J. Taylor, *Petra and the Lost Kingdom of the Nabataeans* (I.B. Tauris, 2001).

700 Gibson, *Qur'anic Geography.* 131-186

701 G. Markoe, *Petra Rediscovered: Lost City of the Nabataeans* (Harry N. Abrams, 2003).

702 Taylor, *Petra and the Lost Kingdom of the Nabataeans.* 151

703 M. Sartre, *The Middle East under Rome* (Belknap Press of Harvard University Press, 2005). 133 ff.

704 G.K. Young, *Rome's Eastern Trade: International Commerce and Imperial Policy 31 Bc - Ad 305* (Taylor & Francis, 2003). 89

705 This is discussed at length in Dan Gibson's 'Quranic Geography'. See: Gibson, *Qur'anic Geography.* 221-237

706 Ibid.

707 Ibid. 375

708 Young, *Rome's Eastern Trade: International Commerce and Imperial Policy 31 Bc - Ad 305.* 89

709 See, for example: Origins, "Archaeologists Discover That Earliest Known Arabic Writing Was Penned by a Christian | Ancient Origins."

710 A. Knysh, *Islam in Historical Perspective* (Taylor & Francis, 2016). 28

711 M. York, *Pagan Ethics: Paganism as a World Religion* (Springer International Publishing, 2015). 28

712 A. El-Zein, *Islam, Arabs, and Intelligent World of the Jinn* (Syracuse University Press, 2009). 35

713 See Section 3.1.2. for an extended discussion of the paganism that was in view in the Islamic texts.

714 P. Crone and H. Siurua, *The Qur'ānic Pagans and Related Matters: Collected Studies in Three Volumes* (Brill, 2016). XIV

715 For a comprehensive discussion of the phenomenon of religious syncretism, see: A.M. Leopold and J.S. Jensen, *Syncretism in Religion: A Reader* (Taylor & Francis, 2016).

716 T. Insoll, *The Oxford Handbook of the Archaeology of Ritual and Religion* (OUP Oxford, 2011). 227

717 S. Codrington, *Planet Geography* (Solid Star Press, 2005). 11

718 See, example, Qur'an 15:45-48

719 Within the Western history the most famous example of this is probably the invasion of the Roman Empire by land-hungry 'barbarian' tribes from north of the Rhine during the 3rd to the 5th centuries.

720 We also see that the primary source record of the era does not consistently point to an invasion taking place. When the incomers are not referred to as Arabs those who discussed them used words denoting their identity as migrants (Magaritai in Greek and Mahgraye in Syriac). An Arabic version of this term is Mujahiroun (i.e. those who participated in a *Hijra* or migration). See Section 7.1

721 J. Culpeper, *History of English* (Routledge, 2005). 3

722 The Mamluks of Egypt is another example of this trend. They were hired as slave-mercenaries but eventually took over the Kingdom. See: T. Philipp and U. Haarmann, *The Mamluks in Egyptian Politics and Society* (Cambridge University Press, 1998).

723 I. Shahîd, *Byzantium and the Arabs in the Fifth Century* (Dumbarton Oaks Research Library and Collection, 1989). 474

724 Ball, *Rome in the East: The Transformation of an Empire*. 110

725 I. Shahîd, *Byzantium and the Arabs in the Sixth Century* (Dumbarton Oaks Research Library and Collection, 1995).155

726 M. Sicker, *The Pre-Islamic Middle East* (Praeger, 2000). 173

727 It is interesting to note that the policy of hiring Arab mercenaries coincides with a general abandonment of many Roman border fortresses that were initially designed to act as a bulwark against the Arab tribes of the interior. See: J.H.W.F. Liebeschuetz, *East and West in Late Antiquity: Invasion, Settlement, Ethnogenesis and Conflicts of Religion* (Brill, 2015). 298

728 Qur'an 30:2-4. The Quran: English Meanings and Notes. Al-Muntada Al-Islami. Available in the original Arabic and several English translations at www.quran.com/3

729 G. Böwering, P. Crone, and M. Mirza, *The Princeton Encyclopedia of Islamic Political Thought* (Princeton University Press, 2013). 219

730 D and Walker, *Muhammad in History, Thought, and Culture: An Encyclopedia of the Prophet of God [2 Volumes]*. 257

731 Patricia Crone, "The First-Century Concept of *Hijra*," *Arabica* 41, no. 3 (1994).

732 While taking the souls of those who were engaged in wronging themselves, the angels asked: 'In what circumstances were you?' They replied: 'We were too weak and helpless in the land.' The angels said: 'Was not the earth of Allah wide enough for you to emigrate in it?' For such men their refuge is Hell - an evil destination indeed; except the men, women, and children who were indeed too feeble to be able to seek the means of escape and did not know where to go, maybe Allah shall pardon these, for Allah is All-Pardoning, All-Forgiving. He who emigrates in the way of Allah will find in the earth enough room for refuge and plentiful resources. And he who goes forth from his house as a migrant in the way of Allah and His Messenger, and whom death overtakes, his reward becomes incumbent on Allah. Surely Allah is All-Forgiving, All-Compassionate. Qur'an 4:97-100. The Quran: English Meanings and Notes. Al-Muntada Al-Islami. Available in the original Arabic and several English translations at www.quran. com/4/97 ff.

733 Crone, "The First-Century Concept of *Hijra*." 355

734 It is quite possible that a surviving example of this sentiment can be found in Qur'an 8:72: "Indeed, those who have believed and emigrated and fought with their wealth and lives in the cause of Allah and those who gave shelter and aided - they are allies of one another. But those who believed and did not emigrate - for you there is no guardianship of them until they emigrate." The Quran: English Meanings and Notes. Al-Muntada Al-Islami. Available in the original Arabic and several English translations at www. quran.com/8/72

735 Crone, "The First-Century Concept of *Hijra*." 356

736 For an excellent anthology of the earliest non-Arab responses to the incomers, see: Penn, *When Christians First Met Muslims: A Sourcebook of the Earliest Syriac Writings on Islam.*

737 M. Bonner, *Arab-Byzantine Relations in Early Islamic Times* (Taylor & Francis, 2017)., Chapter 2

738 Liebeschuetz, *East and West in Late Antiquity: Invasion, Settlement, Ethnogenesis and Conflicts of Religion.* 298

739 Richard C. Martin, *Encyclopedia of Islam and the Muslim World. Vol. 1 Vol. 1* (New York: Macmillan Reference USA, 2004). 117

740 Robert Hoyland makes it clear that there were many Jews, Christians and pagans who participated on the Arab side throughout the early period of Arab dominance. See: Hoyland, *In God's Path: The Arab Conquests and the Creation of an Islamic Empire.*

741 All of these terms would only be retroactively applied to the conquest period, many decades after the events actually took place. We are, therefore, dealing with a classic case of historical back-projection here.

[742] Crone, "The First-Century Concept of *Hijra*." 359 ff.

[743] Perhaps the best example of this in history is the way in which the Mongol invaders (13th to 15th century) eventually adopted the cultures (e.g. Chinese, Islamic, Slavic etc.) of the territories they conquered. See: M. Prawdin, *The Mongol Empire: Its Rise and Legacy* (Taylor & Francis, 2017).

[744] K. Brown and S. Ogilvie, *Concise Encyclopedia of Languages of the World* (Elsevier Science, 2010). 58

[745] There is, in fact, still a village in Syria (Maaloula) where Aramaic survives as a spoken language. See: E. Coghill, *The Rise and Fall of Ergativity in Aramaic: Cycles of Alignment Change* (OUP Oxford, 2016). 164 ff.

[746] H. Elton, *Frontiers of the Roman Empire* (Taylor & Francis, 2013). 64

[747] Anderson, *The Qur'an in Context: A Christian Exploration.* 41

[748] E. El-Badawi, *The Qur'an and the Aramaic Gospel Traditions* (Taylor & Francis, 2013). 33

[749] E. Scott, *A Guide to the Phantom Dark Age* (Algora Publishing, 2014). 115

[750] B. Bitton-Ashkelony, D. Krueger, and P.R.S.D. Krueger, *Prayer and Worship in Eastern Christianities, 5th to 11th Centuries* (Taylor & Francis, 2016). 40 ff.

[751] I. Peña, *The Christian Art of Byzantine Syria* (Garnet Publishing, 1997). 221

[752] The Stylites ('pillar dwellers') were Christian hermits, particularly prevalent in Syria, who spent their days on stone pillars, preaching and exhorting the faithful to acts of devotions. The most famous of them, Simeon the Stylite, was in modern terms a mega-celebrity who drew thousands of people to his sermons. It is not difficult to see how the act of calling people to be faithful to God from a pillar could inspire the Islamic minaret and 'call to prayer'. For more about the 'Pillar Dwellers', see: W.M. Johnston, *Encyclopedia of Monasticism* (Taylor & Francis, 2013). 93

[753] Dumper and Stanley, *Cities of the Middle East and North Africa: A Historical Encyclopedia.* 120

[754] Sahih Muslim Book 19, *Hadith* 4340. Available online at: https://sunnah.com/muslim/32

[755] Abraham is mentioned 69 times and Moses 136 times in the Qur'an

[756] For an overview of how the Abrahamic tradition has been appropriated by Islam, see: M. Lodahl, *Claiming Abraham: Reading the Bible and the Qur'an Side by Side* (Baker Publishing Group, 2010).

[757] For the role played by the 'Ishmael traditions' within Islam, see: R. Firestone, *Journeys in Holy Lands: The Evolution of the Abraham-Ishmael Legends in Islamic Exegesis* (State University of New York Press, 1990).

[758] For an overview of the Qur'anic treatment of the confrontation between Moses and pharaoh, see: B.M. Wheeler, *Prophets in the Quran: An Introduction to the Quran and Muslim Exegesis* (Bloomsbury Academic, 2002). 173-197

[759] E.A. Hamid, *The Qur'an and Politics: A Study of the Origins of Political Thought in the Makkan Qur'an* (International Institute of Islamic Thought, 2004). 56

[760] Cf. the ongoing Arab-Israeli conflict and the rise of anti-Semitic attacks in parts of Europe with a growing Muslim population. See: R. Israeli, *Muslim Anti-Semitism in Christian Europe: Elemental and Residual Anti-Semitism* (Taylor & Francis, 2017).

[761] The friendship between Arabs and Jews around the idea of monotheism is a major theme in: Donner, *Muhammad and the Believers: At the Origins of Islam.*

[762] This is a major theme in the 'Armenian Chronicle' (circa 660-670 CE) attributed to a bishop named Sebeos. Thomson and Howard-Johnston, *Armenian History Attributed to Sebeos.*

[763] El-Hibri, *Parable and Politics in Early Islamic History: The Rashidun Caliphs.* 416

[764] This distancing from the Jewish people took place both in the *hadiths* (with countless anti-Jewish passages) and the Qur'an itself. In the latter it is done through the declaration that the Jews are the 'worst enemies' of the Muslims. Qur'an 5:82. The Quran: English Meanings and Notes. Al-Muntada Al-Islami. Available in the original Arabic and several English translations at www.quran.com/5/82

[765] See: H. Lazarus-Yafeh, *Some Religious Aspects of Islam: A Collection of Articles* (Brill, 1981). 72 ff.

[766] For an overview of the pre-Islamic state of Middle Eastern Christianity, see: K. Cragg, *The Arab Christian: A History in the Middle East* (Westminster/John Knox Press, 1991). 31-51

[767] Olaf H. Schumann, "Jesus the Messiah in Muslim Thought," (2002). 12

[768] Cf. Qur'an 4:48. The Quran: English Meanings and Notes. Al-Muntada Al-Islami. Available in the original Arabic and several English translations at www.quran.com/4/48

[769] D. Morgan, *Essential Islam: A Comprehensive Guide to Belief and Practice* (Praeger/ABC-CLIO, 2010). 43

[770] W.A. Dyrness et al., *Global Dictionary of Theology: A Resource for the Worldwide Church* (InterVarsity Press, 2009). 167

[771] S.J. Grenz, *Theology for the Community of God* (Eerdmans Publishing Company, 2000). 248

[772] J.G.R. Forlong, *Encyclopedia of Religions* (Cosimo, Incorporated, 2008). 133

[773] For an overview of the history and legacy of this council, see: D.E. Henderson and F. Kirkpatrick, *Constantine and the Council of Nicaea: Defining Orthodoxy and Heresy in Christianity, 325 Ce* (Reacting Consortium Press, 2016).

[774] See: R. Price and M. Gaddis, *The Acts of the Council of Chalcedon* (Liverpool University Press, 2005).

[775] Ibid. 131

[776] R.E. Olson, *The Story of Christian Theology: Twenty Centuries of Tradition & Reform* (InterVarsity Press, 1999). 232

777 The Coptic Orthodox Church in Egypt is the largest Monophysite church still in existence.

778 *Encyclopedia of World Religions*, (Encyclopaedia Britannica, Incorporated, 2008). 796

779 Because of their belief in the dual nature of Christ Nestorians are sometimes known as 'diaphysites' from 'dia' and 'physis' (i.e. 'two natures').

780 M. Saghy and E.M. Schoolman, *Pagans and Christians in the Late Roman Empire: New Evidence, New Approaches (4th-8th Centuries)* (Central European University Press, 2018). 59

781 F. Sanders, K.D. Issler, and G.L. Bray, *Jesus in Trinitarian Perspective: An Introductory Christology* (B & H Academic, 2007). 86

782 In fact, the very first ecumenical council, at Nicaea in 325 CE, was not called by church authorities but by the Emperor Constantine to try and ensure unity between the Christians of the Roman Empire. See: E. Ferguson et al., *Encyclopedia of Early Christianity* (Taylor and Francis, 1992). 238

783 K. Parry, *The Blackwell Companion to Eastern Christianity* (Wiley, 2010). 252

784 S.G. Hall, *Doctrine and Practice in the Early Church* (W.B. Eerdmans, 1992). 240

785 J.F. Kelly, *History and Heresy: How Historical Forces Can Create Doctrinal Conflicts* (Liturgical Press, 2012). 71 ff.

786 Nestorianism would, for example, flourish in the Sassanian Empire (Persia), well beyond the reach Roman Imperial power. The Nestorian 'Church of East' became a major part of the religious life in this part of the world before it was eventually all but wiped out with the growth of Islam. See: B. Ye'or and M. Kochan, *Islam and Dhimmitude: Where Civilizations Collide* (Fairleigh Dickinson University Press, 2002). 33

787 R.J. Teske and J.E. Rotelle, *Arianism and Other Heresies* (New City Press, 1995). 68

788 A. Louth and A. Casiday, *Byzantine Orthodoxies: Papers from the Thirty-Sixth Spring Symposium of Byzantine Studies, University of Durham, 23-25 March 2002* (Ashgate Variorum, 2006). 15

789 A.E. McGrath, *Christian Theology: An Introduction* (Wiley, 2011). 275

790 I.M. Studies et al., *The Arian Christian Doctrines: The Origins of Christianity* (CreateSpace Independent Publishing Platform, 2010). 83

791 This is certainly not a new insight. In fact, some of the earliest orthodox responses to Islam pointed out its theological debt to Arius. See: C. Block, *The Qur'an in Christian-Muslim Dialogue: Historical and Modern Interpretations* (Taylor & Francis, 2013). 144

792 Qur'an 3:45. The Quran: English Meanings and Notes. Al-Muntada Al-Islami. Available in the original Arabic and several English translations at www.quran.com/3/45

793 Qur'an 3:47. The Quran: English Meanings and Notes. Al-Muntada Al-Islami. Available in the original Arabic and several English translations at www.quran.com/3/47

794 Qur'an 3:55. The Quran: English Meanings and Notes. Al-Muntada Al-Islami. Available in the original Arabic and several English translations at www.quran.com/3/55

795 *They say: "Why are not Signs sent down to him from his Lord?" Say: "The signs are indeed with Allah: and I am indeed a clear Warner. And is it not enough for them that we have sent down to thee the Book which is rehearsed to them? Verily, in it is Mercy and a Reminder to those who believe."* (Qur'an 29:50-51) The Quran: English Meanings and Notes. Al-Muntada Al-Islami. Available in the original Arabic and several English translations at www.quran.com/29/50

796 Qur'an 5:116. The Quran: English Meanings and Notes. Al-Muntada Al-Islami. Available in the original Arabic and several English translations at www.quran.com/3/55

797 McGrath, *Christian Theology: An Introduction.* 275

798 Qur'an 3:59. The Quran: English Meanings and Notes. Al-Muntada Al-Islami. Available in the original Arabic and several English translations at www.quran.com/3/59

799 Many readers will, for example, be familiar with the Arabic 'N' painted on Christian houses targeted for expropriation by ISIS in areas that they conquered.

800 Most Arab Christians would refer to themselves as 'Masihi' (which is derived from the Arabic word for 'Messiah', i.e. 'Masih'). This word is therefore a direct correlate for the English word 'Christian' which is derived from the Greek word for 'Messiah', i.e. 'Christos'.

801 See, for example, Matthew 2:23: "…and he went and lived in a town called Nazareth. So was fulfilled what was said through the prophets: "He will be called a Nazarene." Holy Bible (NIV, New International Version) Zondervan

802 An obvious exception would be the modern US-based Protestant denomination known as the 'Church of the Nazarene'.

803 John 1:46: "Can anything good come from Nazareth?" Holy Bible (NIV, New International Version) Zondervan

804 Marjanen, Luomanen, and Ebrary, "A Companion to Second-Century Christian "Heretics"." 258

805 Qur'an 5:115: And [beware the Day] when Allah will say, "O Jesus, Son of Mary, did you say to the people, 'Take me and my mother as deities besides Allah?'" The Quran: English Meanings and Notes. Al-Muntada Al-Islami. Available in the original Arabic and several English translations at www.quran.com/5/115

806 P. Schaff, *Nicene and Post-Nicene Fathers: First Series, Volume Iii St. Augustine: On the Holy Trinity, Doctrinal Treatises, Moral Treatises* (Cosimo Classics, 2007). 102

807 For a full overview of the strange (from the perspective of orthodox Christians) Christianity that emerges from the pages of the Qur'an, see: White, *What Every Christian Needs to Know About the Qur'an*. 105-144

808 Luxenberg, *The Syro-Aramaic Reading of the Koran: A Contribution to the Decoding of the Language of the Koran.*

809 See, for example, Qur'an 5:112-114. It is easy to see how this passage could have started life as a liturgy for the celebration of the Mass: "When the disciples said: O Jesus, son of Mary! Is your Lord able to send down for us a table spread with food from heaven? He said: Observe your duty to God, if ye are true believers. They said: We desire to eat of it and our hearts be at rest, and that We may know that you have spoken truth to us, and that We may be witnesses thereof. Jesus, son of Mary, said: 'O God, our Lord, send down for us a Table laden with food out of heaven, that shall be for us a recurring festival, the first and last of us, and a miracle from You. And provide us our sustenance, for You are the best of providers!" The Quran: English Meanings and Notes. Al-Muntada Al-Islami. Available in the original Arabic and several English translations at www.quran.com/5/112 ff.

810 A.R. Hybel, *Ideology in World Politics* (Taylor & Francis, 2013). 27

811 D.T. Irvin and S. Sunquist, *History of the World Christian Movement: Volume 1: Earliest Christianity to 1453* (Bloomsbury Academic, 2002). 182

812 I. Shahîd, *Byzantium and the Arabs in the Fourth Century* (Dumbarton Oaks Research Library and Collection, 1984). 76

813 Winthrop S. Hudson, *The Story of the Christian Church* (New York: Harper, 1958). 28

814 As is evidenced, example, in the thriving Arab Jewish culture that existed at the dawn of the Islamic era See: L. Salaymeh, *The Beginnings of Islamic Law: Late Antique Islamicate Legal Traditions* (Cambridge University Press, 2016). 95

815 In this sense we can call Islam as it eventually developed a deeply syncretistic religion. See Section 6.4 for a discussion of some of the streams that fed into the 'final product'.

816 See Section 7.3

817 Litvak and Bengio, "The Sunna and Shi'a in History Division and Ecumenism in the Muslim Middle East." 23

818 Barnaby Rogerson, *The Heirs of Muhammad: Islam's First Century and the Origins of the Sunni-Shia Split* (Woodstock, NY: Overlook, 2008). 324

819 *Jerusalem Studies in Arabic and Islam Volumes 22 and 23.* 78

820 Foss, *Arab-Byzantine Coins: An Introduction, with a Catalogue of the Dumbarton Oaks Collection.* 34

821 D. Stathakopoulos, *A Short History of the Byzantine Empire* (I. B. Tauris, 2014). 75

822 See, for example: K. Shillington, *Encyclopedia of African History* (Taylor & Francis, 2013). 889

823 M. Bonner, *Jihad in Islamic History: Doctrines and Practice* (Princeton University Press, 2008). 61

824 We thus see many Christian documents from this era, actively decrying the broad religious settlement that was being enacted by the Arab rulers.

825 Because of this the reign of Muawiya was beset by rebellion and civil war. See: Campo, *Encyclopedia of Islam*. 241

826 Ruthven and Nanji, *Historical Atlas of Islam*. 34

827 P.F. Bang and W. Scheidel, *The Oxford Handbook of the State in the Ancient near East and Mediterranean* (OUP USA, 2013). 528

828 We can see traces of this 'nation building' agenda in the designation of those who follow the message of Muhammad as the 'best of people' (i.e. nation). Qur'an 3:110. The Quran: English Meanings and Notes. Al-Muntada Al-Islami. Available in the original Arabic and several English translations at www.quran.com/3/110

829 See Section 4.3.6

830 See Sections 7.7 and 7.8

831 See Section 5.3.3 for a discussion of how Muhammad is presented as a war leader in the accepted Islamic historical tradition.

832 Bonner, *Jihad in Islamic History: Doctrines and Practice*. 61

833 G.H. Adel, M.J. Elmi, and H. Taromi-Rad, *Hadith: An Entry from Encyclopaedia of the World of Islam* (Unknown Publisher, 2012). 186

834 Berkey, *The Formation of Islam: Religion and Society in the near East, 600-1800*. 146

835 Knysh, *Islam in Historical Perspective*. 67

836 A. Mikaberidze, *Conflict and Conquest in the Islamic World: A Historical Encyclopedia [2 Volumes]: A Historical Encyclopedia* (ABC-CLIO, 2011). 965

837 F. Robinson, *The Cambridge Illustrated History of the Islamic World* (Cambridge University Press, 1996). 13

838 Donner, *Muhammad and the Believers: At the Origins of Islam*. 99

839 Gibson, *Qur'anic Geography*. 221-237

840 This is a charge that is present in the pages of the Qur'an itself: "And among them are those who listen to you, but We have placed over their hearts coverings, lest they understand it, and in their ears deafness. And if they should see every sign, they will not believe in it. Even when they come to you arguing with you, those who disbelieve say, "This is not but legends of the former peoples." Qur'an 6:25. The Quran: English Meanings and Notes. Al-Muntada Al-Islami. Available in the original Arabic and several English translations at www.quran.com/6/25

841 M. O'Connell and E.R. Dursteler, *The Mediterranean World: From the Fall of Rome to the Rise of Napoleon* (Johns Hopkins University Press, 2016). 38

842 Johnson, *The Oxford Handbook of Late Antiquity* . 120

843 F.E. Peters, *Mecca: A Literary History of the Muslim Holy Land* (Princeton University Press, 2017). 125

[844] See Section 4.2.2

[845] The many different ways in which the *hadiths* feel entirely out of place in central Arabia were discussed in Section 4.2.3

[846] Gibson, *Qur'anic Geography.* 221-237

[847] See Section 6.4 for an overview of the many scriptural strands that were woven into what eventually became the Qur'an

[848] Schadler, *John of Damascus and Islam: Christian Heresiology and the Intellectual Background to Earliest Christian-Muslim Relations.*

[849] Meri, *Medieval Islamic Civilization: An Encyclopedia.* 848

[850] Qur'an 3:85. The Quran: English Meanings and Notes. Al-Muntada Al-Islami. Available in the original Arabic and several English translations at www.quran.com/3/85

[851] See Section 5.3.3

[852] Qur'an Chapter 9. The Quran: English Meanings and Notes. Al-Muntada Al-Islami. Available in the original Arabic and several English translations at www.quran.com/9

[853] Tarif Khalidi, *Images of Muhammad: Narratives of the Prophet in Islam across the Centuries* (New York, NY: Doubleday, 2009). 87

[854] V.J. Cornell, *Voices of Islam: Voices of Tradition* (Praeger Publishers, 2007). 49

[855] This principle is known as the 'Law of Abrogation', see: Abdullah Saeed, "Interpreting the Quran Towards a Contemporary Approach," (2006). 77 ff.

[856] Berkey, *The Formation of Islam: Religion and Society in the near East, 600-1800.*

[857] Khalidi, *Images of Muhammad: Narratives of the Prophet in Islam across the Centuries.* 37

[858] H.M. Fattah and F. Caso, *A Brief History of Iraq* (Facts On File, 2009). 87

[859] Ibid. 87

[860] Lapidus, *A History of Islamic Societies.* 46

[861] Aaron W. Hughes, "Muslim Identities: An Introduction to Islam," (2013). 107

[862] A.K. Bennison, *The Great Caliphs: The Golden Age of the 'Abbasid Empire* (Yale University Press, 2014). 54

[863] C. Melchert, *The Formation of the Sunni Schools of Law: 9th-10th Centuries C.E* (Brill, 1997). 199

[864] M. Islam, *Decline of Muslim States and Societies: The Real Root Causes and What Can Be Done Next* (Xlibris US, 2008). 112

[865] S.A. Nigosian and S.A. Nigosian, *The Zoroastrian Faith: Tradition and Modern Research* (McGill-Queen's University Press, 1993). 47

[866] S. Dalley, *The Legacy of Mesopotamia* (Oxford University Press, 1998). 77

[867] C.E. Fonrobert and M.S. Jaffee, *The Cambridge Companion to the Talmud and Rabbinic Literature* (Cambridge University Press, 2007). 89

868 M. Khadduri and H.J. Liebesny, *Origin and Development of Islamic Law* (Lawbook Exchange, 2010). 105

869 "Lo! Those who disbelieve after their (profession of) belief, and afterward grow violent in disbelief: their repentance will not be accepted. And such are those who are astray. Lo! Those who disbelieve, and die in disbelief, the (whole) earth full of gold would not be accepted from such a one if it were offered as a ransom (for his soul). Theirs will be a painful doom and they will have no helpers." (Qur'an 3:90-91) The Quran: English Meanings and Notes. Al-Muntada Al-Islami. Available in the original Arabic and several English translations at www.quran.com/3

870 Dhalla, *Zoroastrian Civilization: From the Earliest Times to the Downfall of the Last Zoroastrian Empire... 651 A. D (Classic Reprint).* 276

871 Sahih Bukhari Vol. 4, Book 52, *Hadith* 260. Available online: https://sunnah.com/bukhari/56/226

872 See Qur'an 4:15 and 24:2

873 Sahih Bukhari Book 65 *Hadith* 4556. Available online at: https://sunnah.com/urn/42340

874 Sahih Bukhari Volume 8 Book 82 *Hadith* 817. Available online at: https://sunnah.com/bukhari/86/57

875 Sunan Ibn Majah Volume 3 Book *Hadith* 1944. Available online at: https://sunnah.com/urn/1262630

876 V. Schomp, *The Ancient Persians* (Marshall Cavendish Corporation, 2009). 85

877 D.C. Snell, *Life in the Ancient near East, 3100-332 B.C.E* (Yale University Press, 1997). 142

Chapter 9 - Whereto from Here?

878 A.G. Hasan, *American Muslims: The New Generation Second Edition* (Bloomsbury Academic, 2002). 95

879 R. Van Voorst, *Jesus Outside the New Testament: An Introduction to the Ancient Evidence* (Eerdmans Publishing Company, 2000).2

880 This is a group of scholars who regularly propose revisionist interpretations of the life of Jesus and the early years of Christianity. Ibid. 2

881 Heather Kerrigan, *Historic Documents of 2015* (2016). 11

882 The Independent, "Channel 4 Cancels Controversial Screening of Islam: The Untold Story Documentary after Presenter Tom Holland Is Threatened," (2012).

883 'After darkness I hope for light' – Job, The Vulgate

26915484R00200

Printed in Poland
by Amazon Fulfillment
Poland Sp. z o.o., Wrocław